The Ark and The Dove
Adventurers

GEORGE CALVERT, FIRST LORD BALTIMORE

by Daniel Mytens, the Elder

The Ark of Maryland, *painted by Peter Egli. (On exhibit at Historic St. Mary's City.)*

1. Master's cabin
2. Great cabin
3. Steerage
4. Gun room
5. Bread room
6. Gun deck
7. Cook room
8. Orlop deck
9. Hold
10. Sail locker
11. Bosun's locker
12. Powder room
13. Light room
14. Shot locker
15. Pumps
16. Capstan
17. Knights (for halyards)
18. Tiller
19. Whipstaff
20. Cargo hatches
21. Riding bitts (for anchor cable)
22. Anchor cable
23. Material for building barge
24. Six tons of wine
25. 106 tons of beer
26. Salt beef, pork, fish, and other provisions
27. Boxes of tools
28. Ship's guns
29. Guns for fort

The Ark of Maryland, *also known as the* Ark of London. *(From a painting by Peter Egli, now on display at the Historic St. Mary's City Visitor's Center.)*

THE ARK

AND

THE DOVE
ADVENTURERS

By The Society of
The Ark and The Dove

With a New Addenda
Pages 285-289

Edited by

George Ely Russell
&
Donna Valley Russell

GENEALOGICAL PUBLISHING CO., INC.

Addenda: Additions and Corrections, pages 285-289
added 2012

Published by Genealogical Publishing Co., Inc.
3600 Clipper Mill Rd., Suite 260
Baltimore, Maryland 21211
in collaboration with The Society of The Ark and The Dove

Library of Congress Catalogue Card Number 2005931566

ISBN 978-0-8063-1762-5

Made in the United States of America

CONTENTS

FOREWORD

The Founding of Maryland

In 1632 King Charles I of England granted a princely tract of land in Northern Virginia — nearly nine million acres — to Cecil Calvert, second Lord Baltimore. The charter included the most extensive powers awarded to any English subject of the day. Behind this gracious act was the king's gratitude for Cecil's father's years of faithful service to the crown. Cecil was the eldest son and heir of Sir George Calvert (1578/9–1632), a Yorkshire gentleman who, though baptized an Anglican, converted to the Church of Rome in 1625, and on that account could no longer swear allegiance to the king. The required oath ruled out any superior loyalty on earth, and as a newly minted Roman Catholic he could not in good conscience bypass his obligation to the Pope. The English king regretfully bade Calvert farewell, and rewarded him for his years of faithful service by elevating him to the Irish peerage as Baron Baltimore presumably because Irish peers did not sit in the English House of Lords.

Sir George Calvert had long been involved in overseas colonization. He was a stockholder in the Virginia Company and had established a colony called Avalon in Newfoundland. But the extreme climate there rendered it unsatisfactory from his point of view, and out of gratitude for Calvert's past service to the crown, King Charles gratified his wish to try again, this time in a warmer climate, and granted him a large tract of land from the Potomac River up to the 40th parallel of north latitude. The monarch also allowed him to draw up the charter, and the draft incorporated the extraordinary powers long enjoyed by the Bishop of Durham. The bishop also served as the Earl of the County Palatine of Durham and was vested with political as well as ecclesiastical powers that enabled him to protect Northern England from Scottish incursions in the Middle Ages.

At this juncture, George Calvert suddenly died on 17 April 1632, and the charter passed to his son, Cecil Calvert. Tradition has it that King Charles himself inserted the name "Maryland" (in Latin "Maria Terra") in honor of his beloved French Queen, Henrietta Maria, known in England as

Queen Mary.

Cecil, now the Lord Proprietor of Maryland, set about at once to launch the colonization of his American palatinate. His extensive acres in North America would produce no income for him until he could recruit and transport a substantial number of colonists to make clearings in the forest and plant tobacco that could bring a good price in England. He purchased supplies to see them through the first year: clothing, food, axes for felling timber, and agricultural tools, as well as cannons, muskets, gunpowder, and swords for defense. Lord Baltimore also arranged for transport for settlers to the New World in the 358-ton *Ark* and the 26-ton *Dove*, spending in all, according to his own account, some £40,000 — a very large sum in those days.

Persecution of Roman Catholics in England

When Queen Elizabeth I began her 45-year reign in 1558, she endeavored to make the English establishment a church for all of her subjects by preserving its ancient Catholic essence, mediated from apostolic days through the Middle Ages. She engrafted upon it important insights of the sixteenth-century Reformation so as to make it acceptable to moderate Protestants. Her intent was to ensure religious peace by making the Church of England broad enough to accommodate both Papists and Protestants. Eschewing the continental use of thumbscrew and rack to ferret out heresy and schism, she refused to "make windows in men's souls" as long as they would worship together. As a result, the Elizabethan Church of England became perhaps the most Catholic and certainly the "roomiest" church in Christendom. To be sure, anyone found guilty of supporting the forcible overthrow of the English church and state was apprehended, tried, and, if found guilty, executed for treason, but all others who regularly attended church were spared persecution.

Her devout hope was that the recurring rhythms of praise, petition, and penitence, grounded in the continual recalling of God's saving deeds as proclaimed in holy scripture and the *Book Of Common Prayer*, and made present in their lives in sign, symbol, and the sacraments would shape and form her subjects' faith. This hope was largely fulfilled except for a minority of hard-line popish recusants and Protestant dissenters who dug their heels in and refused to conform. By the first half of the seventeenth century, the rising tide of Puritanism in England posed an ever-increasing threat to the Elizabethan Settlement. As long as King James lived, and as long as his son, King Charles, was in power, the rising tide of Puritanism in England was checked, and English "persecution" was relatively mild compared to the extreme form in France and Spain. This situation resulted in Cecil Calvert finding relatively few of his co-religionists, especially the landed ones, who were willing to leave their comfortable homes in England and risk an overseas voyage to a wilderness three thousand miles away.

Cecil Calvert was, however, remarkably successful in overcoming his countrymen's fear of living under the government of a Roman Catholic landlord. He attracted many settlers by offering them free land and the customary political rights that landholders in England enjoyed. Calvert also promised real religious liberty for virtually all Christians. In order to ensure peaceful co-existence, he did not make Maryland a Roman Catholic colony — a step that would have given the London authorities an excuse for terminating his charter. Instead, he attempted a hitherto untried experiment to create a colony in which church and state were separated. He followed Queen Elizabeth's policy of not making windows in men's souls, and also promised settlers that his government would do nothing to prevent or assist the voluntary building of churches. If inhabitants wanted the ministrations of the clergy of their choice, they were at liberty to have them, but only if they would provide voluntary support and not expect income from public taxes.

Considering the fact that Roman Catholic countries at that time were noted for extreme religious intolerance, it is anomalous that religious liberty and the separation of church and state should first have happened in America under a Roman Catholic proprietor. Roger Williams in Rhode Island provided another early example of the same, but as Maryland was settled two years earlier, this was the place where these twin principles that later became essential to the American way of life gained their first foothold in English America.

In Maryland, under the rule of the first Lords Baltimore, everyone could expect to be treated fairly and equally. When the Jesuits sought to acquire land directly from the Indians, Calvert intervened and prohibited any ecclesiastical society from doing so without a license from the governor. When the Jesuits supposed that they were exempt from certain laws, as they would have been in a Roman Catholic colony, the Lord Proprietor made it clear that English common law, not Roman canon law, prevailed in Maryland. This did not mean that Lord Baltimore was disloyal to the Church of Rome. It signaled his determination to secure the future of Maryland by avoiding even a suspicion that his was a Roman Catholic colony.

Commendable as it is in our eyes, this avant-garde experiment was too far ahead of its time. After 1689 when the government of Maryland was taken away from Lord Baltimore during the Glorious Revolution and his province made a Royal Colony, the Church of England was made the established church of the colony. But the concept was not entirely forgotten, and became a part of the American way of life at the time of the American Revolution. It was then that the spirit of the early Calverts ultimately triumphed.

The Voyage of the *Ark* and the *Dove*

Making their departure from the Isle of Wight on 22 November 1633, the *Ark* and the *Dove* sailed past the Scilly Isles into the English Channel, where the winds increased and the sea grew "more boisterous." Then they encountered "fierce tempest" that rent the mainsail in two from top to bottom, so that all control of the rudder was lost. Meanwhile, the *Dove* disappeared from sight and was not heard from again for several months. It was so badly damaged that it returned to England for repairs and eventually rejoined the *Ark* in the Antilles. After the hurricane subsided, the *Ark* enjoyed three months of delightful weather. Continuing past the Straits of Gibraltar and the Madeiras, it picked up the Portuguese trade winds that wafted them comfortably to the West Indies. The only untoward incident occurred when wine was distributed in order to celebrate Christmas, and twelve passengers who drank too freely subsequently died and were buried at sea. After reaching Barbados, the *Ark* and the *Dove* continued past St. Lucia, Guadaloupe, Montserrat, and Nevis, and spent ten days at St. Kitts. They then rounded Cape Hatteras and in due course entered the Chesapeake Bay. Stopping at Point Comfort to show the Virginia authorities their charter from the king, they proceeded up the bay, entered the Potomac River (which they declared to be the most beautiful river they had ever seen, in comparison to which the Thames "seemed a mere rivulet"). Landing at the first island they encountered, St. Clement's Island, they claimed the land for King Charles of England, erected a great wooden cross, and with hearts overflowing with gratitude to Almighty God, celebrated a Mass. It was 25 March 1634, the Feast of the Annunciation of the Blessed Virgin Mary, and also ever since known as "Maryland Day."

As St. Clement's Island contained only 400 acres (too small for the settlement they intended to make), they sailed back down the Potomac and entered St. Mary's River, capable by their estimates of serving as an anchorage for three hundred ships of the largest size. And, to avoid any appearance of injustice that might afford opportunity for hostility, they purchased from the Indian king some thirty miles of land.

The Society of The Ark and The Dove

The first landing of the adventurers at St. Clement's Island in 1634 was not entirely forgotten. We have an account of a commemoration, said to be the fourth one, in observance of Maryland Day in 1855. Those attending came by steamship from Baltimore and Washington. After a procession (said to have been fatiguing "by reason of the heat of the sun and the excessive dust," they stopped at the site of the first governor's residence. After band music and an "elegant ode" sung by a choir, letters were read from distinguished Marylanders such as Charles Carroll of Riversdale, Chief Justice Roger Brooke Taney, and Edward Lloyd (former President of the Maryland Senate). Then came an hour-long patriotic address followed by band music. George Washington Parke

Custis (Washington's stepson and Robert E. Lee's father-in-law) praised the "Maryland Line" for its bravery in the American Revolution, and told them of the confidence General Washington had reposed in them.

But it was not until 1910 that some descendants of the Maryland pioneers, headed by George Norbury MacKenzie, gathered in Baltimore and formed The Society of The Ark and The Dove. They informed their fellow citizens of the "important part" the early settlers played in the development of the entire country. A badge, a flag, and a seal were selected. The badge was described in the Baltimore *Sun*, 6 April 1910, as showing "representation of a spread eagle to convey the Spirit of patriotism," and an ark and a dove resting on the bosom of the eagle. The society presented copies of a portrait of Leonard Calvert, the first Governor of the Province of Maryland, painted by Florence Maccubbin, to various libraries, schools, and colleges in the Baltimore area. The society presented the original painting to the state of Maryland and it hangs in the State House in Annapolis.

Since its founding, the Society has made contributions to a great many projects of historical importance in the State. The Society's Mission Statement, adopted in 1997 and revised in 2002, is as follows: The Society of The Ark and The Dove was founded in 1910 to perpetuate the memory of the first families of Maryland, and to provide opportunities for fellowship for all those who trace their descent from Lord Baltimore and from those who came on the *Ark* and the *Dove* in 1634 to settle the Proprietary Province of Maryland. The society also encourages research in early Maryland history and promotes its dissemination by enlisting knowledgeable speakers for its assemblies and by contributing to the support of such appropriate institutions as the St Clement's Island - Potomac River Museum, the Historic St Mary's City Foundation, the Maryland Historical Society, and Kiplin Hall, the ancestral home of Sir George Calvert in Yorkshire, England.

Canon *Arthur Pierce Middleton*, Ph.D.

INTRODUCTION

Purpose and Scope. In this book are provided documented accounts of the first settlers of Maryland in 1634, followed by compiled genealogies of their descendants, if any, extended to the fifth generation when possible. Emphasis is placed upon citing the primary documentary record sources which establish the genealogical links and the vital statistics.

Identification of Passengers. Because there were no recorded passenger lists for the two ships which brought the first settlers from England to Maryland in 1634, alternative record sources have been exploited in order to reconstruct the rosters of crew and passengers. We acknowledge the prior work of Harry Wright Newman whose 1959 book *The Flowering of the Maryland Palatinate* (reprinted 2004, Clearfield Co., Baltimore), provided documented lists of the gentlemen adventurers, their transportees, and the crew, plus biographies of the adventurers, and several accounts of some of their descendants.

Primary Documentation. The several authoritative records series upon which this study is largely based are as follows: the Maryland Land Patent Books; the minutes, proceedings, and records of the Maryland Prerogative Court, Chancery Court, Provincial Court, and the Assembly; the land, probate, court, tax, and other records of the original counties; and the registers of the earliest churches. Countless other sources are cited in the footnotes supporting the factual data presented in this book.

Arrangement and Numbering. The first part is devoted to Sir George Calvert, Lord Baltimore, the founder of Maryland, and his descendants. In the second part are presented, in alphabetical order, the gentlemen adventurers and other settlers who are known to have left descendants, often followed to the fifth generation. Descendants are serially numbered for reference and identification purposes. Superscript numerals after given names denote that person's generation of descent. In the third part are listed and described the passengers who are not known to have had descendants. Also included are some later arrivals previously and erroneously claimed as 1634 settlers, and some now disallowed spurious or doubtful claims of descendants.

Abbreviations. The following standard abbreviations are used, mainly in the lists of children and in the footnotes.
b. = born   bp. = baptized   bur. = buried   c = about   Co. = County   d. = died
dau. = daughter   d.s.p. = died without issue   fn. = footnote   gent. = gentleman
£ = pounds sterling   m. = married   unm. = unmarried

Additions and Corrections. The Society will appreciate being advised of any needed additions or corrections, if supported by primary documentary record citations.

George Ely Russell, CG, FASG, FNGS
Donna Valley Russell, CG, FASG

ACKNOWLEDGEMENTS

The Society of The Ark and The Dove thanks Patricia Dockman Anderson and Stephen Brewster for their help in compiling the material in this book.

The Society thanks the members of the Society who volunteered considerable time to this book: Mr. William T. Conklin III, Mr. Iredell W. Iglehart, Mrs. Edwin N. Jenkins, Mr. Henry C. Mackall, Mrs. Richard K. Marshall, Mrs. Barrett L. McKown, Canon A. Pierce Middleton, Mr. Gordon P. Smith, and Mr. A. Thomas Wallace.

The Society also acknowledges the basic work of Harry Wright Newman, entitled *The Flowering of the Maryland Palatinate* (1961).

The Ark and The Dove
Adventurers

PART ONE

SIR GEORGE CALVERT'S FAMILY

1. **Sir George**[1] **Calvert**, Baron of Baltimore, son of Leonard and Alice (Crossland) Calvert, was born c1578 at Bolton Castle, Yorkshire, and died in London on 15 April 1632. He was buried at St. Dunstan's-in-the-West, London.[1] He married first at St. Peter's, Cornhill, London, on 22 November 1604 **Anne Mynne**, who died 8 August 1621, aged 42 years, 9 months, 18 days, daughter of George Mynne of Hertingfordbury, Hertfordshire, and his wife Elizabeth Wroth. He married second **Joane** [-?-], who sailed from Jamestown, Virginia, to England with several of Lord Baltimore's children in the *St. Claude*, which wrecked off the English coast before October 1630, with the loss of all aboard.[2]

A persistent tradition about the Calvert family has been disproved by modern research; it misstated that Sir George and Anne (Mynne) Calvert were the parents of a daughter who married a Mr. Brainthwaite and was the mother of William Brainthwaite who settled on Kent Island and died in 1649. No satisfactory documentation has been found to support this allegation. William Brainthwaite, who died c1649/50 without issue, was probably a son of Robert and Ann (Carter) Brainthwaite and grandson of Edward Brainthwaite who married a member of the Calvert family.[3]

George Calvert matriculated at Trinity College, Oxford, on 28 June 1594 at the age of 14, receiving his Bachelor of Arts degree on 23 February 1596/97. He served as Under Secretary of State, was Clerk of the Privy Council in 1605, and was knighted on 29 September 1617. He was a member of Parliament and from February 1618/19 to 1625 was Secretary of State. He was a member of the Virginia Company and in 1622 was admitted to the New England Company.

In 1622 he was granted all of the Province of Newfoundland. In 1623 he was assigned the southeast peninsula, which he called Avalon, over which he was given almost royal authority. He became a Roman Catholic and in February 1624/25 resigned all his preferments. On 16 February

---

1. John Frederick Dorman, *Adventurers of Purse and Person, Virginia, 1607-1624/5. Vol. 1: Families A-F.* 4th ed.(2004), [hereafter Dorman], 468-469.

2. Dorman, 469, citing the Sloane Papers, British Museum, London.

3. *Biographical Dictionary of the Maryland Legislature*, 1:159-160. John Bailey Calvert Nicklin, "The Calvert Family," *Maryland Genealogies*, 1:132-170 [hereafter Nicklin] does not recognize the Calvert-Brainthwaite marriage.

1624/25 he was made a member of the Irish peerage as Baron Baltimore of Baltimore. He visited Newfoundland with his wife and family (except for Cecil) in 1628, taking with him some 40 colonists. The climate was too harsh for Lady Baltimore, who went to Virginia and lived at Jamestown.

Returning to England, Lord Baltimore requested a charter for land south of the James River, but the King declined; instead, he granted Baltimore land north and east of the Potomac River. The Charter of Maryland gave him sweeping powers, with only two limitations: he could not make any laws that contravened the laws of England, and he had to secure the advice and consent of the free men of the Province.

Lord Baltimore never came to Maryland. He was buried on 15 April 1632 at St. Dunstan's-in-the-West, London, leaving a will dated 14 April 1632 and proved 21 April 1632. His oldest son and heir Cecil received title to the Charter on 20 June 1632.[4]

Children of George and Anne (Mynne) Calvert:[5]

+ 2. Cecil[2] Calvert, b. 1605.
   3. Anne Calvert, bp. 1 April 1607, d. after 1672, m. by 1632 William Peasley, went to Newfoundland, later returned to England.
   4. Dorothy Calvert, bp. 18 Aug. 1608; bur. 13 Jan. 1623/4; no issue.
   5. Elizabeth Calvert, bp. 18 Nov. 1609; probably lost at sea with her stepmother.
+ 6. Leonard Calvert. [See his account in Part Two: Families of the Passengers.]
+ 7. Grace Calvert, bp. 5 Feb. 1611/12.
   8. George Calvert, bp. 8 July 1613; d. unm. in Maryland 1634; mentioned in Father White's Journal as a passenger and was present at a conference with the Chief of the Patuxon [sic] 20 June 1634.[6]
   9. Francis Calvert, living 1627/28; d. without issue, probably lost as sea with his stepmother.
+ 10. Helen Calvert, bp. 5 Dec. 1615.
   11. Henry Calvert, bp. 8 March 1617/18; d. unm. 1635.
   12. John Calvert, bp. 31 Jan. 1618/19; bur. 1 Feb. 1618/19.

Child of George and Joane Calvert:[7]

   13. Philip Calvert, b. 1626, d. 1682; m. (1) Anne Wolseley and (2) Jane Sewell; held several offices in Md. and served as Governor 1660-1661.

2. Cecil[2] Calvert, 2nd Lord Baltimore, son of Sir George and Anne (Mynne) Calvert, was born 8 August 1605 and died 30 November 1675.

---

4. Dorman, 468.

5. Dorman, 469-470.

6. *Archives,* 5:164; Harry Wright Newman, *The Flowering of the Maryland Palatinate* (Washington: the author, 1961; Baltimore: Clearfield Co., reprinted 2004), 179-180.

7. Nicklin, 138.

He was buried in St. Giles-in-the-Fields, Middlesex.[8] He married, by settlement dated 20 March 1627/28, **Anne Arundell**, daughter of Sir Thomas Arundell, Lord Arundell of Wardour, a Count of the Holy Roman Empire, and his wife Anne (Philipson) Thurgood, at Tisbury, Wiltshire.[9] She died 23 July 1649, age 34.

Cecil entered Trinity College, Oxford, in 1621 and was admitted to Gray's Inn on 8 August 1633. As heir to his father's Maryland Charter, he lived in England but promoted the settlement of Maryland.[10]

Children of Cecil and Anne Calvert:[11]

14. Georgiana[3] Calvert, b. Aug. 1629, d. in infancy.
15. Mary Calvert, b. 18 July 1633, d. aged 2 weeks.
16. George Calvert, b. 15 Sept. 1634, d. 6 June 1636.
17. Frances Calvert, b. Nov. 1635, d. 27 Dec. 1635.
18. Anne Calvert, b. 9 Oct. 1636, d. 6 May 1661.
+ 19. Charles Calvert, b. 27 Aug. 1637.
20. Mary Calvert, b. 30 Nov. 1638, d. 24 Sept. 1671; m. c1650 Sir William Blakiston of Gibside, Durham, 2nd Bart.
21. Cecilius Calvert, b. 23 Feb. 1638/39; d. 4 Feb. 1640/41.
22 Elizabeth Calvert, bur. 16 Jan. 1711/12; administration on her estate granted to brother Charles 25 Jan. 1711/12.

7. Grace[2] Calvert, daughter of Sir George and Anne (Mynne) Calvert, was baptized 5 February 1611/12 and married about 1630 Sir **Robert Talbot**, 2nd Baronet of Cartown, County Kildare, Ireland, and brother of the Duke of Tyrconnell. Sir Robert became a baronet in March 1633, and was a Member of Parliament between June and October 1634. He was attainted [accused of treason] in 1642 but was restored to his estates in 1665. He died by 13 May 1671 when administration on his estate was granted. Grace Calvert was living on 22 November 1675 when her brother Cecil bequeathed a ring to her.[12]

Children of Sir Robert and Grace (Calvert) Talbot:[13]

23. Robert[3] Talbot, whose line became extinct.
24. Richard Talbot, created Earl and then Marquess and then Duke of Tyroconnell; had two daughters, but both died without issue.

---

8. Nicklin, 138.

9. Dorman, 470, citing monumental inscription, Tisbury, Wilts., in Arthur Collins, *The Peerage of England* (4th ed., London, 1768), 6:598-599.

10. *Ibid.*

11. Nicklin, 139; Dorman, 470.

12. Dorman, 471.

13. "Talbot of Carton," *Burke's Extinct and Dormant Baronetcies of England, Ireland, and Scotland* (1841); reprint GPC, 1985, 614.

25. Sir William Talbot, 3rd Baronet, came to Md. in 1670 and was made Principal Secretary of the Province. On the death of his father he returned to Ireland and died after June 1671.

+ 26. Frances Talbot, d. 1718.

27. [possibly] George Talbot of Md., d. without issue.

10. **Helen² Calvert**, daughter of Sir George and Anne (Mynne) Calvert, baptized 5 December 1615, married **James Talbot** of Ballyconnell, County Cavan, Ireland, son of Walter Talbot. James was High Sheriff of County Cavan and lost his estates when Cromwell invaded Ireland. He moved to Dublin for a short time, until all Catholics were ordered to leave the city on pain of death. In 1666 he was a signer of the Remonstrance of the Roman Catholic Nobility and Gentry of Ireland to King Charles II. In later years James Talbot lived at Castle Rubey, County Roscommon.[14]

Child of James and Helen (Calvert) James Talbot:

+ 28. George³ Talbot.

19. **Charles³ Calvert**, 3rd Lord Baltimore, son of Cecil and Anne (Arundell) Calvert, was born 27 August 1637 and died 21 February 1715. He was buried at St. Pancras, Middlesex. He married first in 1656 **Mary Darnall**, daughter of Ralph Darnall of Loughton, Hertfordshire. He married second in 1666 **Jane Lowe**, daughter of Vincent Lowe of Denby, Derbyshire, and widow of Henry Sewell. Charles married third 6 December 1701 **Mary (Thorp) Banks**, a widow; she died 13 March 1710. He married fourth in 1712 **Margaret Charleton**, daughter of Thomas Charleton of Hexham, Northumberland. She died 30 July 1732, having married as her second husband Lawrence Eliot of Yapton Place, Sussex.[15]

Charles Calvert was Receiver General of Maryland in 1660, and was appointed Governor of Maryland by his father from 1661-1675, Secretary of the Province 1666-1669 and 1673-1674, and Collector of the Patuxent. He stayed in Maryland until the boundary dispute with William Penn of Pennsylvania required his presence in England in 1684, where he remained until his death.[16]

Children of Charles and Jane (Lowe) Calvert:[17]

29. Cecil⁴ Calvert, b. 1667, bur. 1 July 1681.

30. Clare Calvert, b. 1679, d. 1693, m. cousin the Hon. Edward Maria Somerset, grandson of Sir John and Mary (Arundell) Somerset. Clare died before the

---

14. Dorman, 472.

15. Nicklin, 139.

16. Dorman, 473-474.

17. Nicklin, 139-140.

last festivities of the wedding day had ended.[18]

31. Anne Calvert, b. 1673, d. 10 Feb. 1731; m. (1) 26 May 1694 at St. Giles-in-the-Fields her sister's widower, Edward Maria Somerset. He d. without issue and she m. (2) John Paston of Horton, Gloucestershire. No issue.
+ 32. Benedict Leonard Calvert, b. 21 March 1679.
33. Charles Calvert, b. c1690, d. 1733.[19]

26. Frances[3] Talbot, daughter of Sir Robert and Grace (Calvert) Talbot, died in 1718, married her cousin **Richard Talbot,** born 1637 and died 1703, son of John and Lady Catherine (Plunket) Talbot. Richard was appointed Auditor General of Ireland shortly before the [Glorious] Revolution of 1689.[20]

Children of Richard and Frances (Talbot) Talbot:[21]

34. Richard[4] Talbot, d. without issue.
35. Robert Talbot, d. without issue.
+ 36. John Talbot.
37. Valentine Talbot, m. Mary Tobin, dau. of James Tobin of Ballaghtobin, County Tipperary, Ire.

28. George[3] Talbot, son of James[3] and Helen (Calvert) Talbot, died after 1687. He married **Sarah [-?-].** He came to Maryland and on 11 June 1680 was granted the Manor of Susquehanna, or *New Connaught*, made up of some 32,000 acres in Cecil County. He was a member of the Upper House of Assembly and was Surveyor General of Maryland.

On 31 October 1684 he stabbed Christopher Rousby to death on board HMS *The Quaker.* He was put into irons and taken to Virginia, where he was imprisoned in Gloucester County. He escaped to Cecil County where he hid in the mountains near his estate. He surrendered and was tried by the General Court in Virginia in April 1687, but was granted a pardon by King James II dated 9 September 1686 and released.[22]

Children of George and Sarah Talbott:

38. James[4] Talbot, evidently d. without issue.
39. Helen Talbot.
40. Margaret Talbot.

32. Benedict Leonard[4] Calvert, 4th Lord Baltimore, son of Charles and

---

18. *Maryland Historical Magazine*, 22:328fn.
19. Not recognized by Dorman.
20. "Talbot of Malahide," *Burke's Peerage, Baronetage, Knightage* (1956 ed.), 2122-2123.
21. *Ibid.,* 2133.
22. Dorman, 475-476.

Jane (Sewell) Calvert, was born 21 March 1679 and died 16 April 1715. He was buried at Epsom, Surrey, England.[23] On 2 January 1698 he married Lady **Charlotte Lee,** daughter of Edward Henry Lee, Earl of Lichfield, by his wife Lady Charlotte Fitzroy, the natural daughter of King Charles II by his mistress, Barbara (Villiers) Palmer, the Duchess of Cleveland. After Lord Baltimore died, Charlotte Lee married second Christopher Crewe on 6 December 1719; she died 21 January 1721 and was buried at Woodford in Essex.[24]

Children of Benedict Leonard and Charlotte (Lee) Calvert:
+ 41. Charles[5] Calvert, b. 29 Sept. 1699.
  42. Benedict Leonard Calvert, b. 20 Sept. 1700; d. unm. 1 June 1732.
+ 43. Edward Henry Calvert, b. 31 Aug. 1701.
  44. Cecilius Calvert, b. 6 Nov. 1702, d. unm. 1765.
+ 45. Charlotte Calvert, b. 6 Nov. 1702 [twin?].
+ 46. Jane Calvert, b. 19 Nov. 1703.
  47. Barbara Calvert, b. 3 Oct. 1704, d. young.
  48. Anne Calvert.

36. **John[4] Talbot,** son of Richard and Frances (Talbot) Talbot, married **Frances Wogan,** daughter of Colonel Nicholas Wogan of Rathcofy.[25]

Children of John and Frances (Wogan) Talbot:
  49. Richard[5] Talbot, b. 1766, d. 24 Oct. 1788; m. Margaret O'Relly, dau. of James; she d. 27 Sept. 1834.
  50. Nicholas Talbot, officer in Austrian Service; killed at Battle of Collin, 1757, unmarried.

41. **Charles[5] Calvert,** 5th Lord Baltimore, son of Benedict Leonard and Charlotte (Lee) Calvert, was born 29 September 1699 and died 24 April 1751. He was buried at Erith in Kent. On 20 July 1730 he married **Mary Janssen,** daughter of Sir Theodore Janssen and sister of Stephen Theodore Janssen, Lord Mayor of London.[26] Charles was succeeded in the title and estate by his only son Frederick, 6th Lord Baltimore, a minor.[27]

By an unknown woman, he was the father of an illegitimate son, whom he acknowledged in his will:[28]
+ 51. Benedict[6] Calvert, b. c1724.

---

23. Nicklin, 140.
24. *Ibid.*
25. "Talbot of Malahide," 2133.
26. Nicklin, 141.
27. *Maryland Gazette,* 10 July 1751.
28. Nicklin, 141, 159-160.

Children of Charles and Mary (Janssen) Calvert:
+ 52. Frederick Calvert, b. 6 Feb. 1732.
  53. Frances Dorothy Calvert, b. 1734, d. 1736.
+ 54. Louisa Calvert.
  55. Charles Calvert, b. 21 Jan. 1737.
+ 56. Caroline Calvert.

43. **Edward Henry⁵ Calvert**, son of Benedict Leonard and Charlotte (Lee) Calvert, was born 31 August 1701 and died in April or May 1730. He married **Margaret [-?-]**, who married second on 15 October 1741 James Fitzgerald of the Middle Temple, London.[29]
   Child of Edward Henry and Margaret Calvert:
   57. Frances Maria⁶ Calvert, bp. 29 Feb. 1727.[30]

45. **Charlotte⁵ Calvert**, daughter of Benedict Leonard and Charlotte (Lee) Calvert, was born 6 November 1702 and died in 1744. She married **Thomas Brerewood, Jr.**, son of Thomas Brerewood, Sr., of Horton, Bucks, who came to Baltimore County and died leaving a will dated 8 August 1741, proved 10 February 1746, naming his daughter-in-law the Honorable Charlotte Brerewood, who had conveyed to him by deed of settlement dated 30 August 1730 10,000 acres in Baltimore County called *My Lady's Manor* or *Lord Baltimore's Gift*. Brerewood's "daughter," the said Charlotte, was named his executrix in England and his grandson William Brerewood was appointed his executor in Maryland. Neither was to molest Mrs. Elinor Turner in a settlement the testator made to her on 4 April 1740. A codicil dated 10 Feb. 1746 stated that his grandson William had died and William Dullan, merchant of Joppa, was appointed executor in Maryland.[31]
   Children of Thomas and Charlotte (Calvert) Brerewood:
   58. William⁶ Brerewood, d. by 1746.
   59. Francis Brerewood.

46. **Jane⁵ Calvert**, daughter of Benedict Leonard and Charlotte (Lee) Calvert, was born 19 November 1703, died 12 or 15 July 1778, and was buried at Westminster Abbey, London. On 4 May 1720, at St. Paul's

---

29. *Maryland Historical Magazine*, 28:336fn.

30. *Ibid.*, fn 335 cites St. Margaret's Parish, Anne Arundel Co., Md., but this record was not found among the published records of that church.

31. Md. Wills, 25:1-4.

Cathedral, she married Capt. or Col. **John Hyde** of Kingston Lisle, Berks.[32] He was baptized at St. Paul's Covent Garden on 8 September 1695, the son of Frederick Hyde and Ellen (Hemming) Hyde. He was an officer in a Regiment of the Guards.[33] He died before 17 February 1746 and was buried at Southampton, England.[34]

    Children of John and Jane (Calvert) Hyde:

    60. John[6] Hyde.

    61. Henry Hyde.

    62. Frederick Hyde, Captain, R.N., d. by 2 July 1764; mentioned 15 Aug. 1763 in will of uncle Cecilius Calvert.

    63. Philip Hyde.

    64. Catherine Hyde, m. Rev. Thomas Willis (1743-1789).

    65. Mary Hyde.

    66. Jane Hyde, m. Walter Joyce; issue.

+ 67. [daughter], m. David Graham of Md.

51. Benedict[6] Calvert, son of Charles Calvert by an unknown wife, was born c1724 in England and died at *Mount Airy*, Prince George's County, Maryland, on 9 January 1788. On 21 April 1748 he was married in St. Anne's Church, by the Reverend John Gordon, to **Elizabeth Calvert**, born 24 February 1730 in Anne Arundel County, died July 1798 at *Mount Airy*, daughter of Charles and Rebeccca (Gerard) Calvert.[35] The marriage record identified Benedict as Collector of H.M. Customs for Patuxent District, and Elizabeth as only surviving daughter of the late Hon. Charles Calvert, deceased, formerly Governor of the Province.

    Children of Benedict and Elizabeth (Calvert) Calvert:[36]

    68. Rebecca[7] Calvert, b. 25 Dec. 1749, d. in infancy.

    69. Eleanor Calvert, b. c1753, d. in Va. 28 Sept. 1811; m. at *Mount Airy* 2 Feb. 1744 John Parke Custis (1753-1781).

    70. Charles Calvert, b. 3 Oct. 1756, d. unm. 30 Jan. 1777 at Eton.[37]

    71. Elizabeth Calvert, d. 1814; m. 15 Jan. 1780 Dr. Charles Steuart.

    72. Edward Henry Calvert, b. 7 Nov. 1766, d. 12 July 1846; m. 1 March 1796

---

    32. Calvert Papers #81 contains the original marriage contract between Capt. John Hyde and Jane Calvert.

    33. Bryden Hyde states that this Capt. John Hyde was not the same John Hyde mentioned in Mrs. Russell Hastings' article in the *Maryland Historical Magazine* of December 1927. That John Hyde, of London, was a sea captain and merchant, who owned land in Maryland, and who had three sons: John, Herbert, and Samuel. *Ibid.*

    34. *Ibid.*, cites Westminster Abbey Registers.

    35. *Society of Colonial Wars*, 2:209. *Anne Arundel Co. Church Records*, 101.

    36. Nicklin, 160-161; Rebecca's baptism in *Church Records*, 102. *Maryland Gazette*, 27 April 1748.

    37. *Maryland Gazette*, 28 April 1744.

Elizabeth Biscoe (1780-1857).
73. George Calvert, b. 2 Feb. 1768, d. 28 Jan. 1838 at *Riversdale*, Prince George's Co.;[38] m. Rosalie Eugenia Stier, b. Antwerp, Belgium, d. 13 March 1821.
74. Philip Calvert, d. young.
75. Leonard Calvert, d. young.
76. Cecilius Calvert, d. young.
77. John Calvert, d. after 1788.
78. William Calvert, d. after 1788.
79. Ariana Calvert, d. 24 May 1784 at *Mount Airy,* age 20.[39]
80. Robert Calvert, d. young.

52. Frederick⁶ Calvert, 6ᵗʰ Lord Baltimore, son of Charles and Mary (Janssen) Calvert, was born 6 February 1732 and died without legitimate issue on 4 September 1771 at Naples, Italy. He married on 9 March 1753 Lady **Diana Egerton,** born 1732, died 1758, daughter of Scrope Egerton, Duke of Bridgewater.[40]
Illegitimate children of Frederick Calvert by Hester Whalen of Ireland:
81. Henry⁷ Harford, b. 5 Apr. 1758, d. 1834; m. (1) June 1792 Louisa Pigou, dau. of Peter Pigou; (2) June 1806 Esther Ryecroft, b. c1775, d. 1853. He was the last proprietor of Md., but did not bear the title Lord Baltimore due to his illegitimacy.[41]
82. Frances Mary Harford, b. 28 Nov. 1759, d. Florence, Italy, 18 March 1822; m. 21 July 1784 William Frederick Wyndham, b. 1710, d. 1763, son of Charles Wyndham.[42]
Illegitimate children of Frederick Calvert by Elizabeth Dawson of Lincolnshire:
83. Sophia Hales, b. 1765.
84. Elizabeth Hales.
Illegitimate child of Frederick Calvert by Elizabeth Hope of Munster, Germany:
85. Charlotte Hope, b. 1770 Hamburg.

54. Louisa⁶ Calvert, daughter of Charles and Mary (Janssen) Calvert, married **John Browning,** who had been Secretary to her father. The Hon. Louisa Browning, widow, died 15 November 1821 at Horton Lodge, Epsom Parish, Surrey. She was buried in the family vault at Epsom

38. *Maryland Gazette*, 1 Feb. 1838.
39. *Ibid.*, 10 June 1784.
40. Nicklin, 141-2.
41. *Biographical Dictionary of Maryland Legislature*, 411-412; Vera Foster Rollo, *The Proprietorship of Maryland: A Documented Account* (1989) [hereafter Rollo].
42. Nicklin, 142; Rollo, 288, 296-297.

Church.[43]

Child of John and Louisa (Calvert) Browning:
86. Charles[7] Browning, b. July 1765; issue.

56. **Caroline**[6] **Calvert**, daughter of Charles and Mary (Janssen) Calvert, married **Robert Eden**, Governor of Maryland, who died in 1784. She died in 1786.
Children of John and Caroline (Calvert) Eden:[44]
87. Frederick Morton[7] Eden.
88. William Eden.
89. Catherine Eden, b. 6 June 1770.

67. [–?–][6] **Hyde**, daughter of Captain John and Jane (Calvert) Hyde, died by 4 February 1757. She married first **David Graham** of Maryland, who died on a voyage to England in 1754. She married second **Benjamin Young, Jr.** of Maryland, but had no issue by him. He married second Mary Dulany, by whom he had issue.[45]
Child of David and [–?–] (Hyde) Graham:
90. Catherine[7] Graham, b. by 9 July 1752, d. by 12 Oct. 1760 at home of uncle Charles Graham of Calvert County.[46]

---

43. Rollo, 77, 346; *Maryland Gazette*, 7 Feb. 1822.
44. Rollo, 98; Catherine's birth in *Maryland Gazette*, 7 June 1770.
45. Mrs. Russell Hastings, "Calvert and Darnall Gleanings from English Wills," *Maryland Historical Magazine*, 22:340 fn.
46. *Ibid.*

PART TWO

FAMILIES OF THE PASSENGERS

Introduction. In this section are provided biographical accounts of the passengers known to have had families. Basic information is given for their children, grand children, and great grandchildren, insofar as known, plus the vital data for the fifth-generation descendants. Note that the superscript numeral following the progenitor's given name is the generation number and that the descendants are serially numbered.

JAMES BALDRIDGE

1. **James[1] Baldridge** came on the *Ark* and the *Dove* in 1633. He married **Dorothy** [-?-], who was living on 4 February 1646/7 when she sued Richard Duke for 100 pounds of tobacco.[47] Newman states that James Baldridge, gentleman, and his brother Thomas Baldridge, arrived in the Province before 1637, but there is no record to prove how or when they arrived in the Province.[48] James Baldridge served as Sheriff of St. Mary's County, and as a member of the first Maryland General Assembly in 1637.[49]

At an Admiralty Court case on 21 August 1645 James Baldridge, then of Westminster, County Middlesex, yeoman, aged 55, testified about Leonard Calvert taking possession of the Isle of Kent.[50] On 3 April 1651 Virginia Governor William Berkeley granted James and Thomas Baldridge 840 acres of land in Northumberland County, Virginia.[51]

James Baldridge died leaving a will dated 26 November 1658 and proved in Westmoreland County, Virginia, on 10 January 1658/9. He named Daniel Sisson, and wife Dorothy.[52] Dorothy Baldridge died leaving a will dated 2 November 1662, proved 11 March 1662/3, in which she

47. *Archives of Maryland*, 10:96.

48. Harry Wright Newman, *The Flowering of the Maryland Palatinate* [hereafter "Newman, *Flowering*"], 167.

49. John Bennett Boddie, *Virginia Historical Genealogies* (Baltimore: Genealogical Publ. Co., 1965), 26-27.

50. Public Record Office (England), document HCA 13/60, abstracted in Peter W. Coldham, *More English Adventurers and Emigrants, 1625-1777* (Baltimore: Genealogical Publishing Co., 2002), 5.

51. Newman, *Flowering*, 168.

52. Westmoreland Co. Wills, 1:106, abstracted in Augusta B. Fothergill, *Wills of Westmoreland County, Virginia, 1654-1800* (reprint, Baltimore: Clearfield Co., 1990), 4.

named grandson Charles Baldridge, William Baldridge (son of her nephew James Baldridge), Joshua, son of Thomas Butler, John Stands and Stephen, and three grandchildren: Elizabeth, Ann, and Mary Baynham. Thomas Butler, her son-in-law, was named executor.[53]

James Baldridge was the father of:[54]

+   2. Jane[2] Baldridge, m. Thomas Butler.
+   3. [-?-] Baldridge, m. Capt. Alexander Baynham.
+   4. William Baldridge, m. Elizabeth [-?-].

2. **Jane[2] Baldridge**, daughter of James and Dorothy Baldridge, first married by 1650 to **Thomas Butler**, who died by 27 February 1678. Her second marriage was to **John Berryman**, who died by 28 April 1680. Her third marriage was to **Joseph Harvey** by 26 October 1681.[55] Thomas Butler, probably the oldest son of Thomas and Joan (Mountstephen) Butler, was brought to Virginia by John Hallowes by 1650.[56]

Thomas and Jane were the parents of:[57]

+   5. Joshua[3] Butler.
+   6. Thomas Butler.
    7. [possibly] John Butler, who was assigned land in 1670.

3. **[-?-][2] Baldridge**, daughter of James and Dorothy Baldridge, died by November 1662, having married **Alexander Baynham**. Alexander Baynham was born c1620. He gave his age as approximately 35 in 1655. He was in Maryland by 1642, and in 1649 moved to the Northern Neck of Virginia with John Hallowes, John Tew, the Baldridges and others. He was living on 18 March 1662/3. No will has been found.[58]

Alexander and [-?-] (Baldridge) Baynham were the parents of:

    8. Mary[3] Baynham.
    9. Elizabeth Baynham.
    10. Anne Baynham.

4. **William[2] Baldridge**, son of James and Dorothy Baldridge, was born c1631. He gave his age as twenty-four when he made a deposition on 1 October 1655.[59] In about 1650 he went with his parents to Virginia, and

---

53. Westmoreland Co. Wills, 1:188, abstracted in Fothergill, 6.

54. Newman, *Flowering*, 169.

55. Boddie, *Historical Genealogies*, 27.

56. Boddie, 26.

57. Boddie, 27.

58. Newman, *Flowering*, 335.

59. Beverly Fleet, *Virginia Colonial Abstracts*, 3 volumes (reprint, Baltimore: Genealogical Publishing Co., 1988), 1:654.

he died by July 1659. He married **Elizabeth** [-?-].[60] He left a will dated 20 March 1658/9 and proved 20 July 1659. He named Daniel Hutt and Edmund Lindsey who were to have minor legacies, and then left everything to his wife Elizabeth and his son Charles. In a codicil dated 21 March 1658/9, he left three cows to the three children of his brother-in-law Alexander Baynham.[61]

William Baldridge was the father of:[62]

11. Charles[3] Baldridge.

5. Joshua[3] Butler, son of Thomas and Jane (Baldridge) Butler, was named in his grandmother's will in 1662. He died in King George County, Virginia, in 1725. Joshua had at least one son:[63]

12. Joshua[4] Butler. In 1735 he and Grace Ripley conveyed land to Thomas Turner of Hanover Parish, King George Co., Va.

6. Thomas[3] Butler, son of Thomas and Jane (Baldridge) Butler, was born c1650, probably in Virginia, and died in Westmoreland County, Virginia, after 2 May 1714. His wife has not been positively identified, but he may have married **Anne Lancelott**, daughter of John and Anne (Gray) Lancelott. Thomas Butler died leaving a will dated 2 May 1714. He named his son William, son James, daughter Elizabeth Baker, grandsons Thomas, John, and James Butler (sons of John), and [grand-daughter] Ann Baker, daughter of Elizabeth.[64]

Thomas Butler was the father of:

+ 13. John[4] Butler, m. Katherine Price.
  14. William Butler.
+ 15. James Butler.
  16. Elizabeth Butler, deeded land by Nathaniel Gray 1707; m. [-?-] Baker.
  17. Thomas Butler, deeded land by Nathaniel Gray 1707.

13. John[4] Butler, son of Thomas and Anne (Lancelott) Butler, died by January 1712. He married **Katherine Price**, daughter of Meredith Price. John Butler died leaving a will proved 28 January 1712, naming his wife Katherine, brothers William and James, John Baker, and sons Thomas, John, and James. John and Katherine were the parents of:[65]

60. Newman, *Flowering*, 334.
61. Westmoreland Co. Wills, 1:93, cited in Newman, *Flowering*, 334.
62. Newman, *Flowering*, 334.
63. Boddie, *Historical Genealogies*, 27.
64. Boddie, *Historical Genealogies*, 28.
65. Boddie, *Historical Genealogies*, 28.

18. Thomas⁵ Butler, living 2 May 1734.
19. James Butler, d. cJan. 1749; m. and had issue.
20. William Butler, d. c1731; m. and had issue.
21. John Butler, acquired 100 acres by 1714 will of grandfather Thomas Butler.

15. James⁴ Butler, son of Thomas and Anne (Lancelott) Butler, was born by 1690 in Westmoreland County, Virginia. He died in Stafford County, Virginia after 24 April 1732. He married **Katherine** [-?-], who died after 1732. James and Katherine were the parents of:

22. William⁵ Butler, m. by 1738, Mary Mason; d. probably in Stafford Co., Va., after 1753.

Major THOMAS BALDRIDGE

1. Major **Thomas¹ Baldridge** arrived about the same time as his brother James [see above], although there is no indication of exactly how or when they arrived. He attended the Second Assembly of 1637.⁶⁶ Newman traced his career in Maryland down to 1650 and stated that he moved to Northumberland County, Virginia, where he was a Justice of the Peace in 1652. He died intestate in 1654 in Westmoreland County, Virginia. He married **Grace Beman**, who married second, John Tew.⁶⁷ On 20 August 1654 John Tew and his wife Grace, widow of Thomas Baldridge, renounced administration of the estate of Thomas Baldridge. On 9 April 1655 James Baldridge, administrator of the estate of Thomas Baldridge, exhibited Baldridge's inventory in court.⁶⁸

Major Thomas Baldridge was the father of:
+   2. James² Baldridge.
+   3. Mary Baldridge, m. Richard Heaberd 1657.

2. **James² Baldridge**, son of Major Thomas Baldridge and Grace (Beman) Baldridge, died in Westmoreland County, Virginia, leaving a will dated 20 April 1664. He married **Elizabeth** [-?-] who survived him. He left a minor son William.⁶⁹ James was the father of:

4. William³ Baldridge, minor 1664.

3. **Mary² Baldridge**, daughter of Major Thomas Baldridge and Grace (Beman) Baldridge, married **Richard Heaberd** in 1657. Richard Heaberd

66. Newman, *Flowering*, 169.
67. Newman, *Flowering*, 170-171.
68. Fleet, *Colonial Abstracts*, 1:654, 666.
69. Newman, *Flowering*, 336.

was in Westmoreland County, Virginia, by 20 November 1655 when Samuel Bonam assigned him a patent for 300 acres on the Potomack River, Northumberland County.[70] On 15 June 1657 intending to marry Mary, daughter of the late Major Thomas Baldridge, he conveyed a great deal of property to Alexander Baynham and Thomas Wilsford for the use of his wife [to be]. He made provision for any future children.[71]

ANAM BENUM

1. **Anam**[1] **Benum**, whose name was variously rendered as Anum/Annum/ Enam/Enim Banum/Benam/Benim/Benham, was born c1617, married **Alice** [-?-] after 1657, and died at Newtown, Queens County, Long Island, New York, shortly before 9 November 1670.

He was employed in England by Mr. Thomas Greene, Esq., gentleman, a Roman Catholic from Bobbing, Kent, who sailed for Maryland in 1633 on the ship *Ark* with servants Anam Benam and Thomas Cooper. Greene claimed them as headrights when he demanded a land warrant.[72]

Having completed his indentured service by 25 January 1637[/8], on that date, styled "planter, of Mattapanient," Annum Benum's proxie was exhibited and he was among the freeholders summoned to appear at the next Maryland Assembly.[73] Mattapanient Hundred in Saint Mary's County was located on the south side of the Patuxent River about two miles upriver from the Chesapeake Bay. By 1639 the Jesuits had cleared the land and built homes there, and were raising food crops to support the work of the mission.[74] On 14 February 1638 Anum Benum, who signed by + mark, was among the six residents of Mattapanient Hundred who chose Henry Bishop as their Burgess or Deputy to the next General Assembly.[75] Bishop was in charge of the fort which had been built to protect the Patuxent River approach.[76]

At the Maryland Provincial Court on 25 January 1637[/8] Annum Benum of Mattapanient, planter, appeared and confessed that he owed

---

70. Fleet, *Colonial Abstracts*, 1:667.

71. Fleet, *Colonial Abstracts*, 1:685.

72. Proprietary Records of the Provincial Court of Maryland, Patent Records, F&B (1) (1640-1658): 17, 41-42; ABH:67; Z&A (2): 346. In 1648 Greene was granted a patent for 2000 acres on the north side of St. Hierom's Creek in St. Mary's Co. He was Governor of Maryland 1647-1649.

73. Maryland Assembly Proceedings, Z:15, in *Archives of Maryland*, 1:3.

74. Charles E. Fenwick, "Mattapany-Sewall Manor," in *Chronicles of St. Mary's* vol. 4, no. 8 (Aug. 1956), 1.

75. Maryland Assembly Proceedings, MC:36, in *Archives*, 1:28.

76. Fenwick.

353 pounds of tobacco to Thomas Cornwallis, Esq., which was to have been paid 10 November last. At Court on 5 February 1637[8] Anum Benum acknowledged that he owed 150 pounds of tobacco to James Cauther. On 6 February 1637[8] he and two other planters of St. Maries acknowledged themselves to owe 780 pounds of tobacco to Mr. Thomas Cornwallis, Esq., to be paid before 10 November next.[77] Anum Benam's sperate debt[78] of 200 pounds of tobacco owed to James Hitches was listed in the 12 December 1638 inventory of Hitches' personal estate. Enam Benam's debt of 500 pounds of tobacco, owed to Justinian Snowe, late of St. Marys, was listed in the 24 May 1639 inventory of Snowe's estate, annotated "received since."[79]

Apparently overwhelmed with debt, in or shortly after 1639 Anum Benum became a fugitive from Maryland. On 8 May 1643 the Maryland Provincial Court addressed a certificate to the President of the New Netherlands and to New England: "We do certifie that Thomas Cornwaleys hath recovered a judgement of Court agst the said Enam Benam, 1630 pounds of tobacco, and that nothing appears on record satisfied toward it."[80]

He next appeared at Gravesend in Kings County, New Netherlands, where on 20 December 1648 he received lot 20.[81] On 22 January 1652/3 he received a lot and plantation in Gravesend from George Jewell.[82] At the New Amsterdam Dutch Church on 25 June 1651 he sponsored the baptism of twin children of Wouter Wael.

In 23 January 1656/7 Enom Benam was named in the divorce proceedings of George Baldwin of Gravesend and his wife Abigail (Sweet) Baldwin. Testimony in the court case established that Benam had persuaded Abigail to forsake her husband, to become his wife, and to bear his child. The New Netherlands Court ordered that Enom pay 200 gilders toward support of the child, and fined him 50 gilders, to be paid from his estate before he could be set at liberty. Abigail Baldwin was ordered to be banished from Gravesend. In 1657 she returned to her native town of Warwick, Rhode Island, resumed her maiden name, and - as Abigail Sweet

---

77. Maryland Provincial Court Proceedings, Z:11, 12, 25, in *Archives*, 4:8, 9, 11. Benum signed by mark +.

78. A debt for which there is hope of recovery.

79. Maryland Provincial Court Proceedings, Z:115, 128, in *Archives*, 4:73, 84-85.

80. Maryland Provincial Court Proceedings, P.R.:99, in *Archives*, 4:204. The certificate also named three Irishmen, also fugitives for debt.

81. Bergen, *Early Settlers of Kings County, New York*.

82. *Gravesend Town Records*.

also known as Abigail Baldwin - married Thomas Bradley.[83]

On 30 August 1660 Benum obtained a patent for 28 morgens of land in Flatlands, New York. Shortly thereafter he relocated to Newtown, Queens County, New York, where Anum Banum was a freeholder on the 4 December 1666 Town Rate.[84] He was again rated there on 26 February 1667.[85] By deed dated 29 September 1667 Anum Banum purchased from George Jewell a house, barns, outhouses, lot, orchard, yard, meadows, and all other privileges situated before Mashpeath Kill, bounded west by Laurens Pieterszen, east by John Woollstoncroft, and south by Thomas Wandell.[86] Also on 29 September 1667 Anum Banum and John Burroughes witnessed Nicolas Genengs' assignment of a lot lying against Maspeag Kill to John Woollstoncroft.[87] By a warrant dated 6 November 1667 the New York governor required Aynam Baynam and others living at Mashpeth Kills on land formerly belonging to Mr. Robert Clarke to appear at Fort James on 9 November, bringing their deeds or evidences proving the titles to their land.[88]

Enim Benham died at Maspeth Kill, Newtown, Long Island, shortly before 9 November 1670, on which date his widow Alice Banum and John Grissell of Mashpeth [now Maspeth] sold land formerly belonging to Enam Banum, recently deceased, to Mark Dale for 200 guilders.[89]

Child by Abigail (Sweet) Baldwin:

+   2.   George[2] Baldwin *alias* Benham, b. Gravesend, Long Island, 1656.

There were probably additional children by wife Alice Benham.

2. **George[2] Baldwin *alias* Benham**, illegitimate son of Anum Benum and Abigail (Sweet) Baldwin of Gravesend, Kings County, New York, was born ca. 1656. He died in Hempstead, Queens County, Long Island, New York, in January or February 1730/1. In about 1678 he married **Mary Ellison**,

---

83. Documentary records in this case are quoted in full in the Baldwin genealogy in Herbert F. Seversmith's *Colonial Families of Long Island, New York, and Connecticut* (Washington, D.C.: author, 1939), 212-217, 221.

84. "Newtown Town, Long Island, Records, 1659-1688." original p. 78, in *New York Genealogical and Biographical Record* 63 (1932): 365.

85. "Newtown Town Records," 19, in *NYGBR* 63:362.

86. "Newtown Town Records," original p. 13, in *NYGBR* 63:361.

87. "Newtown Town Records," 11, in *NYGBR* 63:11.

88. Orders, Warrants, Letters, Etc., of the Colony of New York, volume 2 (1665-1668), page 189, in *New York Historical Manuscripts: English, General Entries* (Baltimore: Genealogiclal Publishing Co., 1982), 154.

89. The land was bounded north by orchards of Grissell and Alice Banum. The deed was witnessed by John Watkins and John Clarke. "Newtown, Long Island, Town Records, 1659-1688," original p. 170, in *New York Genealogical and Biographical Record* 64 (1933): 31.

daughter of Thomas and Martha Honor (Champion) Ellison of Hempstead.

As "George Baldwin *alias* Benham," at Huntington, Long Island, Court on 21 February 1680/1 he was a party in a dispute with Jonathan Rogers relative to a barrel of cider, at which time he signed by mark on a document discharging Rogers from debts due to him. Henceforth called "George Baldwin," on 21 December 1681, he acknowledged having received from Joseph Baldwin his part of the estate of "my desesed father [*sic*, foster father] Georg Baldin" of Hempstead. At Huntington Court on 1 March 1682/3, stating his age as about 27 years, he testified in a suit between Henry Soper and Jonathan Rogers. At Hempstead on 3 March 1683/4 he registered his cattle earmarks. He contributed toward the patent of 1696, and was listed with his wife in the 1698 census of Hempstead, then owning a large amount of land.[90]

His wife Mary apparently having predeceased him, George Baldwin made his will on 9 January 1730/1. It was proved at New York City on 25 February 1730/1.[91]

George and Mary (Ellison) Baldwin's twelve children and many descendants are identified in Seversmith's *Colonial Families of Long Island* 198-210, and will not be repeated here.

JOHN BRISCOE

1. Doctor **John**[1] **Briscoe** was born c1612 at Crofton Hall, County Cumberland, England, the fourth son of Leonard Briscoe.[92] His death date is not known. He married, date unknown, **Elizabeth Dubois**, who was probably born in England of Huguenot ancestry. Doctor Briscoe was probably an Anglican, but his descendants married into Roman Catholic families of Maryland.[93] He accepted the invitation of Cecil Calvert to come to Maryland as one of the Gentlemen Adventurers on the *Ark* and the *Dove* Expedition. A Briscoe descendant is stated to have had a letter

---

90. Records summarized in Seversmith, 197-198.

91. Will abstracted in *Collections of the New York Historical Society*, 3:18.

92. Richard St. George, *Visitation of the County of Cumberland in the Year 1615,* London: The Harleian Society, 1872. Vice-Admiral and Mrs. William S. Pye, "The John Briscoe Story," *National Genealogical Society Quarterly* [hereafter *NGSQ*], 46:120-127, refutes the "negative article" published 25 years earlier by Alexander H. Bell, *NGSQ*, 21:73-76, which questions whether a Doctor John Briscoe ever came to Maryland and whether the person referred to in Maryland records was or was not a John Biscoe.

93. Alice Ijams Williams, "Briscoe Notes," typescript in possession of R. W. Barnes.

dated 1 September 1633 in which Cecil Calvert wrote to "Dr. John Briscoe, M. D., Brikskaugh, Newbiggin, Cumberland," telling him that the *Ark* and the *Dove* would sail from Gravesend on 1 October, and inviting him to join the expedition.[94]

John Briscoe was a member of the court that met at St. Mary's City.[95] In 1642 the name of John Brisquett appears twice in an assessment.[96] John Briscoe should not be confused with a contemporary named John Biscoe. The ancestor of the Briscoe family is usually referred to as Doctor.

Some sources say that Doctor John had a son, John Jr., who was the father of Philip Briscoe, but if the latter was in fact born in 1648 he is most likely to have been a son and not a grandson of the Doctor. Pye states that Philip was a son of Doctor John. Alice Ijams Williams, using data compiled by Katharine Spencer Heywood of Pittsburgh, Pennsylvania, in 1854, states that Doctor John and Elizabeth DuBois Briscoe had at least three children.

Children of John and Elizabeth (DuBois) Briscoe:

    2. George[2] Briscoe, probably d. unmarried.
+ 3. John Briscoe.
+ 4. Philip Briscoe, b. c1648.

3. **John[2] Briscoe**, son of Dr. John and Elizabeth (Dubois) Briscoe of County Cumberland, birth unknown, died testate in St. Michael's Hundred, St. Mary's County, by November 1718, when his will was proved. He married **Ann [-?-].**[97]

He made his will on 9 May 1718, proved 11 November 1718. He named his wife Ann and children: Thomas, John, James, Mary, and Anna. Jas. Edmonds and Bryan Dulsey (Dussey) were witnesses.[98] No inventory or account of the administration of the estate have been found filed in the Prerogative Court.

John Briscoe is believed by some to have had a daughter Elizabeth who married Captain Thomas Attaway. A study of other sources has failed to

---

94. Pye, 121.

95. *Archives of Maryland*, 72 volumes (Baltimore: Maryland Historical Society, 1888-1990) [hereafter *Archives*] 2:391.

96. *Archives*, 3:120, 123.

97. St. Mary's Co. Rent Roll #1:12, states she was a daughter of Thomas Jackson. However, subsequent research has established that Anne Jackson, daughter of Thomas Jackson, married first, John Biscoe, and second, Owen Smithson. The spelling Biscoe is consistently used. Maryland Administrations, 2:431; Baltimore Co. Land Records, IS#L:256, HWS#1-A:392.

98. Maryland Prerogative Wills [hereafter Md. Wills], as abstracted by Jane Cotton Baldwin in *Maryland Calendar of Wills*.

find proof of the marriage.[99]

John Briscoe was the father of:

5. Thomas[3] Briscoe, d. c1697 when his estate was valued at 35,374 lbs. tobacco.[100]
6. Dr. John Briscoe, probably the John Briscoe, Jr. who with Philip Briscoe witnessed the will of Susanna Briscoe on 5 Feb. 1739/40.[101] He may have married Elizabeth DeCourcey. The son Walter sometimes ascribed to him is more likely the son of Walter #95.
7. James Briscoe.
8. Mary Briscoe.
9. Anna Briscoe.

4. Philip[2] Briscoe, son of Doctor John and Elizabeth, was born c1647/48 and died in Charles County by January 1724/5. About 1719 he made a deposition giving his age as about 72, saying he saw a bounded white oak in a gully belonging to Luke Barber, where he himself lived some 50 years earlier.[102] He married **Susannah Swann**, daughter of Edward Swann. She died by July 1740 in Charles County.[103] On 19 June 1707 she signed the inventory of the estate of her brother James Swann of St. Mary's County.[104]

Philip Briscoe was one of the coroners of Charles County, and later one of the Magistrates, Justices and Chief Civil Officers of Charles County. He also served on the vestry of King and Queen Anglican Parish, St. Mary's County, in 1692 and 1697.[105] He was a delegate to the Lower House of the Assembly, representing Charles County, 1699-1700.[106]

His will was dated 25 April 1724, proved 29 January 1724/5, and named wife Susannah, who was devised the dwelling plantation *Morris' Venture* for life, then to son John; to son Philip the 80 acres "bought from Father Swann;" son Edward was devised *Hitchen* and 111 acres of *Love's*

---

99. William Crockett Parsons, *Ancestry of the Descendants of Thomas Attaway Reeder of St. Mary's County, Maryland* (1979); June Cooper Reynolds, *Notes on a Brady Family* (Greenville: A Press, 1985); Mary E. Ramey, "Brissko-Brisco-Briscoe and Some Family Connections," typescript, Maryland Historical Society [hereafter MHS]; Semmes Family Genealogical Collection, MHS; Annie Walker Burns, "Maryland Marriage References," typescript, MHS; and Mary Louise Donnelly, *Colonial Settlers of St. Clements Bay, 1634-1780* (Ennis Tex.: the author, 1996).

100. Md. Inventories and Accounts, 15:170.

101. Md. Wills, 22:122.

102. Md. Chancery Court Records, PC:449.

103. Williams, no page number.

104. Md. Inventories, 27:145.

105. Williams.

106. For more on his career, see Papenfuse, *Biographical Dictionary of the Maryland Legislature*, 169.

Enjoyment; deceased son George (who left a son Leonard) and daughters Sarah Leonard [*sic*], Judith Ashcom, Susanna Compton and Ann Wood. Son James was devised 200 acres of *Love's Enjoyment*.[107] At his death his total estate value was £671.19.9 (including 14 slaves and numerous books). After his debts were paid, a final balance of £490.7.2 remained for distribution. An account of the administration of his estate was filed on 3 December 1725 by John Briscoe, executor. Legacies were paid to wife Susannah, Susanna Compton, Ann Wood, Charles Ashcom, and William Howard.[108]

Susannah Briscoe died in Charles County leaving a will dated 5 February 1739/40 and proved 24 July 1740. She named her brother Samuel Swann, daughter Elizabeth, children of her deceased son John, *viz*.: Samuel Williamson, Philip, James, Hezekiah, John Briscoe, and Martha Willson; her daughter Ann Wood and Ann's daughter Mary; granddaughter Elizabeth Garner; grandson William Howard and all the remaining children of daughter Sarah Howard; granddaughter Sarah Parker; granddaughter Susanna Whitely, and all the remaining children of daughter Susanna Compton; grandsons Briscoe and George Davis; grandson Robert, son of Edward; grandson Leonard; children of deceased daughter Judith Brooke; and grandchildren Rebecca and Williamson Briscoe and Henry Smoot. Sons Philip and James were appointed executors. The will was witnessed by John Briscoe, and Philip Briscoe (both minors).[109] No inventory or account of the administration of the estate of Susannah Briscoe was filed in the Prerogative Court.

Children of Philip and Susanna (Swann) Briscoe:

+ 10. John[3] Briscoe, b. c1678.
+ 11. Philip Briscoe, b. c1679/80.
+ 12. Edward Briscoe, b. c1685.
+ 13. George Briscoe, d. by 1720.
+ 14. Sarah Briscoe, d. 1735.
+ 15. Judith Briscoe, d. by 1739.
+ 16. Susanna Briscoe, m. Matthew Compton.
+ 17. Ann Briscoe.
  18. James Briscoe. On 25 March 1730, James Briscoe of St. Mary's Co., and Ann his wife, conveyed to Peter C. Scallorn of Charles Co. 100 acres of *Love's Enjoyment*. On 1 Feb. 1731 James conveyed 115 acres of the same tract to Abrah. Parker. No wife released dower.

107. Md. Wills, 18:339.
108. Md. Administrations, 7:216.
109. Md. Wills, 22:212.

10. Captain **John³ Briscoe**, son of Philip and Susanna (Swann) Briscoe, was born c1678 and died by 10 May 1734 in Charles County. He married **Eleanor Williamson**, possibly born c1680, died in Charles County c1753.[110]

On 12 June 1722, John Briscoe of Charles County, gentleman, conveyed to Henry Wharton of St. Mary's County, part of *Baltimore's Guift*, which William Digges of Prince George's County had conveyed to him on 23 June 1719. His wife, Eleanor, consented.[111]

Capt. John Briscoe's, inventory was taken on 10 May 1734 and valued at £322.00, with son Samuel Williamson Briscoe named as principal creditor; he and John Briscoe signed as next of kin.[112] Elioner Briscoe, executrix, filed the administration account of the estate of her husband on 12 April 1735. Payments totalling £15.11.6 were taken out of the inventory of £323.0.0. No heirs were named.[113]

On 5 September 1738 John Lewellin of St. Mary's County leased to Eleanor Briscoe for 21 years, 102 acres of *Wood Manor* in Charles County. The lease stipulated that Eleanor was to plant 100 apple trees within 10 years.[114] On 6 September 1754, Samuel Williamson Briscoe, son of Eleanor Briscoe, and Hezekiah Briscoe, son and executor of the said Eleanor, conveyed to John Lewellin 102 acres of *Westwood Manor*.[115]

The children of Captain John and Eleanor (Williamson) Briscoe, named by their grandmother Susannah:[116]
+   19. Samuel Williamson⁴ Briscoe.
+   20. Philip Briscoe.
     21. James Briscoe.
+   22. Hezekiah Briscoe.
+   23. John Briscoe.
     24. Martha Briscoe, m. [-?-] Willson.

11. Doctor **Philip³ Briscoe**, son of Philip and Susanna (Swann) Briscoe, was born c1679/80 and died c1743 in St. Mary's County. He married **Elizabeth [Cole?]**,[117] who died c1767.

Philip Briscoe of St. Mary's County, with acknowledgement of his wife

---

110. Probably the daughter of Samuel Williamson, based on the name of John's first child.
111. Charles Co. Land Records, L#2:24.
112. Md. Inventories, 18:275.
113. Md. Administrations, 13:60.
114. Charles Co. Land Records, 0#2:348.
115. Ibid., A#3:229.
116. Md. Wills, 22:212.
117. No proof found, but George Cole in his will named a daughter Elizabeth. Md. Wills, 11:5, and a son was named George Cole Briscoe by Philip and Elizabeth.

Elizabeth, on 19 June 1725 conveyed to Samuel Swann 80 acres, part of *Eggleston*, formerly belonging to Edward Swann.[118]

The personal property of Philip Briscoe was appraised at £273.19.0 by Luke Barber and William Bond in November 1743. Richard Wanright and Philip Briscoe signed as next of kin, Elizabeth Briscoe filed the inventory on 6 February 1743/4.[119] Payments were £301.15.9. The balance (*sic*) was distributed with one-third going to the widow, and the balance to the orphans [named below].[120]

Children of Philip and Elizabeth Briscoe:

+ 25. Dr. John[4] Briscoe, b. 1717.
+ 26. Philip Briscoe, b. c1719.
   27. Edward Briscoe.
   28. James Briscoe.
   29. Walter Briscoe.
+ 30. George Cole Briscoe.
   31. Elizabeth Briscoe, m. [-?-] Hedges.
   32. Sarah Briscoe.

12. **Edward[3] Briscoe**, son of Philip and Susanna (Swann) Briscoe, born c1685 and died in 1726, having married **Susanna Gerard**.

Edward Briscoe died leaving a will dated 7 December 1725; proved 19 February 1725/6. He named his wife Susanna as executrix and his children Philip, Robert (devised *Love's Enjoyment*), Edward (devised *Hitchen*), John, George, Lydda, and Priscilla, and a posthumous child. William Wood, George Saint Clare, and Matthew Parlow were witnesses.[121] The estate of Edward Briscoe of Charles County was appraised by John Chunn Jr., and Benjamin Chunn, and was valued at £194.16.7. Philip Briscoe and Thomas Masser signed as creditors. John Briscoe Sr., Susanna Briscoe Sr., and John Briscoe Jr., signed as next of kin.[122] Susannah Briscoe, executrix, filed the account of the administration of the estate of her husband on 21 August 1727. Payments totaled £2.8.1 and were made to Thomas Reed and Samuel Hanson.[123]

---

118. Ibid., L#2:227.

119. Md. Inventories, 28:518.

120. Md. Administrations, 21:446. Often the amount of money distributed in accounts exceed the amount cited in the inventory. Probably additional inventory was found and not reported.

121. Md. Wills, 18:444.

122. Md. Inventories, 11:424.

123. Md. Administrations, 8:347.

Children of Edward and Susanna (Gerard) Briscoe:[124]
+ 33. Philip[4] Briscoe, b. 1718.
   34. Robert Briscoe.
   35. Edward Briscoe, schoolmaster on 14 April 1741, sold to Jacob Wood 100-
       acre *Hitchen.*
+ 36. John Briscoe, b. 1721.
+ 37. George Briscoe, d. by 1755.
   38. Lydda Briscoe.
+ 39. Priscilla Briscoe.
+ 40. James Briscoe, b. 1726.

13. **George[3] Briscoe**, son of Philip and Susanna (Swann) Briscoe, died by
March 1720. He married **Mary** [-?-], who married second, William Tippolls
of Charles County.
   Samuel Williamson and Francis Clarke appraised the personal estate of
George Briscoe on 9 March 1720 and set a value of £152.1.1 on his
personal estate. Philip and Susanna Briscoe [probably his parents] signed
as next of kin. Mary Briscoe, administratrix filed the inventory on 6 June
1721.[125] On 5 July 1726, Mary, wife of William Tippolls, filed the account
of the administration of the estate of George Briscoe of St. Mary's County.
His personal estate had been appraised at £152.15.1[126]
   Child of George and Mary Briscoe:
      41. Leonard[4] Briscoe.

14. **Sarah[3] Briscoe**, daughter of Philip and Susannah (Swann) Briscoe, died
May 1735. She married first **Thomas Truman** and second **William Stevens
Howard.**
   Thomas Truman of Prince George's County died leaving a will dated 15
September 1717, proved 14 January 1717/8. He named his mother, Mrs.
Jane Taney, his oldest son Henry, son James, his own brother Edward,
daughter Jane, nephew Thomas Truman, and wife Sarah, executrix. The
will was witnessed by Thomas Greenfield, and Philip Willisey. A codicil
dated 15 September 1717 stated that his brother Edward was to be
discharged of his debt to the testator if he should convey *Thomas and
Anthony's Choice* to the testator's son James at once.[127] An account of the
administration was filed on 23 October 1719 by Sarah Truman. She

---

124. Sources cited above and "Briscoe Lineage," a series of charts in possession of R. W.
Barnes.
   125. Md. Inventories, 5:70.
   126. Md. Administrations, 7:406.
   127. Md. Wills, 16:649.

reported an inventory value of £602.16.11, and a second inventory value of £98.7.10. Payments totaled £72.15.9. Truman's mother Jane Taney was mentioned, and the legal representatives named were: the widow Sarah and children: Henry, Jane, James, and Thomas.[128]

William Stevens Howard was a son of Edmund Howard, gentleman, of Charles County, whose will dated 3 December 1709 named the children of William Stevens Howard. William married first, Eliza, and was the father of Edmund and Elizabeth.[129] He died in Charles County leaving a will dated 15 December 1733, proved 29 April 1734. He appointed his wife Sarah executrix. He mentioned his eldest son Edmund, a daughter Rachel, wife of Matthew Compton, and his four younger children: William, Elizabeth, Susannah, and Sarah. The will was witnessed by Benjamin Douglas Sr., Philip Jenkins, and Benjamin Douglas Jr.[130] Henry Truman, executor of Sarah Howard [now deceased], the original executor of William Stevens Howard, filed an account of the administration of the estate of William Stevens Howard on 3 June 1736. An inventory value of £474.15.6 was listed and payments totaled £102.12.[131]

Sarah (Briscoe) (Truman) Howard died in Charles County leaving a will dated 16 April 1735 and proved 20 May 1735. She named her sons Henry Truman, James Truman, and William Howard, daughters Elizabeth and Sarah, and grandson Henry Smoot. Later she named her children William, Elizabeth, and Sarah Howard, her deceased husband William Stevens Howard and his son Edmund. Her sons Henry and James Truman were cautioned to behave with tenderness toward Edmund Howard. George Dent and Anne Smoot witnessed the will.[132] Henry Truman administered Sarah Howard's estate on 22 February 1736. An inventory value of £487.13.3 was listed, and payments totaled to £49.18.2. No heirs were named.[133]

Children of Thomas and Sarah (Briscoe) Truman:

+ 42. Henry[4] Truman.
  43. James Truman, d. without issue; will dtd. 26 May, proved 30 Aug. 1744, naming brother William Howard, sisters Elizabeth and Sarah Howard, nephew Henry Smoot, niece Susanna, and nephew James; devised land to nephew Thomas, with nephew James as reversionary heir. Brother Henry was

---

128. Md. Administrations, 2:364.
129. Md. Wills, 13:632, 14:187.
130. Md. Wills, 21:55.
131. Md. Administrations, 15:53.
132. Md. Wills, 21:344.
133. Md. Administrations, 15:306.

executor.[134]
+ 44. Jane Truman.
45. Thomas Truman.
Children of Sarah by William Stevens Howard:
46. William Howard.
+ 47. Elizabeth Howard, b. 1725.
48. Susannah Howard, m. [-?-] Smoot; had son Henry Smoot.
49. Sarah Howard.

15. **Judith**[3] **Briscoe,** daughter of Philip[2] and Susannah (Swann) Briscoe, died by 1739. She married first, by 1723 **Charles Ashcom,** who died in 1726 in St. Mary's County, and second, between 23 March and 5 September 1727, **Thomas Brooke**; after her death Thomas Brooke married second, Sarah Mason.[135] On 21 October 1717 Winifred Ashcom made a will naming her brother Charles, her niece Martha Ashcom, and other relatives.[136]

Martha Dansey, widow and mother of Charles Ashcomb, of St. Mary's County, made a will on 19 February 1723/4. She named her daughter-in-law Judith Ashcom, granddaughters Martha and Susannah Ashcom, and granddaughter Elizabeth wife of William Shelley. She bequeathed to her grandson Samuel Ashcom money in England, and stated that if any of her grandchildren married Roman Catholics they were to forfeit their bequests.[137]

Charles Ashcom of St. Mary's County was the son of Charles and Martha [-?-] Ashcom. He died by March 1726/7,[138] leaving a will dated 20 November 1725 and proved 23 March 1726/7. His wife Judith was named executrix. He named his children Martha, Susannah, Elizabeth (not yet 16), and son Samuel. He left personalty to Joyce Haines, Richard Ward Key, and Philip Key. He named his grandmother Martha Dansey and Elizabeth Shelley. To daughter Martha was devised 100 acres of *Ashcom's*. To son Samuel was devised *Point Patience, Marsh Neck*, and *Town Neck*. The will was witnessed by Grace Clelan, Magdalen Tomlinson, Richard Deaver, Thomas Truman Greenfield, and Ellis Slater.[139] Executrix Judith Brooke filed the inventory of the estate of Charles Ashcom on 5

---

134. Md. Wills, 23:589.
135. Md. Wills, 18:339; Testamentary Proceedings, 18:1, 29:186; Christopher Johnston, "The Brooke Family," *Maryland Genealogies*, 1:91-110.
136. Md. Wills, 14:464.
137. Md. Wills, 18:256.
138. Elise Jourdan, "The Ashcom Family," *Early Families of Southern Maryland*, 3:211-219.
139. Md. Wills, 19:127.

September 1727. John Cartwright and John Burroughs had appraised his personal property at £939.8.9. Elizabeth Greenfield and Elizabeth Jenifer signed as next of kin. An additional inventory value of £36.6.6 was filed 29 May 1728.[140] An account of the administration of the estate of Charles Ashcom of St. Mary's County was filed by executrix Judith, now wife of Thomas Brooke, who filed an account on 29 May 1728. An inventory value of £979.15.8 was listed and payments totaled £116.18.8. Another account was filed on 21 November 1732.[141]

Thomas Brooke was a son of Thomas and Lucy (Smith) Brooke.[142] He died leaving a will dated 2 September 1748, proved 15 June 1749. He named his wife Sarah, his sons Walter and Richard Brooke, and his eldest son Thomas Brooke. He also named his brother Richard Brooke. Elizabeth, Richard, and Isaac Brooke witnessed the will.[143] On 26 November 1750 Sarah Brooke, executrix, filed an account of the administration of the estate. An inventory value of £472.0.0 was cited, and payments totaled £142.17.9.[144]

Children of Judith by Charles Ashcom:

   50. Martha[4] Ashcom, b. by 21 Oct 1717 when named as niece in will of Winifred Ashcom.[145]

+ 51. Susannah Ashcom, b. by 1723.

   52. Elizabeth Ashcom.

+ 53. Samuel Ashcom, b. by 1723.

   Child by Thomas Brooke:

+ 54. Thomas Brooke, b. 1734.

16. **Susanna**[3] **Briscoe**, daughter of Philip and Susanna (Swann) Briscoe, died c1739. About 1704 she married **Matthew Compton**, born c1671, died 1747.

Matthew Compton died leaving a will dated 19 March 1744/5, proved 15 September 1747. He devised to his son Samuel all his estate in Virginia. He named his daughters Susanna Whitely and Elender Slye, and a grandson Matthew Compton Parker. The residue of his estate he bequeathed to his son Matthew. George Briscoe and William Howard

---

140. Md. Inventories, 12:257, 13:102.
141. Md. Administrations, 9:195, 11:525.
142. Johnston, 114; Jourdan, 214.
143. Md. Wills, 27:25.
144. Md. Administrations, 29:142.
145. Md. Wills, 14:464.

witnessed the will.[146]

Children of Matthew and Susannah (Briscoe) Compton:
+ 55. Matthew[4] Compton, b. 26 June 1709.
+ 56. Samuel Compton.
+ 57. Susannah Compton, m. Robert Whitely.
+ 58. Elender Compton, m. John Slye.
   59. [possibly] daughter who m. [-?-] Parker.

17. **Ann**[3] **Briscoe**, daughter of Philip[2] and Susanna (Swann) Briscoe, married first **John Davis**, and second, by 1724, **Samuel Wood**.[147]

John Davis, son of John and Mary Davis, died leaving a will dated 23 December 1716, proved 29 March 1717. He named his wife Ann as executrix, and gave to her one-third of his real and personal estate. He also named his sons John, Briscoe, and George, and his daughter Mary.[148] Philip Briscoe and Peter Harris appraised the personal estate of John Davis on 26 April 1717, and valued it at £88.6.3.[149] Ann Wood, wife of Samuel Wood, filed the account of administration of the estate of John Davis of St. Mary's County on 3 June 1718, listing payments of £19.8.10.[150]

Samuel Wood of St. Mary's County, planter, died leaving a will dated 22 February 1757/8 and proved 4 July 1758. He named his daughter Ann Briscoe, and son Samuel Wood, as well as a grandson Jared Briscoe. The residue was bequeathed to Samuel's son Jonathan Wood, who was not to forget his two poor sisters, Susanna Suit and Elizabeth Banner. Son Jonathan was executor. David Dick, James Brady Jr., and James Broadey, [Jr.?] witnessed the will. Jonathan Wood, executor, filed the account of the administration of the estate of Samuel Wood of St. Mary's County on 24 October 1759. John Eden was paid. George Briscoe and David Dick were sureties for the estate.[151]

Children of John and Ann (Briscoe) Davis:[152]
+ 60. John[4] Davis.
   61. Briscoe Davis.
   62. George Davis.
   63. Mary Davis.

Children of Samuel and Ann (Briscoe) Wood:

---

146. Md. Wills, 25:150.
147. Donnelly, *Colonial Settlers*, 78.
148. Ibid., 78 cites Md. Wills, 14:235.
149. Md. Inventories, 27B:125.
150. Md. Administrations, 1:54.
151. Md. Wills, 30:527.
152. Donnelly, 78.

64. Jonathan Wood.
65. Samuel Wood.
66. Anne Wood, m. [-?-] Briscoe; probably had child Jared Briscoe.
67. Susanna Wood, m. [-?-] Suit.
68. Elizabeth Wood, m. [-?-] Banner.

19. **Samuel Williamson[4] Briscoe**, son of Capt. John and Eleanor (Williamson) Briscoe, may have married **Margaret [-?-]**. He was still alive on 2 August 1775 when with his brother Philip he conveyed to William Compton a 30-acre part of *Willion*.[153]

Child of Samuel Williamson and Margaret Briscoe:
69. Philip[5] Briscoe.

20. **Philip[4] Briscoe**, son of Captain John and Eleanor (Williamson) Briscoe, was born c1710 and died by 1756 when his will was probated. He married **Chloe Hanson**, daughter of Samuel and Elizabeth (Story) Hanson.[154]

Eleanor Briscoe of Charles County, widow, in her will signed 2 February 1753, bequeathed a negro boy to her grandson Hanson Briscoe, son of Philip and Chloe Briscoe. If he died without issue, the negro was to pass to his brother John Hanson Briscoe.[155] On 2 August 1755 Philip Briscoe of St. Mary's County, and Samuel Briscoe of Charles County, planters, conveyed to William Compton 30 acres, part of tract called *Willion*, as cited above. Chloe, wife of Philip, released her right of dower.

Children of Philip and Chloe (Hanson) Briscoe:
70. Hanson[5] Briscoe.
71. Dr. John Hanson Briscoe, b. Chaptico, Md.; d. 7 Sept. 1796; m. c1780 Elizabeth Attaway Bond. Elizabeth d. at Chaptico 5 June 1816.[156]

22. **Hezekiah[4] Briscoe**, son of Captain John and Eleanor (Williamson) Briscoe died by August 1757. He married **Susannah Wilson**, who married second, on 18 November 1758, William Compton.[157]

Samuel Amery and Joseph Dyson appraised the personal property of Hezekiah Briscoe's estate on 20 August 1757. No value was cited; Samuel and Philip Briscoe signed as next of kin. Susannah Briscoe filed the

---

153. Charles Co. Land Records, A3:371.
154. Harry Wright Newman, *Charles County Gentry* (Baltimore: GPC, 1971), 232.
155. Md. Wills, 29:110.
156. *Maryland Gazette*.
157. Jourdan cites Trinity Parish records.

inventory on 21 October 1757.[158] An account was filed on 12 September 1759 showing the administration of the estate of "Philip" Briscoe, with an inventory of £290.16.10, and filed by Susanna Briscoe, now wife of William Compton. Payments in the account of Philip Briscoe's estate totaled £359.13.1, and the representatives were the widow, and four children: Eleanor Wilson Briscoe, age 8; Margaret, age 6; Mary, age 4; and Elizabeth, age 2.[159]

Children of Hezekiah and Susanna (Wilson) Briscoe:[160]

72. Eleanor Wilson[5] Briscoe, b. 21 Sept. 1750; m. Hanley/Hendley Smoot by 1770.[161]
73. Margaret Briscoe, b. 30 Nov. 1752.
74. Mary Briscoe, b. 15 March 1755, probably the Mary Briscoe, sister of Eleanor Briscoe, who m. John Nathan Smoot.[162]
75. Elizabeth Briscoe, b. 17 Dec. 1756.

23. **John[4] Briscoe**, son of Captain John and Eleanor (Williamson) Briscoe, was born c1707 and died in Calvert County in 1742. He married **Mary Hanson**.[163]

Captain John Briscoe of Charles County, was living on 14 March 1738/9 when John Lewellin of St. Mary's County leased part of *Wood Manor* to him (originally for 21 years); the lease was amended on 14 March 1738 to run for the lifetimes of Mary, wife of John Briscoe, and their son Samuel Briscoe.[164]

Captain John Briscoe died leaving a will dated 30 December 1741, proved 15 February 1741/2, naming wife Mary, children Eleanor, Samuel, Elizabeth, and an unborn child, as well as his brothers Samuel and Philip. The estate of Captain John Briscoe was inventoried on 4 December 1742 by Samuel Chunn and Peter Wood; William Williams and Gustavus Brown signed as creditors, and Samuel and Philip Briscoe signed as next of kin. The property was valued at £477.8.0. The inventory was filed by Mary Briscoe, executrix on 3 February 1742.[165] Mary Briscoe filed an account on

---

158. Md. Inventories, 64:62.
159. Md. Administrations, 44:34. The question of the apparent contradiction cannot be resolved, but the children named below were listed in Trinity Parish as having been born to Hezekiah and Susanna, but as the children of "Philip" in Hezekiah's administration account.
160. Jourdan, *Early Families of St. Mary's County*, 5:91, cites Trinity Church records.
161. Hodges Marriage Index, #5, at MSA; *Ibid.*, 92.
162. Hodges cites Trinity Parish records.
163. Md. Wills, 22:424.
164. Charles Co. Land Records, O2:387.
165. Md. Inventories, 27:299.

12 July 1746.[166]
  Children of John and Mary (Hanson) Briscoe:
  76. Eleanor[5] Briscoe.
  77. Samuel Briscoe, d. testate, Charles Co., 1786; m. Anne Warren Dent.[167]
  78. Elizabeth Briscoe.
  79. Capt. John Briscoe, b. c1741; d. St. Mary's Co. 29 May 1822; m. Jane L. Key.[168]

25. Doctor **John[4] Briscoe**, son of Doctor Philip and Elizabeth (Cole) Briscoe, was born March 1717 and died 7 December 1788. He married **Elizabeth [McMillan?]**, born May 1730, died 5 July 1774. He married second **Ann [-?-]**.

John Briscoe died in Berkeley County, [now West] Virginia, leaving a will dated 6 January 1785 and proved in January 1789. He named his wife Ann, children Hezekiah, Sarah Slaughter, Parmenas, John, Elizabeth Baker, and Fra[nces?] Davis. Son John was to be executor. Thomas Hart Sr., Thomas Hart Jr., and George Smallwood witnessed the will.[169]

  Children of Dr. John and Elizabeth Briscoe:
  80. John[5] Briscoe.
  81. Hezekiah Briscoe.
  82. Parmenas Briscoe, b. 1 May 1749; d. 27 Sept. 1824, Nelson Co., Ky.; m. Ann Briscoe, b. possibly 5 Feb. 1760, d. by 1810.
  83. Sarah Briscoe, m. [-?-] Slaughter.
  84. Elizabeth Briscoe, m. [-?-] Baker.
  85. Fra[nces?] Briscoe, m. [-?-] Davis.

26. **Philip[4] Briscoe**, son of Philip and Elizabeth (Cole) Briscoe, was born c1719. He married first, by 16 November 1759, **Mary [-?-]**, administrator of Francis Parham of Charles County.[170] He married second, **Nancy Foster**. Philip Briscoe went to Kentucky, but returned to Maryland.

Philip and Mary Briscoe have been generally accepted as having been the parents of:
  86. Bolivar[5] Briscoe.
  87. Hezekiah Briscoe.
  88. Jeremiah Briscoe.
  89. Rebecca Briscoe.
  Children of Philip and Nancy (Foster) Briscoe:

---

166. Md. Administrations, 20:349.
167. Charles Co. Wills, 9:227.
168. *Historic Graves* by Ridgely; *The Key Family*, 55-69.
169. Transcript filed with applications #586, #615.
170. *Ibid.*, 44:25.

90. William Briscoe.
91. Robert Briscoe.
92. George Briscoe.
93. Parmenas Briscoe.
94. Walter Briscoe, b. 21 May 1741; d. 1784; m. Eleanor (or Elizabeth) Compton Trinity Parish 13 May 1762.[171]
95. Philip Briscoe.
96. Henry Briscoe.
97. Kate Briscoe, m. Joseph Summerhill.
98. Sarah Briscoe, m. [-?-] Swan.

30. **George Cole[4] Briscoe**, son of Dr. Philip and Elizabeth (Cole) Briscoe, was born c1733 in Maryland and died in Jefferson County, West Virginia, on 7 June 1805. He married **Frances [McMillan?]**, born in Prince William County, Virginia, and died in Berkeley County, [West] Virginia, on 24 June 1795.[172]

Child of George Cole and Frances Briscoe:
99. John McMillan[5] Briscoe, b, c1760, Frederick Co., Va.; d. 18 Aug. 1807, Nelson Co., Ky.; m. Maria Horner.

33. **Philip[4] Briscoe**, son of Edward and Susanna (Gerard) Briscoe, died in Charles County in 1750. On 1 November 1748 in Trinity Parish, Charles County, he married **Cassandra Chunn**.[173] She later married Erasmus Gill.

Philip Briscoe died leaving a will dated 2 August 1750 and proved 20 October 1750. He named wife Cassandra, daughter Susanna, brother Robert Briscoe, sister Susannah Anderson, and brothers George and James Briscoe. Wife Cassandra and brother George were named executors.[174] Robert Horner and James Nevison appraised the personal estate of Philip Briscoe of Charles County on 12 January 1750, assessing his goods at £365.0.6. George and Cassandra Briscoe, executors, filed the inventory on 14 January 1750.[175] On 11 May 1752 his executors George Briscoe and Cassandra Briscoe, now the wife of Erasmus Gill filed an account of the administration of the estate. The representatives were the widow and one child, both unnamed in an account filed in 1756, but legatees George and Samuel Briscoe were named.[176] An account filed on

171. Jourdan, *Colonial Records*, 14.
172. *MHM*, 21:43, 45, 47, 51, 53 (Bible Records of Hezekiah Briscoe).
173. Jourdan, *Colonial Records*, 2.
174. Md. Wills, 27:437.
175. Md. Inventories, 44:326.
176. Md. Administrations, 32:254, 40:154.

25 October 1756 showed that Cassandra, now wife of Erasmus Gill as the surviving executrix, with Mathew Compton and George Elgin as sureties, had distributed a balance of £360.10 to Cassandra and Susannah.[177]

Child of Philip and Cassandra (Chunn) Briscoe:

100. Susannah[5] Briscoe.

36. **John[4] Briscoe**, son of Edward and Susanna (Gerard) Briscoe, was born in 1721 and died after May 1749. He married first **Ann Wood**, daughter of Samuel and Ann (Briscoe) Wood, on 27 November 1746 in Trinity Parish, Charles County.[178] He may have married second **Mary [Greenfield?]**. John and Ann Briscoe signed the inventory of William Wood's estate as kin on 2 May 1749.[179]

Children of John and Ann (Wood) Briscoe:

101. James[5] Briscoe, b. c1745, d. Charles Co. by Nov. 1800; m. Elizabeth Sothoron.[180]
102. Ralph Briscoe, b. 24 Nov. 1747; d. Missouri, 1835; m. Ann Mackall, b. 1750, d. Frederick Co. by 1792.
103. Jared Briscoe, named in the will of his grandfather Samuel Wood on 4 Feb. 1758.

Child of John and Mary (Greenfield) Briscoe:

104. Truman Briscoe, m. Henry Co., Va., 1782, Katharine Dunn.[181]

37. **George[4] Briscoe**, son of Edward and Susannah (Gerard) Briscoe, died by July 1755. He married **Mary [Warren?]**, who married second, [-?-] Musgrave.

John Clagett and Joshua Brisey appraised George Briscoe's personal property on 4 July 1755 at a value of £248.16.11. James Briscoe signed as next of kin, and Mary Briscoe, administrator, filed the inventory on 1 October 1755.[182] Mary Musgrave, late Mary Briscoe, filed an account of the administration of George Briscoe's estate on 7 July 1760. Payments totaled £59.19.[183] The account showed that Mary Musgrove, administrator, had distributed a balance of £240.16.11. The "representatives were not known to this office."[184]

---

177. Md. Balance Books (of Final Distributions), 2:40.
178. Jourdan, *Colonial Settlers*, 7.
179. Md. Inventories, 40:92.
180. Charles Co. Wills, AK11:609.
181. Dorothy Ford Wulfeck, *Marriages of Some Virginia Residents, 1609-1800* (GPC).
182. Md. Inventories, 59: 227.
183. Md. Administrations, 46:73.
184. Balance Books, 3:38.

39. **Priscilla[4] Briscoe**, daughter of Edward and Susanna (Gerard) Briscoe, married 1750, **Richard Anderson** who died 1778. Richard and Priscilla (Briscoe) Anderson were the parents of at least one son:

    105. Col. Richard[5] Anderson, b. 16 Jan. 1752, St. Mary's Co.; d. 22 June 1835, Philadelphia, Pa.; m. Ann Wallace, 31 July 1787.

40. **James[4] Briscoe**, son of Edward and Susanna (Gerard) Briscoe, was born in 1726 and died by September 1750 in Frederick County. His wife has not been identified. James Briscoe of Frederick County died by 19 September 1750 when John Clagett and Samuel Beall appraised his goods and chattels at £160.19.11. John Briscoe and Samuel Sotheron signed as next of kin, and James Sotheron Briscoe filed the inventory on 11 April 1751.[185] On 31 May 1751 an account of the administration of his estate was filed by James Sothoron Briscoe of St. Mary's County. Payments totaled £139.11.1. A second account was filed on 9 June 1752.[186]

    Children of James Briscoe:

    106. James Sothoron[5] Briscoe, d. by Nov. 1774; m. Mary [-?-].[187]
    107. John Briscoe.
    108. Nathan Briscoe.
    109. Mary Briscoe, m. Jonathan Swann.

42. **Henry[4] Truman**, son of Thomas and Sarah (Briscoe) Truman, died in Prince George's County by March 1756. He married **Anne Magruder**, daughter of Alexander and Susannah (Busey) Magruder.[188]

Henry Truman died leaving a will dated 30 September 1755, proved 23 March 1756. He named his wife Anne and children: Thomas, James, Henry, Alexander, and Edward. He named tracts *Brittington, Dawson's Purchase, Buttington*, and *Thomas and Anthony's Chance*. The will was witnessed by Fielder Gantt, John Stone Hawkins, and James Sothoron Briscoe. Undated and unvalued lists of debts for Henry and Anne Truman were filed c1761-2.[189]

Anne Truman died in Prince George's County, leaving a will dated 8 April 1760, proved 24 June 1760, and witnessed by Priscilla Hawkins, James Sothoron Briscoe, and Thomas Truman. She named her children Thomas, James, Sarah, Henry, Jane, Alexander, and Edward. Son Thomas

---

185. Md. Inventories, 45:43.
186. Md. Administrations, 30:208, 32:239.
187. Md. Wills, 40:60.
188. Henry C. Peden, Jr., *Truman and Related Families of Early Maryland* (1987), 22.
189. Md. Wills, 30:60; Md. Inventories, 75:209, 213.

was executor. Thomas Truman filed an account of the administration of the estate of Henry Truman on 24 March 1762, valuing it at £1346.1.1. On the same day he filed an account of the widow, who left a personal estate worth £1271.12.8.[190] Thomas Truman, with John Stone Hawkins and James Briscoe as sureties, distributed the estate of Ann Truman, with a balance of £1186.9.3, to Ann's children: Thomas, James, Leonard, Chloe, Clara, Sarah, Henry, Jane, Alexander, and Edward.[191]

Children of Henry and Anne (Magruder) Truman:
110. Thomas[5] Truman, d. by 1777.
111. James Truman, b. c1742; d. 22 Dec. 1789; m. Elizabeth Gordon.[192]
112. Henry Truman.
113. Alexander Truman, b. 1750/1 (his age in 1789); m. Margaret Reynolds, 1781.[193]
114. Edward Truman, b. c1753.
115. Sarah Truman, m. Samuel Compton of Charles Co.[194] [See #56 on page 39.]
116. Jane Truman, m. Capt. Alexander Howard Magruder.[195]
117. Leonard Truman.
118. Chloe Truman.
119. Clara Truman.

44. Jane[4] Truman, daughter of Thomas and Sarah (Briscoe) Truman, was not named in her mother's 1735 will, so probably died before 1735. She married **Barton Smoot**, born 1711, died 1760, son of Barton and Sarah (Hawkins) Smoot. Barton married second, Susanna (Clarke) Mackall, daughter of George Clarke,[196] who survived him.[197]

Barton Smoot died leaving a will dated 19 January 1760 and filed 7 March 1760. He left the use of his personal estate to his [unnamed] wife, and at her death to be divided among his children. His wife was to be executrix. Jn° A. Clarke, William Watts, and Elizabeth Guyther witnessed the will. On 26 September 1761 Thomas Watts and John Wherritt valued the personal property at £721.2.1. George Guyther and William Guyther signed as next of kin, and Susanna Smoot, filed the inventory on 21 August 1761, and the administration account on 30 October 1765.

190. Md. Wills, 31:1121; Md. Administrations, 47:393, 398.
191. Balance Books, 5:188.
192. Prince George's Co. Wills, T1:638.
193. Peden, *Truman and Related Families*, 29-30.
194. Compton bible record.
195. Peden, *Truman and Related Families*, 27.
196. George Clarke's will dtd. 13 Nov. 1751 calls her Smoot.
197. Harry Wright Newman, *The Smoots of Maryland and Virginia* (1936), 97.

Payments totaled £45.13.10, but no heirs were named.[198] Susanna Mackall Smoot filed an account of the administration of the estate of Barton Smoot on 30 October 1765. Payments totaled £45.13.10, but no heirs were named in the account.[199]

Susanna Smoot's will dated 26 September 1780 devised to sons William Barton Smoot and Thomas Smoot the dwelling house and adjoining lands. Also mentioned were daughters Elizabeth Smoot, Susanna Smoot, Hannah Watts, and Tabbs grandchildren.[200]

Children of Barton and Jane (Truman) Smoot:[201]

120. Henry[5] Smoot, b. by 1735, named in the will of grandmother Sarah (Briscoe) (Truman) Howard; m. Jane [-?-]; and d. in Charles Co., leaving will dated 8 Oct. 1759 and proved 28 Nov. 1759, naming wife Jane, executrix, and brothers and sister Barton, Thomas, and Eleanor Smoot. If his wife should be with child, then the negroes left to his brothers and sister should go to his child. Jn° Fendall, William Leigh, and Jos. Thompson witnessed the will. His personal property wss valued at £444.7.3 as appraised on 20 Dec. 1760 by John Fendall and John Marshall. George Clarke Smoot and Francis Smoot signed as next of kin. Jean [or Jane] Smoot filed the inventory 27 July 1761.[202]

121. George Clarke Smoot.

122. William Barton Smoot.

123. Thomas Smoot, d. without issue.

124. Eleanor Smoot, m. [-?-] Tabbs.

125. Hannah Smoot, m. Joshua Watts.

126. Elizabeth Smoot, m. Benjamin Philpot.

127. Susanna Mackall Smoot.

47. **Elizabeth[4] Howard**, daughter of William Stevens and Sarah (Briscoe) Howard, was born in 1725 and died 2 September 1803. On 6 December 1744 she married **Alexander Magruder,** born 1713 and died in October 1779, son of Alexander and Susanna (Busey) Magruder.

Children of Alexander and Elizabeth (Howard) Magruder:[203]

128. Alexander Howard[5] Magruder, b. 15 Sept. 1745, m. Jane Truman [see above]; served in Revolutionary War, and administered Oaths of Fidelity in Prince George's Co. Jane m., second, John Mackall in Calvert Co., 1788.[204]

---

198. Md. Wills, 30:812; Inventories, 74:262; Administrations, 53:234.

199. Md. Administration Accounts, 53:234.

200. St. Mary's Co. Wills, JJ#1:167.

201. Peden, *Truman and Related Families*, 35.

202. Md. Wills, 30:351; Inventories, 76:283.

203. Jourdan, 2:166.

204. Peden, *Truman and Related Families*, 27-28.

129. Leonard Magruder, b. 4 Apr. 1763; d. 25 Feb. 1795; m. Susanna Priscilla Hawkins.[205]

51. Susannah⁴ Ashcom, daughter of Charles and Judith (Briscoe) Ashcom, was born by 1723. She married **John Reeder**, born 1705, died 1777. In his will, John Reeder named the following children:[206]

130. Thomas⁵ Reeder, m. Draden Reeder (dau. of Thomas Reeder who d. 1773).
131. William Reeder, may have moved to Loudoun Co., Va.; m. and had two daughters and one son.
132. John Reeder, b. 1750s; d. 1804; m. Mary [-?-]; settled in Washington Co.
133. Benjamin Reeder, b. 1760, served in Revolutionary War, moved to Va., and then to Overton Co., Tenn.; had issue.
134. Ann Reeder, m. [-?-] Biscoe.
135. Susanna Reeder, m. first cousin Nathaniel Ashcom.
136. Amy Reeder, m. [-?-] Biscoe.
137. Elizabeth Reeder, m. [-?-] Thompson.
138. Henrietta Reeder.

53. Samuel⁴ Ashcom, son of Charles and Judith (Briscoe) Ashcom, was born by 1723 and died by December 1754. He married **Sarah** [perhaps **Brome**], who married, second, **Abraham Neverson**.

Abraham Neverson and wife Sarah filed the inventory of Samuel Ashcome's estate on 17 December 1754; Edward Cole and Thomas Mattingly appraised the personal property at £589.11.10. Anne Brome and Thomas Brome signed as next of kin.[207] On 16 August 1755 Sarah Neverson, administrator, and wife of Abraham Neverson, filed account of administration of the estate, listing payments totalling £545.19.7. The distribution was as follows: one-third to widow, and residue to orphans of the deceased: Ann, John, Sarah, Charles, Samuel, and Nathaniel.[208]

Children of Samuel and Sarah Ashcom:
139. Ann⁵ Ashcom, b. c1741, age 14 in 1755.
140. John Ashcom, b. c1744, age 11 in 1755.
141. Sarah Ashcom, b. c1745, age 10 in 1755.
142. Charles Ashcom, b. c1746, age 9 in 1755; d. St. Mary's Co. by May 1772; m. Margaret [-?-].[209]
143. Samuel Ashcom, b. c1750, age 5 in 1755.

---

205. Francis B. Culver, *Society of Colonial Wars in State of Maryland* (1940).

206. Elise Greenup Jourdan, "The Ashcomb Family," *Early Families of Southern Maryland*, 160.

207. Md. Inventories, 58:320.

208. Md. Administrations, 38:185.

209. Md. Inventories, 110:71; Testamentary Proceedings, 44:383.

144. Nathaniel Ashcom, b. c1752, age 3 in 1755.

54. Thomas⁴ Brooke, son of Thomas and Judith (Briscoe) Brooke, was born 1734 and died 1789 in Washington County. He married by 1765 **Elizabeth** [-?-], who died between 25 August 1784 and 1 April 1785.[210]

In 1774 Thomas Brooke was appointed to a committee to represent Frederick County, and in 1775 he was appointed to the Frederick County Committee of Observation. Later he served on the Washington County Committee. He was the first surveyor of Washington County.

Children of Thomas and Elizabeth Brooke:
145. Thomas⁵ Brooke, d. in the Carolinas.
146. William Pitt Brooke, d. 1816, m. and had issue.
147. Clement Brooke, b. 1770; d. 1836, Zanesville, Ohio; m. Anne Dillon.
148. Rachel Brooke, m., first, William Darrell, and, second, William Collard.
149. Susan Brooke, m. William Lee.
150. Judith Briscoe Brooke, m. James Lindsay.
151. Ann Greenfield Brooke, m. [-?-] Winder.
152. Elizabeth Brooke, m. John Simonson; had issue.

55. Matthew⁴ Compton, son of Matthew and Susanna (Briscoe) Compton, was born 26 June 1709 and died 14 March 1770. He married **Rachel Howard**, born c1714 and died 23 May 1789, daughter of William Stevens and Sarah (Briscoe) Howard.[211]

Matthew Compton died in St. Mary's County leaving a will dated February 1770 and proved 3 September 1770. He named wife Rachel as executrix, and children: Barton, Alexander, Edmund Howard, Stephen, Matthew, John, and Susanna Compton. Robert Slye Wood, Henry Morris, and Samuel Briscoe witnessed the will.[212] On 24 October 1770 Robert Slye Wood and Leo. Briscoe appraised Compton's personal property at value of £130.4.9. William and Matthew Compton signed as next of kin; filed on 10 October 1771.[213]

Children of Matthew and Rachel (Howard) Compton, most of whose births were recorded in Trinity Parish:[214]
153. William⁵ Compton, b. 4 March 1733 [not recorded in Trinity Parish]; d. 5 Dec. 1807; m. Susannah Wilson, widow of Hezekiah Briscoe, 18 Nov. 1758. She d.

210. Christopher Johnston, "The Brooke Family," *Maryland Genealogies*, 118-121.
211. Compton bible, submitted with application #519.
212. Md. Wills, 38:53.
213. Md. Inventories, 107:184.
214. Jourdan, *Colonial Records*, 9.

19 July 1807.[215]

154. Elizabeth Compton, b. 21 May 1742.
155. Matthew Compton, b. Dec. 1744.
156. John Compton, b. 28 Feb. 1747; d. Kentucky 10 Jan. 1803; m. 12 Feb. 1771, Elizabeth Briscoe, b. 18 March 1751, d. 4 Nov. 1790.[216]
157. Susanna Compton, b. Feb [-?-].
158. Barton Compton, b. 3 Dec. [-?-] .
159. Alexander Compton, b. 16 Sept. 1755.
160. Edmund Howard Compton.
161. Stephen Compton.

56. Samuel[4] Compton, son of Matthew and Susanna (Briscoe) Compton, is probably the Samuel Compton who died in Charles County by April 1765. He married **Sarah Truman** [#115 on page 35], daughter of Henry Truman. She married, second, Thomas Compton.

Samuel Compton died leaving a will dated 30 November 1764, proved 16 April 1765. He named his wife Sarah as executrix, and son Henry Truman Compton. William Compton, George Willson, and John George Stinson witnessed the will.[217] Samuel Amery and Samuel Turner appraised the personal estate of Samuel Compton at £333.8.7. Zach Compton and William Compton signed as next of kin; it was filed on 18 June 1765 and the account on 11 May 1769, listing payments totalling £369.6.9, and naming two legatees: herself and son Truman Compton.[218]

Child of Samuel and Sarah Compton:
162. Henry Truman[5] Compton, b. 1763; d. 1836; m. Ann Swann, 17 Nov. 1797.

57. Susannah[4] Compton, daughter of Matthew and Susannah (Briscoe) Compton, was born in Charles County c1716 and died in Loudoun County, Virginia, by 29 December 1787. She married **Robert Whitely**, who died in Fairfax County, Virginia, by 19 April 1744.

Child of Robert and Susannah (Compton) Whitely:
163. William[5] Whitely, b. c1737; d. by 12 Dec. 1789; m. after 10 April 1769 Susanna Tyler, b. Fairfax Co., Va., c1748, d. Loudoun Co., Va., by 12 Dec. 1789.

58. Elender/Eleanor[4] Compton, daughter of Matthew and Susanna (Briscoe) Compton,[219] married before 1734 **John Slye** of Charles County.

---

215. Jourdan, *Colonial Records,* 14.
216. Bible filed with application #617.
217. Md. Wills, 33:280.
218. Md. Inventories, 87:262; Administrations, 59:267.
219. Matthew Compton's will. Md. Wills, 25:150.

He was born c1694-1695,[220] only son of Robert, Jr., and Priscilla (Goldsmith) Slye of St. Mary's County.[221] He died at *Lapworth*, Newport Parish, Charles County, shortly before 10 May 1777.[222] His widow Eleanor Slye died in Charles County shortly before 25 January 1783.[223]

Children of John and Eleanor (Compton) Slye:[224]

164. Mary[5] Slye, b. 8 May 1734; d. Woodford Co., Ky., 8 Feb. 1808; m. by 1751, Philip Wood.[225]

165. Thomas Gerard Slye, b. c1735;[226] d. Charles Co., shortly before 3 July 1764;[227] m. c1762 Elizabeth (Sothoron) Wight.[228]

166. Robert Slye, b. Newport Parish, Charles Co., 15 11th month [Jan.] 1745[/46];[229] m. (1) Trinity Parish, 3 June 1773, Elizabeth Stoddert;[230] m. (2) Henrietta [-?-].[231]

167. Susanna Slye, b. Newport Parish, 1 9th month [Nov.] 1749;[232] d. Union Co., Ky., cApril 1828; m. (1) c1766 Leonard Burch; m. (2) by 1775, Nathaniel Harris.[233]

60. John[4] Davis, son of John and Anne (Briscoe) Davis, died by March 1734. He married **Ann Reeder**, daughter of Benjamin and Elizabeth (Attaway) Reeder.

John Davis died leaving a will dated 21 December 1733, proved 6 March 1734 naming daughter Martha (who was in Virginia), daughter Elizabeth wife of William Elliott, daughter Ann wife of Thomas Notley Goldsmith, son Adelard, grandson John Elliot, daughter Elinor wife of John Murphy and her son Thomas Truman Murphy, and his children Elinor, Violetta,

---

220. Was age 57, his deposition 30 Dec. 1752. Charles Co. Court Records, B#3 (1752-1753): 343-344.

221. Named in father's will dated 18 April 1698, St. Mary's Co. Wills, 6:207.

222. Date on which his will was proved. Charles Co. Wills and Accounts, AF#7 (1777-1782): 2-3.

223. The date on which her personal estate was appraised. Charles Co. Wills and Accounts, B#1 (1782-1785): 339-340.

224. Three surviving children named in his will dated Jan. 1775, and in the final administration account filed 2 Aug. 1777. Charles Co. Wills and Accounts, AF#7:2-3, 39.

225. Family records and research findings, Evlin K. Kinney, M.D., Miami Beach, Fla., letters 1988 and 1993.

226. His orphaned son John Sothoron Slye named as grandchild in 1775 will of John Slye.

227. Md. Inventories, 86:5.

228. Md. Administration Accounts, 59:421, 425.

229. Newport Parish Register.

230. Trinity Parish Register.

231. Henrietta identified as his widow in 1799. Charles Co. Administration Accounts, 1798-1806, 106-108. Nine children named in the account.

232. Newport Parish Register.

233. Family records and research findings, Nan Overton West, Lubbock, Texas, letter 1995.

Arabela, Rebecca, and Sarah.[234] The inventory of his estate, filed 24 May 1734 by Ann Davis, executrix, was valued at £166.9.6. His sons-in-law Elias Smith and Joseph Kine signed as next of kin. An account of administration was filed on 17 September 1735. Out of an inventory of £137.15.6, she made payments totalling £24.1.6.[235]

Children of John and Ann (Reeder) Davis:[236]

168. Martha[5] Davis, in Virginia in 1733.
169. Elizabeth Davis, d. after May 1758, m. William Elliott.[237]
170. Ann Davis, d. by April 1746; m. Thomas Notley Goldsmith.[238]
171. Adelard Davis.
172. Elinor Davis, m. John Murphy.[239]
173. Violetta Davis.
174. Arabella Davis.
175. Rebecca Davis.
176. Sarah Davis.

WILLIAM BROWN

1. **William**[1] **Brown**, passenger on the *Ark* and the *Dove*, was born c1623 (giving his age as c20 in 1643), and came to Maryland in 1633 as a servant of Captain Thomas Cornwallis.[240] He died c1665/6. He married **Margaret** [-?-]. A Roman Catholic, he settled in Bretton Bay, St. Mary's County. Jn° Thimbelby and William Brown gave a power of attorney to George Manners to take legal action against John "Hollis" (Hallowes) c1648/9.[241] On 2 December 1659 he was named as executor in the will of John Thimbelby. Thimbleby left property to the Roman Catholic Church, to John Brown, and to Margaret wife of William Brown, as well as making other bequests. He left all his land in Maryland to his goddaughter Mary Brown.[242] William "Broune" of St. Mary's County died leaving a will dated 27 February 1665 and proved 26 July 1666. He named his children John and Mary who were to share his personal property in equal proportions, but Mary was also to have the personalty given to her by her godfather

234. Md. Wills, 20:900.
235. Md. Inventories, 18:329; Administrations, 13:326.
236. Mary Louise Donnelly, Colonial Settlers of St. Clements Bay (1634-1780), 1996, 78.
237. Donnely, 79.
238. *Ibid.*
239. *Ibid.*
240. Newman, *Flowering*, 178; Md. Land Warrants, 1:110; Md. Land Patents, ABH:94.
241. Newman, *Flowering*, 178; *Archives*, 10:7.
242. Md. Wills, 1:80.

John Thimbleby. John Warren and Edward Clarke were named overseers of the will. Peter Roberts and George Shaw witnessed the will.[243]

Children of William and Margaret Brown:
+   2. John[2] Brown, d. 1701/2.
+   3. Mary Brown, m. Thomas Kerbley/Kirtly.

2. **John[2] Brown**, son of William and Margaret Brown, died 1701/2. His wife's name is not known. A member of the Anglican Church, he settled at Bretton Bay. He was the father of at least two children:
    4. John[3] Brown, of *Brown's Purchase.*
    5. Jane Brown.

3. **Mary[2] Brown**, daughter of William and Margaret Brown, died c1675. She married **Thomas Kerbley/Kirtly**. Thomas Kerbley remarried and died intestate in 1697. His former brother-in-law, John Brown, was surety for Kerbley's widow, Elizabeth. John Thimbleby named his goddaughter Mary Brown in his will of 1659. Mary and Thomas Kerbley were the parents of at least one son:[244]
    6. William[3] Kerbley, d. soon after mother.

LEONARD CALVERT

1. **Leonard[1] Calvert**, son of Sir George Calvert, 1st Baron Baltimore, and Anne (Mynne) Calvert, was born in England in 1606, baptized 21 November 1610, and died in Maryland 9 June 1647. He married in England, **Anne Brent**, daughter of Richard and Elizabeth (Reed) Brent of Larke Stoke and Admington in Gloucestershire, and sister of Mary, Giles, Fulke, and Margaret Brent, who came to Maryland in 1638.[245]

Leonard went to Avalon but returned to England in 1628. He was admitted to Gray's Inn 8 August 1633. As agent for his elder brother, who fitted out the *Ark* and the *Dove* for the voyage across the Atlantic to settle Maryland, he and his brother George sailed with the party from Gravesend, England, reaching Maryland 3 March 1633/4. Upon landing, the party founded the city of St. Mary's, 25 March 1634. Leonard was Lieutenant-General of the province and commissioned Governor in 1637.[246]

---

243. Md. Wills, 1:257.
244. Newman, *Flowering*, 321.
245. Nicklin, 143-144.
246. Dorman, 470-471.

On his deathbed, Leonard Calvert appointed his sister-in-law, Margaret Brent, his executrix and the attorney for his estate in Maryland, directing her to "Take all, & pay all."

Children of Leonard and Anne (Brent) Calvert:

+ 2. William[2] Calvert.
+ 3. Anne Calvert.

2. **William[2] Calvert**, son of Leonard and Anne (Brent) Calvert, was born c1642 in England and died in Maryland on 10 January 1682, drowned while trying to ford the Wicomico River. He married before 5 November 1662 **Elizabeth Stone**, daughter of Governor William Stone. She was living in Virginia with her son Richard about 1698.[247]

Arriving in Maryland in 1661, he received a large grant of land from his uncle Cecil and inherited certain property of his father's. He was Principal Secretary of Maryland and was also a member of the Assembly and the Council, and served as Deputy-Governor of Maryland.[248]

The inventory of The Honorable William Calvert's personal property was taken on 13 July 1682 by Thomas Spinke and James Pattison, and was valued at £662.18.2. The account was filed 30 April 1686 by administrator Elizabeth Calvert, the widow.[249]

On 26 September 1668 Charles Calvert of St. Mary's County, son and heir of William Calvert, and Elizabeth Calvert, widow and relict, conveyed to Joshua Doyne of St. Mary's County 600 acres of 50,000-acre *Nanjemoy,* taken up by William Stone, father of Elizabeth.[250]

Children of William and Elizabeth (Stone) Calvert:[251]

+ 4. Charles[3] Calvert, b. 1662.
+ 5. Elizabeth Calvert, b. 1664.
  6. [perhaps] William Calvert, b. 1666, living 1696 in St. Mary's Co. Witnessed will of William Robinson of St. Mary's Co. 29 Nov. 1696.[252]
+ 7. [perhaps] George Calvert, b. 1668.
  8. [perhaps] Richard Calvert, b. 1670, d. unm. 1718.

3. **Anne[2] Calvert**, daughter of Leonard and Ann (Brent) Calvert, was born in England c1644 and died c1714. She married first **Baker Brooke**, born

---

247. Dorman, 474, citing Md. Chancery Court, 2:706.

248. Nicklin, 144-145.

249. Md. Inventories & Accounts, 7C:206, 8:479.

250. Charles Co. Land Records, P:36.

251. Nicklin, 144-145; Md. Chancery Court, CL:868.

252. Ella Foy O'Gormon, *Descendants of Virginia Calverts*, n.d., 63.

at Battle, Sussex, England 16 November 1628, died testate 1679; second, her cousin **Henry Brent** of Calvert County, who died 1693; third, Col. **Richard Marsham**, justice of Prince George's County, who died testate in 1713.[253]

Baker Brooke of Delabrooke Manor, Calvert County, died leaving a will dated 19 March 1678/79, proved 26 March 1679/80. He devised to wife Anne part of *Delabrooke Manor, Freehold,* and *Longfield* for life. To son Charles was devised part of said manor and to son Leonard part of *Brooke's Manor* and *Haphazard.* To daughter Mary was devised one-half of *Brooke's Partition*, and to son Baker was devised the residue of all real estate. Baker Brooke also mentioned his brother Colonel Thomas Brooke and the latter's daughter Mary. The will was witnessed by Henry Carew and Geritt Van Swearingen. On 7 July 1679 Henry Darnall and C. Boteler appraised the estate at 71,923 pounds of tobacco. On 4 August 1679 his executrix Anne, now wife of Henry Brent, filed an account, with distribution to the widow. Another account was filed on 9 December 1687, showing payments of 135,126 pounds of tobacco.[254]

Henry Brent of Calvert County died by 6 August 1694 when his estate was appraised by Raphael Heywood and Richard Fenwick, and valued at £239.1.0. Mrs. Anne Brent filed an account on 30 April 1695. As the wife of Richard Marsham, Anne filed other accounts, one c1697, and others on 10 November 1698 and 18 July 1699.[255]

Children of Baker and Anne (Calvert) Brooke:

    9. Charles[3] Brooke, d. unm. in 1698.

+ 10. Leonard Brooke, d. 1718.

+ 11. Baker Brooke, d. 1698.

+ 12. Mary Brooke, d. 1763.

4. **Charles[3] Calvert**, son of William and Elizabeth (Stone) Calvert, was born c1662 and died in 1733. In 1721 Charles, of St. Mary's County, made a deposition giving his age as c57 years.[256] He married first in 1690 **Mary Howson**, daughter and coheir of Robert Howson of Stafford County, Virginia, where Calvert lived for a while. He married second **Barbara Kirke**, daughter of Martin and Mary Kirke of St. Mary's County. Barbara married second Andrew Foy. In her will of 1734, Mary mentioned her

253. Dorman, 474-475.

254. Md. Wills, 10:1; Md. Inventories & Accounts, 9:390, 10:9; see also *Archives,* 3:342, 5:94.

255. Md. Inventories & Accounts, 13A:126, 13:291, 15:186, 17:144, 19:160, 23:22.

256. Chancery Court, CL:656.

daughter Barbary Calvert.[257]

Charles Calvert left a will dated 25 October 1733, proved 31 December 1733, bequeathing one shilling each to daughters Sarah and Ann, and providing a maintenance for Barbary, daughter of Martin Kirk, until she comes of age or marries. Wife Barbara was appointed executrix and residuary legatee. Witnesses were James Smith, James Keirk, Andrew Foy, and Joseph Kirk.[258]

Children of Charles and Mary (Howson) Calvert:

+ 13. Sarah Howson[4] Calvert, b. c1694.
+ 14. Ann Calvert, b. c1696.

5. **Elizabeth**[3] **Calvert**, daughter of William and Elizabeth (Stone) Calvert, was born in 1664 and died after 1684. She married, shortly before 24 December 1681 as his first wife, Captain **James Neale** of Wollaston Manor, Charles County, who died in 1725, son of Captain James and Anne (Gill) Neale. He married second in 1687 Elizabeth Lord, and died testate between 1 April 1725 and 11 October 1727.[259]

Child of Elizabeth (Calvert) and James Neale:

+ 15. Mary[4] Neale.

7. **George**[3] **Calvert**, son of William and Elizabeth (Stone) Calvert, was born c1668 and died after 1739. He married c1690 **Elizabeth Doyne**, and possibly **Anne Notley** and **Hannah Neale**.[260] He was in Stafford County, Virginia, by 8 October 1690 when he entered a complaint against John Tarkinson for debt.[261]

Children of George Calvert:[262]

16. Charles[4] Calvert, b. 1691.
+ 17. John Calvert, b. c1692.
+ 18. George Calvert, b. c1694.
19. [possibly] James Calvert.
20. Elizabeth Calvert.
21. William Calvert.
22. [possibly] Thomas Calvert.

10. **Leonard**[3] **Brooke**, son of Baker and Anne (Calvert) Brooke, died in St.

---

257. Nicklin, 145; Dorman, 477.
258. Md. Wills, 20:860-861.
259. Dorman, 477-478; Md. Wills, 19:246.
260. Nicklin, 146; Dorman states that perhaps "George" is the son of William.
261. Stafford Co. First Court Order Book, 102.
262. Nicklin, 146; O'Gorman recognizes only sons John and George.

Mary's County in 1718. He married **Ann Boarman**, daughter of Major William Boarman of Charles County.[263] Leonard Brooke died leaving a will dated 1 November 1716 and proved 2 April 1718. To daughter Eleanor was devised the tract *Hardshift,* to daughter Jane *Haphazard,* an unnamed tract to daughter Anne and the residue of real and personal estate to son Charles. He mentioned cousins Richard and Leonard Brooke and brother-in-law Raphael Neale. An account was filed on 24 March 1718 by Raphael Neale, the surviving executor, including an inventory valued at £336.9.9, with payments of £66.16.6.[264]

Children of Leonard and Anne (Boarman) Brooke:

    23. Charles[4] Brooke, d. unm. by 1 July 1761.[265]

+ 24. Eleanor Brooke, d. 1760.

+ 25. Jane Brooke.

+ 26. Anne Brooke.

11. Baker[3] Brooke II, son of Baker and Anne (Calvert) Brooke, died in 1698. He married **Katherine Marsham**, daughter of Richard Marsham. Katherine married second Samuel Queen. Luke Gardiner and John Fenwick appraised the personal property of Baker Brooke on 28 May 1698, valuing it at £317.4.0.[266]

Children of Baker and Katharine (Marsham) Brooke:[267]

    27. Baker[4] Brooke, d. without issue.

+ 28. Richard Brooke.

+ 29. Anne Brooke.

+ 30. Leonard Brooke.

12. Mary[3] Brooke, daughter of Baker and Anne (Calvert) Brooke, died testate in 1763. She married **Raphael Neale**, who was born in 1683 and died in 1743, son of Anthony and Elizabeth (Roswell) Neale.

On 7 May 1731 Raphael Neale of Charles County, gent., with consent of his wife Mary, conveyed to John Lancaster and Elizabeth his wife, daughter of Raphael Neale, land adjoining Arthur Turner.[268]

Raphael Neale died leaving a will dated 20 July 1743 and proved 10 December 1743. He named his daughters Elizabeth Lancaster, Mary Taney, Henrietta Neale, Monica Diggs, and Ann Thompson; his Hoskins

---

263. Christopher Johnston, "The Brooke Family," *Maryland Genealogies,* 1:91-112.

264. Md. Wills, 14:486; Md. Administrations, 1:368.

265. Johnston, 99.

266. Md. Administrations, 16:8.

267. Johnston, 99, *Archives,* 3:342, 5:94.

268. Charles Co. Land Records, M2:246.

grandchildren; Mary Hoskins now Boarman; and other grandchildren Ann Hoskins, Mary Boarman, Raphael Taney, and John and Joseph Lancaster. His wife was appointed executrix.[269]

Mary Brooke Neale died leaving a will dated 29 September 1760, proved 24 May 1763. She named her daughters Ann Thompson, Mary Taney, and Henrietta Brooke; her grandchildren Eleanor and Raphael Thompson, Mary Eleanor Combs, John Francis Taney, Raphael Brooke, and John and Eleanor Digges, and sons-in-law John Lancaster, Edward Digges, Thomas Taney, and Basil Brooke.[270]

Children of Mary (Brooke) and Raphael Neale:

+ 31. Elizabeth[4] Neale, d. 1743.
+ 32. Mary Neale.
+ 33. Henrietta Neale, d. 1774.
+ 34. Ann Neale.
+ 35. Monica Neale.
+ 36. Eleanor Neale.

13. **Sarah Howson[4] Calvert**, daughter of Charles and Mary (Howson) Calvert, was born c1694 in Stafford County, Virginia, and died after 1754. She married c1718 **Nathaniel Jones** of Westmoreland County, Virginia. He was born c1696 and died 1754, the son of John Jones, who died 1715 in Westmoreland County, Virginia.[271] Nathaniel died testate by 26 March 1754.[272]

Children of Sarah (Calvert) and Nathaniel Jones:[273]

37. John[5] Jones, b. c1720, d. 1762; m. 16 Aug. 1744 Eleanor Moss.
38. David Jones, m. 18 Feb. 1763 Mary Boswell.
39. Nathaniel Jones.
40. Charles Jones, d. testate by 2 March 1771.
41. Calvert Jones, d. testate by 7 April 1791.
42. Mary Jones, m. [-?-] Peck.
43. Frances Jones, named in will of her brother Calvert.
44. Sarah Jones, m. [-?-].

14. **Anne[4] Calvert**, daughter of Charles and Mary (Howson) Calvert, was

---

269. Charles Co. Wills, AC4:178.

270. Christopher Johnston, "The Neale Family of Charles County." *Maryland Genealogies*, 2:248-265.

271. O'Gorman, 68.

272. Westmoreland Co., Va., Deeds & Wills, 12:75-78.

273. Dorman, 479. The wills for Charles and Calvert in King George Co., Va., 1:317a-318; 2:128.

born c1696 in Stafford County, Virginia, and died after 1740. She married there c1714 **Thomas Porter,** who died testate by 8 April 1740.[274]

Children of Anne (Calvert) and Thomas Porter:[275]

45. Anne[5] Porter, b. 13 Oct. 1717, d. 22 Sept.1727.
46. Calvert Porter, b. c1718; m. Elizabeth Cash.
47. Thomas Porter, b. c1720; in Revolutionary War.
48. Benjamin Porter, bp. 1 May 1725; in Revolutionary War.
49. Nicholas Porter, b. c1727; in Revolutionary War.
50. Joseph Porter, b. 7 Aug. 1726; m. 26 Feb. 1756 Jemima Smith.
51. Henry Porter, bp. 1 May 1728.
52. Charles Porter, b. c1729.
53. Howson Porter, b. c1730, d. 11 April 1755; m. 1 Jan. 1745/6 John Stark, who m. (2) 29 May 1756 Hannah Eaves.
53. Anne Porter, b. 15 March 1731/32.
54. John Porter, b. 4 Aug. 1734, d. 14 July 1754.

15. **Mary[4] Neale,** daughter of James and Elizabeth (Calvert) Neale, born c1782, died after 13 May 1730. She married first by 10 April 1702 **Charles Egerton,** who was born by 1677, son of Charles and Anne (Porter) Egerton of *Piney Neck,* St. Mary's County. She married second in 1707 **Jeremiah Adderton,** son of James and Mary (Porter) Adderton, baptized privately on 15 July 1682 at St. Andrews Parish, Penrith, Cumberland, England,[276] and died by 19 May 1713. She married third by 9 April 1715 **Joseph Van Swearingen,** born c1682 and died by 11 October 1722, and fourth by 1 April 1725 **William Deacon.**[277]

On 10 April 1702 James Neale of *Wollaston Manor* conveyed to Charles Egerton, who had lately married James' daughter Mary, all the lands he had received as the marriage portion of Elizabeth Calvert: 600 acres, part of 2000 acres patented by William Calvert. On 5 March 1705 Mary Egerton posted an administration bond on the estate of Charles Egerton; his personal estate was appraised by Charles Beckwith and William Harbert on 5 April 1706, valuing it at £315.4.10. Mary Adderton filed an account on 17 May 1708, citing payments of £43.17.4.[278]

Jeremiah Adderton was Justice of the Peace of St. Mary's County; his will named a son James; a posthumous son Jerermiah was born in 1713.[279]

274. Dorman, 479, citing Stafford Co. Will Book, M:285.
275. Dorman, 480.
276. *Francis Haswell, The Registers of St. Andrew's Parish Church, Cumberland,* (1938-40), 3:30.
277. Dorman, 480-481; Francis B. Culver, "Egerton Family," *Maryland Genealogies* 1:417-429.
278. Md. Testa. Pro., 19C:40; Md. Inventories & Accounts, 26:255, 28:221.
279. St. Mary's Co. Wills, 1:7.

The widow Mary, now wife of Joseph Van Swearingen, filed an account on 12 July 1718 showing payments of £8.0.0. As wife of William Deacon, Mary filed another account on 13 May 1730, with a final account dated 28 June 1755, giving Mary her thirds; the [unnamed] representatives, all of age, received the balance.[280]

Joseph Van Swearingen's inventory filed on 11 October 1722 showed a value of £884.8.4, with payments of £26.10.7. Administratrix Mary Deacon filed another account on 13 June 1723.[281]

William Deacon, in his will dated 19 June 1758, proved 7 January 1760, made bequests to friend Mrs. Mary Johnston, nephew William Deacon, and sister Mary Deacon of Portsmouth, England.[282]

Children of Mary (Neale) by Charles Egerton:
55. James[5] Egerton, b. c1703, d. 1768; m. Mary Baker, dau. of John Baker.
56. Charles Egerton, d. c1738, wife unknown. Issue.
Children of Mary (Neale) by Jeremiah Adderton:
57. James Adderton.
58. [probably] Jeremiah Adderton, who later appears in North Carolina.[283]

17. **John[4] Calvert,** son of George and Elizabeth (Doyne) Calvert, was born c1692 in Maryland and died 1739 in Prince William County, Virginia. He married c1711 **Elizabeth Harrison**, possibly a daughter of Benjamin Harrison, 3rd, of Virginia. She was born 1693 in Charles City County, Virginia, and died c1720 in Prince William County.[284] He probably moved to Virginia after his marriage.

Children of John and Elizabeth (Harrison) Calvert:[285]
59. George[5] Calvert, b. 1712, d. 19 May 1782 Culpeper Co., Va.; m. (1) c1740 Anne Crupper (c1718-c1776), sister of Gilbert Crupper of Prince William Co., Va., and (2) Mary Deatherage, d. 1810, widow of Robert Deatherage and dau. of Francis and Susannah (Dabney) Strother of St. Marks Parish, Culpeper Co., Va.[286]
60. Thomas Calvert, b. 1714; m. 1734 Sarah Harrison.
61. Burr Calvert, m. Adah Fairfax.
62. Cecilius Calvert.
63. William Calvert.

---

280. Md. Administrations, 1:34, 10:249, 38:19.
281. Md. Administrations, 4:244, 5:142, 15:228, 16:324, 38:20.
282. Md. Wills, 30:819.
283. Jeremiah is not recognized by Dorman, 481.
284. Nicklin, 146-147; O'Gorman, 70-71.
285. Nicklin, 147.
286. Nicklin, 147; O'Gorman, 76.

64. [possibly] Obed Calvert.
65. Elizabeth Calvert.
66. Jacob Calvert, b. c1720 Stafford Co., Va., d. 1772; m. c1750 Virginia Sarah Crupper.

18. **George⁴ Calvert**, son of George and Elizabeth (Doyne) Calvert, was born c1694 and died 3 December 1771 in Prince William County, Virginia. He married first in 1725 there or in Stafford County **Sytha Elizabeth Harrison,** who died by 1741. He married second c1741 **Esther [-?-].**[287]

In 1771 Obed Calvert signed the administrator's bond of Esther Calvert, widow.[288]

Children of George and Sytha (Harrison) Calvert, as reported by O'Brien with no documentation:

67. Obadiah⁵ Calvert, b. c1719, d. 1805 Prince William Co., Va.; m. Mary Gosling.[289]
68. George Calvert, d. 1802.
69. John Calvert, b. Stafford Co., d. 1788 Prince William Co., Va.
70. William Calvert, b. 22 Feb. 1732.
71. Humphrey Calvert, d. 1802 Stafford Co., Va.

24. **Eleanor⁴ Brooke**, daughter of Leonard and Anne (Boarman) Brooke, d. 1760. She married **Clement Gardiner,** who died in 1747. It should be noted that Thomas Richard Gardiner states that this Clement Gardiner married Eleanor Middleton, widow of Richard Brooke, but offers no supporting evidence. Johnston does not recognize any such connection and states that when Charles Brooke died by 1760, his land was divided among his sisters.[290]

The estate of Clement Gardiner was administered by Eleanor Gardiner, who filed an account on 27 June 1748, citing an inventory of £771.19.2 with payments of £827.17.9. Distribution was one-third to the widow and the residue to the legal representatives: Richard Brooke, Ann, Eleanor, Mary, and Jean Gardiner.[291]

The estate of Eleanor Gardiner, with a balance of £960.14.5, was

---

287. Mildred Bower O'Brien, "Calvert," 6. This account contains little or no documentation and must be used carefully. No further information as to the source of this item.

288. John Bailey Calvert Nicklin, "An Index of Calverts (1664-1799," *Genealogy of Virginia Families from the William and Mary Quarterly Historical Magazine,* (1982), 1:542-554.

289. O'Brien, 8.

290. Thomas Richard Gardiner. *Gardiner Generations and Relations, Vol. 1: Gardiner Generations* (1991), 34.

291. Md. Administrations, 25:68.

distributed as shown on an account filed on 6 August 1765 by Richard Boarman, executor. John Smith and Jean Gardiner were his sureties, with legatees daughters Monica Queen, Ann Boarman, and Mary Boarman. An unidentified Sarah Mages was bequeathed 1,000 pounds of tobacco.[292]

Children of Clement and Eleanor (Brooke) Gardiner:[293]

72. Monica[5] Gardiner, b. 1716, d. 1772; m. (1) Richard Brooke, son of Richard and Clare (Boarman) Brooke, and (2) Henry Queen.[294]

73. Mary Gardiner, b. 1717, m. [-?-] Boarman.

74. Eleanor Gardiner, b. 1719, d. 1760.

75. Anne Gardiner, b. 1702; m. Richard Basil Boarman.

76. Jane Gardiner, b. 1722, d. 1760.

25. **Jane[4] Brooke**, daughter of Leonard and Anne (Boarman) Brooke, married **John Smith**, son of John and Dorothy (Brooke) Smith of St. Mary's County.

John Smith of St. Mary's County died leaving a will dated 11 August 1735, proved 3 March 1735/36. He named his son Benjamin, to whom was devised the tract *Sharp* in Prince George's County, and son Leonard and brother Basil. His wife Jean/Jane was appointed executrix, with brother Basil and Clement Gardiner as overseers. Daniel Hodgkin, Clement Gardiner, and Samuel Bellwood witnessed. Jane Smith filed an account on 22 August 1738, noting assets of £432.14.3 and payments of £23.2.8.[295]

Children of John and Jane (Brooke) Smith:[296]

77. Benjamin[5] Smith, d. Charles Co. June 1777; m. Mary Neale.

78. Leonard Smith, d. 1794 testate; m. Elizabeth Neale, dau. of Dr. Charles Neale.

26. **Anne[4] Brooke**, daughter of Leonard and Anne (Boarman) Brooke, married after 1 November 1718 **William Neale**, son of Roswell and Mary (Brent) Neale. On the above date Leonard Brooke wrote his will devising to daughter Ann a tract of land in the fork of the creek that ran into Colonel Henry Lowe's landing.[297]

William Neale of Charles County died leaving a very detailed will dated

292. Md. Wills, 31:7, dtd. 18 Jan. 1760, proved 16 Oct. 1760; Balance Books, 4:130.

293. Gardiner, 35.

294. Johnston, 104

295. Md. Wills, 21:519, Md. Administrations, 16:299.

296. Francis B. Culver, *Society of Colonial Wars in the State of Maryland: Genealogies of the Members and Services of Ancestors.* (1940), 2:15.

297. Harry W. Newman, *Md. Semmes and Kindred Families,* [hereafter *Semmes*] (1956), 309.

3 February 1763 and proved 8 February 1763. He directed that he be buried at Chapple Point beside the graves of his two children. To sons Raphael, Leonard, Charles, and Francis Ignatious he devised the tract whereon I live, called *Chandler's Hope* and *Chandler's Addition* near Port Tobacco Creek, specifying that only the sons surviving to age 21 and not "becoming religious" should inherit the lands equally. To son Francis Ignatious he devised lot no. 1 in Port Tobacco where my tobacco storehouse stands, plus two other lots. To his wife Ann he devised the use of one-third of his lands during her life. He bequeathed slaves to wife Ann and to daughters Clare and Eleanor Neale. To son William Chandler Neale was bequeathed 20 pistoles if he ever returns to this part of the world. He forgave his son-in-law William Matthews' debts. Wife Ann and son-in-law William Matthews were appointed executors. William Matthews was appointed guardian and trustee to the minor children.[298]

Anne Brooke Neale's will, proved 7 January 1786, named her son William Chandler Neale, daughter Eleanor Boarman, son Reverend Leonard Neale, and her Matthews grandchildren: Joseph, Ignatius, Anne, Margaret, and William Matthews. She also bequeathed £5 to a monastery in Arles, France.[299]

Children of William and Anne (Brooke) Neale:[300]
- 79. William[5] Chandler Neale, Jesuit, d. 1799 Manchester, England.
- 80. Leonard Neale, 2nd Archbishop of Baltimore, d. 1817.
- 81. Charles Neale, Jesuit, d. Mt. Carmel, Md. 1823.
- 82. Frances Ignatius Neale.
- 83. Raphael Neale, d. 1784; m. Sarah Howard whom he met in England.[301]
- 84. Clare Neale, b. 1738, m. (1) Henry Brent, and (2) George Slye of St. Mary's Co.[302]
- 85. Mary Neale, m. William Matthews.
- 86. Eleanor Neale, m. (1) John Holmes, and (2) Raphael Boarman.

28. Richard[4] Brooke, son of Baker and Katherine (Marsham) Brooke, died by August 1719. He married **Clare Boarman**, daughter of Major William Boarman of Charles County. She married second Richard Sherburne of St. Mary's County, by whom she had a son Nicholas.[303]

---

298. Md. Wills, 31:918.
299. *Semmes*, 310.
300. Ibid.
301. Ibid., 318.
302. Johnston, "Neale Family," 2:263.
303. Johnston, 103.

Richard Brooke died leaving a will dated 5 December 1718, proved 3 August 1719. He gave his entire estate to his wife and two children, Richard and Baker. To the children of his deceased uncle, Leonard Brooke, he devised any interest he may have had in *Dellabrooke Manor*, except *Hardship*. His brother Leonard was named executor on behalf of his two [minor] children, and his wife executrix on her own part. Robert Elliott, William Cabinet, and John Farnile witnessed the will. Leonard Brooke filed an account on 27 July 1720, showing assets of £457.6.4. and payments of £47.4.7. A second account filed on 9 September 1724 showed payments of £14.17.9, and a third account dated 19 November 1726 included payments of £182.18.3 and distribution of one-third of the balance to the widow.[304]

Clare (Boarman) (Brooke) Sherburne's will was dated 21 February 1745 and proved 6 August 1747. She named her three sons Richard and Baker Brooke, and Nicholas Sherburne, the latter appointed executor; John Miles witnessed.[305]

Children of Richard and Clare (Boarman) Brooke:

87. Richard[5] Brooke, d. 1754 testate; m. Monica Gardiner, who m. (2) Henry Queen.
88. Baker Brooke, d. 1756, m. Mary Simpson, daughter of William; no issue.

29. **Anne[4] Brooke,** daughter of Baker and Katherine (Marsham) Brooke, married in 1710 Benedict Leonard Boarman, who was born c1687 in Charles County, and died there by March 1757. Boarman deposed in 1745 giving his age as 58 years.[306]

Benedict Boarman died leaving a will dated 28 July 1754 and proved 11 March 1757, in which he named wife Anne and sons Benedict Leonard, Richard Basil, George, and Joseph, and three unmarried daughters, Mary, Elenor, and Jane, as well as daughter Catherine Gardiner. His wife was appointed executrix, with witnesses Marsham Queen, Ingns. Doyne, and William Matthews.[307]

Children of Benedict Leonard and Anne (Brooke) Boarman:[308]

89. Leonard[5] Boarman, b. c1737, d. Charles Co. 1794; m. Elizabeth Jenkins.
90. Richard Basil Boarman, d. St. Mary's Co. 1782; m. Anne Gardiner.
91. George Boarman, d. 9 April 1768; m. Mary [-?-].

---

304. Ibid., Md. Wills, 15:178; Md. Administrations, 3:88, 6:91, 8:74.
305. Johnston, 99-100; Md. Wills, 25:152-153.
306. Semmes, 309.
307. Md. Wills, 30:277.
308. Semmes, 310.

92. Joseph Boarman.
93. Catherine Boarman, m. [-?-] Gardiner.
94. Mary Boarman.
95. Elenor Boarman, d. unm. testate, will dtd. 22 July 1794; proved 12 Oct. 1795.
96. Jane Boarman, d. unm. testate, will dtd. 20 Sept. 1779, proved 26 April 1783.

30. **Leonard⁴ Brooke**, son of Baker and Katherine (Marsham) Brooke, was born c1690 and died in Prince George's County c1736. In c1722 he married **Anne Darnall**, born c1705 in Prince George's County, died June 1779.

Leonard Brooke died leaving a will dated June 1735 and proved 4 May 1736, appointing his wife executrix, and naming sons Leonard, Richard, Oswald, and Baker, and daughters Ann, Katherine, Jane, Mary, and Henrietta. Henry Hill, John Bowie, and Mary Ann Hill witnessed the will. An account was filed on 30 August 1744 by Anne Brooke, who reported an inventory valued at £628.2.1, with payments totalling £56.3.2. The heirs were his children: Ann, Baker, Catherine, Jane, Leonard, Mary, Henrietta, and Richard.[309]

Children of Leonard and Anne (Darnall) Brooke:[310]

97. Richard⁵ Brooke, b. c1725, d. Charles Co. c1771; m. Elizabeth Neale (1730-1770).
98. Capt. Leonard Brooke, b. 1728, d. c1785; m. (1) Anne Darnall, dau. of Henry Darnall, and (2) Elizabeth [-?-].[311]
99. Baker Brooke, d. Charles Co. 4 June 1771 testate; wife unidentified.
100. Oswald Brooke, not mentioned in 1744 distribution of father's estate.
101. Ann Brooke, d. by 16 Sept. 1773 leaving personal property worth £314.15.0. Leonard Brooke filed an account on the above date; after making payments of £39.9.3 he distributed the balance of £307.16.10 equally to Katherine Brooke and the children of Richard Brooke.[312]
102. Katherine Brooke.
103. Jane Brooke.
104. Mary Brooke.
105. Henrietta Brooke.

31. **Elizabeth⁴ Neale**, daughter of Raphael and Mary (Brooke) Neale, died in 1743. She married c1730 **John Lancaster**, son of John and Fanny (Jerningham) Lancaster. John died in 1760, after marrying second Mary

---

309. Md. Administrations, 20:451.
310. Johnston, 104, and will of deceased.
311. Johnston, "The Brooke Family," 1:108.
312. Md. Administrations, 68:47; Balance Books, 6:221.

(Gardiner) Neale, widow of Henry and daughter of John Gardiner.[313]

On 7 May 1731 Raphael Neale and wife Mary, for love and five shillings, conveyed to Capt. John Lancaster and wife Elizabeth 494 acres of land. On 14 June 1743, Lancaster petitioned the Charles County Court to mark the boundaries; he repeated his petition on 13 November 1744.[314]

On 9 September 1743, Wilfred Gardiner made a will naming his mother Mary Slye, brother George Slye, and sisters Mary Lancaster and Ann Neale; the two sisters were to share his lands called *Cannoe Neck* and *Hilleary*. John Lancaster and Henry Neale were appointed executors.[315] At a court held 13 November 1744, John Lancaster was appointed one of the three overseers of the highway from Pickawaxon Church to Henry Neale's Landing.[316]

John Lancaster died in Charles County leaving a will dated 31 January 1759, proved 21 May 1760. He gave £30 to the poor and a slave to James Ashby. He named wife Mary Lancaster, daughter Mary Bradford, grandson John Holmes, sons Raphael, Joseph and John, and daughter Katherine Combs, plus his own brother Joseph Lancaster. He appointed George Slye and Henry Neale to divide his personal estate among his children. Sons John and Joseph were appointed executors, with John and Ann Scrogin and William Tyere witnessing.[317] On 5 September 1760 John Lancaster's inventory was filed, with appraisers Nathaniel Harris and John Marshall valuing the estate at £2037.16.1. Raphael Lancaster and Mary Bradford signed as kinsmen.[318]

Children of John and Elizabeth (Neale) Lancaster:[319]

106. John[5] Lancaster, b. c1759, d. Nov. 1794; m. Mary [Pye?], who d. Dec. 1803.[320]
107. Joseph Lancaster.
108. Raphael Lancaster, b. c1732; d. 1802; m. c1764 Eleanor Bradford, dau. of John Bradford and Ann [possibly Darnall].
109. Mary Lancaster, m. [-?-] Bradford.
110. [daughter], m. [-?-] Holmes; had son John.
111. Katherine Lancaster, m. [-?-] Combs.

32. Mary[4] Neale, daughter of Raphael and Mary (Brooke) Neale, married

313. Semmes Genealogical Collection, Md. Historical Society.
314. Charles Co. Land Records, M2:246, 39:565, 1744-1745:222.
315. Md. Wills, 23:528.
316. Ibid. 1744-1745:175.
317. Md. Wills, 31:43.
318. Md. Inventories, 70:213.
319. *Society of Colonial Wars*, 2:23.
320. Ibid., 2:23.

Thomas Taney of St. Mary's County, who died leaving a will dated 1 December 1762, proved 1 June 1762 [*sic*]. He named his sons Raphael, Michael Thomas and John Francis Taney, and daughter Mary Eleanor Combs; also grandchildren Charles Taney and Raphael Combs. Wife and son John Francis appointed executors. John Smith, John Gray, and Mary Pike witnessed.[321] Thomas Forrest and John Abell appraised the personal estate by 30 October 1765 and valued it at £38.0.0; Mary Taney and J. Francis Taney signed as next of kin. Administrator John Taney filed an account on 7 July 1764, citing a new inventory of £50.1.0 and payments of £2.14.3.[322]

Children of Thomas and Mary (Neale) Taney:[323]

112. Raphael[5] Taney.
113. John Francis Taney.
114. Michael Thomas Taney.
115. Mary Eleanor Taney, m. William Combs. [See #36 on page 207.]

33. **Henrietta[4] Neale**, daughter of Raphael and Mary (Brooke) Neale, died in 1774. She married **Basil Brooke,** son of Roger; Basil was born 16 November 1717 and died in 1761[324] leaving a will dated 14 May 1761 and proved 13 July 1767, naming sons Raphael, Roger, and James. Wife Henrietta was appointed executrix. Will Hamersley, Henry Bradford, and Raphael Lancaster witnessed.[325]

Henrietta's will was dated 27 June 1773 and proved 16 June 1774, and named her four children Raphael, Roger, James, and Ann; also her sister Ann Thompson. Son Raphael was executor, with John Lancaster Sr. and Jr. witnessing.[326]

Children of Henrietta (Neale) and Basil Brooke:[327]

116. Raphael[5] Brooke.
117. Roger Brooke.
118. James Brooke.
119. Anne Brooke.

34. **Anne[4] Neale**, daughter of Raphael and Mary (Brooke) Neale, married

321. Md. Wills, 31:666.
322. Md. Inventories, 87:315; Md. Administrations, 51:179.
323. Johnston, "Neale Family," 2:259 for his marriage, not children.
324. Johnston, "Brooke Family," 107.
325. Md. Wills, 35:407.
326. Ibid., 39:697.
327. Johnston, "Brooke Family," 107.

James Thompson, Jr.[328] He died in St. Mary's County leaving a will dated 10 August 1749 and proved 18 September 1750, naming sons Raphael Francis and James Charles, daughter Mary Elisabeth, and wife Anne. He bequeathed cattle to his brother Francis, and appointed his parents executors [although they did not serve]. John Shiercliff, Elizabeth Neale, and Philip Greenwell witnessed. Samuel Briscoe and William Hamersley valued his estate on 17 September 1755 at £21.15.0, with Francis Thompson and Mary Roach signing as kin. Administrator Anne Neale filed the inventory on 3 March 1756 and her account on 18 July 1757, listing payments of £1179.11.10. Distribution was to the widow and orphans: Raphael Francis age 13, James Charles age 10, and Mary Elizabeth age 8.[329]

Children of James and Anne (Neale) Thompson:

120. Raphael Francis[5] Thompson, b. c1744.
121. James Charles Thompson, b. c1747.
122. Mary Elizabeth Thompson, b. c1749.

35. **Monica**[4] **Neale**, daughter of Raphael and Mary (Brooke) Neale, married **Edward Digges** by 20 July 1743, when she was called daughter in the will of her father, and on 29 September 1760 her mother named son-in-law Edward Digges and grandchildren Eleanor and John Digges.[330]

Edward Digges of St. Mary's County died leaving a will dated 10 June 1769 and proved 18 December 1769. He named his brothers William and Henry Digges, daughters Elizabeth, Elinor, Anne, and Mary Digges, and sons John and Edward Digges, and sons-in-law Charles and John Whorton. He appointed his three daughters and brothers-in-laws Raphael Neale and George Slye executors. On 10 March 1770 William Jordan and John Shanks, Jr. valued his personal estate at £2285.12.5, with John Digges and H. Digges signing as kinsmen. Wilfred Neale and wife Elizabeth, Eleanor Digges, Raphael Neale, and George Slye, the executors, filed the inventory on 17 March 1770. The first account, filed 28 November 1771, cited payments of £1830.14.5; a second account filed 11 July 1774 showed additional payments of £357.2.4, and a third filed on 1 August 1775, £240.16.6.[331]

Children of Monica (Neale) and Edward Digges:

---

328. As a daughter of Raphael Neale, dcd., she drew lot #4 in a division of *Wollaston Manor* on 11 July 1755. Charles Co. Land Records, A3:359. Md. Wills, 31:993.

329. Md. Wills, Md. Inventories 60:371; Md. Administrations, 41:78.

330. Md. Wills, 23:294, 31:993.

331. Md. Wills, 37:461; Md. Inventories, 103:230; Md. Administrations, 66:67, 73:1, 73:249.

123. John[5] Digges.
124. Eleanor Digges.
125. Elizabeth Digges, m. Wilfred Neale.
126. Mary Digges.
127. Edward Digges.
128. Ann Digges.

36. **Eleanor[4] Neale**, daughter of Raphael and Mary (Brooke) Neale, married **Bennett Hoskins**, born c1701 in Port Tobacco Parish, Charles County, son of Philip and Ann (Matthews) Hoskins.[332]

He died leaving a will dated 21 February 1733/4 and proved 22 April 1734. He appointed his father-in-law Raphael Neale executor and asked that an agreement between the testator and Edward Neale involving two tracts of land be carried out. Richard Cooke, William Neale, Jr., and John Lancaster witnessed. On 27 May 1734 Robert Yates and Jos. Douglas valued his personal estate at £153.17.3, with John Lancaster and William Neale signing as kin. Raphael Neale, executor, filed the inventory on 3 July 1734. An account was filed on 31 October 1735 with payments of £38.16.2.[333]

Children of Eleanor (Neale) and Bennett Hoskins:[334]

129. Mary Anne[5] Hoskins, m. Richard Bennett Boarman by 1743; d. Charles Co. 1792.
130. Ann Hoskins.

THOMAS CORNWALLIS

1. **Thomas[1] Cornwallis**, Esq., immigrated to Maryland on the *Ark* in 1633.[335] A younger son of Sir William and Catherine (Parker) Cornwallis, he was born c1605 in County Norfolk, England.[336] Returning to England in 1659, he died testate in County Norfolk shortly before 4 March 1675/76, the date his will was proved. He married first [name unknown] by 1638. His second wife, whom he married in 1654, was **Penelope Wiseman**,

---

332. George Ely Russell, "Col. Philip Hoskins (c1650-1718) of Port Tobacco, Charles Co., Md," *National Genealogical Society Quarterly* 51 (1963): 30.

333. Md. Wills, 21:53. Md. Inventories, 128.297. Md. Administrations, 14:89.

334. Named in 1743 will of grandfather Raphael Neale. Md. Wills, 23:294.

335. Md. Land Patents, ABH:244; 4:623.

336. *Burke's Dormant and Extinct Peerages*, 137-138; G. Andrews Moriarty, "Early Generations of Cornwallis of Brome," *New England Historical and Genealogical Register* 110 (April 1956): 122-127; Robert Barnes, *British Roots of Maryland Families* (Baltimore: Genealogical Publ. Co., 1999), 136-138.

daughter of John Wiseman of Terrells Hall, County Essex, England. She was still living in 1688.

A major investor and entrepreneur, he transported at least 71 servants to Maryland in the period 1643-1651, had extensive land holdings, held several public offices, and was the chief military officer.[337]

Children of Thomas Cornwallis:[338]

2. William[2] Cornwallis, b. c1659; d. c1679;[339] Clerk of the Prerogative Office 1678-1679.[340]

3. Thomas Cornwallis, Jr., b. 1661; d. 1731; of Ewarton, Co. Suffolk, England.

4. Frances Cornwallis, m. Samuel Richardson, clergyman.

ANN COX

Mrs. **Ann Cox**, a widow, immigrated to Maryland in 1633 and received a special grant of 500 acres from Lord Baltimore. She later married Thomas Green, Esq.[341] [See his account below.][342]

WILLIAM EDWIN

1. **William[1] Edwin** was probably born c1612 and died by October 1663. He

---

337. His career and records are summarized in Newman, *Flowering*, 188-189; and in Edward C. Papenfuse *et al*, *Biographical Dictionary of the Maryland Legislature, 1635-1789* (Baltimore: Johns Hopkins University Press, 1979), 1:234-235. His testimony in 1645 concerning Richard Ingle's plundering of his Maryland estate in 1644 is found in Public Record Office (England) Chancery Court document C2/Chas. I/C15/23, abstracted in Peter W. Coldham, "Genealogical Gleanings in England," *National Genealogical Society Quarterly* 69 (1981): 120-121. His additional testimony concerning Maryland is provided in a 1645 Admiralty Court case. PRO document HCA 13/60, abstracted in Coldham, *More English Adventurers and Emigrants, 1625-1777* (2002), 4-5. Information about his estate, named *Cross Manor*, is provided by John M. Elliott, "Cornwaley's Cross Manor," in *Chronicles of St. Mary's* vol. 13, no. 7 (July 1965): 1-5.

338. *Harleian Society Publications: Visitation Series, vol. 85, Norfolk Visitations*, 56 (Cornwallis).

339. Md. Land Patents, 20:147.

340. Donell M. Owings, *His Lordship's Patronage - Offices of Profit in Colonial Maryland* (Baltimore: Md. Historical Soc., 1953), 142. But this was the *alias* name assumed by the notorious William Vanhaesdunk Riddlesden, an English convict transported to Md. in 1720. He gained access to the Land Office, pretended a right to Thomas Cornwallis's land, and forged title documents which he used when selling the land. For details, see George Ely Russell, "Mr. William Vanhaesdunk Riddlesden *alias* William Cornwallis, 'A Person of Matchless Character in Infamy'," *Maryland Magazine of Genealogy* 4 (1981): 57-60.

341. Md. Land Patents, ABH:12; 2:444.

342. The erroneous claim by Edwin W. Beitzell in *Maryland Historical Magazine* 46 (1951): 189, that Ann was a sister of Maryland settlers Thomas and Richard Gerard, is refuted by David Spalding, "Thomas Gerard of Md. and Va.: Old World Roots," *Chronicles of St. Mary's*, vol. 7, no. 7 (July 1959): 1-8.

was transported to Maryland in 1633 by Richard Gerard,[343] and married first, **Mary Whitehead**, declaring his intention to marry her on 26 March 1637, by the first marriage license in the colony.[344] Mary died after 1658. Willliam returned to England and brought back his second wife **Marguerite/Margaret** [-?-], who survived him.

William was literate and kept an inn. At the Second Assembly of January 1637/8 he was described as a planter. He applied for his land rights in 1648 and was granted fifty acres called *St. William*. He was later Constable of St. George's Hundred.[345] William was entitled to 100 acres for his second entry into Maryland, which passed to his wife Marguerite.

William left an undated will which was proved 13 October 1663. He appointed his [unnamed] wife as executrix, who had lifetime rights to the dwelling plantation, and then to his eldest son Michael. To granddaughter Mary Hall and William Grengo he bequeathed personalty. William Price and William Grengo were witnesses.[346] Thomas Dent filed the inventory on 11 January 1663/64, with Robert Cager and Henry Ellery approving, but no next of kin signed, nor did any administrator.[347] Margaret Edwin, the widow, was living on 26 September 1665 when she assigned her rights to the 350 acres of land from the second patent, located at Pokomoke and called the *Golden Lyon*, to her son William, orphan. The additional acres were assignments from several persons, not specified.[348]

Children of William and Mary (Whitehead) Edwin:

   2. Michael[2] Edwin settled on the Eastern Shore. On 26 July 1718 he was paid out of the estate of his brother Edwin, and on 11 Dec. 1718 he was paid by the state of Daniel Dunsay of Kent Co.[349]
   3. Elizabeth Edwin [cited by Newman with no attribution].
+ 4. Mary Edwin, m. James Hall.

Child of William and Margaret Edwin:
+ 5. William Edwin.

4. **Mary[2] Edwin**, daughter of William and Mary (Whitehead) Edwin, was born in St. Mary's County in December 1637 and died there by 1663. She married between 1657 and 1662 **James Hall**, who was transported to Maryland in 1657.

---

343. Md. Land Patents, ABH:5, 66.

344. Newman, *Flowering of the Maryland Palatinate*, 197.

345. Ibid., 197-8.

346. Md. Wills, 1:197.

347. Md. Testamentary Proceedings, 1D:163, 17.

348. Newman, *Flowering,* 199; Md. Testamentary Proceedings, 7:265.

349. Md. Administrations, 1:261, 267.

Children of James and Mary (Edwin) Hall:[350]

+ 6. Mary[3] Hall.
   7. Thomas Hall of Pocomoke, alive 31 March 1685.[351]

5. **William[2] Edwin,** son of William and Margaret Edwin, settled in Kent County, where he received a grant for 140-acre *Edwin's Addition.* Sometime between 29 January 1674/5 and 24 January 1684/5 he married **Mary Ricaud,** daughter of Benjamin Ricaud and half-sister of Christopher Hall.[352] He probably married second **Mary Lewis** on 14 December 1714 in St. Paul's Parish.[353] Mary (Lewis) Edwin married second Thomas Richards.

William died leaving a will dated 30 October 1716, which devised to brother Michael 100-acre *Tree Neck* near Swann Creek. He named wife Mary and his son William, not yet 18. John Blackinton and Edward Davis appraised the personal property on 5 February 1716, valuing it at £55.10.5. Michael Edwin signed as kinsman. An account of the administration was filed by executrix Mary Richards on 26 July 1718, now wife of Thomas Richards, stating that Michael Edwin was paid. On 21 September 1714 the administration account of Thomas Ricaud listed a payment to William and Margaret Edwin and Robert Hodges, who married Tamar, all children of Mary, sister of the deceased.[354]

Children of William and Mary (Ricaud) Edwin:[355]
   8. William[3] Edwin, b. after 1698, prob. d. without issue.
   9. Mary Edwin, prob. m. William Hall in St. Paul's Parish, Kent Co., 14 June 1716.[356]
   10. Margaret Edwin.
+ 11. Tamar Edwin, m. Robert Hodges.

6. **Mary[3] Hall,** daughter of James and Mary (Edwin) Hall and sister of Thomas Hall of Pocomoke, was born in St. Mary's County between 1657 and 1662 and died in Calvert County after 31 March 1685. She married **Joseph Dawkins,** born c1637 in England and died in Calvert County in

---

350. Newman, *Flowering,* 199.

351. Md. Wills, 4:86.

352. Newman, *Flowering,* 303.

353. *Eastern Shore Vital Records,* 1:21.

354. Md. Wills, 14:170; Md. Inventories and Accounts, 39A:3 36B:17; Md. Administrations, 1:260.

355. Newman, *Flowering,* 303; Md. Inventories and Accounts, 33B:227, 36B:17, 37A:12.

356. *Eastern Shore Vital Records,* 1:25.

May 1685.[357]

Joseph Dawkins died leaving a will dated 31 March 1685 and proved 9 May 1685. He devised to son Joseph 196-acre *Dawkin's Reserve* and to son Joseph 200-acre *Joseph's Place*. Wife Mary was appointed executrix with rights to the home plantation for life. Also named were son James, daughter Mary (wife of James Duke), and Thomas Hall of Pocomoke, brother-in-law. Witnessing were Jn° Stewart and Thomas Owens. An account was filed on 9 August 1686 by Margaret [second wife?], listing an inventory of £63.3.0, with payments amounting to 12,630 pounds of tobacco.[358]

Children of Joseph and Mary (Hall) Dawkins:

+ 12. Mary[4] Dawkins, m. by 31 March 1685 James Duke.
+ 13. Joseph Dawkins, b. c1673.
+ 14. William Dawkins.
+ 15. James Dawkins.

11. **Tamar[3] Edwin**, daughter of William and Mary (Ricaud) Edwin, married before 1709 **Robert Hodges**, born c1687, son of William Hodges. On 3 March 1725/26 Robert Hodges, age c38, deposed regarding the bounds of *Langford's Neck*.[359] He died by April 1735.

On 20 February 1709 Robert and Tamar Hodges sold to Richard Gibbs a 100-acre parcel of land. On 19 November 1723 John Wilson of Kent County, tailor, and wife Mary conveyed to Robert Hodges of Kent Co., planter, 150-acre *Gray's Inn* on the west side of Gray's Inn Creek. On the same day Robert and Tamar conveyed to John Wilson 150-acre *Prevention of Inconvenience*.[360]

Robert Hodges died in Kent County leaving a will dated 30 November 1735, proved 30 April 1735. He devised to his four oldest sons *Prevention of Inconvenience*. He also named sons Samuel and James, and six daughters, and appointed wife Tamar executrix. Witnesses were Benjamin Cleaver, John Heavin, and William Newton.[361]

Children of Robert and Tamar (Edwin) Hodges:[362]

+ 16. William[4] Hodges, b. c1711.
  17. John Hodges, may be the one who m. Ann Burrells or Bussells 18 Sept. 1746,

357. Culver, *Society of Colonial Wars*, 2:52.
358. Md. Wills, 4:86; Md. Inventories and Accounts, 9:146.
359. Kent Co. Land Records, JS W:544.
360. Ibid., JS N:183, JS W:338, 340.
361. Md. Wills, 21:419. No inventory or account was filed for his estate.
362. F. Edward Wright, *Eastern Shore Vital Records*, (1993), 1:25, 2:23, St. Paul's Parish.

St. Luke's Parish, Queen Anne's Co.[363]
18. Martha Hodges, b. 15 Jan. 1715.
+ 19. Robert Hodges, b. 1718.
20. Priscilla Hodges, b. 9 Sept. 1720.
21. Stephen Hodges, b. 28 Feb. 1722, d.in Kent Co., will dated 13 Oct. 1788, proved 22 Oct. 1789; devised to nephew James Hodges, son of James, his portion of *Prevention of Inconvience,* and half of his personal estate to brother James Hodges and the other half to sister Sarah Hodges and niece Mary Miller equally. No executor was named. William Ringgold, Benjamin Yearly, and Robert Hodges were witnesses.[364]
+ 22. Samuel Hodges, b. 1724.
23. Rebecca Hodges, b. 26 Nov. 1726.
24. Sarah Hodges, b. 4 Aug. 1728.
+ 25. James Hodges.
26. [daughter].
27. [daughter].

12. **Mary**[4] **Dawkins,** daughter of Joseph and Mary (Hall) Dawkins, married by 31 March 1685 **James Duke**, who was born by 1670 and died in Calvert County in 1731. The Calvert County Rent Roll states that he conveyed part of *Rich Level* to Richard Hellen and William Dawkins in December 1729.[365]

James died leaving a will dated 10 November 1731, proved 21 December 1731, in which he devised to son James part of *Brooke Place Manor.* To granddaughter Martha was devised the dwelling plantation, *Rich Level,* and then to pass to grandson Benjamin. To grandson Samuel Rowland (son of Samuel) was devised the tract *Shirt Come Off.* To daughter Martha Gray and son Andrew Duke were bequeathed 1 shilling each, while daughter Catherine Beall was bequeathed 20 shillings. Wife was bequeathed one-third of his estate. Witnessing were Grace Hambleton, William Dawkins, and John Dorrumple. James Duke, executor, filed the inventory on 25 November 1732, exhibiting the appraisal by John Dorryumple and William Dawkins, which totaled £80.3.11. William Gray and Samuel Rowland signed as kinsmen. The administration account was filed on 31 May 1734, with payments of £10.3.11.[366]

---

363. *Eastern Shore Vital Records,* 2:57.
364. Kent Co. Wills, 7:241.
365. Md. Rent Rolls, B:7.
366. Md. Wills, 20:364; Md. Inventories, 16:623; Md. Administrations, 12:309.

Children of James and Mary (Dawkins) Duke:[367]

28. James[5] Duke, (c1694-1754); m. (1) Martha Mackall, dau. Benjamin and Barbara; m. (2) Esther Parran, wid. of John Parran. Will dtd. 6 Feb. 1754, proved 20 March 1754. Magistrate of Calvert Co. last 20 years of life. Devised *Brooke Place Manor* to son James and *Duke's Mill* to son Benjamin.[368]
29. Martha Duke, m. William Gray (1681-1738) on 16 Oct. 1706 at Christ Church. Gray d. testate naming children.[369]
30. Andrew Duke, may be the one who received a payment from the estate of John Chittam of Calvert Co. on 7 Dec. 1723.[370]
31. Mary Duke, m. Samuel Rowland.
32. Catherine Duke (1699-1736; m. Ninian Beall, Jr., b. c1696, son of Thomas Beall, immigrant.
33. Elizabeth Duke, b. 22 Dec. 1705.

13. Joseph[4] Dawkins, son of Joseph and Mary (Hall) Dawkins, was born c1673 in Calvert County and died there in April 1715. In 1696 he married **Sarah [-?-].** He and his son William were named in the 1700 will of his brother James Dawkins.

Joseph Dawkins died leaving a will dated 30 December 1714, proved 2 April 1715, naming his brother William, and children William, Joseph, James, Mary, Sarah, Margaret (not yet 16), and Dorcas. Son William was executor and residuary legatee. Overseers were Colonel John Mack and the testator's brothers William Dawkins and Jn° Howe. Witnesses were James Duke, Jr., Joseph Pinder, and Andrew Duke. On 17 April 1715 his personal property was appraised by Thomas Howe and David Hellen and valued at £203.10.4. The account filed on 4 April 1715 showed payments of £12.7.8.[371]

Children of Joseph and Sarah Dawkins, baptized at Christ Church, Calvert County:[372]
34. William[5] Dawkins, b. 1698, d. 1756; m. Christ Church 9 Aug. 1702 Mary Mackall (c1700-1757), dau. James and Ann (Brooke) Mackall. She m. (2) John Greaves. William d. testate owning *Joseph's Place* and *Mary's Dukedom.*[373]
35. Joseph Dawkins, b. 21 March 1703/4; d. leaving will dated 18 Jan. 1733, proved 19 March 1733, naming brothers James and William, and cousin

---

367. "Duke," in Jourdan, *Early Families of St. Mary's County*, 5:6-13.
368. Ibid.; Md. Wills, 29:206.
369. Md. Wills, 22:8.
370. Md. Administrations, 5:311.
371. Md. Wills, 14:48; Md. Inventories and Accounts, 36B:167, 36C:107.
372. Jourdan, *Colonial Records of Southern Maryland*, 49, 51.
373. Jourdan, *Colonial Records,* 84; Md. Administrations, 38:238; Md. Wills, 30:209.

Sarah Dare (not yet 16). John Stevens was a legatee. Witnesses were James Dawkins, Daniel Frazier, Jr., and John Crane.[374]

36. James Dawkins, b. 29 Apr. 1708; d. by Sept. 1744; m. Mary [-?-]. He d. testate devising *Bachelor Hall, Haphassard,* and pt. *Mary's Dukedom* to family.[375]
37. Mary Dawkins.
38. Sarah Dawkins.
39. Margaret Dawkins.
40. Dorcas Dawkins.

14. **William⁴ Dawkins**, son of Joseph and Mary (Hall) Dawkins, was born c1675 and died by September 1726 [not on or about 18 June 1701 as has been suggested; his son William was born 1706]. By 1700 he was married to **Ann Smith**, daughter of Richard Smith, and had at least one son.[376] On 13 May 1701 Dawkins administered the estate of Samuel Scott of Calvert County.[377] He is probably the William Dawkins who, with James Dawkins, was mentioned in the will of Robert Kent made 9 October 1693.[378] On 8 November 1700 James Dawkins (#15) named brother William and William's son James in his will.[379]

William Dawkins died leaving a will dated 30 May 1726 and proved 30 September 1726. He appointed his wife Ann executrix, and named children James, Bennet, William, Mary Pattison, Penelope, Elizabeth, and Ann Hellen. Tracts mentioned were *Chelton, Smith, Dorrington, Enlargement of Dorrington,* and *Joseph His Place*. The will was witnessed by William Blackburn, William Walker, and William Gray.[380]

Ann Dawkins of Calvert County died leaving a will dated 24 May 1742 and proved 14 June 1742, which named her children James, William, and Penelope Sollers, to each of whom was bequeathed 1 shilling. Executrixes were granddaughters Elizabeth Dawkins and Penelope Pattison. To them, with Mary Pattison, was bequeathed the residue of the estate. Witnesses were Joseph Sollers and James Mackall. Ann's personal property was appraised at £241.7.8 on 8 July 1742 by John Brome and Gideon Dare, with William Dawkins, Jr., and Robert Sollers signing as kinsmen. Penelope Pattison filed the inventory on 24 January 1742[/43], and the

374. Md. Wills, 21:24.
375. Md. Wills, 23:5.
376. Md. Wills, 14:83; Baltimore Co. Land Records, IS H:22.
377. Md. Inventories and Accounts, 20:116.
378. Md. Wills, 2:255.
379. Md. Wills, 11:79.
380. Md. Wills, 19:7.

account on 17 September 1743 with payments of £55.18.10. Another account was filed on 7 September 1747 by Penelope, now wife of Peter Hellen, Jr., showing payments to Ann's granddaughter Elizabeth Dawkins, son William, and Richard Smith.[381]

Children of William and Ann (Smith) Dawkins, recorded at Christ Church:[382]

> 41. James[5] Dawkins, b. 1 Aug. 1695.
> 42. Ann Dawkins, b. 1698, d. by Sept. 1747; m. James Hellen, son of David and Susanna Hellen, b. 27 Dec. 1688. Children bp. Christ Church.[383]
> 43. Bennet Dawkins, b. 2 Oct. 1704; d. leaving will dated 10 March 1727, proved 29 June 1728, naming sisters Elizabeth and Penelope; devised to brother William (executor) rights to *Smith's Purchase*. Witnesses: Thomas Brickenden, William Dawkins, and Joseph Dawkins. On 4 Nov. 1730 William Dawkins, Jr. filed an administration account, showing an inventory value of £110.12.9 and payments of £192.17.7. Legatees were Elizabeth and Penelope Dawkins, with the balance to the accountant.[384]
> 44. William Dawkins, b. 13 Sept. 1706; d. testate c20 Jan. 1746; m. Dorcas Mackell, who m. (2) Samuel Dare. William d. owning *Ashton Chance, Ashton Addition, Smith's Purchase*, and *Blinkhorne's Desire.* [385]
> 45. Mary Dawkins, d. 1730-1734; m. (1) James Pattison, who d. 1729; m. (2) Benjamin Tucker who d. 1734.[386]
> 46. Penelope Dawkins, m. by 1742 [probably Joseph] Sollers.
> 47. Elizabeth Dawkins.

15. **James[4] Dawkins,** son of Joseph and Mary (Hall) Dawkins, died by June 1701. He married c1694 **Anne Brooke,** daughter of Roger and Mary (Woolseley) Brooke. She married second James Mackall, and died by March 1733.[387]

James Dawkins died leaving a will dated 8 November 1700 and proved 18 June 1701. He named his wife Anne, and stated if a child was born it was to have half of his estate. Also named were nephews William (of Joseph) and James (of William). Witnesses were Roger Brooke, Jos. Sherwood, and Edm. Hungerford. The inventory was taken by George Young, Sr., and Daniel Phillips, who valued it at £290.6.1. The account filed on 1 April 1703 by executrix Anne, now wife of James Mackall, cited

---

381. Md. Wills, 22:474; Md. Inventories, 27:252; Md. Administrations, 19:489, 24:142.
382. Jourdan, *Colonial Records*, 50.
383. Jourdan, *Colonial Records*, 71.
384. Md. Wills, 19:436; Administrations, 10:543.
385. Judgments, 39:703; Md. Wills, 21:30, 25:11.
386. Md. Administrations, 10:536.
387. Md. Wills, 4:40, 6:384; Md. Inventories and Accounts, 20:213, 32:25.

payments of £36.17.19 to William and James Dawkins.[388]

On 31 March 1709 Roger Brooke conveyed 178-acre *Brooke's Reserve* in Prince George's County to his daughter Anne Mackall.[389]

Anne Mackall died in Calvert County leaving a will dated 17 January 1733, proved 19 March 1733/34. She named daughters Mary and Dorcas Dawkins, Dorothy Mackall, and sons James, John, and Benjamin Mackall, and William Dawkins (bequeathed £10 by his uncle James Dawkins). Witnesses were John Dorrumple and William Holloway. Anne's personal property was valued at £359.3.0 by C. Clagett and John Dorrumple; no next of kin signed the inventory filed 22 August 1734 by John Mackall, executor. The account was filed 2 September 1735.[390]

Children of James and Anne (Brooke) Dawkins:
  48. Mary[5] Dawkins.
  49. Dorcas Dawkins.
  50. William Dawkins [probably b. posthumously].

16. **William[4] Hodges**, son of Robert and Tamar (Edwin) Hodges, was born c1711. On 9 October 1761 William Hodges, age about 50, deposed regarding the bounds of the tract *Huntingfield.*[391] He and **Frances Bradsha** were married 23 December 1736.[392] On 21 August 1735 Morgan Hurtt of Kent County and wife Mary conveyed to William Hodges of same 45-acre *Hurst Direction* on the west side of Gravesend Creek.[393]

William Hodges died in Kent County leaving a will dated 19 October 1776, proved 25 April 1777. He named wife Frances, daughters Hannah Winters and Sarah Hodges, and two granddaughters, Sarah Hodges and Elizabeth Frances Hodges.[394]

Children of William and Frances (Bradsha) Hodges:[395]
  51. William[5] Hodges, b. 31 Jan. 1739.
  52. Robert Hodges, b. Jan. 1741.
  53. [daughter], b. 4 Oct. 174?.
  54. Frances Hodges, bur. 17 Dec. 1767.
  55. Rebecca Hodges, b. 3 Jan. 1747, bur. 17 Dec. 1767.
  56. Hannah Hodges, b. 21 March 1752, m. by 19 Oct. 1776 [-?-] Winters.

388. Md. Wills, 11:79; Md. Inventories and Accounts, 23:25.
389. Prince George's Co. Land Records, C:258.
390. Md. Wills, 21:30; Md. Inventories, 18:456; Administrations, 13:281.
391. Kent Co. Land Records, DD 1:612.
392. *Eastern Shore Vital Records,* 2:45.
393. Kent Co. Land Records, JS 18:167.
394. St. Paul's Parish, *Eastern Shore Vital Records.*
395. Ibid., 2:24, 3:13.

57. Samuel Hodges, b. 2 Oct. 1755.
58. Sarah Hodges, b. 7 May 1758.

19. **Robert⁴ Hodges**, son of Robert and Tamor (Edwin) Hodges, was born 27 August 1718 and died by November 1767. He married **Sarah Ayres**. On 28 November 1767 his estate was appraised by James Jarvis and James Claypole and valued at £65.7.0. William and Stephen Hodges signed as kinsmen. The widow as administrator filed the inventory on 18 April 1768. A list of debts totaled £35.9.6 was filed 18 June 1768. Payments made by 18 June 1768 and on 3 July 1769 were £91.17.7 and £63.6.2.[396]

Children of Robert and Sarah (Ayres) Hodges:[397]
59. Sarah⁵ Hodges, b. 29 April 1766.
60. Frances Elizabeth Hodges, b. Jan. 1768.

22. **Samuel⁴ Hodges**, son of Robert and Tamar (Edwin) Hodges, was born 25 December 1724 and died by May 1772. By 1 February 1763 he married **Dorothy Browne**, daughter of John and Jane (Coursey) Browne of Kent County. Jane Brown, widow, made her will on 1 February 1763 naming her children, including Dorothy Hodges.[398]

Dorothy Hodges of Kent County died leaving a will dated 18 January 1772 and proved 19 February 1772. She named her children Samuel, Mary, Rebecca, and an infant son not yet baptized. Thomas Kiper was named as guardian. Samuel Grant, John Gibbons, and Mary Gibbons witnessed. The estate was appraised at £140.12.11 on 6 April 1772 by John Williamson and Thomas Jemima, with William Browne and Joseph Browne signing as next of kin. William Hodges, administrator, filed the inventory on 12 June 1772 and listing payments of £21.2.8, stating also that there were three children.[399]

On 10 May 1772 Samuel Hodges' estate was appraised by John Williamson and Thomas Pernam and valued at £217.11.11. William Ringgold, Sr., and John Blackiston signed as creditors, with James Hodges and Stephen Hodges signing as kinsmen. William Hodges filed an account of Samuel Hodge's estate on 6 October 1772, listing payments of £239.0.8 and again mentioning the three children. A list of debts totalling £26.16.0

396. Md. Inventories, 97:146; Md. Administrations, 59:319, 62:176.
397. *Eastern Shore Vital Records,* 3:13.
398. Md. Wills, 38:440.
399. Md. Wills, 38:517; Md. Inventories, 111:56.

was filed on 6 October 1772, and the same day a distribution of the estate was made, with a balance of £208.18.3; Lovering Marriott and Thomas Slipper were sureties. Representatives were not named.[400]

Children of Samuel and Dorothy (Browne) Hodges:

61. Samuel[5] Hodges.
62. Mary Hodges, m. Walter Tolley Miller, St. Paul's Parish, Kent Co., 1786. Walter d. testate by 1797.[401]
63. Rebecca Hodges.
64. [son], b. shortly before 18 Jan. 1722.

25. **James[4] Hodges**, son of Robert and Tamar (Edwin) Hodges, died in Kent County by February 1818. His wife is unknown. He inherited from his brother Stephen Hodges one-half of his personal estate.[402]

James Hodges died leaving a will dated 17 September 1816, proved 17 February 1818. He left his entire estate to his son James for his lifetime, with the remainder to James Ringgold and Capt. Thomas Harris. After son James' death, the real estate was devised to his children, with a parent's share for any child who died leaving issue. His entire personal estate was bequeathed to the children of son James. To daughter Ann Gale and to the children of his deceased daughter Martha Gale he bequeathed £100. Son James was appointed executor, with James Collins, Sr., Samuel Wickes, and James Collins, Jr. witnessing.[403]

Children of James Hodges:

65. James[5] Hodges, Jr., living 1788-1816.
66. Ann Hodges, m. Kent Co. by license dated 7 Sept. 1797 Thomas Gale.
67. Martha Hodges, d. by Sept. 1816, m. William Gale.

CUTHBERT FENWICK

1. **Cuthbert[1] Fenwick**, possibly but not proven to be a son of George and Barbara (Mitford) of Langshawes, Northumberland,[404] was born c1614 and died by December 1655. He was transported to Maryland in 1633/34 as a servant of Thomas Cornwalys.[405] He married first, by 1649, [-?-]

---

400. Md. Inventories, 111:56, 110:151; Md. Administrations, 67:158; Balance Books, 6:157.

401. *Eastern Shore Vital Records*, 4:3; Kent Co. Wills, 7:575.

402. Kent Co. Wills, 7:241.

403. Kent Co. Wills, 10:150.

404. Robert W. Barnes, *British Roots of Maryland Colonists*, 191-192.

405. Md. Land Patents, ABH:94, 244; 4:523. See Newman, *Flowering*, 200-201, for discussion of Fenwick's arrival circumstances and year.

[possibly Cornwaleys],[406] and second, Mrs. **Jane (Eltonhead) Moryson**,with whom Cuthbert signed an antenuptial contract on 1 August 1649.[407] She was widow of Robert Moryson of Kecoughtan, Virginia, was related to William Eltonhead of Maryland,[408] and immigrated to Maryland by 1649.[409] She died by December 1660.

Fenwick, a Roman Catholic, was a member of the Assembly in 1637/38 and later. He was a Justice of Saint Mary's County Court in 1644, and in 1638/39 had a commission to seize illegal traders. He was executor and sole legatee by the will, proved 4 January 1639, of Michael Lums of St. Jerome's, St. Mary's County.[410] In 1650 he held *St. Inigoes Manor* in trust for the Society of the Jesuits. In 1651 he was granted absolute lordship of the 2,000-acre *Fenwick Manor* in Resurrection Hundred, St. Mary's County. Fenwick's public career and other activities are summarized by Newman[411] and the *Biographical Dictionary of the Maryland Legislature, 1635-1789.*[412]

Cuthbert Fenwick's will dated 6 March 1654[/55] named his wife Jane and minor children: Cuthbert, Ignatius, Robert, Richard, John, and Theresa. He bequeathed personalty to Mr. Starkey, Mr. Fitzherbert, and brother [-in-law William] Eltonhead. No executor was named. Francis Anketill and Eliza Gerrard witnessed the will.[413] Jane Fenwick, widow of Cuthbert Fenwick, died at Patuxent in Calvert County leaving a will dated 24 November 1660 and proved 12 December 1660. She named sons Robert (eldest son, not yet 18), Richard, and John as heirs to *Little Fenwick* and *Monsieur's Plantation*. Theresa Fenwick was to have personalty at age 16. Her stepsons Cuthbert and Ignatius were mentioned. She bequeathed personalty to the Roman Catholic Church and mentioned the children of her sisters Conoway and Marra. Cuthbert Fenwick, William Mill, and John Bogue were appointed overseers, and the will was witnessed by John Wright, John Turner, and Edmund Scott.[414]

Children of Cuthbert Fenwick by his first wife:

---

406. *Biographical Dictionary of the Maryland Legislature, 1635-1789*, 1:319.

407. *Archives*, 41:262.

408. *Biographical Dictionary of the Maryland Legislature, 1635-1789*, 304 (Eltonhead), 319 (Fenwick).

409. Md. Land Patents, Q:115.

410. Md. Wills, 1:7.

411. Newman, *Flowering*, 200-203.

412. *Biographical Dictionary*, 319.

413. *Md. Calendar of Wills*, 1:219.

414. Md. Wills, 1:114.

2. Thomas[2] Fenwick, living in 1649;[415] not mentioned in father's 1654 will.
+ 3. Cuthbert Fenwick, b. 1640.
4. Ignatius Fenwick, b. 1646; no further record.
5. Theresa Fenwick, under age 16 in 1660; no further record.

Children of Cuthbert and Jane (Eltonhead) Fenwick:
6. Robert Fenwick, b. c1651; d. 1676.
+ 7. Richard Fenwick, b. c1653.
8. John Fenwick, unmarried; d. 1720. On 1 Mar. 1696 he and Thomas Dillon appraised the estate of John Currey of St. Mary's County.[416] On 8 Oct. 1686 John Fenwick, tailor, received payment from estate of Robert Browne Jr.[417] Will dated 20 Mar. 1720, proved 28 May 1720, bequeathed £12.0.0 to a priest, named cousins [*i.e.*, nephews] John, Cuthbert, Ignatius, Richard, and Enoch Fenwick as heirs and executors. They were to have residue of estate "as though they had but one mother."[418] Account of administration of Fenwick's estate filed by five executors 26 Oct. 1720.[419] A second account filed 19 May 1721.[420]

3. Cuthbert[2] Fenwick, son of Cuthbert Fenwick by his first wife, was born in 1640. Before he died he conveyed part of *Fenwick Manor* to his half-brother Richard Fenwick.[421] He died in Calvert County shortly before 16 January 1676, on which date Thomas Tennant and David Davis valued his personal property at 13,103 pounds of tobacco.[422] Richard Fenwick filed an account of the administration of Cuthbert's estate on 27 October 1677, listing payments totalling 15,459 pounds of tobacco.[423]

Child of Cuthbert Fenwick by an unidentified wife:[424]
+ 9. Anne[3] Fenwick, b. 1670.

7. Richard[2] Fenwick, son of Cuthbert and Jane (Eltonhead) Fenwick, was born in c1653 and died in April 1714. He was twice married.[425] He was one of the appraisers of the estates of John Gawdard [Goddard?] of St. Mary's County on 20 January 1700, Stephen Gough on 22 January 1700,

---

415. *Archives*, 4:509.
416. Md. Inventories and Accounts, 15:84.
417. Md. Inventories and Accounts, 10:145.
418. Md. Wills, 15:339.
419. Md. Administration Accounts, 3:138.
420. Md. Administration Accounts, 3:408.
421. Md. Provincial Court Land Records, at MSA, WRC:49.
422. Md. Inventories and Accounts, 3:42.
423. Md. Inventories and Accounts, 4:515.
424. Christopher Johnston, "Chart of the Fenwick Family," Johnston Collection, MHS.
425. Wives not identified, Christopher Johnston, "Chart of the Fenwick Family."

and Henry Jarboe on 26 April 1709.[426] Richard Fenwick died in St. Mary's County leaving a will dated 1 April 1714 and proved 26 April 1714. He named his sons Richard, Cuthbert, John, Enoch, and Ignatius as joint executors and heirs to his entire estate. Sons by his first wife and sons by his second wife were to share equally in the division. Sons Enoch and Ignatius were minors. Any disagreement would be settled by the testator's brother, John Fenwick. Joseph Alvey, George Plowden, and Cuthbert Sewell witnessed the will.[427] On 10 May 1714 Fenwick's estate was appraised by John Miles and Thomas Dillon and valued at £142.9.4. John Fenwick, Sr., and Cuthbert Sewell approved the inventory.[428] On 21 May 1715 the five named executors filed an account of the administration of the estate. Payments totaled £42.16.5. Elizabeth Alvey received an orphan boy, which had been given to her by the deceased.[429] In June 1715 his niece Anne Head and Martin Yates deposed concerning Richard's ownership of certain land.[430]

Children of Richard Fenwick by his unidentified first wife:[431]
+ 10. Richard[3] Fenwick, d. 1722.
+ 11. Cuthbert Fenwick, d. 1729.
+ 12. John Fenwick, d. 1738.

Children of Richard Fenwick by his unidentified second wife:
+ 13. Enoch Fenwick, d. 1758.
+ 14. Ignatius Fenwick, d. 1732.
  15. Elizabeth Fenwick, m. Joseph Alvey, Jr.

9. **Anne[3] Fenwick,** daughter of Cuthbert Fenwick, [Jr.], was born in 1670, was married twice, and died in 1727. Her first husband was **John Sewell,** and her second husband, whom she married by March 1708, was **Adam Head,** born c1675.[432] Adam was the son of Adam Head who died c1698. He may have died by June 1739 and appears to have married a second wife, also named Ann.[433]

John Sewell of *Resurrection Manor*, St. Mary's County, died intestate leaving minor children. On 8 March 1708 an account of the

---

426. Md. Inventories and Accounts, 20:65, 85; 29:434.

427. Md. Wills, 13:699.

428. Md. Inventories and Accounts, 36A:196.

429. Md. Inventories and Accounts, 36C:55.

430. Md. Chancery Records, CL:237-238.

431. Christopher Johnston, "Chart of the Fenwick Family."

432. Christopher Johnston, "Chart of the Fenwick Family."

433. Mary Louise Donnelly, *Colonial Settlers of St. Clement's Bay, 1634-1780* (Ennis, Texas: the author, 1996), 124.

administration of his estate was filed by his relict, "now wife of Adam Head." An inventory of £131.16.7 was reduced by payments totalling £44.13.8.[434] Anne Head, age about 45, deposed in June 1715 that during her minority her uncle and guardian had certain land in his possession. At the same time Adam Head, age about 40, deposed concerning his wife and her uncle.[435] Anne Head of St. Mary's County died leaving a will dated 22 May 1727 and proved 7 June 1727. She devised the tract *Prevention* to her husband Adam Head and at his death to her two daughters Eliza Herbert and Priscilla equally. Edward Cole, John Holland, and Mary More witnessed the will. No executor was named.[436]

The following records may refer to Adam Head, husband of Anne Fenwick, or, more likely, to their son Adam Head. Adam Head died intestate some time before 22 June 1739 when Charles Joy and Samuel Abell appraised his personal effects at £69.11.6. Francis Herbert, Elizabeth Herbert, and Priscilla Head signed as kinsmen. Ann Head, administrator, filed the inventory on 22 June 1739.[437] The account of the administration of the estate of Adam Head was filed by Anne Head on 14 March 1742. Payments of £83.9.8 were made to several people including Frances Herbert. The distribution was made, with one third going to the widow, and the residue to the orphans Cuthbert, Jane, Anne, and Sarah Head.[438]

Children of John and Anne (Fenwick) Sewell:[439]
16. John[4] Sewell, b. c1692.
17. Mary Sewell, b. 1694; m. Leonard Green.[440]
18. Cuthbert Sewell, b. c1696; d. without issue in St. Mary's Co. by 7 Mar. 1723[/24], the date his will was proved, making bequests to sisters Mary Green, Priscilla Head, and Elizabeth Herbert, and to father-in-law Adam Head, and appointed brother Leonard Green executor.[441] Green filed account of administration 4 Aug. 1725.[442]

Children of Adam and Anne (Fenwick) Head:[443]
19. Priscilla Head, unmarried in 1739.

---

434. Md. Inventories and Accounts, 29:102.
435. Md. Chancery Records, CL:237-238.
436. Md. Wills, 19:200.
437. Md. Inventories, 24:377.
438. Md. Administration Accounts, 19:376.
439. Christopher Johnston, "Chart of the Fenwick Family"; Donnelly, *St. Clement's Bay*, 124.
440. See #18 Leonard[3] Green later in this work.
441. Will dated 31 Jan. 1723/24. Md. Wills, 18:235.
442. Md. Administration Accounts, 7:98.
443. Christopher Johnston, "Chart of the Fenwick Family."

+ 20. Elizabeth Head, m. Francis Herbert.
+ 21. Adam Head.

10. **Richard³ Fenwick**, son of Richard Fenwick by his unidentified first wife, died in 1722. He married **Dorothy Plowden**. She died in 1724, a daughter of George and Margaret (Brent) Plowden.[444] Mr. Richard Fenwick died intestate shortly before 20 July 1722, on which date his personal estate was appraised by Edward Cole and George Jenkins at a value of £299.10.11. Cuthbert and Enoch Fenwick signed as kinsmen, and Dorothy Fenwick filed the inventory on 8 August 1722.[445] An account of the administration of Richard Fenwick's estate was filed on 8 August 1723 by Dorothy Fenwick, the administrator. Assets totaled £299.10.4. A number of payments were made, but no heirs were named.[446]

Dorothy Fenwick of St. Mary's County died leaving a will dated 1 April 1724 and proved 19 June 1724. Her brother Edmund Plowden was to be executor and have the care of her estate which was to be divided among all children equally as they came of age or married. George Jenkins, Peter Joy, and John Fenwick witnessed the will.[447] John Read and George Jenkins appraised Dorothy Fenwick's personal estate, valuing it at £277.8.6. Cuthbert Fenwick and Cuthbert Fenwick, Jr., signed as kinsmen. Edmund Plowden filed the inventory on 11 September 1724.[448] Dorothy Fenwick's estate had disbursed £25.9.5 when the accounting of the administration was filed by Edmund Plowden on 16 June 1725.[449]

Children of Richard and Dorothy (Plowden) Fenwick:[450]
+ 22. Ann⁴ Fenwick, m. Athanatius Ford.
   23. Cuthbert Fenwick, unmarried, d. St. Mary's Co., Sept. 1762. Will dated 1 Sept., proved 8 Sept. 1762. To cousin Benedict Fenwick, son of George, devised 238-acre *Swamp Island* in Beaver Dam Manor. To cousin Cuthbert Fenwick, living with testator, son of Bennett, devised remaining part of his lands. Bequeathed 1,000 pounds of tobacco annually to Elizabeth Barnes, and livestock to Rebecca, wife of William King, and cousins Benedict and Cuthbert Fenwick. Remainder of estate to be divided between two cousins

---

444. St. Mary's Co. Wills, PC#1:285. The 1709 will of George Plowden of St. Mary's Co. bequeathed personalty to daughter Dorothy. Md. Wills, 13:618. It should be noted that Chester H. Brent [in *Descendants of Col. Giles Brent* (1946), 100] states, without supporting evidence, that Dorothy Plowden married Col. James Fenwick.
445. Md. Inventories, 7:315.
446. Md. Administration Accounts, 5:204.
447. Md. Wills, 18:285.
448. Md. Inventories, 10:117.
449. Md. Administration Accounts, 6:436.
450. Donnelly, *St. Clements Bay*, 88.

when they reached age 21. Brother Bennett Fenwick appointed executor.[451] On 8 Sept. 1762 personal estate appraised at a value of £343.5.4. Creditors and kinsmen George and Athanatius Ford and James Bute approved inventory, which was filed 4 Mar. 1763 by executor Bennett Fenwick.[452] On 10 Feb. 1764 Bennett Fenwick filed account of administration of estate, listing payments of £140.15.3,[453] and balance of £417.4.4 remaining.[454]

11. **Cuthbert**[3] **Fenwick**, son of Richard and his unidentified first wife, died in 1729. He married first [name unknown], and second, by 17 January 1715, **Elizabeth Brooke**, daughter of Robert and Grace Brooke.[455] The will of Robert Brooke of Calvert County, dated 17 January 1715 and proved 10 April 1716, devised to daughter Eliza[beth] Fenwick 100 acres on the north side of Island Creek.[456] The [undated] will of Grace Brooke, proved 30 October 1725, named daughter Elizabeth Fenwick and grandson Cuthbert Fenwick.[457]

Cuthbert Fenwick of St. Mary's County died shortly before 23 March 1729, the date on which his [undated] will was proved, He bequeathed 10 shillings each to his two eldest [unnamed] daughters, and personalty to daughter Elizabeth, wife [unnamed], and sons Bennett and Cuthbert. To son Cuthbert was devised the dwelling plantation. To son Robert and his heirs was devised a tract at Hervy Town. He mentioned grandchildren Robert and Mary Brooke, who were to have personalty bequeathed to them by their grandmother. His wife and son Cuthbert were appointed executors. Adam Head, Philip Clarke, and Cuthbert Fenwick witnessed the will. The widow claimed her thirds [*i.e.*, one-third dower share in entire personal estate].[458]

On 20 May 1730 Mr. Cuthbert Fenwick's personal estate was appraised at £285.15.8. The inventory was approved by kinsmen John and Cuthbert Fenwick and filed on 11 July 1730 by Mrs. Elisabeth Fenwick, the executrix.[459] Also filed on 11 July 1730 was Elisabeth Fenwick's account of the administration of the estate. She listed disbursements of £16.9.0,

---

451. Md. Wills, 31:782.
452. Md. Inventories, 80:167.
453. Md. Administration Accounts, 50:366.
454. Md. Balance Books, 4:29.
455. Johnston, "Chart of the Fenwick Family."
456. Md. Wills, 14:207.
457. Md. Wills, 18:424.
458. Md. Wills, 19:888.
459. Md. Inventories, 15:603.

and identified the legal representatives as five [unnamed] orphans.[460]
Children of Cuthbert Fenwick:[461]

+ 24. Robert[4] Fenwick.
  25. Cuthbert Fenwick, Jr., named in 1725 will of grandmother Grace Brooke; d. unmarried by 29 Jan. 1745/46, date estate inventoried, value £172.11.5, approved by kinsman Robert Fenwick, filed 4 June 1746 by administrator Benjamin Fenwick;[462] account filed 21 July 1747 listed legal representatives: Robert, Benjamin, and Joseph Fenwick, John, Clement, and Ann Spaulding, Robert Brooke, John Michell, Thomas Tanney, and Matthias Burn.[463]
+ 26. Bennett Fenwick, b. 1728.
+ 27. George Fenwick, d. 1772.
+ 28. Jane Fenwick, m. Robert Brooke.
  29. Elizabeth Fenwick, m. Clement T. Spalding (1706-1759).
  30. Joseph Fenwick, d. 1758. Will proved 6 Dec. 1758 bequeathed negro woman Terresia to Cudbert [*sic*] Fenwick, son of Robert Fenwick of Harvy Town.[464] Administrator Robert Fenwick filed inventory 26 March 1759, approved by kinsmen Benjamin Fenwick and Elisabeth Spalding.[465] Administration account filed 29 Nov. 1760; distribution to heirs, all of age: Robert Fenwick, Benjamin Fenwick, John Feilds, John Bapt. Mattingly, Clem. Spaulding, Robert Brooke, and John Taney.[466]
  31. Anne Fenwick, daughter by Elizabeth Brooke, m. before 1759, John Baptist Mattingly.[467]

12. **John**[3] **Fenwick**, son of Richard Fenwick and unidentified first wife, died in 1733. He married **Winifred** [-?-]. The personal estate of Mr. John Fenwick of St. Mary's County was appraised on 15 March 1733 by John Read and Philip Clark. They set a value on it of £154.15.2. Edmund Plowden and Cuthbert Fenwick approved the inventory as kinsmen, and Winifred Fenwick filed it on 4 June 1734.[468] Winifred Fenwick filed the administration account on 22 August 1735, showing distribution to herself (one-third dower right), and residue to orphans Jane, Doryty [*sic*], and Mary Fenwick.[469]

---

460. Md. Administration Accounts, 10:416.

461. Johnston, "Chart of the Fenwick Family."

462. Md. Inventories, 33:45.

463. Md. Administration Accounts, 24:20.

464. Md. Wills, 30:624.

465. Md. Inventories, 66:220.

466. Md. Administration Accounts, 46:157.

467. Margaret K. Fresco, *Marriages and Deaths St. Mary's County Maryland 1634-1900* (Ridge, Md.: the author, 1982), 203.

468. Md. Inventories, 18:315.

469. Md. Administration Accounts, 13:317.

Children of John and Winifred Fenwick, all minors in 1735:
32. Jane⁴ Fenwick.
33. Dorothy Fenwick.
34. Mary Fenwick.

13. **Enoch³ Fenwick**, son of Richard Fenwick and unidentified second wife, died in 1758. Donnelly suggests that he married **Cassandra Brooke**.⁴⁷⁰ Application #652 states that he married, second, **Elizabeth Miles**. Enoch Fenwick of St. Mary's County died leaving a will dated 30 January 1758 and proved 8 November 1758. To eldest son Enoch, Jr., he bequeathed Negro boy Joseph. To second son John he bequeathed a bed and a cow. He bequeathed 5 shillings to daughter [Mrs.] Joseph. The remainder of his estate was bequeathed to youngest son Ignatius Fenwick, who was appointed executor. The will was witnessed by Edward Cole, Cuthbert Fenwick, and Thomas King.⁴⁷¹ On 2 February 1759 Thomas Forrest and Francis Boarman appraised Fenwick's goods and chattels, valueing them at £369.2.4. Joseph Fenwick and William Josephs approved the inventory as kinsmen, and executor Ignatius Fenwick filed the inventory on 8 March 1759.⁴⁷²

    Children of Enoch Fenwick:
+ 35. Enoch⁴ Fenwick, b. 1714.
+ 36. John Fenwick.
    Children of Enoch and Elizabeth (Miles) Fenwick:
   37. Ignatius Fenwick, b. 1731.
+ 38. Elizabeth Fenwick, m. Charles Ganyott and William Joseph.

14. **Ignatius³ Fenwick**, son of Richard Fenwick and unidentified second wife, was born in c1695 and died in St. Mary's County in 1732. He married **Eleanor/"Ellen" Clark**, who died by November 1737. Eleanor Fenwick filed the inventory of Ignatius Fenwick on 8 March 1732[/33]. His personal property had been appraised on 6 December 1732 by William Canaday and Thomas Hebb, who valued his goods and chattels at £426.16.4. As kinsmen, John and Enoch Fenwick approved the inventory.⁴⁷³ The administration account was filed by Eleanor Fenwick on 22 July 1734, showing distribution of one-third to [Eleanor] and the balance to the orphans: Ignatius, Philip, John, George, Richard, and

---

470. Donnelly, *St. Clement's Bay*, 89.
471. Md. Wills, 30:582.
472. Md. Inventories, 66:234.
473. Md. Inventories, 17:23.

Eleanor Fenwick.[474]

Ellen Fenwick of St. Mary's County left a will dated 7 August 1737 and proved 1 November 1737, leaving personalty to her daughter Ellen, 20 shillings each to sons Philip and John, and the residue of the estate to her four children Ignatius (appointed executor), George, Richard, and Ellen. The will was witnessed by George Clarke, Matt. and James Burne.[475] On 4 January 1737/38 James Waughop and John Lynch appraised the goods and chattels of Ellen Fenwick at £453.2.7. Philip Fenwick and George Clarke approved as kinsmen, and executor Ignatius Fenwick filed the inventory on 23 January 1737/38.[476] He filed the administration account on 6 July 1738.[477]

Children of Ignatius and Eleanor (Clark) Fenwick:

+ 39. Philip[4] Fenwick, d. 1749.
+ 40. John Fenwick, m. Elizabeth Guyther.
  41. George Fenwick, d. 1768; m. Belinda [-?-], who m., second, Robert Fenwick. James Pike and Joseph Jenkins appraised personal estate of George Fenwick on 15 July 1769, at £242.9.7. Cousin Enoch Fenwick and Jeremiah Edmonds were mentioned. Belinda Fenwick, administrator, now wife of Robert Fenwick, filed the inventory on 15 July 1769.[478] Belinda, wife of Robert Fenwick, filed account of administration of George Fenwick's estate on 18 July 1769. An inventory of £242.9.7 was shown, and payments totaled £104.6.7. No heirs were named.[479]
+ 42. Richard Fenwick, d. 1758.
  43. Eleanor Fenwick.
+ 44. Col. Ignatius Fenwick, b. c1712.

20. **Elizabeth[4] Head**, daughter of Adam and Anne (Fenwick) Head, died by May 1759. She married **Francis Herbert**, son of William and Elinor (Pattison) (Angell) Herbert.[480] James Pattison of St. Mary's County, in his will dated 23 September 1697 and proved 1 April 1698, devised land on St. Jerome's Plain to his grandson Francis Herbert.[481]

Francis Herbert died in St. Mary's County shortly before 24 December 1754, the date on which his [undated] will was proved. He bequeathed

474. Md. Administration Accounts, 12:454.
475. Md. Wills, 21:825.
476. Md. Inventories, 23:19.
477. Md. Administration Accounts, 16:223.
478. Md. Inventories, 102:239.
479. Md. Administration Accounts, 62:156.
480. Mary L. Donnelly, *Colonial Settlers of St. Clement's Bay, 1634-1780* (Ennis, Texas: the author, 1996), 124.
481. Md. Wills, 6:85.

slaves to wife Elizabeth and appointed her executrix. He gave slaves to son Francis, to whom he devised *Jerome's Plains*. He directed the sale of his lands on Patuxent [River]. He directed that 5,000 pounds of tobaco be divided among his children Michael, William, Priscilla, and Mary Herbert, and bequeathed the balance of his estate to be divided among his wife and nine children. His will was witnessed by Geo. Leigh, John Cossey, and Richard Thomson.[482] His personal estate was appraised on 1 April 1755 by George Leigh and Benjamin Williams, valued at £253.7.9 plus £1.19.0. The inventories were approved by kinsmen Cuthbert and Michael Herbert and filed on 15 April 1755 by executrix Elizabeth Herbert.[483] She filed administration accounts on 14 February 1756[484] and 21 August 1757, the second account listing payment of the balance of the estate of their uncle Mark Herbert [brother of Francis] to Priscilla, Michael, William, and Margaret Herbert, and to the wife of William Spalding. The balance of Francis Herbert's estate was distributed to the widow and children: Ann, Jane, Cuthbert, Elizabeth Spalding, Michael, William, Priscilla, Margaret Herbert (all of age), and Francis Herbert, age 15.[485] The estate of Francis Herbert, with a balance of £210.18.5, was distributed on 21 August 1757 by executrix Elizabeth Herbert, with George Fenwick, Sr., and Cuthbert Fenwick as sureties. The widow and Francis Herbert were legatees, and the residue was distributed equally among Michael, William, Priscilla, and Mary Herbert.[486]

Elizabeth Herbert died in St. Mary's County leaving a will dated 20 April 1759 and proved 7 May 1759. She named her youngest son Francis Herbert, sons Michael and William, and daughters Priscilla and Mary Herbert. She also named a son Cuthbert Herbert and daughters Jane Fenwick and Elizabeth Spalding. Son William was appointed executor and guardian to son Francis. The will was witnessed by Elizabeth Milburn and Thomas Lowe.[487] Mrs. Elisabeth Herbert left personal property worth £130.19.4, as appraised on 2 June 1760 by George and Joseph Leigh. The inventory was approved by kinsmen Cuthbert Herbert and Elisabeth Spalding.[488] Priscilla and Mary Herbert filed the account of administration

---

482. Md. Wills, 29:293.
483. Md. Inventories, 60:217, 359.
484. Md. Administration Accounts, 39:62.
485. Md. Administration Accounts, 41:185.
486. Md. Prerogative Court Balance Books, 2:68.
487. Md. Wills, 30:687.
488. Md. Inventories, 69:123.

of the estate of Elizabeth Herbert on 8 October 1761.[489] Elizabeth Herbert's estate, with a final balance of £139.6.2, was distributed to the legatees: Francis and Cuthbert Herbert, Jane Fenwick, Elisabeth Spalding, and Priscilla and Mary Herbert. The residue went equally to Michael, William, Priscilla, and Mary Herbert.[490]

Children of Francis and Elizabeth (Head) Herbert:

45. William[5] Herbert, d. St. Mary's Co., before 25 Feb. 1760, when estate inventory filed by Priscilla and Mary Herbert, approved by kinsmen Francis and Michael Herbert.[491] Account dated 8 Oct. 1761 lists distribution of £137.5.8 to Priscilla, Michael, Mary, and Francis Herbert.[492]
46. Michael Herbert.
47. Priscilla Herbert.
48. Mary Herbert.
49. Jane Herbert, m. [-?-] Fenwick.
50. Elizabeth Herbert, m. by 1757 William Spalding.[493] On 14 Apr. 1767 she filed account of administration of estate of William Spalding of St. Mary's Co., sureties George and Bennett Fenwick, estate balance £226.8.1, "representatives unknown to [Prerogative] office."[494]
51. Cuthbert Herbert.
52. Francis Herbert, age 15 in 1757.

21. **Adam[4] Head,** son of Adam and Anne (Fenwick) Head, died by 1739. He married **Anne** [-?-], who survived him.[495] Adam Head of St. Mary's County died shortly before 22 June 1739, the date his personal estate was appraised by Charles Joy and Samuel Abell, valued at £69.11.6, the inventory approved by kinsmen Francis and Elisabeth Herbert and Presilea Head.[496] On 14 March 1742 an account of the administration of Adam Head's estate was filed by administratrix Anne Head, showing a balance of £83.9.8 to be distributed to the widow (one-third) and the residue to the orphans: Cuthbert, Jane, Anne, and Sarah Head.[497]

Children of Adam and Anne Head:

53. Cuthbert[5] Head, m. Martha Gristy; d. testate, Nelson Co., Ky., before 18

---

489. Md. Administration Accounts, 47:213.
490. Md. Prerogative Court Balance Books, 3:109.
491. Md. Inventories, 68:174.
492. Md. Administration Accounts, 47:229; Md. Balance Books, 3:111.
493. Md. Administration Accounts, 41:185.
494. Md. Administration Accounts, 56:85; Md. Balance Books, 5:21.
495. Donnelly, *St. Clement's Bay,* 124.
496. Md. Inventories, 24:377.
497. Md. Administration Accounts, 19:376.

Nov. 1811 (date will proved).[498]
54. Jane Head.
55. Anne Head.
56. Sarah Head.

22. **Ann**[4] **Fenwick**, daughter of Richard and Dorothy (Plowden) Fenwick, married **Athanatius Ford**.[499] In March 1768 he was age 40, a tenant of lots 42-45 in Beaverdam Manor in St. Mary's County.[500] Ford died by 1798 and John Smith advertised he would settle the estate.[501]

Athanatius and Ann (Fenwick) Ford had the following children baptized by Father Walton, S.J. of St. Francis Xavier Church, St. Mary's County:[502]
57. Athanatius[5] Ford, bp. 8 Mar. 1767.
58. Teresa Ford, bp. 3 Apr. 1771.
59. Sarah Ford, bp. 17 Aug. 1772.

24. **Robert**[4] **Fenwick**, son of Cuthbert Fenwick, died in St. Mary's County, in 1779. He married by 1763 **Susanna Hopewell**, granddaughter of Mark Heard.[503] She died in St. Mary's County in 1785. Robert Fenwick died leaving a will dated 11 Mar 1778 and proved 30 Nov 1779. He left the use of his whole estate, real and personal to his wife Susannah during her widowhood, and then directed that his personal estate be equally divided among his twelve [named, see below] children. Wife Susanna and son Cuthbert Fenwick were appointed executors. Edward and Aaron Abell and Richard Evans witnessed the will.[504]

Susanna, wife of Robert Fenwick, may be the Susanna Fenwick who died leaving a will dated 17 January 1785 and proved 31 August 1785. She named two daughters Mary and Ann Fenwick, and appointed son Bennet Fenwick as executor. She also mentioned her "six [other] children." John Abell, Sr., and Ann [Grenall?] witnessed the will.[505]

Children of Robert and Susanna (Hopewell) Fenwick:
60. Cuthbert[5] Fenwick.
61. Thomas Fenwick, d. Washington Co., Ky., 1816; m. St. Mary's Co., 3 July

498. Donnelly, *St. Clement's Bay*, 124.
499. Donnelly, *St. Clement's Bay*, 88.
500. Rent Roll in Timothy J. O'Rourke, *Catholic Families of Southern Maryland* (Baltimore: Genealogical Publishing Co., 1985), 46.
501. *Maryland Gazette* (Annapolis), 7 June 1798.
502. Parish Register, in O'Rourke, *Catholic Families of Southern Maryland*, 2, 8, 10.
503. Md. Provincial Court Land Records, at MSA, DD#2:359, 401.
504. St. Mary's Co. Wills, JJ#1:115.
505. St. Mary's Co. Wills, JJ#1:338.

1774, Elizabeth Thomas.
62. Elizabeth Fenwick.
63. Bennett Fenwick, d. 1800.
64. Ann Fenwick.
65. Mary Fenwick.
66. Susanna Fenwick.
67. Rebecca Fenwick.
68. Joseph Fenwick.
69. John Fenwick.
70. Francis Fenwick.
71. Nicholas Fenwick.

26. **Bennett⁴ Fenwick**, son of Cuthbert Fenwick, was born in 1728 and died in 1771. His [unidentified] wife predeceased him. He died in St. Mary's County leaving a will dated 19 May 1770 and proved 5 February 1771. He named his children Cuthburt, Francis, Michael, Richard, Elizabeth, Mary, Dorety, Henryritea Maria, and Priscella. He mentioned the estate of his brother Cuthburt, and appointed his son Richard as executor and as guardian of sons Francis and Michael. Ignatius Clarke, Joseph Walker and James Roach witnessed the will.[506]

Massey Leigh and Jo. Milburn appraised the personal estate of Bennett Fenwick on 17 April 1771, and valued his property at £520.19.1. Mary Ann Fenwick and Cuthbert Fenwick approved the inventory as kinsmen. Executor Richard Fenwick filed the inventory on 20 April 1771.[507] Richard Fenwick filed an account of the administration of Bennett Fenwick's estate on 1 Jan 1773. He cited the inventory given above, and listed payments of £111.13.5.[508] On the same day Richard Fenwick, with Samuel Bellwood and William Fenwick as sureties, distributed a balance of £468.1.11 to Bennett's children, Elizabeth, Mary, Richard, Dorothea, Henrietta, Francis, Michael, and Priscilla.[509]

Children of Bennett Fenwick and his wife:[510]
72. Cuthbert⁵ Fenwick, may have d. before 1773 (not listed in the distribution).
73. Richard Fenwick.
74. Francis Fenwick.
75. Michael Fenwick.
76. Elizabeth Fenwick.
77. Mary Fenwick.

506. Md. Wills, 38:358.
507. Md. Inventories, 107:97.
508. Md. Administration Accounts, 68:209.
509. Md. Balance Books, 6:256.
510. Johnston, "Chart of the Fenwick Family."

78. Dorothy Fenwick.
79. Henrietta Maria Fenwick.
80. Priscilla Fenwick.

27. **George⁴ Fenwick**, son of Cuthbert Fenwick, died in 1772. He married by 1757, **Jane Jenkins**, daughter of William Jenkins of St. Mary's County and sister of Thomas Courtney Jenkins of Baltimore County who died leaving a will dated 30 September 1757 and proved 1 November 1757, naming his sister Jane Fenwick.[511]
George Fenwick died leaving a will dated 15 July 1769 and proved 27 April 1772. He named his children William, George, and Jean, and mentioned the tract *Chance's Conclusion*. Wife Jane and son George were named executors. Ignatius and Richard Fenwick and Henrietta Magee witnessed the will.[512] Jane Fenwick, executrix, filed the inventory of his personal estate on 10 August 1772. John Smith Sr. and Zachariah Forrest appraised the personal property at £379.2.3, Benjamin and Robert Fenwick signed as kinsmen.[513] Account of the administration of the estate of George Fenwick was filed on 20 June 1774 by Jane Fenwick. Assets of £379.2.3 were listed, and payments totaled £83.3.5.[514] On the same day the account was filed, Jane Fenwick, with Ignatius and Cuthbert Fenwick as sureties, distributed a balance of £375.18.11 to the widow and three children.[515]

Children of George and Jane (Jenkins) Fenwick:[516]

81. Benedict⁵ Fenwick, d. by 2 Apr. 1769, will dated 2 May 1763 left land to mother, named his brothers William and George Fenwick and his sister Jean Fenwick; also named William King, Justinian Moore, and John B. Lucas. Brother William named executor. Ignatius Fenwick of Enoch, John E. Greenwell, and Enoch Fenwick witnessed will.[517] John Smith and Thomas Forrest appraised his personal estate at £164.14.6 on 25 Apr. 1769. Ignatius Fenwick [son] of Enoch, and Jane Fenwick signed as kinsmen. William Fenwick, executor, filed inventory 10 Nov. 1769.[518] William Fenwick filed account of administration 30 Aug. 1770. An inventory of £164.14.6 was listed

---

511. Md. Wills, 30:368.
512. Md. Wills, 38:604.
513. Md. Inventories, 110:99.
514. Md. Administration Accounts, 70:315.
515. Md. Balance Books, 7:20.
516. Johnston, "Chart of the Fenwick Family."
517. Md. Wills, 37:251.
518. Md. Inventories, 102:183.

and payments totaled £79.7.5.[519]

82. William Fenwick.
83. George Fenwick, b. 1749, d. 1811; m. Margaret Medley.
84. Jean or Jane Fenwick.

28. **Jane⁴ Fenwick**, daughter of Cuthbert and Elizabeth (Brooke) Fenwick, died in 1759. She married **Robert Brooke**, born c1692, died 1753, son of Robert Brooke.[520]

Robert Brooke died leaving a will dated 1748 and proved 15 September 1753. He named his wife Jane and sons Robert, Will, Francis, Henry, and Charles. He named daughters Mary Fenwick, Sarah, Barbara, and Jane Brooke. Roger Brooke deposed that he wrote Robert Brooke's wishes on a half sheet of paper.[521] Jane Brooke filed an account of the administration of the estate of Robert Brooke on 2 [month not given] 1755. The inventory value was listed as £639.2.7, with payments of £82.4.3 deducted from that amount. The family was mentioned, but no heirs were named.[522]   Jane Brooke of Calvert County died leaving a will dated 19 May 1758 and proved 21 March 1759. She named her children Robert, Henry, Mary Fenwick, Charles, Sarah, Barbara, Jane, and Francis Brooke. Charles Brooke was the executor. John Spicknall and [Saint?] Card witnessed the will.[523] Charles Brooke, executor, filed the inventory of Jane Brooke's personal estate on 29 March 1760. It showed that on 11 February 1760 J. Brome and James Duke had appraised the goods at £316.15.0. Roger and Barbara Brooke had signed the inventory as kinsmen.[524] Charles Brooke filed the first account of the administration of the estate on 31 May 1760, showing payments of £48.13.8, the second account on 13 July 1763 (mentioning Charles Neal as a legatee), and the third on 10 November 1763 (mentioning Samuel Roundell and Henry Darnall as legatees).[525] On 31 May 1760 Charles Brooke distributed a balance of £320.6.10 of Jane Brooke's estate. Sarah and Henry Brooke were named as legatees. Distribution of the balance went to Charles, Barbara, and Jane Brooke.[526]

---

519. Md. Administration Accounts, 64:228.
520. Christopher Johnston, "The Brooke Family," in *Maryland Genealogies*, 1:107-108.
521. Md. Wills, 29:145.
522. Md. Administration Accounts, 37:217.
523. Md. Wills, 30:643.
524. Md. Inventories, 68:193.
525. Md. Administration Accounts, 46:84, 49:286, 50:31.
526. Md. Balance Books, 3:40.

Children of Robert and Jane (Fenwick) Brooke:
85. Robert[5] Brooke.
86. William Brooke.
87. Francis Brooke.
88. Henry Brooke.
89. Charles Brooke.
90. Mary Brooke, m. Philip Fenwick.
91. Sarah Brooke.
92. Barbara Brooke.
93. Jane Brooke.

35. Enoch[4] Fenwick, son of Enoch and Cassandra (Brooke) Fenwick, was born in 1714 in St. Mary's County, where he died in 1787. He married **Susanna Ford** who died in St. Mary's County in 1784.

Enoch Fenwick died leaving a will dated 2 February 1787 and proved 17 April 1787. To his grandson Enoch Millard, son of Joseph and Rebecca Millard, he devised his 396-acre dwelling plantation known as *Squabbles Ridge and Addition*, as well as 108-acre *Swamp Island*. To son Joseph Fenwick and daughter Rebecca Millard was devised the tract *Saint Peter's Hills*. He named his grandson Joshua Millard. Wife Elizabeth was to have the tract *Sebastian*. He named his grandchildren Enoch Fenwick, son of Philip, Mary Fenwick, Enoch Medley, and Elizabeth Medley. He also mentioned a possible unborn child. Son[-in-law] Joseph Millard was to be executor. Timothy Bowen, William Fenwick, and Ignatius Brown witnessed the will.[527] In the *Maryland Gazette* issue of 2 August 1787 Joseph Millard, executor, advertised he would settle the estate of Enoch Fenwick of St. Mary's County, deceased.

Children of Enoch and Susannah (Ford) Fenwick:[528]
94. Philip[5] Fenwick, b. by 1733, d. 1782, m. Rebecca Greenwell.
95. Rebecca Fenwick, b. 1742-1748, d. 30 Nov. 1799, m. Joseph Millard.
96. Elizabeth Fenwick, m. Benedict/"Bennett" Medley.

36. John[4] Fenwick, "Sr.," son of Enoch and Cassandra (Brooke) Fenwick, died by October 1781. He married **Monica Ford**, born in St. Mary's County, daughter of Robert and Rachel (Howard) Ford.[529] Another source states that Monica was a daughter of Robert and *Teresa* Ford of St. Mary's County.[530]

---

527. St. Mary's Co. Wills, JJ#1:412.
528. Undocumented material supplied by application #652.
529. Donnelly, *St. Clement's Bay*, 89.
530. St. Mary's Co. Wills, TA#1:314.

Robert Ford, in his 1753 will proved 31 January 1754, named the four [oldest] children of daughter Monica and John Fenwick as his grandchildren.[531] John Fenwick filed an account of the administration of the estate of Robert Ford on 12 September 1755, listing distribution of the residue to Ford's Fenwick grandchildren: Robert age 13, Margerit age 12, Mary age 10, Joseph age 6, Ann and Monica both age 3.[532]

John Fenwick, "Sr.," from 1753 on held 151-acre *Revells* and 171-acre *Revell's Backside*, which had been surveyed for Robert Ford.[533] He devised both of these tracts to his son Joseph. John Fenwick died leaving a will dated 19 November 1777 and proved 2 October 1781. He named all of his sons Robert, Joseph, and William, daughters Eleanor, Ann, and Catherine, sons-in-law Philip Combs, Robert Manning, and Ignatius Combs, and his wife Monica. He appointed his wife Monica and son Joseph as executors. Timothy Bowes, John Manning, and Henry Winsatt witnessed the will.[534]

Children of John and Monica (Ford) Fenwick:[535]

97. Robert[5] Fenwick, b. March 1742; d. Franklin Co., Ky., 1807; m. Ann Elizabeth Manning.
98. Margaret Fenwick, b. c1743; m. first, by 1766, James Manning (d. testate 1768),[536] and second, by 1780, Philip Combs.
99. Mary Fenwick, b. c10 March 1745; d. St. Mary's Co., Jan. 1813; m. 30 Sept. 1760, Ignatius Combs (1740-1790).[537]
100. Joseph Fenwick, b. c1749; d. Indian Creek, Perry Co., Mo., 1810; m. Chloe James (c1755-1834).
101. Ann Fenwick, b. c1751 [twin].
102. Monica Fenwick, born 22 Oct. 1751 [twin], m. first Robert Manning, and second, by 1782, William Greenwell.
103. William Fenwick, b. 30 Dec. 1759, d. 18 June 1833, m. Elizabeth Morris.
104. Eleanor Fenwick, b. 17 Oct. 1761, d. after 1791. According to application #652 she married first Wilfred Reswick, second, Francis Herbert, and third, Ralph Taney, by whom she had a daughter Dorothy Taney who married Wilfred Manning, born 1774, died 1824.
105. Catherine Fenwick, b. 27 Feb. 1763.

---

531. Md. Wills, 29:88.

532. Md. Administration Accounts, 38:178.

533. St. Mary's Co. Rent Rolls, 43:79; St. Mary's Co. Debt Books 1753-1754.

534. St. Mary's Co. Wills, JJ#1:182.

535. Donnelly, *St. Clement's Bay*, 89; birth dates of last three children recorded St. Andrew's Episcopal Church Register.

536. Md. Wills, 36:446.

537. Information from application #652.

38. **Elizabeth**[4] **Fenwick**, daughter of Enoch and Cassandra (Brooke) Fenwick, married first, **Charles Ganyott**, and second, by 1744, **William Joseph**.[538] Charles Ganyott of St. Mary's County died leaving a will dated 11 November 1744 and proved 6 March 1744/45. His wife Elizabeth was executrix. He devised land to his neighbor John Dent, and gave freedom to servant man Samuel Mitchell. He named his son Charles, not yet 10, daughters Mary, Margaret, Constantia, and a possible unborn child. The will was witnessed by Edward Cole, William Lucas, and Charles Lucas.[539] An account of the administration of Ganyott's estate was filed on 19 April 1749 by the executrix Elizabeth, now wife of William Joseph. Enoch and John Fenwick were sureties. Distribution was to the widow, and the rest to the orphans: Mary, age 14, Margaret, age 11. Also mentioned orphans Constant and Charles, "the last two dead."[540]

Children of Charles and Elizabeth (Fenwick) Ganyott:
106. Mary[5] Ganyott, b. c1735.
107. Margaret Ganyott, b. c1738.
108. Constantia Ganyott, d. by 1749.
109. Charles Ganyott, d. by 1749.

39. **Philip**[4] **Fenwick**, son of Ignatius and Eleanor (Clark) Fenwick, died in St. Mary's County by 15 January 1749/50. He married **Mary Brooke**, daughter of Robert Brooke. She died c1760.

Philip Fenwick left a will dated 13 October 1749 and proved 15 January 1749/50. He named his wife Mary as executrix and named son Robert and daughter Elinor. He mentioned "all my children," and "my three daughters." The will was witnessed by Edward Cole, and Ignatius and Benjamin Fenwick.[541] Fenwick's estate was appraised on 5 April 1750 by Edward Cole and Edmund Plowden, and valued at £172.8.11. Ignatius and Richard Fenwick signed as kinsmen.[542] An account of the administration of Fenwick's estate was filed 31 January 1750 by executrix Mary Fenwick. Payments from the estate totaled £202.6.1. The distribution was to the widow and the orphans: Eleanor, age 10; Robert, age 7; Jane, age 6; Philip, age 3; and Barbara, age 1.[543]

The account of the estate of Mary Fenwick was filed on 5 May 1760 by

---

538. St. Mary's Co. Wills, TA#1:149; Md. Testamentary Proceedings, 31:57.
539. Md. Wills, 24:23.
540. Md. Administration Accounts, 26:47.
541. Md. Wills, 27:183-184.
542. Md. Inventories, 42:215.
543. Md. Administration Accounts, 29:200.

Eleanor Fenwick, executrix. An inventory value of £242.1.0 was cited, and payments totaled to £278.3.11. The account named the orphans of the deceased, the accountant [Eleanor] of age; Robert, age 16; Jennet, age 14; Barbara, age 12; and Philip, age 10.[544]

Children of Philip and Mary (Brooke) Fenwick:[545]
110. Eleanor[5] Fenwick, b. c1740.
111. Robert Fenwick, b. c1743-1744, d. testate, St Mary's Co., by Oct. 1774.[546]
112. Jane or Jennet Fenwick, b. c1744-1746.
113. Barbara Fenwick, b. c1746-1748.
114. Philip Fenwick, b. [probably posthumously] 1750.

40. **John[4] Fenwick, "Jr.,"** son of Ignatius and Eleanor (Clark) Fenwick, died in St. Mary's County in 1790. He married by 1767 **Elizabeth Guyther** who died 1769. She was a daughter of John Guyther.[547] John Fenwick Jr., held 100 acres of *Crofts Rectified* (which had been resurveyed for John Guyther).

Children of John and Elizabeth (Guyther) Fenwick:[548]
115. [probably] Richard[5] Fenwick, b. 1759, d. Washington, D.C., 26 March 1829; m. Anne Arundel Co., 15 June 1784, Ann Welch.
116. John Fenwick.
117. Ignatius Fenwick.
118. Susanna Fenwick, m. by 1796, Joseph (or Josiah) Langley.[549]
119. Mary Fenwick.
120. Elizabeth Fenwick, m. by 1796, Richard Fenwick.
121. Anne Fenwick.
122. Margaret Fenwick.
123. Eleanor Fenwick, m. by 1796 Raphael Taney of St. Mary's Co.[550]
124. Sarah Fenwick, m. St. Mary's Co. license dated 30 Dec. 1796, John Wiseman.[551]

42. **Richard[4] Fenwick,** son of Ignatius and Eleanor (Clark) Fenwick died in 1758-1759. He married **Anne Spalding.** She married second, John Baptist Mattingley. Anne Fenwick, administrator, filed an account of the administration of Richard Fenwick's estate on 16 March 1759. The

---

544. Md. Administration Accounts, 44:270.
545. Johnston, "Chart of the Fenwick Family."
546. Md. Wills, 40:113; Md. Inventories, 121:402.
547. St. Mary's Co. Wills, TA#1:537; Md. Wills, 35:304.
548. Johnston, "Chart of the Fenwick Family"; Md. Chancery Court Papers, at MSA, #911.
549. Md. Chancery Court Papers, at MSA, #911.
550. St. Mary's Co. Wills, TA#1:537; Md. Chancery Court Papers, #911.
551. Md. Chancery Court Papers, #911.

inventory totaled £293.11.8, and payments totaled £353.0.2. Distribution was made with one-third going to the widow, and the residue to the orphans: Eleanor, age 8; Elizabeth, 6; John, 2; and James, age 9 months.[552] Anne, now wife of John Baptist Mattingley, filed a second account on 3 September 1759. The orphans were mentioned, but not named.[553]

Children of Richard and Ann (Spalding) Fenwick:[554]

125. Eleanor[5] Fenwick, b. c1750; m. by 1773, Bennett Spalding who was a brother-in-law of Elizabeth Fenwick.[555]

126. Elizabeth Fenwick, b. c1752, unmarried; will dated 30 Aug. 1771, proved 20 July 1773, named nephew Francis Spalding, sister Eleanor (wife of Bennett Spalding), and niece Ann Spalding; brother-in-law Bennett Spalding executor.[556]

127. John Fenwick, b. c1756.

128. James Fenwick, b. c1758.

44. Colonel **Ignatius[4] Fenwick**, son of Ignatius and Eleanor (Clark) Fenwick, was born c1712 and died in October 1776. He married c1734 **Mary Cole**, born 1716, died 1776, daughter of Edward and Anne (Neale) Cole.[557] Edward Cole of St. Mary's County, in his will dated 26 March 1761, named his grandson Ignatius Fenwick and daughter Mary.[558]

Ignatius Fenwick died in St. Mary's County leaving a will dated 24 January 1776 and proved 8 October 1776. He named his children: Edward, James, Joseph, Henry, Richard, John, Helena, and Elizabeth, Ann Clark and Mary Jenkins. Son James and daughter Helena were appointed executors. Richard Mckay, Kennady Hebb, and William Hebb witnessed the will.[559] His daughter Helena filed an account of the administration of the estate.[560]

Children of Ignatius and Mary (Cole) Fenwick:[561]

552. Md. Administration Accounts, 43:95.

553. Md. Administration Accounts, 43:300.

554. Johnston, "Chart of the Fenwick Family."

555. St. Mary's Co. Wills, TA#1:671; Md. Wills, 39:347.

556. Md. Wills, 39:347.

557. Donnelly, *St. Clement's Bay*, 66.

558. Md. Wills, 31:868.

559. Md. Wills, 41:219.

560. Donnelly, *St. Clement's Bay*, 66.

561. Donnelly, *St. Clement's Bay*, 66; Francis B. Culver, ed., *Society of Colonial Wars in the State of Maryland: Genealogies of the Members and Services of Ancestors* (Baltimore: William & Watkins Co., 1940), 2324.

129. Edward[5] Fenwick, d. c1789, m. by 1757, Ann Hebb.[562]
130. Ignatius Fenwick, b. c1736, m. c1763, Sarah Taney.[563]
131. Richard Fenwick, b. 1747, d. testate, 1778, naming sisters Helena and Elizabeth, and nephew Ignatius Clarke Jr.[564]
132. James Fenwick, b. 1750, d. 1806.
133. Rev. John Ceslas Fenwick, a priest, d. 1814.
134. Joseph Fenwick, b. c1765, d. in Mo.
135. Henry Fenwick, unmarried, d. after 1806.
136. Ann Fenwick, m. [-?-] Clark.
137. Mary Fenwick, d.1807, married [-?-] Jenkins.
138. Helena Fenwick, b. 1756, d. 1817 or 1837, unmarried.[565]
139. Elizabeth Fenwick.

Captain HENRY FLEETE

1. Captain **Henry[1] Fleete** was a son of William Fleete (of Chatham, County Kent, England, and Gray's Inn, London, member of the Virginia Company) and Deborah Scott.[566] He died in Lancaster County, Virginia, in 1660 or 1661. Late in life he married the widow **Sarah Burden**.[567] She married third, by 28 October 1661, Colonel John Walker of Gloucester County, Virginia, and fourth Colonel John Stone.

Henry Fleete came to Virginia c1621. A ship master, factor, and fur trader, he assisted Lord Baltimore's party upon its arrival in Maryland in March 1634, and was rewarded by a grant of 4,000 acres on the west side of St. George's River, on which he settled. By 1643 he moved across the Potomac River to Virginia's Northern Neck, where he patented a total of 13,197 acres in Lancaster and Northumberland Counties, and where he was a burgess for Lancaster County in 1652.[568]

---

562. Md. Chancery Court Papers 1815, #5668; Md. Judgments, 63:117; Md. Chancery Court Records, 16:151-170; 22:167-168, 180.

563. Johnston, "Chart of the Fenwick Family"; Md. Administration Accounts, 48:350, 358.

564. Donnelly, *St. Clement's Bay*, 66.

565. Donnelly, *St. Clement's Bay*, 66.

566. *Berry's Kentish Pedigrees; Famillae Minorum Gentium, Harleian Society Publication*, 40:1297. Will of his mother Deborah (Scott) Fleete of Westminster, widow, dated 27 March 1651, referred to "sums lent me and my son Henry Fleete ... for his last voyage to Virginia." P.C.C. Wills, 5 Bowyer, 1652.

567. Bond of Col. John Walker "to pay unto Mary Burden the natural daughter of Mrs. Sara Fleete" when she is 16 years of age. Lancaster Co. Court Order Book 1656/7-1666, 193. Cited by John Frederick Dorman, *Adventurers of Purse and Person Virginia 1607-1624/5*, 4th ed. (2004), 1:972.

568. A detailed and well documented account of Fleete's Maryland activities is provided by Harry W. Newman, in *The Flowering of the Maryland Palatinate*, 204-209. His history in Virginia and his descendants are described in Dorman, *Adventurers*, 1:970-993.

Henry Fleete died between 12 April 1660, when he attended Lancaster County court, and 8 May 1661, when Mrs. Sarah Fleete was described as a widow.[569] Sarah Walker died in Rappahannock County, Virginia, leaving a will dated 28 January 1668/69 and proved 29 December 1679, in which she named her son Henry Fleete and her Burden and Walker children.[570]
    Child of Henry and Sarah Fleete:
+   2. Henry[2] Fleete, minor in Jan. 1668/69.

2. **Henry[2] Fleet(e)**, son of Henry and Sarah Fleete, was under age 21 in January 1668/69, when his mother's will was made. He died in Lancaster County, Virginia, 1729-1733. Before 18 July 1683 he married **Elizabeth Wildey**, daughter of William and Jane Wildey.[571]
    Henry Fleet was a justice of Lancaster County, Virginia in 1695, sheriff in 1702, and a captain of militia. Fleet died leaving a will dated 31 January 1728/29 and proved 9 May 1733. He named his sons Henry and William, his grandchildren Henry Currell, Major Brent, Fleet, and John Fleet, and his daughters Ann, Judith Hobson, and Margaret Cox. He also named his granddaughters Ann Currell, Sarah Hobson, Judith Hobson, and Eliza Howson. He also named a grandson Fleete Cox. His children William, Judith Hobson, and Elizabeth Currell were appointed executors. Edwin and Ann Conway, and Edwin Conway Jr., witnessed the will.[572]
    Children of Henry and Elizabeth (Wildey) Fleet:[573]
+   3. William[3] Fleet, m. Ann Jones.
+   4. Sarah Fleet, m. William Brent.
+   5. Elizabeth Fleet, m. Abraham Currell.
+   6. Ann Fleet, m. Leonard Howson.
+   7. Judith Fleet, m. William Hobson.
+   8. Margaret Fleet, m. Presley Cox.
     9. Henry Fleet, d. Christ Church Parish, Lancaster Co., Va., 1735, unmarried. Will dated 26 Nov.1735, proved 11 Feb.1736, named mother Elizabeth Fleet, Samuel Hinton, Rebecca Banton, Thomas Edwards, David Pugh, William Mugg, nephews George and John Fleet, and godson Richard Edwards. John

---

569. Lancaster Co. Court Order Book, 1656/7-1666, 119, 143, cited by Dorman, *Adventurers*, 972.

570. Old Rappahannock Co. Records, 2 (1677-1682): 142, cited by Dorman, *Adventurers*, 972.

571. Her parents' wills, Northumberland Co., Va., Order Bk. 1678-1698, 96, 190; Record Bk. 1706-1720, 227-229, cited by Dorman, *Adventurers*, 973.

572. Lancaster Co. Wills, 12:265, Ida J. Lee, *Abstracts of Lancaster Co., Va., Wills, 1653-1800* (1959), 85.

573. W. G. Stanard, "Capt. Henry Fleet and His Family," *Va. Magazine of History and Biography*, 2:70-76.

Carter executor.[574]

3. **William³ Fleet**, son of Henry and Elizabeth (Wildey) Fleet, died in King and Queen County, Virginia, shortly before 10 July 1734.[575] He married, by Lancaster County, Virginia, marriage bond dated 1 November 1718, **Ann Jones**,[576] daughter of William Jones of Middlesex County, Virginia.

William moved from Lancaster County to King and Queen County, Virginia before his death. His estate inventory was recorded on 10 July 1734 by executor Henry Fleet.[577] On 13 March 1734/35 his will, now lost, was proved in Lancaster County, Virginia.[578] His widow was living as late as 14 March 1752 when she petitioned the House of Burgesses for a ferry across the Mattapony River.[579]

Children of William and Ann (Jones) Fleet:[580]

  10. Henry⁴ Fleet, born 10 Oct. 1719,[581] d. without issue; will dated 20 Dec. 1785, proved 15 Oct. 1787, named brother John Fleet and Vincent Brent (executor).[582]

+ 11. Mary Ann Fleet, b. 12 May 1722.

+ 12. John Fleet, b. 12 Aug. 1724.

+ 13. William Fleet, b. 19 Oct. 1726.

  14. Edwin Fleet, b. 22 Aug. 1729, d. by 13 July 1778, evidently unmarried; will dated 27 Apr. 1778, proved 13 July 1778, named brother John and nephews.[583]

  15. George Fleet, b. 15 June 1731.

4. **Sarah³ Fleet**, daughter of Henry and Elizabeth (Wildey) Fleet, died in Lancaster County, Virginia, by 10 March 1717/18.[584] She married **William Brent**, born c1685, who married second, on 7 January 1723/24, Margaret

---

574. Lancaster Co. Wills, 12:358, as abstracted by both Lee and Stanard.

575. Date his estate inventory was recorded.

576. Stratton Nottingham, *Marriage License Bonds of Lancaster Co., Va., From 1701 to 1848* (1927), 27.

577. Lancaster Co. Court Order Bk. 1729-1743, 102.

578. Lancaster Co. Court Order Bk. 1729-1743, 112.

579. Dorman, *Adventurers*, 973, fn 34.

580. Stanard, "Fleet Family"; Dorman, *Adventurers*, 973-974.

581. Christ Church Parish, Middlesex Co., Register.

582. Lancaster Co. Wills, 22:157, as abstracted by Ida J. Lee.

583. Dorman, *Adventurers*, 973.

584. Date of deed of gift by William Brent to his two children by Sarah Brent, deceased. Lancaster Co. Deeds, 11:89-90.

Haynes, and third, by bond dated 9 August 1734, Letitia Wale.[585]
William Brent died leaving a will dated 2 July 1740 and proved 8
August 1740. He named his sons William and James, and daughters Sarah
and Frances Brent, and Elizabeth Hinton; also a friend Robert Biscoe.
William's brother Hugh Brent, James Haynes, Captain William Steptoe,
and cousin James Brent were appointed executors. Isaac Currell, Jane
Heard, and Robert Biscoe witnessed the will.[586]

Children of William and Sarah (Fleet) Brent:[587]

+ 16. Elizabeth[4] Brent, m. c1735, Samuel Hinton.
  17. Major Richard Brent, d. without issue by 1740.

5. **Elizabeth[3] Fleet**, daughter of Henry and Elizabeth (Wildey) Fleet,
married **Abraham Currell** of Lancaster County, Virginia. She died before
her husband who left a will dated in Lancaster County 13 December 1753
and proved 17 June 1757. He named his sons Harry, Spencer, and
Nicholas Currell. His brother, Nicholas Martin, and sons Harry and
Nicholas Currell were appointed executors. Nicholas and William Martin
and Geo. Currell witnessed the will.[588]

Childen of Abraham and Elizabeth (Fleet) Currell:[589]

+ 18. Harry[4] Currell, d. by 17 June 1785.
  19. Ann Currell.
+ 20. Spencer Currell, m. Judith Bridgeford.
+ 21. Nicholas Currell, d. by 15 June 1801.

6. **Ann[3] Fleet**, daughter of Henry and Elizabeth (Wildey) Fleet, married
by Lancaster County, Virginia, bond dated 10 November 1722, **Leonard
Howson**[590] of Wicomico, Northumberland County, Virginia. She died early
and he remarried and left a will, now lost, which was probated in
Northumberland County 13 June 1737.[591]

Child of Leonard and Ann (Fleet) Howson, named in her grandfather
Henry Fleet's 1729 will:

+ 22. Elizabeth[4] Howson, m. 1742, John Ledford.

---

585. Chester H. Brent, *Descendants of Hugh Brent* (Rutland, Vt., 1936), 44; Stratton
Nottingham, *Marriage License Bonds of Lancaster Co., Va., from 1701 to 1848* (Onancock, Va., 1927),
8.

586. Lancaster Co. Wills, 13:177, abstracted by Ida J. Lee, 21.

587. Dorman, *Adventurers*, 1:974.

588. Lancaster Co. Wills, 15:296, abstracted by Ida J. Lee, 62.

589. Dorman, *Adventurers*, 1:974; Brent, *Descendants*, 229.

590. Nottingham, *Bonds of Lancaster County*, 39.

591. Northumberland Co. Court Order Book 1729-1737, 258, cited by Dorman, *Adventurers*,
974.

7. **Judith³ Fleet**, daughter of Henry and Elizabeth (Wildey) Fleet, died in Northumberland County, Virginia, leaving a will dated 4 July 1766, a codicil dated 14 August 1766, and proved 8 September 1766.[592] She married by Lancaster County, Virginia, bond dated 28 June 1723, **William Hobson**[593] of Northumberland County. He was born 28 April 1700, son of Thomas Hobson,[594] and died in Northumberland County leaving a will dated 28 February 1737/38 and proved 10 September 1739.[595]

Children of William and Judith (Fleet) Hobson:[596]
+ 23. Sarah⁴ Hobson, b. 19 May 1725.
+ 24. Judith Hobson, b. 9 Dec. 1727.
+ 25. John Hobson, b. 13 Apr. 1730.
+ 26. Mary Ann Hobson, b. 17 June 1732.
+ 27. Betty Hobson, b. 8 Feb. 1736/37.

8. **Margaret³ Fleet**, daughter of Henry and Elizabeth (Wildey) Fleet, and called Mary in her father's will, married by Lancaster County, Virginia, bond dated 17 October 1723, **Presley Cox**[597] of Cople Parish, Westmoreland County, Virginia. Presley was born c1701, a son of Charnock Cox, and died by 30 September 1766, the date his will dated 18 February 1766 was proved in Westmoreland County.[598] He was a justice of the peace for Westmoreland County in 1737.[599]

Children of Presley and Margaret (Fleet) Cox:[600]
+ 28. Mary Ann⁴ Cox, m. Francis Wright.
  29. Peter Presley Cox, unmarried; will dtd. 6 June 1762, proved 29 June 1762.[601]
+ 30. Fleet Cox, b. 1725.
+ 31. William Cox, b. c1740-1745.

11. **Mary Ann⁴ Fleet**, daughter of William and Ann (Jones) Fleet, was

---

592. Northumberland Co. Record Book 1762-1766, 692.

593. Nottingham, *Bonds of Lancaster County*, 38.

594. Dorman, *Adventurers*, 974.

595. Northumberland Co. Record Book 1738-1743, 48.

596. Dorman, *Adventurers*, 974.

597. Nottingham, *Bonds of Lancaster County*, 17.

598. Westmoreland Co. Deeds and Wills, 14 (1761-1768): 393-395.

599. Louise C. Morrell, *Jamestown to Washington: 12 Generations*, 68.

600. Dorman, *Adventurers*, 975. Francis B. Culver, *Society of Colonial Wars in the State of Md.: Genealogies of the Members and Services of Ancestors* (Baltimore: Williams & Wilkins Co., 1940), 2:94.

601. Westmoreland Co. Deeds and Wills, 14 (1761-1768): 133.

born 12 May 1722.[602] She married first, **Robert Dudley**, and second [-?-] **Tebbs**.

Children of Robert and Mary Ann (Fleet) Dudley:[603]

32. William[5] Dudley, m. 13 Feb. 1773, Ann Pinchback;[604] will dtd. 7 Nov. 1794, proved King and Queen Co., Va., 12 July 1802; had issue.[605]

33. Henry Dudley, capt.-lieut. in Va. State Line; will dtd. 16 Feb. 1788, proved 8 June 1789; resided King and Queen Co., Va.[606]

12. **John**[4] **Fleet**, son of William and Ann (Jones) Fleet, was born 12 August 1724[607] and died in Lancaster County, Virginia, by June 1793. He married by Lancaster County bond dated 19 May 1746, **Mary Edwards**,[608] daughter of Thomas Edwards.[609]

John Fleet was a justice of Lancaster County, a militia colonel, and served in the Virginia State Line during the Revolutionary War.[610] He died leaving a will dated 12 July 1792 and proved 17 June 1793. He named his wife Mary and children: John (to have land the testator had from his uncle Henry Fleet), daughters Elizabeth Christian, Dolly Fleet, and Judy Fleet. He also named John, Mary, Lucy, Richard, Ann, and Benjamin Ingram. His wife, Jn° Fleet and John Christian were appointed executors. Charles Ingram and Jn° Christian witnessed the will.[611]

Children of John and Mary (Edwards) Fleet:[612]

34. Ann[5] Fleet, m. Henry Hinton.

35. Henry Fleet, unmarried; will dtd. 20 Dec. 1785, proved 15 Oct. 1787.[613]

36. Sarah Fleet, m. by Lancaster Co. bond dtd. 16 Apr. 1772, Thomas Ingram;[614] had issue.[615]

37. Dorothy/"Dolly" Fleet, m. by Lancaster Co. bond dtd. 19 July 1781, John

602. Stanard, "Fleet Family," 76.

603. Will of Edwin' Fleet, cited by Dorman, *Adventurers*, 975.

604. *William and Mary College Quarterly Historical Magazine*, 2nd ser., 9:66.

605. Alfred Bagby, *King and Queen Co., Va.* (New York, 1908), 373-374; Dorman, *Adventurers*, 979-980.

606. Revolutionary War pension application, National Archives, claim no. R-13891.

607. Stanard, "Fleet Family," 76, cited by Dorman, *Adventurers*, 975.

608. Nottingham, *Bonds of Lancaster County*, 17.

609. Will of Thomas Edwards dtd. 14 Nov. 1759, proved 15 Feb. 1760; division of estate. Lancaster Co. Wills, 16:80, 116.

610. Dorman, *Adventurers*, 975, fn 58.

611. Lancaster Co. Wills, 22:385, abstracted by Ida J. Lee.

612. Dorman, *Adventurers*, 975.

613. Lancaster Co. Wills, 22:157.

614. Nottingham, *Bonds of Lancaster County*, 41.

615. Dorman, *Adventurers*, 980.

Christopher[616] had issue.[617]

38. Elizabeth Fleet, b. c1753, d. Lancaster Co., 28 Jan. 1840;[618] m. (1) by Lancaster Co. bond dtd. 22 Jan. 1772, Nicholas Pope of Northumberland Co.;[619] m. (2) by bond dtd. 4 July 1782, Rawleigh C. Christian.[620] Had issue by both husbands.[621]

39. Judith Fleet, m. by Lancaster Co. bond dtd. 9 Sept. 1779, Daniel Haynie[622] of Northumberland Co.; had issue.[623]

40. Lucy Fleet, m. by Lancaster Co. bond dtd. 16 June 1781, John Smallwood.[624]

41. John Fleet, of *Fairview*, Lancaster Co.; will dtd. 7 Feb. 1800, proved 19 Jan. 1801.[625]

13. William⁴ Fleet, son of William and Ann (Jones) Fleet, was born 19 October 1726[626] and died by 11 October 1773. He married first, 29 May 1744, **Ann Temple**, who died 7 May 1754, and second, on 9 November 1755, **Susannah Walker**.[627] She was born 25 October 1736, daughter of John and Eliza (Baylor) Walker of *Locust Grove*, King and Queen County, Virginia.[628]

William Fleet lived at *Rural Felicity* and was a justice of King and Queen County. His will was dated 20 April 1763 and proved 11 October 1773.[629]

Child of William and Ann (Temple) Fleet:[630]

42. Ann⁵ Fleet, m. Christopher Tompkins.

Children of William and Susannah (Walker) Fleet:[631]

43. Henry Fleet, d. 24 Dec. 1826,[632] m. Mildred Pierce, had issue.[633]

---

616. Nottingham, *Bonds of Lancaster County*, 14.

617. Dorman, *Adventurers*, 980.

618. Deposed 15 July 1839, aged 86 years.

619. Nottingham, *Bonds of Lancaster County*, 61.

620. Her Revolutionary War widow's pension application, National Archives, claim no. W-18892.

621. Dorman, *Adventurers*, 980-981.

622. Nottingham, *Bonds of Lancaster County*, 36.

623. Dorman, *Adventurers*, 981.

624. Nottingham, *Bonds of Lanvcaster County*, 68.

625. Lancaster Co. Wills, 28:48.

626. Stanard, "Fleet Family," 86.

627. Malcolm H. Harris, *Old New Kent County* (West Point, Va., 1977), 395.

628. Croshaw family, in Dorman, *Adventurers*, 778.

629. Abstracted in William A. Crozier, *Williamsburg Wills, Virginia County Records* (New York, 1906), 3:25.

630. Dorman, *Adventurers*, 976.

631. Dorman, *Adventurers*, 976.

632. *Tyler's Quarterly Historical and Genealogical Magazine* 17:176-177.

633. Dorman, *Adventurers*, 982.

44. William Fleet, b. 18 Dec. 1757; d. at *Goshen*, King and Queen Co., 11 Apr. 1833;[634] m. Sarah (Browne) Tomlin; had issue.[635]
45. Mary Ann Fleet, b. 22 Jan. 1759; d. King and Queen Co., 4 Sept. 1820; m. Philip Pendleton;[636] had issue.[637]
46. John Fleet, d. 1 Dec. 1795, of King and Queen Co.,[638] m. and had issue.[639]
47. Edwin Fleet, m. Frances Pierce;[640] d. before 24 Dec. 1794.[641]
48. Baylor Fleet, d. before 23 Apr. 1832, m. Ann [-?-], had issue.[642]
49. Elizabeth Fleet.

16. **Elizabeth**[4] **Brent**, daughter of William and Sarah (Fleet) Brent, died in 1779.[643] She married first, c1735, **Samuel Hinton**, who died in Lancaster County, Virginia, by 21 June 1771. She married second, by Lancaster County bond dated 30 December 1774, **Thomas Hunton**.

Samuel Hinton of Christ Church Parish, Lancaster County, died leaving a will dated 3 April 1771 and proved 21 June 1771. He named his sons Richard, William, Spencer, Henry, Samuel and Fleete Hinton, and his wife Elizabeth. His sons were appointed executors. John Fleet, Martin Hill, William Currell, and Nicholas Pope, witnessed the will.[644]

Children of Samuel and Elizabeth (Brent) Hinton:[645]
50. Richard[5] Hinton, b. c1736, d. June 1779, m. and had issue.[646]
51. William Hinton, will dtd. Lancaster Co. 2 March 1790, proved 17 Jan. 1791;[647] m. Ann Sydnor; had issue.[648]
52. Spencer Hinton, will dated Lancaster Co. 26 Feb. 1811, proved 17 June 1811.[649]
53. Henry Hinton, will dtd. Lancaster Co. 1 Aug. 1821, proved 19 Nov. 1821;[650]

---

634. Gravestone inscription, cited by Dorman, *Adventurers*, 982.

635. Dorman, *Adventurers*, 982-984.

636. Her death notice, *Enquirer* (Richmond), 29 Sept. 1820.

637. *Virginia Magazine of History and Biography* 44:71, 265; Dorman, *Adventurers*, 984-985.

638. His Revolutionary War pension application, National Archives, claim no. R-14208.

639. Dorman, *Adventurers*, 985.

640. Hanover Co., Va., Deed Book 1783-1792, 24; *Tyler's Quarterly Historical and Genealogical Magazine* 17:177-178.

641. Date executrix Frances Fleet advertised for sale his plantation on Pamunkey River. *Virginia Gazette and General Advertiser* (Richmond), 24 Dec. 1794.

642. Dorman, *Adventurers*, 985.

643. *The Southside Virginian* 5:149.

644. Lancaster Co. Wills, 20:20, abstracted by Ida J. Lee, 115.

645. Dorman, *Adventurers*, 976.

646. Dorman, *Adventurers*, 985-986.

647. Lancaster Co. Wills, 22:286.

648. Dorman, *Adventurers*, 986.

649. Lancaster Co. Wills, 28:116.

650. Lancaster Co. Wills, 28:218.

m. Ann Fleet; had issue.[651]
54. Samuel Hinton, d. by 16 Feb. 1789;[652] m. (2) by Lancaster Co. contract dtd. 13 Nov. 1785, Catherine Sydnor;[653] resided Dinwiddie Co., Va.; had issue.[654]
55. Fleete Hinton, d. Lancaster Co. by 21 May 1778;[655] m. by Lancaster Co. bond dtd. 17 Nov. 1768, Catherine Pope;[656] had issue.[657]

18. **Harry**[4] **Currell**, son of Abraham and Elizabeth (Fleet) Currell, died by 17 June 1785. He married **Amy (Brent) Haynes.**[658] He died leaving a will dated 4 December 1782 and proved in Lancaster County, Virginia, 17 June 1785. He named son Gilbert Currell (not yet 21), brother Nicholas Currell, and grandson William Ford (not yet 21). Gilbert and Nicholas Currell were appointed executors. Robert Ferguson, William James, and Matthias James witnessed the will.[659] His widow Amy left a will dated 2 December 1803 and proved in Lancaster County 29 February 1804.[660]
Children of Harry and Amy (Brent) Currell:[661]
56. Gilbert[5] Currell, will dtd. Lancaster Co. 8 Dec. 1799, proved 20 Feb. 1804.[662]
57. Elizabeth F. Currell, m. by Lancaster Co. bond dtd. 27 May 1773, Daniel Ford;[663] had issue.[664]

20. **Spencer**[4] **Currell**, son of Abraham and Elizabeth (Fleet) Currell, married by Lancaster County, Virginia, bond dated 31 December 1757, **Judith Bridgeford.**[665]
Children of Spencer and Judith (Bridgeford) Currell:[666]
58. Spencer[5] Currell, m. by Lancaster Co. bond dtd. 17 June 1793, Lucy Hinton.[667]
59. [perhaps] Thomas Currell, m. by Lancaster Co. bond dtd. 17 Dec. 1801, Mary

651. Dorman, *Adventurers*, 986-987.
652. Date his will proved, Lancaster Co. Wills, 28:183.
653. Lancaster Co. Deeds, 21:55.
654. Dorman, *Adventurers*, 987.
655. Date his estate was inventoried, Lancaster Co. Wills, 20:142.
656. Nottingham, *Bonds of Lancaster County*, 38.
657. Dorman, *Adventurers*, 987.
658. Dorman, *Adventurers*, 976.
659. Lancaster Co. Wills, 22:77, abstracted by Ida J. Lee, 62.
660. Lancaster Co. Wills, 28:119.
661. Dorman, *Adventurers*, 976.
662. Lancaster Co. Wills, 28:76.
663. Nottingham, *Bonds of Lancaster County*, 28.
664. Dorman, *Adventurers*, 987.
665. Nottingham, *Bonds of Lancaster County*, 18.
666. Lancaster Co. Personal Property Tax List, 1787; Dorman, *Adventurers*, 976-977.
667. Nottingham, *Bonds of Lancaster County*, 18.

George.[668]

21. **Nicholas[4] Currell**, son of Abraham and Elizabeth (Fleet) Currell, died in Lancaster County, Virginia, shortly before 15 June 1801, the date his 6 May 1801 will was proved.[669] He was a Lancaster County militia captain during the Revolutionary War.[670]
   Children of Nicholas Currell:[671]
   60. James[5] Currell.
   61. Ann Currell, m. by Lancaster Co. bond dtd. 25 Jan. 1797, Joseph Ball;[672] had issue.[673]
   62. Elizabeth Currell, m. by Lancaster Co. bond dtd. 1 Feb. 1780, Thomas Lee;[674] had issue.[675]

22. **Elizabeth[4] Howson**, daughter of Leonard and Ann (Fleet) Howson, was named in the 1729 will of her grandfather Henry Fleet. She married in 1742 **John Ledford**.[676] His will was dated in Lancaster County, Virginia, 10 May 1741 and proved 15 November 1754.[677]
   Children of John and Elizabeth (Howson) Ledford:[678]
   63. James[5] Ledford, d. Northumberland Co. before 13 Apr. 1784;[679] m. by Lancaster Co. bond dtd. 9 Jan. 1770, [-?-] Garlington;[680] had issue.[681]
   64. Elizabeth Ledford, m. by Lancaster Co. bond dtd. 16 Oct. 1797, George Norris;[682] had issue.[683]

23. **Sarah[4] Hobson**, daughter of William and Judith (Fleet) Hobson, was born 29 May 1725 and married **Charles Fallin**. He was a son of Charles

---

668. Nottingham, *Bonds of Lancaster County*, 18.
669. Lancaster Co. Wills, 28:49.
670. William L. Hopkins, *Va. Revolutionary War Land Grant Claims, 1783-1850* (Richmond, 1988), 62.
671. Dorman, *Adventurers*, 977, 987-988.
672. Nottingham, *Bonds of Lancaster County*, 3.
673. Dorman, *Adventurers*, 988.
674. Nottingham, *Bonds of Lancaster County*, 47.
675. Dorman, *Adventurers*, 988.
676. Dorman, *Adventurers*, 977.
677. Lancaster Co. Wills, 15:190.
678. Dorman, *Adventurers*, 977, 988-989.
679. Date administration on his estate granted, Northumberland Co. Order Book 1783-1784, 146.
680. Nottingham, *Bonds of Lancaster County*, 47.
681. Dorman, *Adventurers*, 988
682. Nottingham, *Bonds of Lancaster County*, 54.
683. Dorman, *Adventurers*, 988-989.

and Hannah (Harcum) Fallin,[684] was a justice of Northumberland County, Virginia, and left a will dated 1 February 1773 and proved 11 October 1773.[685]

Children of Charles and Sarah (Hobson) Fallin:[686]

65. John Hobson[5] Fallin, b. 25 March 1753; d. testate, Northumberland Co., 31 Jan. 1839;[687] m. by Northumberland Co. license dtd. 4 June 1784, Nancy Davenport;[688] had issue.[689]

66. William Fallin, will dtd. Northumberland Co., 31 Jan. 1783, proved 18 Oct. 1783;[690] m. by Northumberland Co. license dtd. Dec. 1764, Sarah Eskridge;[691] had issue.[692]

67. Frances Fallin, d. Westmoreland Co. before 25 Apr. 1775;[693] m. by Northumberland Co. license dtd. 13 Feb. 1764, Matthew Lamkin[694] had issue.[695]

68. Sarah Fallin.

69. Elizabeth Fallin, m. by Northumberland Co. license dtd. 6 May 1777, Samuel Denny,[696] a captain 1776-1780,[697] administration on his estate granted to Edmund Denny 12 Sept. 1785.[698]

70. Charles Fallin, administration of his estate granted to Thomas Fallin 11 Nov. 1805;[699] m. Hannah Kesterson. Had issue.[700]

24. Judith[4] Hobson, daughter of William and Judith (Fleet) Hobson, was born 9 December 1725. She married, first, **Stephen Chilton**, and, second, by Northumberland County, Virginia, [intention] contract dated 9

684. *Northumberland County Historical Society Bulletin* 14:41-43.

685. Northumberland Co. Record Book 1772-1796, 277.

686. *Northumberland County Historical Society Bulletin* 13:81-88; 14:41-47. Dorman, *Adventurers*, 977, 989-990.

687. Northumberland Co. Records, 30:328-329.

688. *Virginia Magazine of History and Biography*, 47:143.

689. Dorman, *Adventurers*, 989.

690. Northumberland Co. Records, 12 (1783-1785): 95.

691. *Virginia Magazine of History and Biography* 47:32.

692. Dorman, *Adventurers*, 989.

693. Date when her estate appraisal was ordered, Westmoreland Co. Records and Inventories, 5:33.

694. *Virginia Magazine of History and Biography* 47:43.

695. Harold E. Wilkins, *Descendants of Thomas Lamkin* (Boston, 2001), 105-106, 176-180; Dorman, *Adventurers*, 990.

696. *Va. Magazine of History and Biography* 47:47.

697. Margie G. Brown, *Genealogical Abstracts, Revolutionary War Veterans, Scrip Act 1852* (Oakton, Va., 1990), 80.

698. Northumberland Co. Order Book 1783-1785, 381.

699. Northumberland Co. Minute Book 1805-1807, 58.

700. Dorman, *Adventurers*, 990.

December 1769, **Joseph Coleman.**[701]
Children of Stephen and Judith (Hobson) Chilton:[702]
71. Millicent[5] Chilton, b. 26 March 1749.
72. Fleet Chilton, b. 5 March 1751.
73. Molly Chilton, b. 3 June 1753.
74. John Chilton, b. 10 Oct. 1755.
75. William Chilton, b. 12 March 1758.
76. Judith Chilton.
77. Sarah Fleet Chilton.
78. Stephen Chilton, b. 28 Feb. 1767.

25. **John**[4] **Hobson,** son of William and Judith (Fleet) Hobson, was born 13 April 1730. He died in Northumberland County, Virginia, shortly before 8 February 1762, the date his 12 October 1750 will was proved.[703] He married **Winifred Wildey.**
Children of John and Winifred (Wildey) Hobson:[704]
79. Thomas[5] Hobson, m. 1778, Rebecca Eskridge.[705]
80. Mollie Fleet Hobson.

26. **Mary Ann**[4] **Hobson,** daughter of William and Judith (Fleet) Hobson, was born 17 June 1732. She married, first, **William Chilton,** and, second, **Moses Williams.** William Chilton's will was dated December 1748 and proved in Lancaster County, Virginia, 11 August 1749.[706] Moses Williams will was dated 14 September 1772 and proved in Northumberland County, Virginia, 12 October 1772.[707]
Child of William and Mary Ann (Hobson) Chilton:[708]
81. Sallie[5] Chilton, deeded negroes and personalty by mother, 12 May 1777.[709]
Child of Moses and Mary Ann (Hobson) Williams:[710]
82. William Fleet Williams, administration on his estate granted to William Rogers 13 Feb. 1815;[711] possibly m. by Northumberland Co. bond dtd. 28 Jan.

---

701. Northumberland Co. Record Book 7, 526, cited by Dorman, *Adventurers*, 977.
702. St. Stephen's Parish Register, cited by Dorman.
703. Northumberland Co. Record Book 1758-1762, 495.
704. Dorman, *Adventurers*, 978.
705. *Tyler's Quarterly Historical and Genealogical Magazine* 47:142.
706. Lancaster Co. Deeds and Wills, 14:253; Lancaster Co. Order Book 1743-1752, 196.
707. Northumberland Co. Record Book 1772-1776, 51.
708. Dorman, *Adventurers*, 978.
709. Northumberland Co. Record Book 1776-1780, 161-162.
710. Dorman, *Adventurers*, 978.
711. Northumberland Co. Order Book 1811-1816, 281.

1792, Ellen Rogers.[712]

27. Betty⁴ Hobson, daughter of William and Judith (Fleet) Hobson, was born 8 February 1736/37. She married c1753 **John Corbell**. In Northumberland County, Virginia, 13 February 1815, William Corbell was granted administration on the estate of John Corbell.[713]

Children of John and Betty (Hobson) Corbell, recorded at St. Stephen's Parish:[714]

 83. William⁵ Corbell, b. 17 July 1754; will dtd. 8 Nov. 1814, proved 15 Nov. 1814.[715] Had issue.[716]
 84. Molly Corbell, b. 16 May 1756; will dtd. 10 Apr. 1801, proved 14 June 1802;[717] m. [-?-] Corbell. Had issue.[718]
 85. John Corbell, b. 15 Oct. 1758.
 86. Clement Corbell, b. 25 Oct. 1761.
 87. Fleet Corbell, b. 10 Sept. 1764.
 88. Gilbert Corbell, b. 28 Aug.1766, will dtd. 18 March 1799, proved 8 July 1799;[719] m. by Northumberland Co. bond dtd. 31 Dec. 1792, Ann/"Nancy" [-?-] Docksey. Had issue.[720]

28. Mary Ann⁴ Cox, daughter of Presley and Margaret (Fleet) Cox, married **Francis Wright**, son of Richard and Elizabeth (Wigginton) Wright. His will was dated 5 December 1775 and proved in Westmoreland County, Virginia, 26 March 1793.[721]

Children of Francis and Mary Ann (Cox) Wright:[722]

 89. Richard⁵ Wright.
 90. Presley Wright, m. Elizabeth Middleton.
 91. Nancy Wright, m. Matthew Rust.

30. Fleet⁴ Cox, son of Presley and Margaret (Fleet) Cox, was born in 1725 and died by 18 June 1791, the date his 7 January 1791 will was proved in

---

712. Nottingham, *Marriage License Bonds of Northumberland County*, 109, cited by Dorman, 978.

713. Northumberland Co. Order Book 1773-1783, 353.

714. St. Stephen's Parish Register, cited by Dorman, *Adventurers*, 978.

715. Northumberland Co. Record Book 20 (1815-1816): 92.

716. Dorman, *Adventurers*, 990.

717. Northumberland Co. Record Book 16 (1799-1803): 391.

718. Dorman, *Adventurers*, 991.

719. Northumberland Co. Record Book 15 (1794-1799): 628.

720. Dorman, *Adventurers*, 991.

721. Westmoreland Co. Deeds and Wills, 18 (1787-1794): 294-295.

722. Dorman, *Adventurers*, 979.

Westmoreland County, Virginia.[723] He married **Elizabeth Wright,** daughter of Richard and Elizabeth (Wigginton) Wright. He was a justice of Westmoreland County.

Children of Fleet and Elizabeth (Wright) Cox:[724]

92. Fleet[5] Cox, m. Sept. 1787, Elizabeth Downing.[725] Had issue.[726]
93. Peter Presley Cox, d. *Federal Hill,* Westmoreland Co., before 28 Feb. 1820, date his 6 Oct. 1818 will proved;[727] m. (1) by Westmoreland Co. bond dtd. 18 Oct. 1796, Fanny Bailey;[728] m. (2) by bond dtd. 16 June 1802, Sally Gordon;[729] m. (3) by bond dtd. 17 Aug. 1808, Eleanor Jackson.[730] Had issue.[731]
94. John Cox.
95. James Cox, d. 27 Feb. 1837; m. by Westmoreland Co. bond dtd. 12 June 1804, Hannah Jackson (1782-1838).[732]
96. Richard Cox.
97. Betty Cox, d. 26 Apr. 1838; m. 5 Apr. 1787, Thomas D. Downing.[733] Had issue.[734]
98. Mary Cox, m. (1) 4 Dec. 1777, Capt. William Middleton[735] m. (2) by Westmoreland Co. bond dtd. 7 March 1795, Thomas Plummer.[736] Had issue.[737]

31. William[4] Cox, son of Presley and Margaret (Fleet) Cox, married **Ann** [-?-].

Children of William and Ann Cox:[738]

99. George[5] Cox, m. by Northumberland Co. bond dtd. 14 Feb. 1797, Rebecca Beacham.
100. Molly Flood Cox.

---

723. Westmoreland Co. Deeds and Wills, 18 (1787-1794): 191.

724. Dorman, *Adventurers,* 979, 991-993; Louise C. Morrell, *Jamestown to Washington: 12 Generations,* 22, 68.

725. *Virginia Magazine of History and Biography* 47:143.

726. Dorman, *Adventurers,* 991.

727. Westmoreland Co. Deeds and Wills, 24:40-43.

728. Nottingham, *Bonds of Westmoreland County,* 16.

729. *Ibid.*

730. *Ibid.*

731. Dorman, *Adventurers,* 992.

732. Nottingham, *Bonds of Westmoreland County,* 16. Morrell, *Jamestown to Washington,* 68.

733. Nottingham, *Bonds of Westmoreland County,* 20.

734. Downing Bible, *Northumberland Co. Historical Society Bulletin* 4:59-62; Dorman, *Adventurers,* 992.

735. Middleton Bible, *Northern Neck of Va. Historical Magazine* 16:1481; Westmoreland Co. Wills and Deeds, 18:148-149.

736. Nottingham, *Bonds of Westmoreland County,* 54.

737. Dorman, *Adventurers,* 993.

738. Dorman, *Adventurers,* 979.

101. Jane Cox, perhaps m. by Northumberland Co. bond dtd. 11 Feb. 1788, Thomas Beacham.[739]
102. William Presley Cox, m. (1) by Northumberland Co. bond dtd. 23 Dec. 1800, Alice R. [-?-] Travers; m. (2) by bond dtd. 30 Jan. 1809, Sally Cralle.[740]
103. Thomas McFarling Cox, m. by Northumberland Co. bond dtd. 5 July 1799, Alice Claughton.[741]

RICHARD GERARD

1. **Richard**[1] **Gerard**, esquire, second son of Sir Thomas Gerard of Bryn, Lancashire, England, and his wife Frances, daughter of Sir Richard Molyneux of Sefton, Lancashire, was born c1613, and died 5 September 1668 at Ince, Lancashire. He married, first, **Frances Hansby**, daughter of Sir Ralph Hansby of Tickhill Castle, Yorkshire, and, second, **Judith Steward**, daughter of Sir Nicholas Steward of Pattishull, Northamptonshire.[742]

In 1633 Mr. Richard Gerrard went to Maryland on the *Ark* and the *Dove* expedition.[743] He brought in five men, whose land rights he assigned to Ferdinand Pulton, Jesuit. The manor granted to him by Lord Baltimore was assigned by him to the Jesuits.[744] In 1634/35 he was present at a skirmish involving Captain Thomas Cornwallis and Lieutenant Ratcliffe Warren, in which four men were killed. He remained in Maryland for three years,[745] but returned to England before the January 1637/38 General Assembly, from which he was absent.[746]

He raised a troop of foot for the King of Spain, and from 1638 to 1642 he served in the Netherlands. He entered the service of Henrietta Maria (wife of Charles I), who was then at the Hague. Gerard raised the soldiers in the bodyguard that accompanied the Queen from the Hague to Bridlington Bay, Yorkshire. He was commissioned a lieutenant-colonel by the Earl of Newcastle, and fought at the second Battle of Newbury in

---

739. *Ibid.*, 6.

740. *Ibid.*, 22.

741. Nottingham. *Bonds of Northumberland County*, 22.

742. Playfair, *British Family Antiquity*, 4:cxxi; William Dugdale, *Visitation of the County Palatine of Lancaster*, (Chetham Society Publication, vol. 85), (London, 1872), 116.

743. Md. Land Patents, ABH:66.

744. Newman, *Flowering*, 211.

745. According to his testimony taken at Chancery Court in London 18 July 1646. PRO: C2/Chas. I/C15/23. Abstracted by Peter Wilson Coldham in *National Genealogical Society Quarterly* 69 (1981): 121.

746. Newman, *Flowering*, 211.

October 1644. He carried letters between Charles I at Hurst Castle, and Henrietta Maria in France. Upon the Restoration, Gerard was appointed Cup-bearer and Waiter to the Queen Mother. He purchased the Manor of Ince from his cousin Thomas Gerard, and died there. He was buried in Wugan Church.[747]

By his first wife, Richard had one son who died in infancy. By his second wife Judith Steward he had six sons and three daughters, all but two of whom died unmarried:[748]

+ 2. Thomas[2] Gerard, m. Mary Wright.
+ 3. Richard Gerard, m. Jane Prescott.

2. **Thomas[2] Gerard**, son of Richard and Judith (Steward) Gerard, died in 1724. He married **Mary Wright**, and had at least one son:[749]

4. Richard[3] Gerard, d. without issue, 1743; estates inherited by William[4] Gerard [no. 6 below].

3. **Richard[2] Gerard**, son of Richard and Judith (Steward) Gerard, married **Jane Prescott**, daughter of Samuel Prescott. They were the parents of:[750]

+ 5. Richard[3] Gerard, m. Isabella Baldwin.

5. **Richard[3] Gerard**, son of Richard and Jane (Prescott) Gerard, married **Isabella Baldwin**, daughter of John Baldwin. They were the parents of:[751]

6. William[4] Gerard, inherited Ince estate on death of Richard [no. 4 above]; d. unmarried; his estates and Gerard arms passed to sisters.
+ 7. Mary Gerard, m. John Walmesley.
8. Elizabeth Gerard, d. unmarried.

7. **Mary[4] Gerard**, daughter of Richard and Isabella (Baldwin) Gerard, and sister and coheiress of William Gerard, married **John Walmesley**. John Walmesley was succeeded by his only surviving son:[752]

9. Richard[5] Walmesley, m. Sarah Worthington, daughter of James Worthington, and had issue.

---

747. *Dictionary of National Biography*, 7:1103. David Spalding, "Thomas Gerard of Maryland and Virginia," in *Chronicles of St. Mary's*, vol. 7, no. 7 (July 1959): 2, 6, end notes 8-11.

748. *Dictionary of National Biography*, 7:1103; "Walmesley of Wetswood House," *Burke's Commoners*, 1:278-279.

749. "Walmesley," *ibid.*, 279.

750. *Ibid.*

751. *Ibid.*

752. *Ibid.*

RICHARD GILBERT

1. **Richard[1] Gilbert** was transported to Maryland by Leonard Calvert in 1633.[753] He died in St. Mary's County by 1638. He married c1626 **Rose** [-?-], who was born in England c1599 and died in St. Mary's County between 1660 and 1669. Rose Smith gave her age as c59 years when she deposed in 1658. She signed her name on all documents. She was licensed on 23 November 1638 to marry Robert Smith,[754] a planter, who testified that he was not contracted to any woman other than Rose Gilbert.[755]

Richard Gilbert left a wife in England on his initial voyage, and, like other adventurers, returned to bring them to Maryland if conditions in the new colony should prove favorable. He was back in Maryland by 1637, having brought his wife Rose and their two children, as well as two indentured servants, Walter Waterling and Thomas Thomas.

Children of Richard and Rose Gilbert:[756]
+   2. Elizabeth[2] Gilbert, m. William Asbeston.
+   3. Grace Gilbert, m. William Waterling.

2. **Elizabeth[2] Gilbert**, daughter of Richard and Rose Gilbert, married **William Asbeston** by January 1654/55 and died before 1680. He was born c1625[757] and died testate by 11 February 1681/82.

William petitioned the Court on 5 December 1648 stating that he had served his master Thomas Allen for seven years by indenture, and his time of service "expired on Sunday next; that Jn° Hatch (who is accounted and esteemed as the administrator of Thomas Allen, deceased) may be bound and compelled to allow the petitioner his dues. Hatch acknowledged that the petitioner had accomplished his time.[758]

Elizabeth Gilbert was raised by her stepfather, Robert Smith, who in January 1654/55 gave a heifer to his "daughter" Elizabeth Asbeston.[759] In August 1651 William Asbeston leased 50 acres of *Asbeston Oak*[760] on the

---

753. Md. Land Patents, 1:121, ABH:98.

754. Md. Land Patents, 1:133-134.

755. *Archives*, 41:181, 4:51; Newman, *Flowering*, 211-212.

756. Newman, *Flowering*, 212.

757. He gave his age as 26 or 27 years old on 20 Nov. 1652, and 43 years in 1667. *Archives*, 10:197; Newman, *Flowering*, 284.

758. *Archives*, 4:447.

759. Newman, *Flowering*, 284.

760. His patent for this tract was not found.

St. George River to Mark Blomfield; Asbeston also owned land at the lower end of St. Mary's Town.[761] About 1675-1676 he was listed as a creditor of the estate of Joseph Bruffe of St. Mary's County; and in 1679 as a debtor in the inventory of Richard Chillman. An unidentified Samuel Asbeston was also listed in the latter. On 26 August 1679 Winifred Asbeston, goddaughter of Elizabeth Moy, was named as a legatee of the latter's estate; Winifred's legacy was paid to William Asbeston.[762]

William Asbeston died leaving a will dated 12 December 1680 and proved in St. Mary's County on 11 February 1681/82. He named his son William, not yet 21, and daughters Winifred, Isabella, and Mary, with Richard Attwood appointed executor. An inventory of his personal property was taken by Edward Chester and Thomas Doxey, but no date or values were reported. A later inventory cited a value of 16,380 pounds of tobacco, matched by payments totalling the same. Payments went to the children of the deceased: Winifred, Mary, Isabella, Rebecca, and William. On 11 September 1686, Richard Atwood filed a report of the administration, which mentioned only Rebecca Asbeston as legatee.[763]

Children of William and Elizabeth (Gilbert) Asbeston:[764]

    4. Winifred[3] Asbeston.
    5. Mary Asbeston.
    6. Isabella Asbeston.
    7. Rebecca Asbeston, [possibly] m. [-?-] Green.
+   8. William Asbeston, b. 1660.

3. Grace[2] Gilbert, daughter of Richard and Rose Gilbert, was born in England c1628 and died in St. Mary's County by 1672. She almost certainly married in St. Mary's County c1647 **Walter Waterling,** who had been born c1608 and died in 1672.[765] Walter Waterling had been transported by Richard Gilbert c1638 and had completed his time of service by 1642, when he was able to claim land.[766] In 1649/50 he assigned to Robert Smith 100 acres of land, Willima Asbeston witnessing.[767]

Walter Waterling died leaving a will dated 30 August 1672 and proved 14 September 1672, in which he named his daughter Mary Waterling,

---

761. *Archives,* 57:228, 401-402.
762. Md. Inventories & Accounts, 2:91, 5:382-404; 6:319.
763. Md. Wills, 2:167; Md. Inventories & Accounts, 7C:45, 230; 9:88.
764. Newman, *Flowering,* 285.
765. *Archives,* 4:371; Newman, *Flowering,* 283. He gave his age as 40 in 1648.
766. Md. Land Patents, ABH:244; 2:606.
767. Newman, *Flowering,* 283.

grandchildren Grace and Elizabeth Barnes, daughters Grace and Patience, and son [*sic*] John Barnes who was appointed executor. William Asbeston and Henry Smith were witnesses. John Barnes filed an account of the estate on 21 November 1674, naming legatees Mary Waterling and grandchildren Grace and Elizabeth Barnes.[768]

Children of Walter and Grace (Gilbert) Waterling:[769]

  9. Mary^3 Waterling, b. c1648, d. 1740, m. (1) unknown; as a widow she moved to Dorchester Co. in 1678; she or her daughter may have md. Henry Hooper.[770]

+ 10. Grace Waterling, b. c1649.

  11. Patience Waterling, b. c1652, [possibly] m. into family of Capt. Thomas Ennalls, Justice of Dorchester Co. Court.[771]

8. **William^3 Asbeston**, son of William and Elizabeth (Gilbert) Asbeston, was born c1660 and died in May 1737. He married **Mary** [-?-], who married second Robert Jackson.

On 2 August 1718 William Asbeston filed an account of the estate of John Greene of St. Mary's County. William's will was dated 8 February 1736/37 and proved 7 May 1737. He devised to daughter Rachel, wife of William Thomas, *Asbeston Oak.* He also named daughter Elizabeth and granddaughter Mary Thomas, with wife Mary appointed executrix. William Price, William Price, and Charles Rawlins were witnesses. On 25 July 1737 Asbeston's personal property was appraised at £29.15.3, with Charles Smith and Rachel Thomas approving as kinsmen. The widow filed an account on 28 March 1738, which mentioned legacies paid to Rachel Thomas and Mary Thomas. As the wife of Robert Jackson, Mary filed a further account on 3 February 1741/42.[772]

Children of William and Mary Asbeston:[773]

  12. Samuel^4 Asbeston, legatee in 1697 will of John Askins.[774]

+ 13. Rachel Asbeston, m. William Thomas.

  14. Elizabeth Asbeston.

---

  768. Md. Wills, 1;502; Md. Inventories & Accounts, 1:131.

  769. Newman, *Flowering*, 284.

  770. Capt. Arthur Clifton Bushey, Jr., "Richard Gilbert of the Ark and The Dove and His Dorchester County Descendants," typescript, Aug. 1964, at MHS. No further information.

  771. *Ibid.* No proof was found for such a marriage in the abstracts of Md. wills, inventories, or accounts, or Dorchester Co. land records.

  772. Md. Administrations, 1:198; Md. Wills, 21:774; Md. Inventories, 22:409; Md. Administrations, 16:88, 18:533.

  773. Newman, *Flowering,* 286.

  774. Md. Wills, 7:338.

10. **Grace³ Waterling**, daughter of Walter and Grace (Gilbert) Waterling, was born c1649 in St. Mary's County and died in Dorchester County after 1703. She married first by 1672 **John Barnes**, who died there by the summer of 1695. She married second by 30 November 1696 **William Lawyer**. On 23 January 1689 Grace Barnes, wife of John, gave a power of attorney to Benjamin Hunt to acknowledge a deed for 1750 acres of Martin's Hundred, which John Barnes had sold to Henry Hooper.[775]

John Barnes was in St. Mary's County as late as 29 July 1678, but moved to Dorchester County where he died intestate. In August 1695 an administration bond on his estate was executed by his wife Grace, with Cornelius Johnson and Thomas Harvey as sureties. The inventory of his personal property was appraised at £24.10.6. On 10 April 1701 William Lawyer and his wife Grace, and John Barnes of Talbot County and his wife Elizabeth, conveyed to Henry King 200 acres of *Philip's Range*. William Lawyer died by 28 September 1703 when his estate in Dorchester County was appraised at £29.8.6.[776]

Children of John and Grace (Waterling) Barnes:[777]

    15. Walter⁴ Barnes, b. 1666, twin, d. by 1695.
+ 16. Thomas Barnes, b. 1666, twin.
    17. Grace Barnes, b. 1667.[778]
    18. Elizabeth Barnes, b. 1669, m. [-?-] Taylor.
+ 19. Mary Barnes, b. 1672.
+ 20. Matthew Barnes, b. 1673.
+ 21. John Waterling Barnes, b. 1678.

---

775. Dorchester Co. Land Records, 4 Old:70, 167.

776. Newman, *Flowering*, 287; Dorchester Co. Land Records, 5 Old:188.

777. Capt. Arthur Clifton Bushey, Jr., "The Barnes Family of Dorchester County, Md." Ms., 1974, at MHS.

778. The marriage of Grace Barnes and therefore her children are not proved by documentary evidence. Grace and her sister Elizabeth were given bequests by the will of their grandfather Walter Waterling in 1672. Grace could not have married John Pritchett, chemist, because he had a wife Abigail by the time of his will dated 19 December 1711, yet six months earlier his alleged wife Grace, styled a widow, bought a 136-acre tract called *Chetall's Lot* in Dorchester County from William Chettle. Therefore, Grace is not the mother of the children listed in Bushey's "The Barnes Family of Dorchester County, Maryland," a 1974 manuscript housed at the Maryland Historical Society, and they are not eligible for membership in The Society of The Ark and The Dove. Note that while a Grace Pritchett existed in 1711, she is not Grace Barnes, daughter of John Barnes. Further research is required to determine her marriage. No pertinent Pritchetts were found in the land records index from 1703 to 1714, nor were any Grace Pritchetts indexed in the abstracts of wills, inventories, or accounts for the period 1700-1711.

13. **Rachel⁴ Asbeston**, daughter of William and Mary Asbeston, married by 8 February 1736/37 **William Thomas**. They had at least one child, named in the will of William Asbeston:⁷⁷⁹

    22. Mary⁵ Thomas.

16. **Thomas⁴ Barnes, Sr.**, twin son of John and Grace (Waterling) Barnes of Dorchester County, was born c1666 and died by 1706. He married **Hannah Willoughby**, daughter of William Willoughby. Hannah was living with her son Charles as late as 1732.

    Children of Thomas and Hannah Barnes:⁷⁸⁰

    23. John⁵ Barnes, d. 1706. John Robson and Charles Baily filed appraisal of his personal estate 1 Nov. 1707. David Macall and John Creeman filed a second appraisal on 2 July 1708, valuing his goods at £25.16.9. Hannah Barnes filed accounting of the estate on 4 March 1708, which showed payments of £6.18.5.⁷⁸¹

    24. Thomas Barnes, b. c1689, styled "of the Freshes," d. after 1726. One son.

    25. Grace Barnes, b. c1690, m. [Matthew?] Gadd, b. c1672, he d. testate by 11 June 1733, naming six children.⁷⁸²

    26. Charles Barnes, of Hollowing Point, Taylor's Island, b. c1691; m. first Mary Meekins, living in 1734, and sister of Mrs. Elizabeth Mace. He may have married second an Elizabeth [-?-] who m. second Peter Bell. He d. by 15 April 1750, leaving ten children.⁷⁸³

    27. Capt. William Barnes, b. c1694, d. after 1777. Two children.⁷⁸⁴

19. **Mary⁴ Barnes**, daughter of John and Grace (Waterling) Barnes, was born in 1672. She married by 1707 **James Pattison**, who was born in 1654 and died in 1747. James Pattison, age 77, deposed between 12 June and 13 August 1739, and again at age c80 between 6 April and 3 June 1732. At age c88 he deposed again about 17 July 1745.⁷⁸⁵ He may be the James Pattison of Dorchester County who married as a first wife by 29 September 1681, Margaret Hall, widow of Walter Hall, who died 1678.⁷⁸⁶

On 3 May 1706 James Pattison of Dorchester County conveyed to Matthew Barnes of the same county, 50 acres of *Pollard's Point*, part of a tract called *Dover*; David Mackall, attorney for wife Mary, acknowledged

779. Md. Wills, 21:774.

780. Bushey, "Barnes Family."

781. Md. Inventories & Accounts, 28:83, 168; 30:163.

782. Md. Wills, 20:668; Md. Administrations, 13:353.

783. Md. Inventories, 43:513; Md. Administrations, 30:233, 31:194; Balances, 1:13, 48.

784. Bushey, "Barnes Family," "Richard Gilbert" ms.

785. Dorchester Co. Land Records, 12 Old:91, 9 Old:68, 14 Old:44.

786. Md. Land Patents, 28:202.

the deed. On 8 September 1739, James and Mary conveyed part of *Armstrong's Quarter* and part of *Dover, Esquire's Chance*, and *Armstrong's Hogpen* to their children Jacob, Elizabeth, William, and Richard. The deed also mentions James Pattison's daughter Anne Hollings of Calvert County.[787]

James Pattison was dead by 10 December 1747 when William Graham and Henry [Toa-?-] signed an appraisal of his personal property valued at £49.8.0, filed on 15 June 1748 by administrator John Pattison; Althan Patison signed as kinsman. On 11 November 1748, payments totalling £15.10.09 were made to Ennalls Hooper, Richard Pattison, John Pattison, Jr., and William Geoghegan.[788]

Children of James and Mary (Barnes) Pattison:
28. Jacob[5] Pattison, b. c1707; one child.
29. Elizabeth Pattison.
30. William Pattison.
31. Richard Pattison, b. c1710.[789]
32. [possibly] Anne Pattison, m. [-?-] Hollings of Calvert Co.

20. **Matthew[4] Barnes**, carpenter, of *Dover*, Taylor's Island, son of John and Grace (Waterling) Barnes, was born c1673 and died by August 1719. He married c1694 **Sarah Lewis**, daughter of Glode Lewis, born 1679 and alive in 1754. She married second [-?-] Murphy.[790] On 3 May 1706 Matthew Barnes bought from James Pattison, his brother-in-law, 50 acres of *Dover*, called *Pollard's Point*.[791]

Matthew Barnes left a personal estate worth £28.0.0, as appraised on 20 August 1719 by John Robson and Giles Williams. David Macall, Hannah Barnes, and Thomas Nevett approved the inventory. Mary Fairbrother, wife of Oliver Fairbrother, filed the administration account on 16 March 1720, which reflected payments made to Margaret Cragg and Thomas Nevitt, but no heirs were named.[792]

On 23 February 1753 the widow Sarah Murphy conveyed to her grandson William Barnes one-half of 25-acre *Sarah's Lot* on Taylor's Island. The tract included the land where William Barnes' father, John,

787. Dorchester Co. Land Records, 6 Old:108, 10 Old:102.
788. Md. Inventories, 36:229; Md. Administrations, 25:233.
789. Dorchester Co. Land Records, 15 Old:483.
790. Bushey, "Barnes Family," ms.
791. Dorchester Co. Land Records, 6 Old:108.
792. Md. Inventories, 3:196; Md. Administrations, 3:337.

lived.[793]

Child of Matthew and Sarah (Lewis) Barnes:[794]

33. John[5] Barnes, planter, b. c1695, d. testate May 1749; m. Elizabeth Pollard, b. 1701, d. after 1754, dau. of Tobias and Jane (Robson) Pollard. 9 children.

21. **John[4] Waterling Barnes**, "merchant of Clemens Bay and Boston," son of John and Grace (Waterling) Barnes, was born in 1678 and died in 1738. He married **Elizabeth** [-?-] who survived him and to whom he left his home in Boston.[795] John was in St. Mary's County in 1713 when he witnessed the will of John Coode.[796]

Children of John Waterling and Elizabeth Barnes:[797]

34. Katharine[5] Barnes.
35. Edward Barnes.
36. John Barnes.
37. Henry Barnes.
38. Elizabeth Barnes.
39. William Barnes.

THOMAS GREENE

1. **Thomas[1] Green(e)**[798] came to Maryland with the *Ark* and the *Dove* expedition in 1634 and died before 23 January 1651/2. He married first **Ann Cox**, who also came on the *Ark* and the *Dove*, and second, by 1647, **Winifred Seybourne**, widow of Nicholas Harvey. She married third 1654 Robert Clarke.[799] Green, a Roman Catholic, was a friend of Father Thomas Copley, and supported the Jesuits against Lord Baltimore. (It is highly unlikely that he was the boatswain who married Millicent Brown on 2 April 1743.[800]) "Mrs. Ann Cox" received a special grant of 500 acres

---

793. Dorchester Co. Land Records, 14 Old:681.

794. Bushey, "Barnes Family," ms.

795. Bushey, "Richard Gilbert," ms.

796. Md. Wills, 14:646.

797. Bushey, "Richard Gilbert," ms.

798. The surname Green is spelled variously Greene in official records.

799. Md. Patents, AB&H:6. In "Thomas Gerard and His Sons-in-Law," by Edwin W. Beitzell, *Md. Historical Magazine*, 46:[1946], 189, the author claims that Anne Gerard was the sister of Richard and Thomas Gerard and came on the *Ark* and *Dove* with her brother Richard, as the widow of [-?-] Cox, but no proof was given for this claim. Walter V. Ball, *John Wheeler, 1630-1693, of Charles County, Maryland, and Some of His Descendants*, hereafter Ball; H: 67,403; *Biographical Dictionary*, 1:373-374.

800. This is surely an error in *Biographical Dictionary*, 1:373; the marriage is not recognized by Newman in *Flowering, 214-216.*

from Lord Baltimore in 1633.[801] Mrs. Winifred Seybourne came into Maryland in 1638.[802] Thomas Green served in the General Assembly from 1637 to 1650, and on 9 June 1647 was appointed Governor by Leonard Calvert, but was superceded by William Stone in 1648, and Green was discharged from all offices in 1650 for usurping authority. He named his plantation *Bobbing* after his ancestral home in Kent.[803]

On 18 November 1650 Green executed a deed of trust, describing himself as a "faithful Christian" and desiring the prayers of the Holy Church; he named his wife Winifred and children Thomas, Leonard, Robert, and Francis Greene, assigning to them his whole estate, to be managed by friends Henry Adams and James Langworth. Winifred was to possess every part of his estate during her natural life, except for 1,000 pounds of tobacco to be delivered to friend Thomas Copley. His sons were to be maintained out of his estate until age 18. At the end of ten years, Winifred was instructed to give the first part of her estate to son Thomas; after 13 years, one-fourth of the estate to son Leonard; after 15 years son Robert was devised one-third of the estate, and at the end of 17 years, son Francis was devised half of the remaining estate. Richard Willen and Alice Smith witnessed the document. He died by 23 January 1651.[804]

Children of Thomas Green by wives Ann Cox and Winifred (Seybourne), the first two probably by Anne:[805]

    2. Thomas[2] Green, b. c1642; d. without issue.
+ 3. Leonard Green, b. c1645.
+ 4. Robert Green, b. c1647.
+ 5. Francis Green, b. c1649.

3. Leonard[2] Green, son of Governor Thomas and probably Ann (Cox) Green, was born c1645, and died in 1688. He married **Anne** [-?-], who married second Charles Evans.[806] Green represented St. Mary's County in the Lower House of the Assembly from 1682 to 1684, and also served as Constable and Deputy Sheriff in St. Mary's County. In 1683 he was

---

801. Md. Patents, AB&H:12, 2:444; called the first wife of Thomas Greene, Esq.

802. Md. Patents, 6:67, 2:346.

803. *Biographical Dictionary*, 1:373-374.

804. Md. Patents, 1:188; *Archives*, 1:83; Semmes, 135; Ball, Wheeler; Robert Barnes, *Baltimore County Families, 1659-1759* (1989).

805. Ball, *Wheeler*; Robert Barnes, *Baltimore Families, 1657-1759* (1989); *Semmes*, 135, and based on the ages of his children cited in his deed of trust, and the fact that they were to claim their inheritances at age 18.

806. *Biographical Dictionary*, 1:373; Charles Co. Land Records, Q1:39; *Semmes*, 138.

appointed to the commission for the advancement of trade in the province.[807]

John Watson and Henry Lawrence, on 16 September 1688, appraised the personal estate of Leonard Green at £238.12.6; three servants were included in the inventory: Ralph Taylor, Thomas Richardson, and Katherine Haveing.[808]

Children of Leonard and Anne Green:[809]

    6. Thomas[3] Green, m. by 22 Feb. 1709 Mildred, widow of William Shircliffe, and d. leaving a will dated 9 Jan. 1749/50, bequeathing his entire estate to his wife. Her will was written three days later, and devised all her real estate to her grandson, Joseph Alvey, but if he died without issue, the land was to pass to her grandson Henry Shircliffe. One shilling was left to her daughter Tecla Green [born Tecla Shircliffe], who married Thomas Green [#10 below]. Mildred also named grandson Henry Miles. Both wills were proved in St. Mary's Co. on 6 Feb. 1749/50.[810]

+   7. Winifred Green, m. Francis Wheeler.
+   8. Mary Green, m. Francis Marbury.
+   9. Margaret Green, m. Joseph Alvey.

4. **Robert[2] Green**, son of Governor Thomas and Winifred (Seybourne) Green, was born in 1647 and was alive in 1713. He married **Mary Boarman**, daughter of William and Sarah Boarman. He may have married second **Katherine Severen**.

Robert Green conveyed 100 acres of *Thompson's Rest* [part of *Green's Inheritance*] to his daughter Mary, wife of John Thompson, on 8 June 1703. Robert's wife Mary acknowledged the deed in open court. On 21 August 1703 they conveyed part of *Green's Inheritance* to Richard Combs. The tract had been patented by Leonard, Robert, and Francis Green. Both Robert and Mary signed by mark.[811] Robert Green may have moved to Culpeper County, Virginia.[812]

Children of Robert and Mary (Boarman) Green:[813]

+ 10. Thomas[3] Green, b. 1683.
+ 11. Elizabeth Green, m. Andrew Simpson.
+ 12. Mary Green, m. John Thompson.

---

807. *Archives*, 7:610.
808. Md. Wills, 4:313; Md. Inventories & Accounts, 10:82.
809. *Biographical Dictionary*, 1:373; Semmes, 138.
810. Md. Wills, 27:187-188.
811. Charles Co. Land Records, Z:24, 70.
812. Ettie Tidwell McCall, *McCall-Tidwell and Allied Families*. Atlanta, 1931, 487.
813. Semmes, 140.

13. Sarah Green, m. Patrick McAtee.
14. Ann Green, m. [-?-] Clark.
15. William Green, b. 28 Dec. 1694. This man has been confused with a William Green, b. 1690, son of Robert of Baltimore Co.[814]
16. Robert Green, d. *s.p.* 1749.
+ 17. James Green, m. Elizabeth Dyer.

5. **Francis² Green**, son of Governor Thomas and Winifred (Seybourne) Green, was born in 1649 and died in 1707, having married **Elizabeth** [-?-]. He died in Charles County leaving a will dated 16 September 1707, proved 7 May 1708, naming his wife Elizabeth and devising to son Leonard 100 acres of 800-acre *Green's Inheritance;* to son Francis: all my land on "the Old Woman's Branch;" to son Giles: the land between Leonard and Francis; and to Clare: personalty. His wife and Leonard were appointed executors; witnessing were William Chandler, Thomas Nation, and John Carment. Elizabeth Green, executrix, filed an account of the administration on 7 August 1707; two inventories of his personal property totaled £230.11.0 and £25.17.5, and payments amounted to £27.17.5.[815]

Children of Francis and Elizabeth Green, born in Charles County:[816]
+ 18. Leonard³ Green, b. 30 May 1691.
19. Verlinda Green, b. 16 Aug. 1692; m. Thomas Sanders.
+ 20. Francis Green, b. 23 April 1694.
+ 21. Clare Green, m. Jacob Clements.
+ 22. Giles Green, b. c1698.

7. **Winifred³ Green**, daughter of Leonard and Ann Green, married **Francis Wheeler**, son of John Wheeler. Francis was born c1670 and died by February 1735/36. In June 1726 he deposed, giving his age as c50, and again in 1730 as between 50 and 60 years.[817]

On 14 October 1718 Francis Wheeler and wife Winifred conveyed 90 acres of *Major's Choice* in Prince George's County to their daughter Mary Noble, wife of Joseph. On 9 November 1730 Francis and Winifred conveyed 70 acres of the same tract to son Leonard, and on 23 February 1731 Francis conveyed 100 acres of *Wheeler's Design* to sons Clement and Ignatius.[818]

---

814. See Barnes, *Baltimore Families,* 276.
815. Md. Wills, 12:132; Md. Inventories & Accounts, 27:50.
816. Charles Co. Church Records: 30; *Semmes,* 142.
817. Ball, 44.
818. Prince George's Co. Land Records, F:220, Q:221, 419.

Francis Wheeler died leaving a will dated 3 November 1735 and proved 18 February 1735/36. He devised part of *Major's Choice* to son William; if William died without issue, the reversionary heir was son Leonard, with reversion to Leonard's son John, and finally to son Francis. Francis was to have the residue of the tract, with reversion to Clement. To son Ignatius was devised 80 acres in *Calvert Manor* near the head of Aqua Creek, with reversion to Leonard's son Ignatius. Also named were granddaughter Mary Noble and daughter Ann Jones. Peter Robinson, Henry Jones, James Johnson, and William Presley witnessed. John Hawkins and William Hawkins valued the personal property at £89.10.3, with William Wheeler and Mary Noble signing as kinsmen. Leonard, Francis, Clement, and Ignatius, the accountants, filed the inventory on 21 May 1736.[819]

Children of Francis and Winifred (Green) Wheeler; births recorded in St. John's Parish:[820]

+ 23. Leonard[4] Wheeler, b. 1691.
+ 24. Mary Wheeler, b. 1693.
+ 25. Charity Wheeler, b. 1699.
+ 26. Francis Wheeler, b. 25 Jan. 1701 (twin).
   27. Winifred Wheeler, b. 25 Jan. 1701 (twin).
   28. William Wheeler, b. 1704; alive in 1755.
+ 29. Clement Wheeler, b. 1706.
+ 30. Ignatius Wheeler, b. 1709.
   31. Ann Wheeler, b. 1712; m. [-?-] Jones.

8. **Mary**[3] **Green,** daughter of Leonard and Ann Green, died 11 February 1713. She married **Francis Marbury,** who married second, Frances Heard on 14 September 1714. They attended King George's Parish Church. Francis was born in England c1661, based on a deposition he made on 2 March 1725 giving his age as 64, and again in June 1726 as c65 years. He was a Justice of the Prince George's County Court in December 1724. He died in Prince George's County in January 1734/35.[821]

He died leaving a will dated 1 January 1734/35 and proved 22 January 1734/35. He named the following children: Leonard, Martha Ann, Susannah, Barbara Frazer, Luke, Lucy Hatton, Mary Ann, Eliza Davidson (wife of John), Tabitha Hoye, Eusebius, Eli, and William. Sons

819. Md. Wills, 21:511; Md. Inventories, 21:340; Md. Administrations, 15:302.

820. Helen W. Brown, *Indexes of Church Registers, 1686-1885* (1979): St. John's Church, King George's Parish, 151-152.

821. King George's Parish, 245; Prince George's Co. Land Records, I:645, M:26.

Leonard and Luke were appointed executors. Two codicils were dated 5 January and 6 January 1734/35. The will was witnessed by Thomas Waller, Francis Hargis, and John Moreis. John Hawkins and Henry Massey appraised the personal property at £566.12.9, with Eaveline Marbury and Eliazer Marbury signing as kinsmen. Leonard and Luke Marbury filed the inventory on 19 April 1735. An administration account was filed on 25 May 1738, showing payments of £484.17.11, to four daughters the [unnamed] wives of Joseph Hatton, John Davidson, James Smallwood, and James Hoy, and Eusebius, William, and Eleazor Marbury. Susanna Marbury was the only legatee under age.[822]

Children of Francis and Mary (Green) Marbury (order uncertain):[823]

32. Elizabeth[4] Marbury, m. John Davidson on 5 Feb. 1732/3 at St. John's Church; he was a schoolmaster, b. c1689 and d. by 5 July 1746.[824] Her father in his will dtd. 1. Jan. 1734/5 named Davidson overseer and devised to Elizabeth *Appledore*.

+ 33. Tabitha Marbury, m. James Hoye.

+ 34. Lucy Marbury, m. Joseph Hatton.

+ 35. Barbara Marbury, m. Daniel Frazer.

36. Leonard Marbury, b. 31 Jan. 1708, m. Penelope [-?-].

+ 37. Luke Marbury, b. 10 March 1710.

+ 38. Mary Ann Marbury, b. 8 Feb. 1713.

9. **Margaret**[3] **Green**, daughter of Leonard and Ann Green, married **Joseph Alvey** of St. Mary's County.[825] Margaret Alvey filed an account of the administration of her husband's estate on 20 July 1729. His personal estate was valued at £83.18.3, with Leonard and Elinor Alvey signing as kinsmen.[826]

Margaret Alvey died leaving a will dated 16 May 1736 and proved 3 June 1746. She named all of her children, appointing son Joseph executor. John Shircliffe and Henry Bryan appraised the estate on 1 July 1746, valuing it at £30.6.1, with Arthur and Elinor Alvey signing as kinsmen. The administration was filed on 3 May 1748, showing payments of £10.6.4.[827]

Children of Joseph and Margaret (Green) Alvey:[828]

822. Md. Wills, 21:309; Md. Inventories, 20:353; Md. Administrations, 16:236.

823. Md. Wills, 23:309.

824. Chancery Records, 8:45; Md. Inventories, 32:294; Md. Administrations, 25:106.

825. Donnelly, *Colonial Settlers*, 28.

826. Md. Inventories, 15:143.

827. Md. Wills, 24:422; Md. Inventories, 33:319; Md. Administrations 24:291.

828. Donnelly, 28.

+ 39. Leonard[4] Alvey.
   40. Joseph Alvey, m. Elizabeth Fenwick.
   41. Arthur Alvey, alive 1749.
   42. Mary Alvey.
   43. Elinor Alvey.
   44. Margaret Alvey, m. George Graves by 1746.[829]

10. Thomas[3] Green, son of Robert and Mary (Boarman) Green, was born in 1683 and died in 1760. He made a deposition on 1 August 1743 giving his age as 60, and mentioning his deceased father Robert Green.[830] He married **Tecla Shircliffe**, who died 1773.

Thomas Green of Charles County died leaving a will dated 27 August 1759 and proved 12 March 1760. He devised to sons Thomas, Nicholas, Ralph, Dudley, Peter, William, and Melchizedek, *Green's Inheritance*, adding that if son Bennett got no part of *Boarman's Manor* [presumably from his grandfather], then he was to share in the devise to the other sons. To wife Tecla and daughter Mary was bequeathed the residue. Witnessing were William Hamilton, Patrick Hamilton, and Henry Simpson. William Comes and Angus McKay valued the personal estate on 10 June 1760 at £104.9.1, from which payments of £9.3.7 were made by Ralph Green, acting executor.[831]

   Children of Thomas and Tecla (Shircliffe) Green:[832]
   45. Bennet[4] Green, b. c1710, living in 1773; m. Anne [-?-]; no known issue.
   46. Thomas Green, m. Henrietta [-?-].
+ 47. Nicholas Green, m. Susannah [-?-].
   48. Ralph or Raphael Green, m. Elizabeth [-?-].
+ 49. Thomas Dudley Green, m. Mary Semmes.
   50. Peter Green, m. Appolonia [-?-].
   51. William Green, m. Eleanor [-?-].
   52. Thomas Melchizedek Green.
   53. Mary Green.
   54. Joseph Green, d. *s. p.*; m. Jane [-?-], who m. (2) Ignatius Simpson.

11. Elizabeth[3] Green, daughter of Robert and Mary (Boarman) Green, died by May 1718; she married **Andrew Simpson** by 9 November 1702.[833] He was born c1665 in Charles County, where he died by December 1744.

---

829. Md. Testamentary Proceedings, 32:109.
830. Charles Co. Land Records, 39:619; *Semmes*, 142.
831. Md. Wills, Md. Inventories, 70:197; Md. Administrations, 57:47.
832. *Semmes*, 150.
833. Charles Co. Land Records, Z2:71, 89.

On 9 November 1702 Robert Green, with acknowledgement by his wife Mary, in consideration that a marriage had taken place between Andrew Simpson and their daughter Elizabeth, conveyed to Simpson 100 acres of land.[834] Elizabeth died by 9 May 1718 when Andrew Simpson entered into a bond with Juliana (Goodrick) Price, widow, whom he was soon to marry. Juliana Simpson, age 63, deposed in November 1745 that she was a daughter of Robert Goodrick and formerly married to Robert Price.[835]

Andrew Simpson died in Charles County, leaving a will dated 2 November 1744 and proved 3 December 1744. He bequeathed personalty to children Thomas, Joseph Green, Ann Clark, Mary, and Clare, and 5 shillings to grandson Jno. Semmes, son of Cleburn Semmes. The residue of his estate was bequeathed to wife Juliana, who was appointed executrix. Witnessing were Jos. Semmes and William Hogan.[836]

Children of Andrew and Elizabeth (Green) Simpson:[837]
+ 55. Thomas[4] Simpson, b. 21 May 1702.
+ 56. Joseph Green Simpson, d. by 1750.
   57. Ann Simpson, m. [-?-] Clark.
   58. [daughter], d. by 1744; m. Cleborne Semmes.
+ 59. Mary Simpson, m. James Semmes.
   60. Clare Simpson.

12. **Mary**[3] **Green**, daughter of Robert and Mary (Boarman) Green, married by 8 June 1703 **John Thompson**. Robert Green conveyed 100 acres of *Thompson's Rest* (part of *Green's Forest*) to his daughter Mary, wife of John Thompson. On 11 August 1713 John and Mary conveyed 183 acres of *Green's Forest* to John Clements, Jr., and William Clements.[838]

John Thompson of Charles County died leaving a will dated 2 March 1733, proved 8 May 1739, which named his sons Thomas, William (father of Joseph), John, and daughters Winifred, Ann, Magdalen, and Susanna. Sons Thomas and William were appointed executors. Witnesses were John Beale, Johanna Beale, and Thomas Morris.[839]

Children of John and Mary (Green) Thompson:
   61. Thomas[4] Thompson.

---

834. Ibid., Z:27.

835. Ibid., H2:173; 40:468.

836. Md. Wills, 23:659. No land was mentioned, suggesting it went to his oldest son by primogeniture customs.

837. *Semmes*, 172, 176-177.

838. *Semmes*, 140; Charles Co. Land Records, Z:24, D2:53.

839. Md. Wills, 22:66.

+ 62. William Thompson, b. c1705-1712.
  63. John Thompson.
  64. Winifred Thompson.
  65. Ann Thompson.
+ 66. Magdalen Thompson, m. Ignatius Hagan.
  67. Susanna Thompson.

17. **James**[3] **Green**, son of Robert and Mary (Boarman) Green, died in 1776. He married first at St. John's at Broad Creek, King George's Parish, on 26 July 1727 **Elizabeth Dyer**, daughter of Patrick and Comfort (Barnes) Dyer. Elizabeth was born 22 January 1711/12 and was living in 1760. Green married second **Eleanor** [-?-].

James Green of Prince George's County died leaving a will dated 15 November 1774 and proved 23 August 1776. He devised *Strife* to his wife for life, then to son Basil; son John was devised 10 acres in Mattawoman Swamp, and to Basil was bequeathed a gun. Eleanor refused the executorship and demanded her thirds; Basil assumed the administration and filed his account on 6 May 1777, citing an inventory of £220.13.7 and payments of £227.19, with distribution to the widow and nine unnamed children.[840]

Children of James Green, at least first seven by Elizabeth (Dyer):[841]

+ 68. Catherine[4] Green, b. 16 Feb. 1729/30.
  69. Mary Green, b. 30 March 1732; m. [-?-] Bowling.
  70. Elizabeth Green, b. 7 May 1734.
  71. Charity Green, b. 5 Oct. 1736.
+ 72. James Green, b. 4 Oct. 1738.
  73. Rebecca Green, b. 4 April 1741.
  74. Thomas Edelen Green, b. 9 March 1755/56, moved to Washington Co., Ky. by 1800.
  75. Basil Green, m. Mary Ann Lanham.
  76. John Green.

18. **Leonard**[3] **Green**, son of Francis and Elizabeth Green, was born 30 May 1691 and died by November 1733. He married first **Mary Sewell**, daughter of John and Anne (Fenwick) Sewell of St. Mary's County.[842] Born in 1694, Mary died soon and Leonard married second, after 4 June 1725, **Prudence (Cooper) Sanders**, widow of Charles and daughter of

---

840. Md. Wills, 41:14; Md. Administrations, 72:429; Balance Books, 7:70.
841. Brown, *Church Records*, 49. Marriage and first seven children recorded there.
842. See #9 Anne[3] (Fenwick) Sewell in Fenwick family above.

Nicholas and Penelope Cooper.[843]

Cuthbert Sewell, by his will proved in St. Mary's County on 7 March 1723/24, devised his interest in *Fenwick Manor, Cuthbert's Fortune,* and *Addition to Cuthbert's Fortune* to his sister Mary Green and appointed Leonard Green executor.[844]

Leonard Green died leaving a will dated 11 October 1733, proved 7 March 1723/24, devising to son Leonard land in St. Mary's County, to sons Cuthbert, John, and Francis land in Charles County, and appointing his wife Prudence executrix. Witnesses were Thomas Sanders, Edward Clements, and Giles Green. Prudence Green left a will, dated 27 September 1757 and proved 21 November 1757. She named her daughters Jane Doyne and Mary Livers, wife of James Livers, and son Francis Green; also grandchildren Ann Livers, Mary Saunders, Jane and Mary Sanders, Mary Simms, and Sarah Doyne. Daughter Mary and son Francis were appointed executors, with Thomas Sanders, John Sanders, and Virlinda Clements witnessing.[845]

Children of Leonard and Mary (Sewell) Green:

+ 77.   Leonard[4] Green.
  78.   Cuthbert Green.
  79.   John Green, d. *s.p.*
  80.   Teresa Green, m. [-?-] Milstead.

Child of Leonard and Prudence (Cooper) Green:

  81.   Francis Green, m. Charity Hagan.

20. **Francis[3] Green**, Jr., son of Francis and Elizabeth Green, was born c1694, according to his deposition made 22 April 1742, declaring his age as 47, and again on 17 April 1749 at age c56;[846] he died in 1761. He married c1711 **Elizabeth Wheeler**, born c1693, daughter of Thomas Wheeler.

Peter Dent appraised Francis Green's personal estate, but no value was recorded. William Clement and Thomas Green signed the inventory as kinsmen, and administrator Leonard Green filed it on 28 March 1761. An account was filed on 11 April 1764 showing payments of £16.3.9. The balance distributed to the unnamed representatives amounted to £54.17.9; they were all of age.[847]

---

843. Prudence Sanders was named in her father's will. Md. Wills, 14:193.

844. Ibid., 18:235.

845. Md. Wills, 20:340, 30:393.

846. Charles Co. Land Records, 39:379.

847. Md. Inventories, 73:103; Md. Administrations, 51:377; Balance Books, 4:55.

Children of Francis and Elizabeth (Wheeler) Green:[848]

   82. Leonard[4] Green, b. 1712; m. Clare [-?-].[849]
   83. Elizabeth Green, b. 1713/14, d. by 1755.
   84. Francis Green, b. 1716; m. Elizabeth [?].[850]
   85. Anastasia Green, b. 1718.
   86. Eleanor Green, b. 1720.
   87. Susanna Green, b. 1722.
+ 88. Ann Green, b. 1724.
+ 89. Henry Green, b. 1726.
   90. Henrietta Green, b. 1728.
+ 91. Benjamin Green, b. 1730.
   92. Ignatius Green, b. 1732.
   93. Clement Green, b. 1735; m. Hannah Thomas.
   94. John Green, b. 1737, m. Elizabeth Bevan.

21. **Clare[3] Green,** daughter of Francis and Elizabeth Green, married **Jacob Clements,** who died in Charles County by November 1755. Jacob Clements died in Charles County leaving a will dated 17 September 1755 and proved 21 November 1755. To wife Clare was devised the plantation *Huckle Berry Garden,* with reversion to son Edward. To sons Jacob and Walter was devised part of *The Reserve,* and to sons John and Charles was devised 100 acres of *Cornwallis' Neck.* Also named were son Francis, daughters Jane, Martha, Clare Sanders, and deceased daughter Elizabeth Wheeler. Wife Clare and son Edward were appointed executors. Witnesses were Joseph Gardner, John Garner, and Thomas McPherson. An account of the administration was filed on 16 March 1758 by executors Charles Clements and Edward Clements [Clare evidently refused] showing an inventory of £912.16.10 and payments of £19.2.11.[851]

   Children of Jacob and Clare (Green) Clements:

   95. Edward[4] Clements, d. unm.; will dtd. 26 March 1764, named brother John Clements, niece Ann Wheeler, and siblings Jacob, Walter, Francis, Hugh, Charles, and Jean [sic] Clements, Clare Saunders and Martha Dyer.[852]
   96. Jacob Clements.
   97. Walter Clements.
   98. John Clements.
   99. Charles Clements.
+ 100. Francis Clements.

---

848. Ball, 29; *Semmes, 148.*
849. Leonard was age 50 on 6 Aug. 1762; Charles Co. Land Records, M3: 56:508.
850. Francis gave his age as 47 on 6 Aug. 1762. Charles Co. Land Records, M3 56:4.
851. Md. Wills, 29:541; Md. Administrations, 41:364.
852. Md. Administrations, 59:416; Md. Wills, 32:276.

+ 101. Martha Clements, m. [-?-] Dyer.
  102. Clare Clements, m. [-?-] Saunders.
+ 103. Elizabeth Clements.
  104. Jane or Jean Clements, evidently d. unm. as her will proved 14 Oct. 1777 named nephews Thomas Dyer and John Clements, nieces Mary and Helen Clements, and Ann Dyer, and sisters Martha Dyer and Clare Sanders; also brothers Walter, Charles, John, and Francis Clements.[853]

22. **Giles**[3] **Green**, son of Francis and Elizabeth Green, was born c1698, based on a deposition he made on 5 July 1762 stating his age as 64.[854] He died in 1792; his wife has not been identified. Giles made a will dated 2 May 1792, proved in Charles County on 18 June 1792. He named his grandson Joseph Green, sons Giles and Charles, grandchildren Elizabeth Green, Sarah Green, and Giles Thomas, daughters Clare Green and Eleanor Macatee, and Leonard Clements. Executors were his sons and grandson Joseph Green [son] of Giles.
  Giles Green was the father of:[855]
  105. Edward[4] Green.
  106. Charles Green, d. *s.p.*
  107. Giles Green, m. Elizabeth Craycroft.
  108. Clare Green.
  109. Eleanor Green, m. [-?-] Macatee.
+ 110. Elizabeth Green, m. Giles Thomas.

23. **Leonard**[4] **Wheeler**, son of Francis and Winifred (Green) Wheeler, was born in 1691 and is probably the man of this name who died in Prince George's County by 1764. He married c1730 **Elizabeth Hanson**, daughter of John and Elizabeth Hanson.[856] He inherited part of *Major's Choice* from his father in 1735 and his sons Ignatius and John were named as reversionary heirs in Francis Wheeler's will.

Leonard died in Prince George's County by 5 January 1764, when Francis King and George Hardey, Jr., appraised his personal estate at £448.7.3, with Leonard Wheeler [not identified] and Elizabeth Wheeler signing as kinsmen. The widow, Elizabeth, administrator, filed an account of the estate on 28 May 1765, showing payments of £52.17.4.[857]

---

853. Charles Co. Wills, AE 6:165.
854. Charles Co. Land Records, M3: 56:214.
855. Charles Co. Wills, AL1:81.
856. Testamentary Proceedings, 40:1.
857. Md. Inventories, 83:145; Md. Administrations, 52:264.

Children of Leonard and Elizabeth (Hanson) Wheeler:[858]
111. Ignatius⁵ Wheeler, b. 23 Jan. 173[?].
112. John Wheeler, named in grandfather's will as second son.
113. Samuel Wheeler, b. 4 Feb. 173[?].
114. George Wheeler, b. 3 Dec. 173[?].
115. Edward Wheeler, b. 10 Oct. 1738.

24. Mary⁴ Wheeler, daughter of Francis and Winifred (Green) Wheeler, was born in 1693 and married **Joseph Noble** on 2 December 1708. A son of Joseph and Catherine Noble, he was born in Cockermouth, Cumberland, England, on 17 April 1689 and died 14 December 1749. Joseph Noble of Prince George's County, gentleman, gave his age as c41 in 1730.[859] On 14 October 1718, Francis and Winifred Wheeler conveyed 90 acres of *Major's Choice* to their daughter Mary, wife of Joseph Noble.

Joseph Noble, Sr., of Prince George's County, died leaving a will dated 6 December 1747 and proved 15 January 1749/50, devising to wife Mary 3 acres of *Littleworth* in St. John's Town, then to son John, he paying son William £5 annually. Other children named were Joseph, Francis, Catherine, Salome, Mary and granddaughter Mary Eleanor Hawkins. Wife Mary was appointed executrix, who agreed to abide by the will, which was witnessed by Jn° Hawkins, Richard Tubman, Jn° Hawkins, Jr., and Priscilla Hawkins. On 26 May 1750 John Hawkins, Jr., and Luke Marbury appraised the estate at £559.13.5. The inventory was approved by John Baynes and Anne Cunning, creditors, and by Joseph Noble and Francis Noble, kinsmen. The document was filed on 26 May 1750. The executrix filed an account on 9 March 1750/51, citing payments of £133.17.4, and naming the children of the deceased: Joseph, Francis, John, and William Noble, Elizabeth Stockett, Catherine Noble, and Mary Baynes.[860]

Children of Joseph and Mary (Wheeler) Noble, recorded at St. John's Church, some dates illegible:[861]
116. Sarah⁵ Noble, b. 8 Nov. 1709; m. 13 May [17-?], William Hawkins.

---

858. St. John's Church Register, 151.

859. Henry Peden, *Maryland Deponents, 1634-1799*, 139; Prince George's Co. Land Records, F:110. Elise Greenup Jourdan in her "Wade Family" states that Mary Wheeler married Zachariah Wade, who died in 1744/5, without documentation. *Early Families*, 4:223.

860. Md. Wills, 27:141; Md. Inventories, 43;105; Md. Administrations, 29:222.

861. Brown, *St. John's Church*, 100-101.

117. Elizabeth Noble, b. 3 May 1712; may have m. (1) [-?-] Luckett, but definitely m. by 1748 Thomas Stockett.[862]
118. Joseph Noble, b. 15 April 1715; m. 5 March 1738/9 Martha Tarvin.
119. Francis Noble, b. 27 Dec. 1719.
120. Catherine Noble, b. 14 Nov. 1721.
121. Salome Noble, b. 23 April 1724; m. by 1750 James Edelen.
122. Mary Noble, b. 31 May 1727; m. 20 Aug. 1749 John Bayne(s).[863]
123. John Noble, b. 5 Feb. 1732.
124. William Fraser Noble, b. 8 Nov. 1735.

25. **Charity**[4] **Wheeler**, daughter of Francis and Winifred (Green) Wheeler, was born in 1699 and died between 1729 and 1735. She married **George Noble** on 27 January 1719/20. George Noble, gentleman, of Prince George's County gave his age as 40 in 1730, placing his date of birth as c1690.[864] He died 14 September 1735, leaving a will dated 6 September 1735, proved 24 November 1735, devising to sons Thomas and George 600 acres bought of Daniel Dulany and 400 acres in Piscataway Manor. To daughters Elizabeth and Anne were devised 300-acre parts of 1000-acre *St. John's Manor*, and lands lying in the Back Woods [Frederick County]: *Wett Work, Spring Garden, Addition, Dry Work*. To son Thomas was bequeathed the house and garden in Roper Lane, White Haven. To son John was devised *Chance* in Swan Neck, but if Thomas and George died without issue, Elizabeth and Ann were named as reversionary heirs to *Chance*. To these five children was bequeathed the entire personal estate, and they were to be under the care of the executors, John Addison and John Abingdon, while minors. Because of the minor children, the estate was not settled until 1756, when the youngest child came of age. On 19 March 1756, John Addison, executor, filed an account showing assets of £1413.10.5, and named only son Thomas and daughter Ann, wife of Zachariah Wade. A distribution of the balance of £470.8.0 to the unnamed representatives was recorded on 31 March 1760.[865]

Children of George and Charity (Wheeler) Noble, all baptized at St. John's Church, some entries incomplete:[866]
125. John[5] Noble, b. 3 Sept. [c1720].
126. Elizabeth Noble, b. 23 Jan. 1722; d. 17 Sept. 1735.

---

862. Prince George's Co. Administrations, DD:41.
863. Md. Wills, 27:141, 34:193; Md. Administrations, 29:222.
864. Peden, *Deponents,*
865. Md. Wills, 21:483; Md. Administrations, 39:80; Balance Books, 3:11.
866. Brown, *Church Records,* 100-101.

127. Anne Noble, b. 16 Feb. 1725/26; m. 3 Nov. [by 1756] Zachariah Wade.
128. Thomas Noble, b. 19 April 1727; d. by June 1762; poss. m. Mary Ann Wade, dau. of Zachariah Wade.[867]
129. George Noble, b. 16 Jan. 1729; d. by May 1761; m. Elizabeth [-?-].

26. Francis[4] Wheeler, twin son of Francis and Winifred (Green) Wheeler, was born 25 January 1701 and was baptized at St. John's Church in King George Parish. Before 1747 he married **Elizabeth** [-?-].
    Child of Francis and Elizabeth Wheeler:
130. Samuel[5] Wheeler, b. 9 April 1747.

29. Clement[4] Wheeler, son of Francis and Winifred (Green) Wheeler, was born in 1706 and died in 1750. He married on 5 February 1732/33 **Elizabeth Edelen**, daughter of Christopher and Jane (Jones) Edelen, born 10 October 1708 at St. John's Church.[868] She filed an account of the administration of his estate on 9 March 1750, showing an inventory value of £120.16.5 and payments of £12.15.9. The children named were: Catherine, Henry, Clement, and Susanna Wheeler.
    Children of Clement and Elizabeth (Edelen) Wheeler:
131. Catherine[5] Wheeler, b. 25 July 1734; m. 20 April 1767 Charles Lansdale.
132. Susanna Wheeler, b. 2 Jan. 1735.
133. Clement Wheeler, b. 13 March 1737.
134. Henry Wheeler, b. by 1750.

30. Ignatius[4] Wheeler, son of Francis and Winifred (Green) Wheeler, was born on 14 October 1709 and died in 1771. He married at St. John's, King George Parish, Prince George's County, on 29 July 1753 **Elizabeth Marbury**, daughter of Francis Marbury.[869] On 4 January 1771 Thomas Marshall and Kenelm Truman Stoddert appraised the personal estate of Ignatius Wheeler at £516.13.10, with Ignatius Wheeler, Jr. and George Noble Wheeler signing as kinsmen; the inventory was filed on 28 March 1771. Hezekiah Wheeler filed an account on 10 December 1771, listing payments of £3.10.0 and a second account on 23 March 1774 of £12.9.3. A final distribution of £634.13.2 was made on 23 March 1774 to heirs "unknown to this office."[870]

---

867. Charles Co. Land Records, CC 2:217.
868. St. John's Church, 38; Md. Wills, 38:524.
869. St. John's Church, 38; Md. Wills, 38:524.
870. Md. Inventories, 106:165; Md. Administrations, 66:220, 68:336; Balance Books, 6:270.

The Ark and the Dove Adventurers

Children of Ignatius and Elizabeth (Marbury) Wheeler, all baptized at
St. John's Church:
135. Luke Marbury[5] Wheeler, b. 24 July 1754.
136. Eleanor Wheeler, b. 28 Dec. 1756.
137. Elizabeth Wheeler, b. 28 Dec. 1759.
138. Ignatius Wheeler, b. 9 Sept. 1763.
139. George Wheeler, b. 1 Aug. 1768.

33. **Tabitha[4] Marbury**, daughter of Francis and Mary (Green) Marbury,
was born in Prince George's County in 1706 and died there on 15
November 1761. In his will dated 1 January 1733/34 her father devised
Tewkesbury and 65-acre *Apple Hill* to her.[871] She married first **James
Hoye**, who was born in 1701 and died in September 1737. Tabitha
married second on 9 February 1738 **William Deakins, Sr.**, who died in
Bladensburg, Maryland, on 22 November 1800.
Child of James and Tabitha (Marbury) Hoye:
140. Paul[5] Hoye, b. 26 March 1736; d. Washington Co. 13 Oct. 1816; m. in 1762
Mariam Fuller, b. 1734 Stafford Co., Va., d. Washington Co. 18 Nov. 1811.
Children of William and Tabitha (Marbury) Deakins:
141. Francis Deakins, b. 12 Nov. 1739; d. 28 Dec. 1804 Washington, D.C.; m.
Eleanor Threlkeld, widow.
142. Leonard Deakins, b. 9 March 1747; d. Georgetown 8 June 1824; m. Deborah
Mauduit Duke, b. Nov.1778, d. 12 Nov. 1846.

34. **Lucy[4] Marbury**, daughter of Francis and Mary (Green) Marbury,
married on 17 October 1710 **Joseph Hatton**, son of William and Mary
Hatton, at St. John's Church, Prince George's County. He was born
c1690, giving his age as c52 in 1742. He died by November 1747. He was
a member of the St. John's Parish vestry from 1713 to 1715.[872]
Joseph Hatton died in Prince George's County leaving a will dated 1
December 1737 and proved 14 November 1747. To wife Lucy he
bequeathed one-third of his personal estate and 100 acres given to him
by his mother Mary Hatton; he also named his father William Hatton
and a sister Penelope Middleton. To son Joseph he devised 400 acres on
Cowpen Branch; to sons Nathaniel and Richard were each devised a 200-
acre part of the home plantation. Also mentioned were daughters Mary
and Elizabeth, and son Joshua. Wife Lucy was appointed executrix, with
John Fraser, Mary Whitmore, and Margaret Whitmore witnessing. Lucy

---

871. Md. Wills, 23:309.
872. Parish register, 88; *Biographical Dictionary*, 1:423.

filed an account on 1 March 1748, showing assets of £483.17.2 and payments of £534.3.1. The following heirs received equal shares: Joseph, Mary, Nathaniel, Elizabeth, and Richard Hatton, with the balance distributed to the widow and to John Hatton, a minor.[873]

Children of Joseph and Lucy (Marbury) Hatton, recorded St. John's Church:[874]

143. Mary[5] Hatton, b. 19 April 1713, d. young.
144. Mary Hatton, b. 25 Dec. 1715.
145. William Hatton, b. 13 April 1718.
146. Joseph Hatton, b. 3 June 1721; m. Mary [-?-].
147. Nathaniel Hatton, b. 3 March 1723.
148. Richard Hatton, b. 2 Aug. 1726.
149. Joshua Hatton.
150. Elizabeth Penelope Hatton, b. 16 [-?-] 1729.
151. John Hatton, b. 9 Aug. 173[?].

35. **Barbara[4] Marbury**, daughter of Francis and Mary (Green) Marbury, married **Daniel Frazer** by 14 August 1725. Their children were all baptized at St. John's Parish:

152. Daniel[5] Frazer, b. 14 Aug. 1725; m. Elizabeth [-?-].
153. [possibly] Elizabeth Frazer, b. 11 July 1728.
154. [possibly] William Frazer, b. 15 June 1731.

37. **Luke[4] Marbury**, son of Francis and Mary (Green) Marbury, was born 10 March 1710[875] and died in October 1758 in Prince George's County. He married c1740 **Elizabeth Beans**. On 3 June 1737 Eusebius, Eliazer, and Luke Marbury sold to John Dawson 227-acre *Mistake*. On 2 March 1740, Luke and wife Elizabeth sold a 100-acre part of *Apple Hill* to Joseph Newton.[876]

On 30 November 1759, Francis King and Smallwood Coghill appraised the personal estate of Luke Marbury at £611.7.5, with William Marbury and Elizabeth Davison signing as kinsmen. The inventory included "things gave to Ignatius Wheeler in Mr. Marbury's lifetime," including a woman Pegg, feather bed, 400 pounds of pork, and two sows with pig. Elizabeth Marbury filed the inventory on 30 May 1759, and filed the

873. Md. Wills, 25:159-161; Md. Administrations, 26:27; Md. Inventories, 35:493.

874. St. John's Parish records, 239, 249, 252, 260 (57 in Brown).

875. About 1742 he made a deposition giving his age as c32. Prince George's Co. Land Records, Y:654.

876. Prince George's Co. Land Records, T:465, Y:143.

account on 21 August 1760, showing payments of £188.6.3. The final balance of £867.5.8 was distributed on 21 August 1760, representatives unknown to Prerogative Court office. In another distribution made 25 June 1761, with a balance of £678.19.5, and William and Colmore Beanes as sureties, the distribution was: one-third to the widow and the balance to three children.[877]

Only known child of Luke and Elizabeth (Beans) Marbury:

155. Luke[5] Marbury, b. 1745; d. Prince George's Co. 1809; m. first cousin Elizabeth Beanes, dau. of William Beanes.[878]

38. Mary Ann[4] Marbury, daughter of Francis and Mary (Green) Marbury, married **Matthew Smallwood**, son of James Smallwood (who died in 1723). On 19 February 1739 Matthew and Mary sold the tract *School House*, which Francis Marbury had devised to Mary, to Smallwood Coghill of Prince George's County.[879]

Matthew Smallwood died leaving a will dated 5 November 1760, proved in Charles County on 4 January 1764. He devised the tract *Friendship* to his son Beane, and also named children Priscilla, Philip, and James. Son Beane, daughter Priscilla, and Joshua Harris were appointed executors. Harris and Priscilla filed an account on 6 April 1765, showing an inventory of £324.7.3 and payments of £269.9.4; a second account with payments of £32.3.3. was filed on 17 September 1768. The balance of £92.17.1 was distributed on 17 September 1768 to the children named in the will plus Francis Green, Martha, and Benjamin equally.[880]

Children of Matthew and Mary (Marbury) Smallwood:[881]

156. Beane[5] Smallwood, living 14 Aug. 1771 when he and wife Mary sold 100-acre *Friendship* to Philip Thomas.
157. Philip Smallwood, b. c1744.
158. Priscilla Smallwood, b. c1746.
159. Francis Green Smallwood, b. c1753.
160. Martha Smallwood, b. c1756.
161. Benjamin Smallwood, b. c1759.
162. James Smallwood.

---

877. Md. Inventories, 66:198; Md. Administrations, 46:88; Balance Books, 3:36, 74.
878. Prince George's Co. Revolutionary Pensions, 204.
879. Arthur L. Keith, "Smallwood Family of Charles County,", *Md. Genealogies*, 2:325-372. Prince George's Co. Land Records, Y:127.
880. Md. Wills, 31:1074; Md. Administrations, 53:39, 58:319; Balance Books, 5:118, 4:119.
881. Keith, 346.

39. Leonard⁴ Alvey, son of Joseph and Margaret (Green) Alvey, died 13 January 1774. He married **Jane** [-?-], who died 24 May 1770.

Children of Leonard and Jane Alvey:[882]

 163. James⁵ Alvey, b. 10 April 1737.
 164. Arthur Alvey.
 165. Thomas Green Alvey, moved to Perry Co., Ind.
 166. Joseph Alvey, moved to Washington Co., Ky.
 167. Travis Alvey.
 168. John F. Alvey, moved to Union Co., Ky.
 169. Robert Alvey, moved to Union Co., Ky.

47. Nicholas⁴ Green, son of Thomas and Tecla (Shircliffe) Green, died by March 1802. He married **Susannah** [-?-]. Nicholas left a will dated in Charles County 31 July 1800, proved 16 March 1802, naming son Solomon, and daughters Dorothy, Eleanor, and Mary.[883]

Children of Nicholas and Susannah Green:

 170. Solomon⁵ Green.
 171. Dorothy Green.
 172. Eleanor Green.
 173. Mary Green.

49. Thomas Dudley⁴ Green, son of Thomas and Tecla (Shircliffe) Green, was born in 1726 and died 22 September 1794 in Baltimore. In 1765 he married **Mary Simms**, born March 1747, daughter of Alexius and Verlinda Simms.[884]

Children of Thomas and Mary (Simms) Green:

 174. Jesse⁵ Green, b. 1766; d. Georgetown, Del., 21 Aug. 1834; m. 1797 Betsy [Gunby?], b. Snow Hill 1 June 1766, d. 1862.[885]
 175. Sarah Green, b. 14 June 1767.
 176. Thomas Green, b. 25 Dec. 1768, d. young.
 177. Catherine Green, b. 1770.
 178. Bennett Green, b. 5 June 1772, d. young.
 179. Teasley Green, b. 24 April 1776, d. young.
 180. Winifred Green, b. 11 Jan. 1778.
 181. Thomas Green, b. 2 Jan. 1781.
 182. Mary Green, b. 18 Jan. 1783.

---

882. Donnelly, 28, cites *The Chronicles of St. Mary's County*, 23:11-13.
883. Charles Co. Wills, AL12:350.
884. *Semmes*, 152.
885. Application #621 cites a General Jesse Green manuscript at Delaware Archives, and cemetery plot at Seaford, Del.

55. Thomas⁴ Simpson, son of Andrew and Elizabeth (Green) Simpson, was born 21 May 1702 and died on 14 December 1761. He married **Mary Wilson**, daughter of Alexander Wilson.
Child of Thomas and Mary (Wilson) Simpson:
    183. Ignatius⁵ Simpson, b. 1706; d. Charles Co. 1793; m. Ann Semmes.

56. Joseph Green⁴ Simpson, son of Andrew and Elizabeth (Green) Simpson, may have been born in Culpeper County, Virginia, and died by 1750.[886] He married on 28 August 1737 **Elizabeth (Keech) Alder**, widow of George Alder.[887] She died in Prince George's County by 21 November 1786.
An account of the administration of the estate of Joseph Green Simpson of Prince George's County was filed on 23 December 1751 by the widow, administratrix, showing an inventory of £137.13.3 and payments of £199.10.10. The heirs of George Alder, former husband of Elizabeth, were mentioned. Of the children of the deceased named, the eldest being ten years old, were: Thomas, John, Sarah, and Andrew Simpson.[888]
Children of Joseph Green and Elizabeth (Keech) Simpson:
    184. Thomas⁵ Simpson.
    185. John Simpson.
    186. Sarah Simpson, b. Culpeper Co., Va. c1742; m. Sampson Bobo, b. c1735 La Rochelle, France, d. 17 April 1804 Spartenburg, S. C.[889]
    187. Andrew Simpson, [possibly] m. Elizabeth [-?-].

59. Mary⁴ Simpson, daughter of Andrew and Elizabeth (Green) Simpson, married **James Semmes** II who died in Charles County in 1787. He had married first Anne Barnes, by whom he had a son Ignatius Semmes.[890] James Semmes owned *Semmes' Amendment* and *Amendment*. In 1778 he subscribed to the Oath of Fidelity in Charles County. He died leaving a will dated 1 April 1785 and proved 26 February 1787, in which he named his wife Mary, sons Joseph (appointed executor) and Thomas, and grandson Joseph Semmes. Ignatius Adams, James Dunnington, and Rhoda Maddox witnessed.[891]

---

886. Ettie Tidwell, *McCall-Tidwell and Allied Families* (Atlanta: 1931), 485.
887. Prince George's Co. Land Records, 17:80.
888. Md. Administrations, 32:64.
889. McCall, 486.
890. *Semmes,* 48.
891. Charles Co. Wills, 9:332.

Children of James and Mary (Simpson) Semmes:

188. Joseph[5] Semmes, b. c1752; d. Charles Co. 1826; m. Henrietta Thompson, b. 13 Jan. 1755, d. Charles Co. 27 May 1833, dau. Richard and Henrietta (Boarman) Thompson.

189. Thomas Semmes, b. 1754; d. Wilkes Co., Ga. 14 June 1824; m. 1779 Mary Ann (Ratcliffe) Brawner.

190. Andrew Green Semmes.

191. James Semmes, officer of the Maryland Line.

62. William[4] Thompson, son of John and Mary (Green) Thompson, was born between 1705 and 1710. He made two contradictory depositions regarding his age: on 1 August 1743 he said he was 38, but on 6 August 1762 he gave his age as 50, stating that his father was John Thompson.[892] His wife is unknown.

He left a will dated 29 April 1767 and proved the same year in Charles County, naming his children James, who was devised the dwelling plantation, with reversion to son Leonard, Joseph, Ignatius, Elizabeth, plus a granddaughter Elender Thompson. Leonard and Elizabeth Thompson, executors, filed an account on 1 March 1769, showing an inventory of £278.82 and payments of £319.7.7. After the legatees were paid, the balance was distributed among all the children, who, besides those named above, were Appolonia, Mary, and Susanna, all of age.[893]

Children of William Thompson by unknown wife:

192. James[5] Thompson, d. 1795 Charles Co.; m. 17 Sept. 1786 Ann Prudence Wills.[894]

193. Joseph Thompson.

194. Ignatius Thompson.

195. Elizabeth Thompson.

196. Leonard Thompson.

197. Appolonia Thompson.

198. Mary Thompson.

199. Susannah Thompson.

66. Magdalen[4] Thompson, daughter of John and Mary (Green) Thompson, died in Frederick County after 1774. She married **Ignatius Hagan** who died in Charles County in 1765, leaving a will dated 25 March 1761 and proved 15 October 1765. He appointed his wife executrix and named children William, Thomas, Joseph, James, Mary,

---

892. Charles Co. Land Records, F3 50:299, 486, M3 56:3, 56:528.

893. Md. Wills, 36:39.

894. Mary Louise Donnelly, *Arnold Livers Family in America*, 51.

Sarah Hagan, Elizabeth Speak, Eleanor Wheeler, and Ann Blanford. James Hagan, Ignatius Smith, and Bazil Hagan witnessed. On 26 November 1765 Joshua Sanders and Richard Belen valued Hagan's personal property at £256.8.0. William Thompson [*sic*] Hagan, signed as kinsman. Magdalen Hagan filed the inventory on 10 November 1766. After all accounts were settled, there was a balance due the estate of £279.14.0 which was distributed to the legatees: James, Mary, and Sarah Hagan, Elizabeth Speak, Eleanor Wheeler, and Ann Blanford on 8 January 1768.[895]

Children of Ignatius and Magdalen (Thompson) Hagan:
200. William[5] Hagan, d. Nelson Co., Ky., by 1800; m. Mildred [-?-].
201. Thomas Hagan.
202. Joseph Hagan.
203. James Hagan.
204. Mary Hagan.
205. Sarah Hagan.
206. Elizabeth Hagan, m. [-?-] Speak.
207. Eleanor Hagan, m. [-?-] Wheeler.
208. Ann Hagan, m. [-?-] Blanford.

68. **Catherine[4] Green**, daughter of James and Elizabeth (Dyer) Green, was born 16 February 1729/30. She married by 1748 **Basil Spalding**, born c1715, died 26 September 1791, son of John Spalding. He had married first Catherine Edelen, daughter of Thomas and Comfort (Barnes) Edelen, but this couple apparently had no children.[896]

Basil Spalding died leaving a will dated 12 September 1791 and proved 5 March 1792. He named his wife Catherine and the following children: Ann, Christianne Young, William, Elizabeth Elder, James, Basil, Edward, and Hilary.[897]

Children of Basil and Catherine (Green) Spalding:
209. Henry[5] Spalding, d. 19 Feb. 1816; m. 1771 Anne Edelen, b. 1746, d. 17 Jan. 1806; both buried St. Joseph Cemetery, Taneytown, Md.
210. John Spalding, b. 1752; d. 1820; m. Anne Bowling.
211. Elizabeth Spalding, b. 1754; d. 30 Aug. 1848 Nelson Co., Ky.; m. Thomas H. Elder, b. 4 Jan. 1748 Frederick Co., Md., d. 27 Dec. 1832 Nelson Co., Ky.
212. William Spalding, b. 1755; d. 1803; m. Mary Lilly.
213. Catherine Spalding, m. [-?-] Young.

---

895. Md. Wills, 33:421, Md. Inventories, 94:252; Balance Books, 5:68.

896. Charles Thomas Roland, *The John Basil Spalding-Miranda Roland Family of Prince George's County.* 1982.

897. Charles Co. Will Book, AK 1:64, asbstracted in *DAR Magazine* 61:856.

214. James Spalding, d. by 1801; m. Mary Edelen.
215. Basil Spalding, Jr., d. 1828 in Charles Co.; m. Teresa (Clements?) Brawner, widow.
216. Edward Spalding.
217. George Hilary Spalding, b. 10 Feb. 1770; d. 1820; m. Elizabeth Marbury Hargroves.
218. Ann Spalding.
219. Christianne Spalding.
220. Mary Elizabeth Spalding, m. Joseph Sansbury by Prince George's Co. license dated 30 Nov. 1798.
221. Raphael Spalding, d. in father's lifetime, leaving one daughter: Mother Catherine, founder of Nazareth in Ky.

72. **James⁴ Green**, son of James and Elizabeth (Dyer) Green, was born 4 October 1738 and died by 10 August 1777, when his personal estate was appraised. He married Elizabeth [-?-], possibly married by 1760 **Elizabeth Edelen**, daughter of Comfort Edelen of Prince George's County.[898]

Children of James and Elizabeth Green:
222. Terry⁵ Green.
223. James Ramon Green.
224. Mary Elizabeth Green.

77. **Leonard⁴ Green**, son of Leonard and Mary (Sewell) Green, died in Charles County in 1755. His wife's name is not known and she may have died before he made his will.[899] Of Charles County, he died leaving a will dated 18 April 1755 and proved 28 April 1755. To his eldest son Leonard was devised 100-acre part of *Phoenix Manor* in St. Mary's County and 75-acre part of *Green's Inheritance* in Charles County. The residue of the latter tract, plus 100-acre part of *St. Matthew's*, and 18-acre part of *The Mount*, were divided among his son Robert and brothers Cuthbert and Francis. Personalty was bequeathed to children Leonard, Robert, Martha, and Mary Ann Sewell, with Joseph Doyne appointed executor. Thomas Hussey Luckett, John Gates, and Thomas McPherson witnessed. John Theobald and Richard Gambra valued the personal estate on 22 May 1755 at £231.8.3, with Frances and Giles Gilbert signing as kinsmen on 17 September 1755. Robert and Jean [*sic*] Doyne filed an account on 29 August 1759 listing payments of £273.1.11.[900]

---

898. Prince George's Co. Wills, 1:513.
899. Semmes, 155.
900. Md. Wills, 29:372; Md. Inventories, 61:115; Md. Administrations, 44:41.

Children of Leonard Green:

225. Benedict[5] Leonard Doyne Green, d. intestate in 1777.
226. Robert Green.
227. Martha Green.
228. Mary Ann Sewell Green.
229. Joseph Green, devised 170-acre *Doyne's Range* by uncle Joshua Green.

88. **Ann[4] Green**, daughter of Francis and Elizabeth (Wheeler) Green, was born in 1724 and married **Patrick Hamilton**, who was born c1717 and died in Charles County in 1790. Patrick Hamilton deposed, age 45, on 6 August 1762, in a case involving Francis Green, who was living five or six years ago, but was now deceased.[901]

Children of Patrick and Ann (Green) Hamilton:

230. Lt. Edward[5] Hamilton, b. 4 June 1762; d. Charles Co. 27 May 1824; m. 19 Jan. 1796 Eleanor Hawkins, b. 16 April 1778, d. 13 Nov. 1807.[902]
231. Elizabeth Hamilton, d. Charles Co. 22 April 1824; m. George Macatee.

89. **Henry[4] Green**, son of Francis and Elizabeth (Wheeler) Green, was born 1726 and died in Harford County in 1797. He married **Elizabeth Wheeler**, daughter of Benjamin Wheeler and widow of David Thomas, who died in 1746.

Henry Green died leaving a will dated 10 April 1795 and proved 16 May 1797. He named his daughter Ann, wife of Bennett Bussey; grandchildren Mary, wife of Henry Cooper, and Elizabeth, Martha, Sarah, and Susannah Green, devising to the grandchildren all the land he had bought from Benjamin Butterworth. Bennett Bussey and Henry Cooper, Jr. were appointed executors, with David Cook, James Denning, and John Love witnessing.[903]

Children of Henry and Elizabeth (Wheeler) Green:[904]

232. Leonard[5] Green, b. 1748; d. by 1797; m. c1776 Elizabeth Wheeler, b. Baltimore [now Harford] Co.
233. Ann Green, m. Bennett Bussey of Harford Co.

91. **Benjamin[4] Green**, son of Francis and Elizabeth (Wheeler) Green, was born 15 January 1730/31 in Charles County and died 16 April 1808 in Harford County. He married **Elizabeth Thomas**, born 14 September 1736 in Charles County and died 23 November 1803 in Baltimore County,

---

901. Charles Co. Land Records, M3 56:4.
902. Application #298 cites a Hamilton Bible, NSDAR Library.
903. Harford Co. Wills, AJ 2:261.
904. Ball, 84.

daughter of David and Elizabeth (Wheeler) Thomas.[905]

Benjamin Green took the Oath of Fidelity in Charles County in 1778 and served as a substitute in the Continental Army for nine months. He died leaving a will dated 4 April 1808 in Harford County and proved 26 April 1808, appointing sons Benjamin and Clement as executors. Other children named were Henrietta, Leonard, Eleanor Bevan, Ann Croskery, Sarah, and Teresa Wheeler, plus grandchildren Michael and Francis Wheeler.[906]

Children of Benjamin and Elizabeth (Thomas) Green, order uncertain:[907]

234. Henrietta[5] Green.
235. Sarah Green, d. unmarried.
236. Leonard Green, m. Mary Wheeler, dau. of Benjamin Wheeler.
237. Eleanor Green, m. Edward Bevan; to Ky. in 1793.
238. Ann Green, m. Bernard Croskery.
239. Clement Green, d. March 1829; m. Rebecca Todd.
240. Benjamin Green, d. Harford Co. March 1820; m. Mary Reynolds, b. Del. 1781.
241. Elizabeth Green, b. c1761; d. 8 Feb. 1802 Harford Co.; m. Benjamin Wheeler.
242. Teresa Green.

100. **Francis[4] Clements**, son of Jacob and Clare (Green) Clements, died about 2 March 1758 in Charles County. He married **Elizabeth Saunders**, who died in 1777. Francis Clements died leaving a will dated 2 March 1758 and proved 16 August 1758. To wife Elizabeth he devised his dwelling plantation, 100-acre *Reformation*. To sons George and John were devised *Saint Matthews* and *Clement's Addition*. Sons Francis, Thomas, and Henry were also given land. Also named were daughters Mary and Martha, with wife Elizabeth appointed executor. Thomas McPherson, Edward Clements, and John Maccatee witnessed the will. The executors, Elizabeth and George Clements [*sic*] filed an account of the administration on 1 September 1759, which showed assets of £530.2.8, from which payments of £82.3.5 were deducted.[908]

Elizabeth (Sanders) Clements died by 18 March 1773 when her executor, George Clements, with John Clements [son] of James, and Thomas Clements, sureties, distributed a balance of £469.7.2. Legatees

---

905. *The Raskob-Green Record Book*, 1921.
906. Harford Co. Wills, AJ C:186.
907. *The Raskob-Green Record Book*.
908. Md. Wills, 30:590; Md. Administrations, 44:367, 47:188.

were: Henry and Thomas Clements, daughter Martha Hilling, George Clements, Mary Smith, goddaughters Tracey Clements, Mary Edelen, Mildred Mudd, and son John. The balance was distributed equally among John, Thomas, and Henry Clements, Henrietta Dyer, and Priscilla Edelen.[909]

Children of Francis and Elizabeth (Saunders) Clements:

243. Henrietta[5] Clements, b. c1722; d. Prince George's Co. 7 Jan. 1777; m. Thomas Dyer, b. King George's Parish 12 Dec. 1715, son of Patrick and Comford Dyer.

244. George Clements.

245. John Clements.

246. Francis Clements, d. Charles Co. with will dtd. 11 June 1760, naming brothers Thomas and Henry who were devised the land left him by his father, and bequests to his mother, brothers George and John (still minors), and sisters Mary and Martha Clements, Henrietta Dyer, Benedicta Mudd, Priscilla Edelen, and Elizabeth Mudd.[910]

247. Thomas Clements.

248. Henry Clements.

249. Mary Clements, m. [-?-] Edelen.

250. Martha Clements, m. [-?-] Hilling.

251. Priscilla Clements, m. by 1760 [-?-] Edelen.

252. Benedicta Clements, m. [-?-] Mudd.

253. Elizabeth Clements, m. [-?-].

101. **Martha[4] Clements**, daughter of Jacob and Clare (Green) Clements, married [-?-] **Dyer**. She was the mother of the following children, named in the will of her sister Jane Clements:

254. Thomas[5] Dyer.

255. Ann Dyer.

103. **Elizabeth[4] Clements**, daughter of Jacob and Clare (Green) Clements, died in 1767; she married **Benjamin Wheeler**.

Child of Benjamin and Elizabeth (Clements) Wheeler:

256. Jacob[5] Wheeler, b. 1712; d. Baltimore Co. by July 1799; m. Ann [-?-].

110. **Elizabeth[4] Green**, daughter of Giles Green, died in 1767. She married first **Giles Thomas** and second [-?-] **Jenkins**.

Child of Giles and Elizabeth (Green) Thomas:

257. Giles[5] Thomas, b. Baltimore Co. 30 Nov. 1763; d. Blacksburg, Va. 21 March 1842; m. Ann (Nancy) Wheeler.

---

909. Balance Books, 6:280.

910. Bowie, *Across the Years*, 222-223.

JOHN HALLOWES

1. **John[1] Hallowes** was baptized 31 December 1615 in Lancashire, England, and died in Westmoreland County, Virginia, in 1657. He married first **Restituta Tew** in Maryland on 2 June 1639, and second **Elizabeth** [-?-], who married second John Sturman and third David Anderson.[911] Restituta, who died after 1655, was a sister of John Tew, whose will dated 2 June 1655, proved in Westmoreland County on 20 July 1655, named his wife Grace, nephew John Hallowes, Jr., and niece Restituta Hallowes.[912] John Hallowes was still in Maryland in November 1642 when he claimed 100 pounds of tobacco for the hire of his boat for one month, and 75 pounds of tobacco for one man pressed to supply Will Macfenin's absence,[913] but he was in Virginia in 1654 when he represented Westmoreland in the Virginia House of Burgesses; at the time of his death he was High Sheriff of the County.[914]

Children of John and Restituta (Tew) Hallowes:

   2. John[2] Hallowes, Jr., d. without issue.

+ 3. Restituta Hallowes, b. Md.

3. **Restituta[2] Hallowes**, daughter of Major John and Restituta (Tew) Hallowes, was born in Maryland and married **John Whetstone**, who died in 1670; she predeceased him. At the time of his death his wife was Ann.[915] John Reynes, clerk of Westmoreland County, Virginia, in an undated will proved 31 August 1664, left all of his estate to John "Whistens." On 11 December 1664 Nicholas Lansdowne's will appointed Colonel Valentine Peyton and John Whitstone overseers [of his minor children].[916] John Whetstone's undated will proved 27 July 1670 named his wife Ann and daughter Restitute Whiston.[917]

Child of John Whetstone and Restituta (Hallowes) Whetstone:

+ 4. Restituta[3] Whetstone.

4. **Restituta[3] Whetstone**, daughter of John and Restituta (Hallowes) Whetstone, was born in Virginia, where she died in 1688, having married

---

911. George H. S. King, *Marriages of Richmond County, Va.*, 1964.

912. Augusta B. Fothergill, *Wills of Westmoreland County, Va., 1654-1800* (1925), 1.

913. *Archives,* 3:119.

914. King, n.p.

915. King. n.p.

916. Fothergill, 7-8.

917. Ibid., 11.

first **Matthew Steele**, who died in 1679, and second **John Manley**, who died c1687 in Westmoreland County, Virginia. Restituta made her will on 30 January 1687, leaving her estate to her three sons.[918]
Child of Matthew and Restituta (Whetstone) Steele:[919]
5. Thomas[4] Steele, b. c1675, d. 1695.
Children of John and Restituta (Whetstone) Manley:
+ 6. William Manley, b. 1686.
7. John Manley, d. without issue.

6. **William[4] Manley**, son of John and Restituta (Whetstone) Manley, was born c1686 in Virginia, and died testate in Westmoreland County, Virginia, in 1716. He married **Penelope Higgins**, b. c1695 and died after 1750. She married second in 1716 Francis Spencer (who died in 1720) and third before March 1725 Andrew Russell[920] (who died testate in 1727),[921] and fourth Richard Osborne.[922] On 9 June 1709 William Manley was granted 216 acres south of John Hallows, north of John Chilton, and east of William Smoot.[923] Manley's will dated 30 May 1716 was proved in Westmoreland County on 26 November 1716.[924]
Children of William and Penelope (Higgins) Manley:
8. Penelope[5] Manley, b. Va., d. 1760 or 1768; m. (1) as his second wife Capt. Richard Barnes, b. c1700, d. c1760; m. (2) Robert Dade. Capt. Barnes m. (1) Frances Ingo.[925] His will dated 15 July 1754 at Lunenberg Parish, Richmond County, was proved 2 March 1761 and named his brother Major Abraham and sons John and Richard, Landon Carter, Col. John Tayloe, wife Penelope, his own children Thomas, Mary Kelsick, Rebecca Beckwith, Elinor, Sarah, and Elizabeth Barnes. Brother Abraham was appointed executor, with William Wilson, John Samford, John Newman, George Wilson, Henry Sisson, and William Ford witnessing.[926] Penelope had six daughters.
9. John Manley, d. 1751; m. Sarah Harrison, widow of Thomas Triplett. John is placed by Newman as having died intestate in Prince William Co., Va., sometime before 20 Nov. 1734, and states that Richard Osborn, gent., was the administrator. Newman bases this assumption on the fact that the

---

918. Newman, *Flowering*, 324. See also Robert T. Bartons, "Virginia Colonial Decisions," *Tyler's Magazine*, 1:66, for a court case about the disposition of this estate.

919. All data from King.

920. Westmoreland Co. Records, book 1721-1731, 86.

921. Westmoreland Co. Deeds, 8:83A.

922. All data from King.

923. D. Eaton, reconstructed plat map, earliest land grants, Westmoreland County.

924. Westmoreland Deeds & Wills, 6:43.

925. Robert K. Headley, Jr., *Wills of Richmond County, Va., 1699-1800* (1983).

926. Headley cites Richmond Co. Wills Book, 6:212, 123.

inventory was part of the estate of a John Manley "deceased."[927] However, Henry C. Mackall of Fairfax, Va., points out that John Manley was not described as deceased, and that Richard Osborn was not called administrator, but merely described as holding part of the estate of John Manley's deceased father William. Osborn had m. William Manley's widow Penelope. John Manley of Truro Parish, Fairfax Co., Va., died leaving a will dated 26 Dec. 1745, proved 25 June 1751, naming his children Penelope, Sarah, Harrison, and John; wife Sarah was appointed co-executrix with his brother Anthony Russell and cousin John Wood.[928] Sarah died in Alexandria by 13 Oct. 1785.[929]

10. Jemima Manley.

NICHOLAS HARVEY

1. **Nicholas**[1] **Harvey** was transported to Maryland in 1633 by Father White, who assigned the head right to Thomas Copley.[930] He died by January 1646. He married second, after August 1644, **Jane** [-?-], called "my now wife" in January 1644/45.[931] Jane, widow of Nicholas Harvey, was married to Thomas Green by 1653.[932]

He may have been the Nicholas Harvy, age 30, among the passengers who took the oath of allegiance and embarked on the ship *Merchant Bonaventure*, James Ricroft, master, bound from London to Virginia, on 2 January 1635.[933] He was back in Maryland in January 1637 when the Lieutenant General exhibited his proxy for Nicholas Harvey at the General Assembly.[934] On 3 January 1639 Leonard Calvert commissioned Nicholas Harvey and "any company of English willing to go along with you so that they exceed 12 in number, sufficiently provided" [with arms] to [make war] on the Maquantequat Indians.[935]

In 1641 Nicholas Harvey again returned to Maryland, transporting his [unnamed] wife, infant daughter Frances, and four men servants.[936] On

---

927. *Flowering*, 325.

928. Fairfax Co. Will Book A:469 ff.

929. Robert K. Headley, Jr., *Genealogical Abstracts from 18ᵗʰ Century Virginia Newspapers* (1987), 13 Oct. 1785.

930. Md. Land Patents, 1:20, 37-38 ("Hervey"); ABH:66.

931. *Archives*, 4:294.

932. Md. Land Patents, 7:62, 427; ABH:216.

933. Peter Wilson Coldham, *The Complete Book of Emigrants, 1607-1660* (Baltimore: Genealogical Publishing Co., 1987), 121-122.

934. *Archives*, 1:3.

935. *Archives*, 3:87.

936. Md. Land Patents, 1:129-130 ("Hervey"); ABH:102.

23 March 1641 Nicholas Harvey attended the session of the Assembly.[937] On 1 September 1641 Lord Baltimore requested that Nicholas Harvey be granted manorial rights. On 17 December 1641 Harvey requested a grant of 1,000 acres on the south side of Patuxent River. The land was surveyed for him; he named it *Saint Joseph Manor*.[938] On 3 September 1642 he attended the Assembly. He held the proxies of Richard Garnett and Lewis Froman. On 6 September 1642 he was appointed to a committee to consider bills to be propounded to the House.[939] On 15 April 1644 he and others were commissioned to restore corn and other goods taken from the Patuxent Indians.[940] On 17 January 1644 Robert Ellyson, chirurgeon, demanded 556 pounds of tobacco from Nicholas Harvey, due Ellyson for physick administered to Jane, the now wife of Nicholas Harvey, during her illness in the months of July and August 1643.[941]

On 27 January 1646 Nicholas Harvey was mentioned as having died.[942] On 28 January 1647 William Wheatley deposed that some time in August 1644, Nicholas Harvey, then being in perfect health, made a will at his house in Patuxent, leaving his entire estate to his daughter Frances, whom he named as sole legatee. The deponent did not know of any other will. The other witness was Henry Spink, one of Harvey's servants. The will was proved at court on 28 June 1647.[943]

The administration of Harvey's estate was complicated. Administration and guardianship were first granted to Cuthbert Fenwick and later to John Dandy. Dandy testified that Harvey had gone to Virginia, leaving some goods with his servant, Henry Spink.[944] The widow, Jane Harvey, to whom he could not have been long married, soon married Thomas Green and settled on Elizabeth River in Virginia, leaving her stepdaughter Frances Harvey in the care of Patuxent neighbors. In March 1654 Jane and Thomas Green conveyed her one-third dower interest in *Saint Joseph Manor* to Edward Lloyd of Severn.[945] On 20 August 1657 Jane Green, wife of Thomas Green of Elizabeth River, Lower Norfolk

937. *Archives*, 1:120.
938. Md. Land Patents, ABH:102.
939. *Archives*, 1:167, 168, 175.
940. *Archives*, 4:269.
941. *Archives*, 4:294.
942. *Archives*, 4:310.
943. *Archives*, 4:318; Md. Wills, 1:11; *Maryland Historical Magazine* 7:174.
944. See *Archives*, volume 4, various references.
945. For additional records and discussion of Nicholas Harvey, see Newman, *Flowering*, 224-226.

County, Virginia, and widow of Nicholas Harvey of Patuxent, agreed to the sale of *St. Thomas's Point* by her husband.[946]

Nicholas Harvey left one daughter by his unidentified first wife:
+   2. Frances[2] Harvey, born 1640-1641; m. George Beckwith.

2. **Frances[2] Harvey,** daughter of Nicholas Harvey, was born in 1640 or 1641 and died in April 1676. She married by 1657 **George Beckwith.**[947] Frances Beckwith, age 18, deposed in 1659.[948] George Beckwith first came to Maryland in 1648 as a retainer of Thomas Hatton, Secretary of State.[949] He immigrated to Maryland again in 1657 and married Frances Harvey, heiress of Nicholas Harvey,[950] by 1 October 1657, on which date he petitioned the provincial court at Patuxent for chattels then in the possession of her guardian, John Dandy.[951] At the provincial court held at Patuxent on 17 February 1657 George Beckwith complained against Ann Maddocks.[952] On 8 February 1658 George and Frances Beckwith sold a 165-acre part of *Saint Joseph's Manor* to Emperor Smith and Abdelo Martin.[953] George Beckwith was licensed on 1 March 1672 to keep a ferry over the Patuxent River between his house and Point Patience. The license was revoked by the Maryland Council on 13 October 1675, and granted to Richard Keene.[954] George Beckwith, gentleman, died at London, England,[955] before the April 1676 death of his wife.

Letters of administration on both of their estates in Calvert County were issued first to John Halls, steward of their *Saint Joseph's Manor,* and later to Cuthbert Fenwick, Esq. The inventory of the estates was taken on 12 April 1676 by Thomas Gantt and John Darnall and valued at 168,725 pounds of tobacco. Distribution was made to the [unnamed] orphans.[956] An account of the administration of the Beckwith's estate was filed on 18 September 1676, listing payments to their steward John

---

946. Md. Land Patents, A&B (1650-1657): 336.

947. See Newman, *Flowering,* 329-333, for a detailed account of George Beckwith.

948. *Archives,* 41:341.

949. Md. Land Patents, ABH:123; Z&A (1637-1651): 613.

950. Md. Land Patents, 5:219; 7:81-82; Q:416.

951. *Archives,* 10:545. Dandy was to be executed on 3 Oct. 1657, having been convicted for murdering his servant. Md. Land Patents, SA&B (1650-1657): 333, 336.

952. Md. Land Patents, A&B (1650-1657): 403. The nature of the suit was not explained.

953. Chancery Court Proceedings, in *Archives,* 51:156.

954. *Archives,* 15:54-55.

955. Md. Inventories and Accounts, 6:46.

956. Md. Inventories and Accounts, 2:179.

Hales.[957] An additional inventory was taken on 14 October 1676 by Thomas Sprigg and John Griggs and valued at £512.2.9. Thomas Banks, administrator, filed the inventory on 18 November 1676.[958] Banks filed an account on 13 July 1677, listing payments totaling 172,295 pounds of tobacco to (among many other persons): Beckwith's daughter Mary who married John Miles, and daughters Elisabeth and Margaret.[959] Some additional personal property of George Beckwith was appraised 26 Apr 1678 by Henry Darnall and John Darnall and valued at £49.19.2. The account mentioned [unnamed] orphans.[960] Banks filed another account on 28 April 1679, listing payments and disbursements totaling 192,857 pounds of tobacco. Distribution was made to son and heir Charles, unmarried daughter Barbara, and daughter Margaret. Also mentioned were two [unnamed] orphans, Elias Nutalls who married one of the orphans, and widow Frances Beckwith.[961] John Hailes filed an additional account in 1679. No heirs were named.[962] Thomas Banks filed an account of the administration of the estates of both George and Frances on 29 April 1680, listing additional payments and receipts.[963] Administrator Thomas Banks of St. Mary's County died by 3 April 1688, on which date Ann Dennis, his relict and executrix, filed an account of the administration of his estate. The account listed payments to: Charles Beckwith (ward of Nicholas Sewell) and Margaret Beckwith (wife of Michael Taney), children of George Beckwith, deceased.[964]

Children of George and Frances (Harvey) Beckwith:

+   3. Charles[3] Beckwith, b. c1669.

     4. [son], d. as a minor.

+   5. Mary Beckwith, m. John Miles.

     6. Elizabeth Beckwith, m. before 28 Apr. 1679 Elias Nuthall,[965] son of John and Elizabeth Nuthall.[966] Nuthall may have died after 1689.[967] On 10 May 1683 Elias Nuthall and wife Elizabeth conveyed 100 acres part of [*Wat's Neck?*]

957. Md. Inventories and Accounts, 2:243.

958. Md. Inventories and Accounts, 2:319.

959. Md. Inventories and Accounts, 4:175; Md. Testamentary Proceedings, 9:242.

960. Md. Inventories and Accounts, 6:9.

961. Md. Inventories and Accounts, 6:46.

962. Md. Inventories and Accounts, 6:400.

963. Md. Inventories and Accounts, 7A:30.

964. Md. Inventories and Accounts, 9:475.

965. Md. Inventories and Accounts, 6:46.

966. *Archives*, 8:507.

967. Elise Greenup Jourdan, "The Nuthall Family," *Early Families of Southern Maryland*, 2:183.

to Richard Ridgell. Nuthall executed two more deeds in November 1688.[968] On 17 Apr. 1689 Elias "Nutwell" was listed as a runaway in list of debtors in inventory of estate of Daniel Clocker of St. Mary's County,[969] and as "worth nothing" in a list of debts due the estate of Mr. Jacob Saith of Talbot County filed 30 April 1702.[970] No further record found in Maryland.

\+   7. Barbara Beckwith, m. Jacob Seth.

\+   8. Margaret Beckwith, m. thrice.

3. **Charles³ Beckwith,** son of George and Frances (Harvey) Beckwith, was born c1669 in Calvert County and died in the period 1712-1717. He married, first, by 1697, **Elizabeth (Hill) (Hopewell) Keen,** daughter and executrix of Francis Hill of St. Mary's County,[971] and widow of Hugh Hopewell,[972] and of Richard Keen of Calvert County.[973] He married, second, by October 1702,[974] **Anne Guyther,** born 1686-1687,[975] daughter of William and Christina Barbara (de Hinojosa) Guyther.[976] She married, second, after March 1730[/31] and before 1732,[977] John Miller of Prince George's County,[978] and died 17 October 1746.[979]

---

968. Md. Provincial Court Land Records, WCR#1:257, 482, 528.

969. Md. Inventories and Accounts, 10:232.

970. Md. Inventories and Accounts, 21:343.

971. Will of Francis Hill of St. Mary's Co., dated 19 Sept. 1696 and proved 19 July 1697, bequeathed entire estate to daughter Elizabeth Hopewell and her three children. Richard Keene witnessed the will. Md. Wills, 7:295. Hills appointed as executrix his daughter Elizabeth Hopewell, afterward wife of Richard Keen. On 10 July 1697 she entered her administration bond with William Taylard and Edward Balson as her securities. Md. Testamentary Proceedings, 17:319, 321; 19A:161.

972. The will of Hugh Hopewell of Calvert Co., dated 3 March 1693 and proved 24 May 1694, devised plantation to wife Elizabeth during minority of son. Md. Wills, 2:325. Hopewell's personal estate was appraised by John Griggs and John Wiseman, value £238.9.0. Relict Elizabeth craved further time. Md. Testamentary Proceedings, 16:91.

973. Md. Testamentary Proceedings, 17:319, 321.

974. He and wife Ann complained against Alexander Deheniosia in Md. Chancery Court 16 Oct. 1702 [Chancery Court Records, 2:477].

975. In her deposition made in October 1736, Ann Miller, then wife of John Miller of Prince George's County, gave her age as about 48 years.

976. The will of widow Christina Barbara Cooper of St. Mary's City, dated 5 Oct. and proved 23 Oct. 1717, named son Nicholas Guyther and daughter Ann Beckwith, and appointed Ann Beckwith co-executor. Md. Wills, 14:651. The executors' bond was dated 23 Oct. 1717. Md. Testamentary Proceedings, 23:156.

977. Ann still called "Beckwith" in her 24 March 1730[/31] deed, but called "Ann Miller, wife of John Miller, lately called Ann Beckwith," in Nov. 1732 court case.

978. John Miller, age 66, made deposition in 1735, Prince George's Co. [Peden, *Md. Deponents 1634-1799*, 131].

979. Paul Beckwith, *The Beckwiths* (Albany: Joel Munsell's Sons, 1891), 30. John Miller renounced administration on her estate 5 Nov. 1746 [Prince George's Co. Administration Bonds, box 13, folder 25].

Charles Beckwith received payment from his father's estate, according to an account filed by administrator Thomas Banks on 28 April 1679.[980] The will of Thomas Bankes of Calvert County, dated 10 November 1684, bequeathed personalty to Charles and Margaret Beckwith.[981] As a ward of Nicholas Sewell and a son of George Beckwith, he received his legacy from the estate of Thomas Banks, according to an administration account filed on 3 April 1688.[982] In October 1696 the Maryland Council ordered that a seal for the newly established Prince George's County be made by Mr. Charles Beckwith of Patuxent.[983] By a note attached to the 30 May 1698 will of John Low of St. Mary's County, his kinsman Marshall Low was bound to Charles Beckwith for five years, to be brought up as a Protestant.[984] On 26 August 1701 he witnessed a deed for land on the west side of the Patuxent River in Prince George's County, sold by Colonel Henry Darnall to John Miller.[985] Included among payments from the estate of Thomas Sedgwick of Calvert County, according to an administration account filed on 16 September 1703, was a payment to Roger Brooke per Charles Beckwith who married the widow of Richard Keen.[986] In St. Mary's County on 5 April 1706 Charles Beckwith appraised the personal estate of Charles Egerton.[987] On 5 April 1711 he appraised the estates of Patrick Buckley and Cornelius Fitsgarald of St. Mary's County.[988] On 20 May 1712 he appraised the estate of Zacharias Vansweringen of St. Mary's County.[989]

Charles Beckwith and wife Ann were listed as plaintiffs on the 8 May 1703 docket of the Maryland Chancery Court.[990] On 10 October 1707 Charles Beckwith was granted a patent for 600-acre *Beckwith's Lodge* in St. Mary's County.[991] Charles Beckwith, shipwright, of St. Mary's County, on 19 June 1710 conveyed to Charles Carroll and Amos Garrett 200 acres of land, part of 5,700 acres originally taken up by Captain William

980. Md. Inventories and Accounts, 6:46.

981. Md. Wills, 4:126.

982. Md. Inventories and Accounts, 9:475.

983. *Archives*, 20:524.

984. Md. Wills, 11:175.

985. Prince George's Co. Land Records, A (1696-1702): 399.

986. Md. Inventories and Accounts, 24:194.

987. Md. Inventories and Accounts, 26:255.

988. Md. Inventories and Accounts, 32B:201, 266; 32C:57.

989. Md. Inventories and Accounts, 33B:16, 209.

990. Md. Chancery Court Records, PC:481.

991. Md. Land Patents, PL2 (1706-1708):146; Md. Certificates of Survey, DD5 (1700-1713):466.

Hawley, and several slaves.[992] On 7 November 1711 he conveyed a 200-acre part of *Hog Neck*, out of the same parcel, and several slaves to Amos Garrett.[993]

Charles Beckwith died intestate after 1712,[994] after which his children and remarried widow settled in Prince George's County. By deed dated 4 November 1727 in Prince George's County, Ann Beckwith conveyed two negroes to her son George Beckwith.[995] On 13 May 1729 Ann paid four pistolls to John Henry for half of lot #59 in Marlborough Town in Prince George's County.[996] On 9 May 1730 Ann Beckwith gave a negro girl to her granddaughter Ann Boswell.[997] On 24 March 1730[/31] Ann Beckwith of Upper Marlborough gave to her son Basil Beckwith the one-acre half lot in Marlborough which she purchased from John Henry.[998] A Maryland Chancery Court case, filed on 25 November 1732 by Thomas Gittings against William Beckwith, heir-at-law of Charles Beckwith, dealt with ownership of the tract *Halley's Mannour* on St. Jerome's Creek in St. Mary's County, mortgaged for the full value by Charles Beckwith. Depositions in the case were made by the following family members, all residents of Prince George's County: on 8 and 9 December 1735, from [sons] Basil Beckwith, age about 25, and George Beckwith, age about 29; and on 29 October 1736, from Ann Miller, age 48, wife of John Miller of Prince George's County; she had conveyed her [widow's] dower right in the land to Gittings.[999]

Children of Charles and Anne (Guyther) Beckwith:

+   9. George[4] Beckwith, b. c1706.
+ 10. Basil Beckwith, b. c1710.
+ 11. William Beckwith, b. c1711.

5. **Mary[3] Beckwith,** daughter of George and Frances (Harvey) Beckwith, was born c1659. She married **John Miles** in Calvert County before 13 July 1677.[1000] John Miles was born 1653 in St. Mary's County and died in March 1697 in St. Mary's County. His will was dated 30 February 1697

---

992. Provincial Court Land Records, PL#3:168.

993. Provincial Court Land Records, TP#4:92.

994. No Maryland estate inventory, administration, or other probate records are found for Charles Beckwith.

995. Prince George's Co. Land Records, M (1726-1730): 253.

996. Prince George's Co. Land Records, M:429.

997. Prince George's Co. Land Records, M:590.

998. Prince George's Co. Land Records, Q (1730-1733): 240.

999. Md. Chancery Court Records, 6:11, 21, 24, 25.

1000. Md. Inventories and Accounts, 4:175; Md. Testamentary Proceedings, 9:242.

and proved 16 March 1697. He devised his home plantation to son James, whom he appointed as executor. He bequeathed the residue of his estate equally to his five other children John, Nicholas, Henry, Edward, and an unnamed daughter. His sons were to be of age at 18 and daughter at 16. Son John was to have charge of the children. Thomas Dillon, Charles Joy, and Cornelius Dunman witnessed the will.[1001]

Four inventories of the personal estate of John Miles of St. Mary's County were made in the period 1698-1700.[1002] Richard Hopewell filed an account of the administration of the estate of John Mills [*sic*] of St. Mary's County on 25 October 1700, listing payments totaling £33.13.0. He filed a second account on 1 May 1702. No heirs were named.[1003]

Children of John and Mary (Beckwith) Miles, according to his will:

    12. James[4] Miles.
+ 13. John Miles, m. Mary Gough.
+ 14. Nicholas Miles/Mills, m. Elizabeth Heard.
+ 15. Henry Miles.
+ 16. Edward Miles.
    17. [daughter].

7. **Barbara**[3] **Beckwith**, daughter of George and Frances (Harvey) Beckwith, married, as his second wife, **Jacob Seth**.[1004] Jacobus [*sic*] Seth was a native of Delaware. He married first, Margaret [-?-], who died by 1679. Seth was naturalized by private law in Maryland 26 April 1684.[1005] He had moved from Delaware first to Dorchester County, and then to Talbot County,[1006] where he died shortly before 17 April 1698.

Jacobus Seth's will was dated in Talbot County 22 December 1697 and proved 17 April 1698. He devised land to sons John and Charles and to daughters Mary and Susanna, and mentioned daughter Eliza[beth]. He appointed Frances Sayer executrix.[1007] On 19 April 1698 his estate, valued at £266.13.7, was appraised by William Hemsley and Arthur Emery.[1008] Administration accounts were filed 30 April 1702 by Richard Bennet, executor of Madam Frances Sayer(s), listing payments of £21.19.7 and

---

1001. Md. Wills, 7:343.

1002. Md. Inventories and Accounts, 16:31, 192; 11B:2, 3.

1003. Md. Inventories and Accounts, 20:53, 348, 387.

1004. Md. Testamentary Proceedings, 11:271.

1005. *Md. Archives*, 13:126.

1006. Sara Seth Clark and Raymond B. Clark, Jr., "Bloomingdale, or Mount Mill, Queen Anne's County," in *Maryland Historical Magazine* 50:209.

1007. Md. Wills, 6:124.

1008. Md. Inventories and Accounts, 16:145.

£247.1.8, and mentioning children Jane, John, Susanna, Elizabeth, and Charles Saith [*sic*]. Also mentioned were legacies to the wives of Robert Robertson and Richard Watts.[1009]

Children of Jacob and Barbara (Beckwith) Seth:
     18. John⁴ Seth, d. young.
+ 19. Charles Seth, b. Feb. 1692.
+ 20. Susannah Seth, m. Owen Sulavant.
+ 21. Elizabeth Seth, m. by 1721, James Barkhurst.
+ 22. Jane Seth, m. by 1721, Nathaniel Comegys.

8. **Margaret³ Beckwith**, daughter of George and Frances (Harvey) Beckwith, was born at *St. Joseph's Manor* in Calvert County, and married first, by 3 April 1688, **Michael Taney**, second, Dr. **Joachim Kierstead**, who died by August 1698, and third, by 15 April 1700, **George Gray**.

The administration account of the estate of Thomas Bankes, filed 3 April 1688, listed a payment to Michael Taney who married Margaret Beckwith, child of George Beckwith.[1010] Michael Taney's will dated 18 May 1692 in Calvert County was proved 21 June 1692. He named his wife Margaret; children Thomas, Michael, John, and Eliza[beth]; cousin Thomas Norris; and kinsman John Taney. He bequeathed half of his personal estate to his wife Margaret and their [unnamed] "youngest daughter born of her." Son Thomas was appointed executor. The will was witnessed by James Duke, Joachim Kirstead, George Young, and Wm. Sturmy.[1011]

Joachim Kierstede was baptized 24 October 1655.[1012] A surgeon of Calvert County, he died by 15 August 1698 when John Taney and Peter Sewell appraised his estate at £496.8.0. Mrs. Keirsted was mentioned.[1013] Margarett Kersted's debt was mentioned in the inventory of the estate of William Head of Calvert County dated 15 June 1698.[1014] Before his marriage to the widow Taney, Dr. Kirsted agreed to "pay to one Margaret Taney the younger [his step-daughter] £200 and four good negroes on the day of the marriage of said Margaret or at the age of twenty-one," and "in the meantime to maintain suitable to her birth and degree." This matter was heard at the Chancery Court on 15 April 1700,

---

1009. Md. Inventories and Accounts, 21:331, 343.
1010. Md. Inventories and Accounts, 9:475.
1011. Md. Wills, 6:1.
1012. Kierstede genealogy, *New York Genealogical and Biographical Record*, vol. 65 (1934).
1013. Md. Inventories and Accounts, 16:236.
1014. Md. Inventories and Accounts, 16:239.

at which time John Bigger, who had been surety on Kersted's bond, complained against George Gray, stating that Joachim Kersted was deceased "leaving his wife Margaret, formerly the widow of Michael Taney, administrator of his estate, who is since married to one George Gray."[1015] Letters of administration on the New York estate of Joachim Kierstede were granted to his nephew Hansa Kierstede, Sr., on 5 July 1710.[1016]

On 7 September 1698 Anthony Demondidier of Baltimore County and wife Mary conveyed 50-acre *Cold Comfort*, 100-acre *Rich Level*, and 145-acre *Roper's Range* to Margaret Kiersted of Calvert County, widow, and to her son Hance.[1017] On 6 March 1699 Demondidier conveyed the same three tracts to Samuel Sickelmore and Henry Wriothesley in trust for the above named Margaret and Hance Keirsted.[1018]

By deed dated 6 November 1708 Hans Kierstead, eldest brother and heir-at-law of Joachim Kierstead, late of Calvert County, conveyed several parcels of land to George Gray.[1019] On 4 April 1711 Margaret Gray, wife of George Gray, filed an account of the administration of the estate of Joakim Kierstead of Calvert County. Payment was due to Margaret Taney, daughter of Michael Taney, deceased.[1020] George Gray died intestate in Calvert County shortly before June 1715 when his inventory was filed, appraised at £343.16.19. After all debts were paid, there was a balance of £344.2.0 to be distributed among his heirs.[1021] On 14 October 1715 Margaret Gray, widow of George Gray of Calvert County, conveyed 50-acre *Cold Comfort* to Thomas Taylor.[1022] Margaret Gray filed an administration account of the estate of George Gray on 7 March 1716. Two inventories, worth £343.16.10 and £1.1.0, were cited.[1023] A second account was filed on 22 May 1728 by John Gray, Margaret's executor. Payments totaled £128.16.5.[1024]

The will of Margaret Gray of Patuxent River in Calvert County was dated 20 November 1719 and proved 9 June 1720. She bequeathed her

1015. Maryland Chancery Court Records, PC:433.
1016. *New York Genealogical and Biographical Record* 65 (1934): 226.
1017. Baltimore Co. Land Records, HW#2:33.
1018. Baltimore Co. Land Records, HW#2:29.
1019. Provincial Court Land Records, PL#3:115.
1020. Md. Inventories and Accounts, 32B:129.
1021. Md. Inventories and Accounts, 36B:183.
1022. Baltimore Co. Land Records, TR#A:257.
1023. Md. Inventories and Accounts, 37C:119.
1024. Md. Administration Accounts, 9:177.

entire estate to her five children: John, George, Elizabeth, Ann, and Jane. Son John was appointed executor, and Colonel John Mackall and Thomas Howe were appointed overseers. The will was witnessed by George Lyons, Thomas Morgan, and William Biddle.[1025] On 22 May 1728 an account of the administration of Margaret Gray's estate was filed by John Gray, executor. An inventory value of £372.2.6 and payments of £28.7.0 were listed.[1026] On 5 November 1728 executor John Gray filed a joint account of his parents' estates, listing disbursements totaling £395.11.7, including payments of their filial portions to: William Meads of Queen Anne's County, who married her daughter Elisabeth Gray; son George Gray; daughter Ann Gray; Thomas Smith, who married her daughter Jane Gray; and son John Gray, the accountant.[1027]

Child of Michael and Margaret (Beckwith) Taney:[1028]
23. Margaret[4] Taney, referred to but not named in father's 1692 will;[1029] unmarried as of 1711.[1030]

Child of Dr. Joachim and Margaret (Beckwith) Kierstead:
24. Hance Kierstead, living in 1698-1699,[1031] but dead by 1708.[1032]

Children of George and Margaret (Beckwith) Gray:[1033]
+ 25. John Gray, m. Dorcas [-?-].
26. George Gray.
+ 27. Elizabeth Gray, m. William Meeds of Queen Anne's County.
28. Anne Gray.
29. Jane Gray, m. Thomas Smith.

9. **George[4] Beckwith**, son of Charles and Anne (Guither) Beckwith, was born ca. 1705-1707. George Beckwith of Prince George's County, age 29, deposed 1736.[1034] At age about 25 he deposed 25 July 1760, naming his brother William Beckwith.[1035] He died in Frederick County, c1788. He married **Ann** [-?-].

On 26 July 1728 Thomas Gittings sold to George Beckwith, carpenter,

1025. Md. Wills, 16:50.
1026. Md. Administration Accounts, 9:179.
1027. Md. Administration Accounts, 9:100.
1028. Newman, *Flowering*, 331.
1029. Md. Wills, 6:1.
1030. Md. Inventories and Accounts, 32B:129.
1031. Demondidier deeds, described above.
1032. When father's eldest brother was father's heir-at-law.
1033. Newman, *Flowering*, 332; 1728 administration account.
1034. Md. Chancery Court Records, 6:25.
1035. Frederick Co. Land Records, G:156-158.

150 acres of *Hartwele*, near Rock Creek.[1036] On 10 June 1761 Daniel Dulany leased to George Beckwith 100-acre *Locust Level*, the lease to run for the lifetimes of George Beckwith and his sons Basil and Benjamin, "and the life of the longest liver of them."[1037]

Children of George and Ann Beckwith:

30. Charles[5] Beckwith, b. Frederick Co., 1736; buried Montgomery Co., 5 May 1799; m. Keziah [-?-]; buried Montgomery Co., 17 June 1802;[1038] her will dated 6 May 1802 named children.[1039]
31. Basil Beckwith.
32. Benjamin Beckwith.

10. **Basil[4] Beckwith**, son of Charles and Anne (Guither) Beckwith, was born 9 April 1703 in Prince George's County. Basil Beckwith of Prince George's County, planter, age about 25 [*sic*], deposed 8 December 1735.[1040] He married on 7 October 1741, **Verlinda Clagett**, daughter of Jonathan Clagett. She died 17 April 1798.[1041]

By deed dated 27 August 1741, Basil Beckwith of Prince George's County, gentleman, sold to Thomas Lee for £130 a half lot in Upper Marlborough Town formerly belonging to John Henry.[1042] Basil Beckwith was living on 15 June 1767 when he and John C. Clagett agreed concerning a 700-acre tract called *Greenland*.[1043]

Children of Basil and Verlinda (Clagett) Beckwith:[1044]

33. Basil[5] Beckwith, b. 4 Apr. 1743; d. unmarried, Frederick Co., Nov. 1767.
34. George Beckwith, b. 26 Sept. 1745; Capt. in Col. Bailey's Regt. in Continental Line; killed in battle.
35. Anne Beckwith, b. 10 June 1748; m. Charles Williams; moved to Bullitt Co., Ky.
36. John Beckwith, b. 7 Oct. 1752; d. Bullitt Co., Ky., 8 Aug. 1825; m. 18 Aug. 1773, Martha Williams, daughter of Joseph and Prudence Williams; had eight children.[1045]

11. **William[4] Beckwith**, son of Charles and Anne (Guither) Beckwith, was

1036. Prince George's Co. Land Records, M:467.
1037. Frederick Co. Land Records, G:64.
1038. Rock Creek Parish Register.
1039. Montgomery Co. Wills, E:4.
1040. Md. Chancery Court Records, 6:24.
1041. Paul Beckwith, *The Beckwiths* (1891), 31.
1042. Prince George's Co. Land Records, Y:392.
1043. Provincial Court Land Records, DD#4:244.
1044. *The Beckwiths*, 31.
1045. *The Beckwiths*, 32-33.

born c1711 in Prince George's County. William Beckwith of Prince George's County gave his age as 25 in 1736.[1046] William died in Prince George's County shortly before 24 July 1738. He married **Elizabeth** [-?-], who was living in 1742.[1047] She married, second, Peter Butler.

William Beckwith moved to Stafford County, Virginia, but returned to Maryland soon after 26 July 1728, on which date William Beckwith of Stafford County, Virginia, purchased 200-acre *Paradice* in Prince George's County from Thomas Gittings.[1048] The personal property of William Beckwith of Prince George's County was appraised on 24 July 1738 by Nathaniel Wickham and William Penson, and valued at £296.13.3. Ann Miller [William's mother] and Basil Beckwith [his brother] signed the inventory as kinsmen. Elizabeth Beckwith filed the inventory on 28 November 1739.[1049] An account of the administrationn of the estate of William Beckwith was filed by his widow, Elizabeth Beckwith, on 26 March 1742. An inventory value of £256 was mentioned, and payments totaled £207.9.5. The heirs were his children, Lucy, Ann, Mary, and William Beckwith.[1050] Elizabeth, wife of Peter Butler, filed a second account of the administration of the estate of William Beckwith on 15 December 1746. Distribution was to the [unnamed] widow, who was the accountant, and to his children, Lucy, Anne, Margaret [*sic*], and William Beckwith.[1051]

Children of William and Elizabeth Beckwith:

37. Lucy[5] Beckwith.
38. Ann Beckwith.
39. Mary [or Margaret] Beckwith.
40. William Beckwith, Jr., m. by 1765, Lucy Watson of Montgomery Co.; living in 1794; four children.[1052]

13. **John[4] Miles**, son of John and Mary (Beckwith) Miles of St. Mary's County, died there in January 1726/27. He married **Mary Gough**.

John Miles' will was dated 3 and proved 23 January 1726/27. He named his wife Mary, and devised the 54-acre dwelling plantation to her for life. To son John, appointed executor, was devised *Summerfield* and

---

1046. Md. Chancery Court Records, 6:24.
1047. *The Beckwiths*, 38.
1048. Prince George's Co. Land Records, M:465.
1049. Md. Inventories, 24:296.
1050. Md. Administration Accounts, 19:107.
1051. Md. Administration Accounts, 23:93.
1052. *The Beckwiths*, 38.

Westfield. Son Henry was to have 92-acre *Cornelius's* and dwelling plantation at mother's decease. Personalty and the residue of the estate were bequeathed to his wife and seven children: John, Mary, Margaret, Elizabeth, Henry, Priscilla, and Anne. Personalty was bequeathed to testator's brothers Nicholas and Edward. To daughter Eleanor Sinnott was bequeathed 2,000 pounds of tobacco. Edward Cole, Charles Joy, and Thomas Oglesby witnessed the will.[1053] Executor John Miles filed an account of administration of the estate of John Miles Senior of St. Mary's County on 5 September 1727. An inventory of £286.3.3 was cited. Payments totaled £5.17.8.[1054] A second account was filed 19 May 1730 by John Miles. Payments totaled £7.10.9. Legatee Eleanor Sinnott was mentioned.[1055]

Mary Miles, widow, died leaving a will dated 3 April 1734 and proved 15 May 1734. She named daughters Margaret, Priscilla, and Anne, granddaughter Mary Sinnett, and son-in-law Joseph Stone, who was appointed executor. John Gaufe and Ann Farthing witnessed the will.[1056]

Children of John and Mary (Gough) Miles:

41. John[5] Miles, b. March 1700; d. St. Mary's Co. by Aug. 1761; m. 1728, Elizabeth Gardiner (1708-c1766), daughter of John and Susanna (Barton) Gardiner; estate inventoried 14 Aug. 1761; account filed 3 Feb. 1764.[1057]
42. Henry Miles, d. as minor prior to 22 June 1727 date of estate inventory; account filed 19 May 1730.[1058]
43. Eleanor Miles, m. (1) Simon Sinnott (d. 1732);[1059] m. (2) by July 1734, James Burn(e).[1060]
44. Mary Miles.
45. Margaret Miles, will dated St. Mary's Co., 12 Dec. 1744; proved 11 Aug. 1746; mentioned children of Michael and Priscilla Burn.[1061]
46. Elizabeth Miles.
47. Priscilla Miles, m. Michael Burn(e) (he d. before Dec. 1744; his estate inventoried 19 Aug. 1745; account filed 13 Feb. 1746).[1062]
48. Anne Miles.

1053. Md. Wills, 19:34.
1054. Md. Administration Accounts, 8:322.
1055. Md. Administration Accounts, 10:257.
1056. Md. Wills, 21:98.
1057. Md. Wills, 23:225-6; Md. Inventories, 74:267; Md. Administration Accounts, 51:3.
1058. Md. Inventories, 12:139; Md. Administration Accounts, 10:529.
1059. Md. Inventories, 17:544.
1060. Md. Administration Accounts, 12:357.
1061. Md. Wills, 24:484.
1062. Md. Inventories, 31:426; Md. Administration Accounts, 23:189.

14. **Nicholas⁴ Miles/Mills**, son of John and Mary (Beckwith) Miles, was named in his father's will. Married by 1706 **Elizabeth Heard**, daughter of John and Susanna Heard.[1063] Died in St. Mary's County shortly before 18 March 1728/29.[1064]

Nicholas Miles and John Heard, as kinsmen, approved the inventory of the estate of John Norrice of St. Mary's County on 30 August 1710.[1065] He witnessed will of James Gant of Brittain's Bay on 10 May 1717.[1066] On 2 October 1717 William Langham of Brittain's Bay, St. Mary's County, named Nicholas Miles as a brother-in-law.[1067] On 5 January 1724/25 he witnessed will of James Wildman of St. Mary's County.[1068] He was bequeathed personalty by the 3 January 1726/27 will of his brother John Miles, Sr., of St. Mary's County.[1069]

The will of Nicholas Mills of St. Mary's County was dated 11 November 1728 and proved 18 March 1728/29. To his wife Elizabeth he devised life use of the dwelling plantation and the residue of his personal estate. To son Nicholas he devised 309-acre *Strife* and *Strife's Addition*. To daughters Mary Millard and Susanna Mills he devised 400-acre *Neal's Lott*. To daughter-in-law Mary Mills he gave use of lands where she now lives during her widowhood. He devised his dwelling plantation to grandson John Mills, with granddaughter Mary Mills as contingent heir if John dies without issue. He bequeathed personalty to daughter Susanna and to the clergy at New Town. Wife and son Nicholas were appointed executors. Witnesses were Cornelius Maning, Mathew Dafft, and James Thompson.[1070] The inventory of his personal estate was made on 18 March 1728[/29] by John Mills and A. Thompson, valued at £270.10.10, approved by kinsmen Nicholas and Susanna Mills, and filed on 4 June 1729 by executors Mrs. Elisabeth Mills and Nicholas Mills.[1071] They filed their account of administration on 5 November 1729, explaining that the estate would be distributed after the legatees are at full age.[1072]

1063. Will of Susanna Heard, widow of John Heard, dated 13 May 1706. Md. Wills, 12:199.
1064. Date his estate was inventoried and his will was proved.
1065. Md. Inventories and Accounts, 32B:1.
1066. Md. Wills, 14:444.
1067. Md. Wills, 14:643.
1068. Md. Wills, 18:346.
1069. Md. Wills, 19:34.
1070. Md. Wills, 19:616.
1071. Md. Inventories, 14:168.
1072. Md. Administration Accounts, 10:176.

Children of Nicholas and Elizabeth (Heard) Mills:
49. [son], m. Mary [-?-]; d. before 1728, leaving children John and Mary Mills.
50. Nicholas^5 Mills, adult in 1728.
51. Mary Mills, m. before 1728, [-?-] Millard.
52. Susanna Mills, unmarried in 1729.

15. Henry^4 Miles, son of John and Mary (Beckwith) Miles, was born c1681 and was named in his father's will. He married **Mary** [-?-]. He may be the Henry Miles who died in Charles County leaving a will dated 25 March 1720 and proved 2 May 1720. He named his wife Mary as executor and his children Mary, Elizabeth, and Henry. The daughters were to be of age at 16 and the son at 18. Benedict Boarman and John Higton witnessed the will.[1073] On 9 May 1720 Benedict Boarman and Randall Garland appraised the goods and chattels of Henry Miles at £47.7.9. Edward Miles, James Hagan, John Boarman, and Richard Edelen approved the inventory.[1074] Mary Miles, executor, filed an account of administration of Henry Miles' estate on 20 March 1723. She cited the inventory above, and listed payments of £8.10.8.[1075]

Children of Henry and Mary Miles:
53. Henry^5 Miles, b. 1702; d. by 22 June 1727 when John Abell and Thomas Blackman appraised his goods and chattels at £19.0.0. Mary Miles and Mary Mils [sic] signed as kinsmen, and John Miles, administrator, filed inventory 29 June 1727.[1076] On 19 May 1730 John Miles filed account of administration of the estate, citing inventory above and listing payments of £5.2.1.[1077]
54. Mary Miles, b. after 1704.
55. Elizabeth Miles, b. after 1704.

16. Edward^4 Miles, son of John and Mary (Beckwith) Miles, was born c1682 and was named in his father's will. He married **Mary Dodd** of Charles County. On 14 July 1719 Thomas Baker, formerly of Richmond County, Virginia, granted to George Dent a quit claim of his rights to lot #2 in Charles County where Richard Dod formerly lived, now in possession of Edward Miles.[1078] On 13 June 1721 Edward Miles, carpenter, sold 40 acres of land lying in the dividend of Thomas Baker to George Dent, and on 14 June 1721 he sold another 50 acres of the same

---

1073. Md. Wills, 16:49.
1074. Md. Inventories, 4:82.
1075. Md. Administration Accounts, 5:396.
1076. Md. Inventories, 12:139.
1077. Md. Administration Accounts, 10:259.
1078. Charles Co. Land Records, H#2:272, 303.

parcel to George Dent.[1079]

Children of Edward and Mary (Dodd) Miles:

56. Henry[5] Miles, d. Charles Co., 1774; m. Eleanor Pidgeon (she d. 1806); his estate appraised 6 June 1774, approved by kinsmen William and Henry Miles, inventory filed by Eleanor 25 July 1774;[1080] she filed administration account 6 May 1775, naming ten children.[1081]
57. John Miles, d. 1774; m. Sarah [-?-]; his estate appraised 13 June 1774, approved by kinsmen Eleanor and William Miles, inventory filed by Sarah 28 July 1774;[1082] she filed administration account 20 May 1775.[1083]
58. Nicholas Miles.
59. Edward Miles.
60. Joseph Miles.

19. **Charles**[4] **Seth**, son of Jacob and Barbara (Beckwith) Seth, was born in February 1692 and died in Queen Anne's County in 1737. He married **Elizabeth Jennings**, who married, second, Nathaniel Connor, and died in 1741. Charles was age 14 when the court ordered him to learn the trade of a carpenter. On 23 March 1714 Charles Seth, planter, in accordance with the will of his father Jacob Seth, conveyed to Charles Blake all his right, title, and interest in 100-acre *Hog's Hole* in Queen Anne's County, which Colonel Peter Sayer sold to Jacob Seth on 17 August 1697.[1084] On 27 March 1717 Charles Seth and wife Elizabeth sold to Philemon Hemsley 50-acre part of *Mount Mill* on the south side of Thomas' Branch.[1085]

Charles Seth's will was dated 23 April 1737 and proved 12 June 1737. He devised all of his real estate to his four underage sons: John, James, Charles, and Jacob; gave personalty to daughter Susannah; and appointed wife Elizabeth executrix, giving to her life use of his estate.[1086] Charles Seth left personal property valued at £549.1.9 by William Campbell and John Downes on 26 September 1737. John Sutiant and John Higgins signed as kinsmen. Elizabeth Seth, executrix, filed the inventory.[1087] On 12 July 1738 Richard Bennett, gentleman, conveyed to John, James, Charles and Jacob Seth, minor sons of Charles Seth, deceased, 200-acre part of

1079. Charles Co. Land Records, H#2:434, 436.
1080. Md. Inventories, 116:379.
1081. Md. Administration Accounts, 72:95.
1082. Md. Inventories, 116:374.
1083. Md. Administration Accounts, 72:93.
1084. Queen Anne's Co. Land Records, IKA:27.
1085. Queen Anne's Co. Land Records, IKA:112.
1086. Md. Wills, 21:771.
1087. Md. Inventories, 24:18.

Bennett's Outlet, being a resurvey of *Hackney Marsh*, to be equally divided among them according to their father's will.[1088] On 11 March 1741 Elizabeth Connor, wife of Nathaniel Conner, filed an account of the administration of the estate of Charles Seth of Queen Anne's County. In addition to the original inventory cited, two more inventories had been filed, totaling £103.13.0 and £105.18.9. The representatives were John, James, Charles, Susanna, and Jacob.[1089]

Children of Charles and Elizabeth (Jennings) Seth:
61. John[5] Seth, b. *Mount Mill*, c1719; d. 1782; m. Lucy Montgomery.
62. James Seth, m. (1) Ann Wilkinson, (2) Hannah Elbert, (3) Jane [-?-]; ship joiner, Philadelphia, Pa., 1753.[1090]
63. Charles Seth, d. Queen Anne's Co., 1769; m. Rachel Clayland; estate distribution named seven children.[1091]
64. Jacob Seth, d. by 1789; m. Mary [-?-].
65. [probably] Susanna Seth, m. (1) Thomas Clayland (he d. 1769),[1092] (2) Andrew Sylvester.

20. **Susannah[4] Seth**, daughter of Jacob and Barbara (Beckwith) Seth, died by July 1737. She married **Owen Sullivan**. Children of Owen and Susannah (Seth) Sullivan:[1093]
66. John[5] Sulavant/Sullivane, d. without issue, Queen Anne's Co., 1769; m. Sarah [-?-]; estate distributed to widow and sisters, 1769.[1094]
67. Eleanor Sullivan, m. [-?-] Floyd; had son Moses Floyd.[1095]
68. Barbara Sullivan, m. by 1757, John Higgins;[1096] had four children.[1097]

21. **Elizabeth[4] Seth**, daughter of Jacob and Barbara (Beckwith) Seth, married by 1721, **James Barkhurst**, and was living on 30 August 1729. James Barkhurst, Senior, of Queen Anne's County, died by October 1731.

On 3 March 1700 James Barkhurst was listed as debtor in the inventory of estate of Captain Benjamin Dolten of London.[1098] On 1 April 1721 Nathaniel Comegys and his wife Jane conveyed to James Barkhurst and

---

1088. Queen Anne's Co. Land Records, RTB:193.
1089. Md. Administration Accounts, 18:538.
1090. Queen Anne's Co. Land Records, RTD:128.
1091. Md. Administration Accounts, 61:221; 63:36; Md. Balance Books, 5:376.
1092. Md. Wills, 37:319; Md. Inventories, 103:98; Md. Administration Accounts, 63:379.
1093. Distribution of son John's estate in 1769.
1094. Md. Administration Accounts, 63:41; Md. Balance Books, 5:375.
1095. Md. Balance Books, 5:375.
1096. Queen Anne's Co. Land Records, RTNB:85.
1097. Md. Balance Books, 5:375.
1098. Md. Inventories and Accounts, 21:38.

wife Elizabeth 132-acre *Emmifield* and 192-acre part of *Sheppard's Discovery*, which Jacob Seth devised to his daughters Jane and Elizabeth.[1099]

James Barhurst's will was dated 30 August 1729 and proved 21 October 1731. To his wife Elizabeth was bequeathed his entire estate during her life or widowhood. If she died the estate was to be divided among his eleven [named] children. William Burroughs, Senior, and Eleanor Blackston witnessed the will.[1100] Elizabeth Barkhurst, executrix, filed the inventory of James Barkhurst of Queen Anne's County on 5 July 1732. His personal property had been appraised by Richard Wells and George Hollyday and valued at £77.7.10. John Hackett, James Barkhurst and Robert Phillips signed as kinsmen.[1101] An additional inventory, showing a value of £6.17.6, was filed on 2 October 1732, approved by Michael Bateman and George Burroughs as kinsmen.[1102] Elizabeth Barkhurst filed an account of the administration of the estate of James Barkhurst on 3 October 1732. Payments totlaled £93.17.8. Distribution was to the widow.[1103]

Children of James and Elizaberh (Seth) Barkhurst:

69. James[5] Barkhurst.
70. Ann Barkhurst.
71. Mary Barkhurst.
72. Rachel Barkhurst, m. St. Luke's Parish, Queen Anne's Co., 2 March 1730/31, George Burris.[1104]
73. Rebecca Barkhurst.
74. Sarah Barkhurst.
75. John Barkhurst.
76. Elizabeth Barkhurst.
77. Charles Barkhurst, m. St. Luke's Parish, Queen Anne's Co., 19 July 1744, Jane Carman.[1105]
78. Susannah Barkhurst.
79. Jane Barkhurst.

22. **Jane[4] Seth**, daughter of Jacob and Barbara (Beckwith) Seth, married as his second wife, **Nathaniel Comegys**, born 1671 in Talbot [now Queen

1099. Queen Anne's Co. Land Records, IKB:56.
1100. Md. Wills, 20:247.
1101. Md. Inventories, 17:74.
1102. Md. Inventories, 17:85.
1103. Md. Administration Accounts, 11:655.
1104. Parish Register.
1105. Parish Register.

Anne's] County, son of Cornelius and Rebecca Comegys.[1106] On 1 April 1721 Nathaniel Comegys of Queen Anne's County and his wife Jane sold to James Barkhurst, planter, and his wife Elizabeth, the land Jacob Seth devised to his two daughters Jane and Elizabeth: *Emminfield*, also *Henfield*, 200 acres, also the upper part of *Sheppard's Discovery*, 200 acres, lately resurveyed and found to contain 132 acres and 192 acres respectively.[1107]

Children of Nathaniel and Jane (Seth) Comegys:

80. John[5] Comegys, d. 1765; m. 27 March 1733, Ann Rochester;[1108] will dated 13 May and proved 6 June 1765, named wife and three children.[1109]

81. William Comegys, m. St. Luke's Parish, Queen Anne's Co., 4 March 1735, Charity Rochester of Anne Arundel Co.[1110]

25. John[4] Gray, son of George and Margaret (Beckwith) Gray, was named in his father's will. He died by March 1741. He married **Dorcas** [-?-].

The will of John Gray of Calvert County was dated 4 January 1739 and proved 31 March 1741. He named his wife Dorcas and Dr. James Somervell as executors. To brother George was devised the tract *Hazard*. John named his children John, George, James, Margaret, and William. John Stennot and William Brickly were witnesses.[1111] An account of the administration of the estate of John Gray was filed on 4 July 1744 by executrix Dorcas Gray. The inventory was valued at £466.7.8 and payments totaled £176.8.8.[1112]

Widow Dorcas Gray died in Calvert County leaving a will dated 30 December 1750 and proved 22 March 1750[/51]. She named her children John, William, and James Gray, daughter Margaret James, and granddaughters Dorcas Wood and Mary Gray. Son John was appointed executor. John and Anne Ramsey and Mary Wanaman were witnesses.[1113] John Gray filed an account of the administration of the estate of Dorcas Gray on 23 December 1754. Assets value totaled £388.9.0, while payments totaled £239.11.1. The account named her deceased children George and Mary, and her living children John, James, William, and Margaret, wife

---

1106. Nancy M. Poeter, *The Comegys Family: Descendants of Cornelius Comegys* ... (Baltimore: Gateway Press, 1981), 112.

1107. Queen Anne's Co. Land Records, IKB:56.

1108. Named in her father Francis Rochester's will. Md. Wills, 25:536.

1109. Md. Wills, 33:221; Md. Administration Accounts, 62:366.

1110. Parish Register.

1111. Md. Wills, 22:328.

1112. Md. Administration Accounts, 20:318.

1113. Md. Wills, 28:42.

of John James.[1114] The estate of Dorcas Gray of Calvert County was distributed by John Gray, administrator, on 21 December 1754. The representatives were not known to the Prerogative Office.[1115]

Children of John and Dorcas Gray:

82. John[5] Gray, d. Clifts, Calvert Co., by Oct. 1757; m. Jane Pattison (her will dated Calvert Co., 16 Nov. 1747);[1116] his will dated 28 Sept. 1757, proved 7 Oct. 1757, named their children.[1117]
83. George Gray, d. before coming of age.
84. James Gray.
85. Margaret Gray, m. (1) Edward Wood of Calvert Co. (d. testate 1743);[1118] she m. (2) by 1749, John James (d. 1764).[1119] Had issue by both husbands.
86. William Gray.
87. Mary Gray, d. before coming of age.

27. **Elizabeth[4] Gray,** daughter of George and Margaret (Beckwith) Gray, married **William Meeds** of Queen Anne's County who probably died by November 1769.

By deed dated 22 August 1732, William Meeds and wife Elizabeth and John Meeds and wife Mary, conveyed to Robert Jarman, planter, 400-acre *Saint Martin's*.[1120] John Meeds of Queen Anne's County made a will on 18 January 1753. To his "cousin" [nephew] John Meeds, son of the testator's brother William, was devised 141-acre *Branford*. After John's wife Rebecca died, his estate was to go to his brother William's children: Elizabeth, Margaret, Mary, Dorcas, and Susanna.[1121]

The will of William Meeds of Queen Anne's County was dated 10 April 1766 and proved 3 November 1769. He named his children: William, John, Elizabeth Hall, Margaret, Mary, Dorcas, and Susanna, and mentioned the tract *Branford*. Son William was appointed executor. The will was witnessed by Thomas Marsh, J. Barniclo, and John Walker.[1122] James Satterfield filed an account of the administration of the estate of William Meeds on 17 August 1770. An inventory value of £62.17.2 was cited. The deceased left four children: Margaret Satterfield, wife of the

1114. Md. Administration Accounts, 37:56.

1115. Md. Balance Books, 1:127.

1116. Md. Wills, 25:224.

1117. Md. Wills, 30:405. Births and deaths of children recorded in Christ Church Parish Registers.

1118. Md. Wills, 23:293; Md. Administration Accounts, 21:396; 27:145.

1119. Md. Administration Accounts, 51:44; Md. Balance Books, 4:29.

1120. Queen Anne's Co. Land Records, RTA:142.

1121. Md. Wills, 28:462.

1122. Md. Wills, 37:371.

accountant; Mary, wife of George Hall; Dorcas, wife of James Sylvester; and Susanna.[1123]

Children of William and Elizabeth (Gray) Meeds:
- 88. William[5] Meeds.
- 89. John Meeds.
- 90. Elizabeth Meeds, m. [-?-] Hall.
- 91. Margaret Meeds, m. James Satterfield.
- 92. Mary, m. George Hall.
- 93. Dorcas Meeds, m. James Sylvester.
- 94. Susanna, unmarried in 1770.

RICHARD LOWE

1. **Richard[1] Lowe** (also Loe) was master of the *Ark* of London in October 1633.[1124] He died at sea in 1639. In 1624 at St. Botolph's without Bishopsgate, he married **Jane Hunte**. At age 34 she married, secondly, William Allen on 12 December 1639 at St. Mary Aldermanbury.

Richard Lowe went to sea as early as 1615 and by 1627 had command of his own ship. By October 1632 he was master of the 358-ton *Ark* of London, which would bring the first colonists to Maryland.[1125]

Children of Richard and Jane (Hunte) Lowe:
- 2. Jane[2] Lowe, b. c1625.
- + 3. Alice Lowe, b. c1627; m. Nathaniel Chesson.
- 4. Elizabeth Lowe, b. c1634; m. at age 15, an unnamed mariner from Shadwell.
- 5. Richard Lowe, Jr., b. c1635; went to sea at age 16 or earlier; d. in Va. 1655 age 20.[1126]

3. **Alice[2] Lowe**, daughter of Captain Richard and Jane (Hunte) Lowe, was born c1627, and in 1646 married Captain **Nathaniel Chesson** who was born c1622. Chesson was slain on 18 February 1652 at the Battle of Portland, survived by his widow, two young daughters, and a seven month old son, Nathaniel (who died at sea at age 22 or 23).[1127]

1123. Md. Administration Accounts, 65:113.

1124. *Archives*, 3:23.

1125. Full account of his career, William W. Lowe, "Two Captains, Two Ships: A 17th Century Chronicle," in *Maryland Historical Magazine*, volume 95, no. 3.

1126. At Prerogative Court of Canterbury in Sept. 1655 administration on estate of Richard Low of Va., bachelor, granted to mother, Jane Allen *alias* Low.

1127. Lowe, "Two Captains ...."

JOHN NEVILLE

1. **John**[1] **Nevill**, a passenger on the *Ark* and the *Dove*,[1128] died by 14 January 1664. In 1637/38 he was styled an Anglican and a mariner.[1129] He married first in England, **Bridget Thorsbey**, whom he transported in 1639 as his wife.[1130] He married second, also in England by 1651, **Joan(na) Porter**, whom he brought to Maryland that year.[1131] She was born c1627, according to a deposition she made in 1661 stating her age as 34.[1132] She married second by 1666 Thomas Hussey, gentleman, by whom she apparently had two daughters. Her sister Margaret was the wife of Francis Pope of Charles County.[1133]

John was granted 400-acre *Nevill's Cross* in Charles County in 1649, 200 acres for himself and 200 acres for his wife Bridget. In 1651 he demanded 400 acres which had been assigned to him by George Asquith and 100 acres more for transporting Joanna, being land he had bought from Thomas Doynes.[1134] He had earlier settled in St. Michael's Hundred, where he owned a tract with Christopher Carnell on Poplar Hill Creek, which they leased to Richard Bennett; it adjoined Nevill's dwelling plantation. He moved to Charles County by 1659, when he bought 300 acres there from John and Mary Jarbo.[1135]

He died testate leaving a will dated 14 January 1664 at Portobacco, and proved 4 February 1664/65, in which he devised to his wife Joanna all his real and personal estate, and to son William his plantation, and bequeathed personalty to daughter Ellen Lambert, and grandson John Lambert.[1136] His personal estate was appraised on 4 September 1675 by Henry Hosier and John Wells and valued at 650 pounds of tobacco.[1137]

Children of John and Bridget (Thorsbey) Neville:[1138]

1128. Md. Patents, 1:121.
1129. Newman, *Flowering*, 239.
1130. Md. Patents, 4:186.
1131. Md. Patents, 2:528, ABH: 27.
1132. Charles Co. Land and Court Records, A1:142.
1133. Newman, *Flowering*, 240-242; Charles Co. Court and Land Records, G:72.
1134. Md. Patents, ABH: 27, 241.
1135. *Archives*, 65:679; Charles Co. Court and Land Records, N:239.
1136. Md. Wills, 1:222.
1137. Md. Inventories & Accounts, 1:446.
1138. There is no evidence that John Neville had a son James who went to Virginia or a son John who went to Talbot Co., Md. His second wife Joanna had an illegitimate daughter, Rachel, born in 1658. Joanna had been in England one or two years before, while John stayed in Maryland. The father of Rachel is unknown. This is confirmed by a lawsuit detailed in *Archives*, 53:380-382, and

+ 2. Ellen[2] Neville, b. c1642.
  3. William Neville, b. c1645 (of age in 1666 when he claimed his estate). On 17 Aug. 1666 of Portobacco, he sold to Thomas Mathews, gent., for 3000 pounds of tobacco the land he inherited from his father, *Huckle Berry Swamp*. In that document his wife Joane released her dower rights. His last definite record was at court in 1674, when he delivered a mare to Edmond Lindsey. It is very unlikely that he is the William Neville who married Sarah Noble of Salem, Mass., in 1694. No children have been identified as his.[1139]

2. **Eleanor/Ellen[2] Neville**, daughter of John and Bridget (Thorsbey) Neville, was born c1642 and died after March 1671/72. She married by 1662 **John Lambert**, who married second by 13 April 1676 Sarah Barker.[1140] He died by 14 November 1717.

Children of John and Eleanor/Ellen (Neville) Lambert, born in Charles County:[1141]

  4. John[3] Lambert, b. 5 Feb. 1663/64; d. testate *s.p.* in 1693/94.
+ 5. Eleanor Lambert, b. Jan. 1667/68.
  6. Elizabeth Lambert, b. Jan. 1667.
+ 7. William Lambert, b. 27 Feb. 1669/70.
  8. Samuel Lambert, b. 16 March 1671/72.

5. **Eleanor[3] Lambert**, daughter of John and Eleanor/Ellen (Neville) Lambert, was born in January 1667/68[1142] and died by 14 November 1717.[1143] She married by 9 January 1692 **John Allen**, born c1663, of Nanjemoy Hundred, Charles County, who was alive on 12 August 1719, when he stated his age as 56 and deposed regarding the tract *Glover's Point*, mentioning his father-in-law John Lambert.[1144]

On 10 March 1710, John Allen conveyed all his slaves, servants, cattle, hogs, and household goods and possessions to his three children, James, George, and Ann Allen, with the provision that he and wife Eleanor

---

Charles Co. Court and Land Records, G:72, when Joanna and her second husband Thomas Hussey on 13 Nov. 1677 gave to Rachel Ashford, "natural daughter of Joannah and wife of Michael Ashford of Charles Co., carpenter" a tract on the west side of Zachiah Swamp called *Moore's Ditch*. (Charles Co. Court and Land Records, C:61, G:72). John Neville had only two children, both by his first wife Bridget.

1139. Newman, *Flowering*, 313; *Archives*, 60:202.
1140. Newman, *Flowering*, 315-320.
1141. Newman, *Flowering*, 315; *Archives*, 60:603-604; Charles Co. Court and Land Records, P:205.
1142. Age 5 in Jan. 1672. Charles Co. Court and Land Records, E:72.
1143. Charles Co. Court and Land Records, H2:131.
1144. Ibid., D2:35.

would have the use of the goods for the rest of their natural lives.[1145]
    Children of John and Eleanor (Lambert) Allen:[1146]
    9. John[4] Allen, b. c1689; alive on 2 Feb. 1718; m. Katherine [-?-]. No known issue.
+   10. James Allen, b. c1691.[1147]
    11. Anne Allen, b. 28 Jan. 1694.[1148]
    12. George Allen, d. by May 1733; prob. m. Barbara [-?-].[1149]

7. **William[3] Lambert**, son of John and Eleanor (Neville) Lambert, was born 27 February 1669/70 in Nanjemoy Hundred, Charles County, and died intestate in 1700. He married **Mary Clark**, eldest child of John and Coniey Clark. Lewis Jones, planter [no known relation] made a deed of gift of land on the west side of Portobacco Creek for natural love and affection to William Lambert on 1 March 1680, with reversion to John Lambert, Jr. and then to Eleanor, daughter of John Lambert, Sr.
    Presumed child of William and Mary (Clark) Lambert:
    13. John[4] Lambert, adopted the spelling "Lambeth" for the family name. He m. (1) Sarah [-?-] and (2) Mary [-?-], who m. (2) by 22 Jan. 1726/27 Philip Tippett.[1150] No known issue.

10. **James[4] Allen**, son of John and Eleanor (Lambert) Allen, was born c1691 and died testate by 11 May 1733. He married first **Verlinda** [-?-] c1712. On 16 November 1716 they conveyed 20 acres at the head of Nanjemoy Creek to Joseph Manning.[1151] He married second **Jane** [-?-], who married second Samuel Gray. James deposed on 20 August 1719 at age 21 concerning the tract of land *St. David's*.[1152]
    James died leaving a will dated 21 March 1732/33 and proved 11 May 1733, devising one-half of his estate to wife Jane and appointing her executrix. Except for a legacy to his brother George, the balance of the estate went to his son William, who was a minor. His inventory totaled £144.14.8.[1153]

1145. Charles Co. Court and Land Records, C2:233.
1146. Newman, *Flowering*, 317.
1147. Md. Wills, 20:665.
1148. Charles Co. Court and Land Records, Q:25.
1149. Md. Inventories, 17:251.
1150. Newman, *Flowering*, 319-20.
1151. Charles Co. Court and Land Records, H2:52.
1152. Ibid., M2:48.
1153. Md. Wills, 20:665; Md. Administrations, 12:343.

Child of James and probably Verlinda Allen:
14. William[5] Allen, b. after 21 March 1712/13.

RICHARD NEVITT

Note: This line has many weaknesses and frequent lapses of documentation which should be resolved by future applicants.[1154]

1. **Richard**[1] Nevitt, possibly the son of Henry and Alice (Armistead), an armorial family, was born in London c1619 or later and died after 1674, without leaving a will or administration. He married **Anne** possibly **Norris**, a servant transported by John Lewger in 1637.[1155] Nevitt was a ward of John Saunders of London, who owned one-fourth of a 50-ton pinnace, the *Dove*.[1156] John Saunders and Richard Nevitt signed on for the voyage to Maryland.[1157] He was residing in St. Clement's Bay or New Towne Hundred, St. Mary's County, in 1646 when he paid rent to Lord Baltimore. He owned 100 acres on Nevett's Creek which flowed into the Potomac River, and on 14 May 1651 had surveyed 300 acres on the north side of the Patuxent River called *Nevitt*, which later fell into Calvert County. He also owned 200-acre *Rocky Point* and 100-acre *Red Bud Thickett*.[1158] He was frequently appointed by the court to appraise estates and was literate; he also served as a sergeant in the militia company of his hundred. He was alive on 23 March 1674 when he was listed as a debtor to the estate of Benjamin Solley.[1159]

Children of Richard and Anne Nevitt:
+ 2. John[2] Nevitt, b. c1641.
+ 3. Richard Nevitt, b. by 1645.

2. **John**[2] **Nevitt**, son of Richard and Anne Nevitt, was born c1641; his death date is not recorded.[1160] He gave his age as c70 on 28 September 1711 when he deposed that the land now held by Richard Vowles on St.

1154. Some undocumented information is based on contributions of Susan Johanson of Springfield, Va., and Vickie S. Connor, supplied to the compiler.

1155. Newman, *Flowering*, 242-5. ABH: 150, 19:150 (Norris).

1156. Newman, *Flowering*, 48.

1157. He is listed as Richard Nevill in Gust Skordas, *The Early Settlers of Maryland* (1968), ABH:35, transported in 1633.

1158. Md. Patents, AB&H: 98, 3, 171. Rent Rolls, O:48, 27-28.

1159. Mary Louise Donnelly, *Colonial Settlers of St. Clement's Bay, 1634-1780* (1996), 180.

1160. He is not the John who signed as the brother on Richard Nevitt's inventory, as had been reported. See #13 and #14 below for that record.

Clement's Bay, St. Mary's County, had formerly been owned by his father Richard Nevitt.[1161] John probably married **Millicent Martin**, daughter of James and Frances Martin.[1162]

In June 1662 he was given a cow and her increase by his godmother, Frances, wife of Walter Pake. On 11 October 1677 he was paid by the estate of Francis Moundefort, and on 9 August 1686 by the estate of William Cole, all of St. Mary's County.[1163] He had surveyed 100-acre *Knevet's Beginning* on 22 October 1681, which he apparently sold to John Heard by 1707, who paid rent on it. On 1 August 1692 Nevitt and wife Millicent sold to John Bayne 200 acres of *Nevitt's Desire*.[1164]

Children of John and Millicent (Martin) Nevitt:[1165]

+   4. Nicholas[3] Nevitt.
    5. Margaret Nevitt, d. unm. in 1723.
+   6. John Nevitt, b. c1670.
    7. Millicent Nevitt, b. c1673, d. unmarried.
+   8. Francis Nevitt.
    9. Ann Nevitt, d. by 1698; m. Peter Jarboe; no issue.[1166]

3. **Richard[2] Nevitt**, son of Richard and Anne Nevitt, was of age in 1666,[1167] so born by 1645. His wife is unknown. He moved to Charles County, but no record of land he owned was found.[1168] Probable child of Richard and Mary Nevitt:[1169]

    10. Mary[3] Nevitt, m. Richard Vowles who may be the man whose will dated 4 April 1724 named children Richard, James, Matthew, John, Mary wife of John Chunn, and wife Mary.[1170]

4. **Nicholas[3] Nevitt**, son of John and Millicent (Martin), may have married **Elinor** [-?-], who received a bequest by the will of her godmother, Dorothy Smith, in 1742. Nicholas died by the fall of 1711 when his personal estate was appraised at £13.12.0 by William Canady and

---

1161. Donnelly, 181. Md. Chancery Records, PC:751. Richard Vowles was the husband of John's brother Richard's daughter.

1162. Donnelly, 181.

1163. Ibid., 180. Md. Inventories & Accounts, 4:406, 9:143.

1164. St. Mary's Co. Rent Roll: 38.

1165. Donnelly, 181.

1166. Ibid., 134.

1167. Newman, 245; no primary source cited.

1168. Newman, 298; *Archives*, 57:99, 60:574.

1169. Chancery Records, 2:751; Newman does not name any children.

1170. Md. Wills, 18:258. Newman does not recognize this marriage.

Christopher Davison. Robert Tunnihill, the administrator, filed an account on 15 July 1711, which showed payments to Nicholas Nevitt, presumably his son, and Mr. Cheseldyne.[1171]
Children of Nicholas and Elinor Nevitt:
11. Nicholas[4] Nevitt.
12. Anne Nevitt.

6. **John**[3] **Nevitt**, son of John and Millicent (Martin) Nevitt, was born c1670 in St. Mary's County; his death date is unknown. He married **Sarah** [-?-], probably the widow of Samuel Harris. Possible children of John and Sarah Nevitt [not proved]:
+ 13. Richard[4] Nevitt, b. c1700.
   14. John Nevitt, b. 1702; d. after 1724 when he approved the inventory of his brother Richard's personal estate.

8. **Francis**[3] **Nevitt**, son of John and Millicent (Martin) Nevitt, died testate by June 1724 in St. Mary's County. He married **Elinor Spink**, daughter of Thomas and Margaret Spink.[1172] William Dant's will made in St. Mary's County on 31 January 1714 named his cousin William Mills, brother Peter Mills, and cousin Elinor Nevitt.[1173] In 1717 Francis Nevitt witnessed the will of Edward Spinke.[1174]

Francis Nevitt's will, dated 20 February 1723/24, made bequests to his daughters Elizabeth and Mary, to be delivered at the time of their marriages. Bequests were also made to Lewis Moor and John Farr, with wife Elinor appointed executrix and bequeathed the residue of the estate. If she died, John Mills and James Thompson were to complete the execution. Witnesses were Charles Dafft and Ezekiel Pain. Charles Neal and Thomas Vanreshwick appraised the personal property at £108.7.4 on 17 March 1723/24, with Margaret Neavett and John Realy [Riley] signing as kinsmen. Apparently the widow died soon, because Mills and Thompson alone filed an account on 4 August 1725, showing payments of £39.1.0, and a second account on 3 August 1726 cited additional payments of £10.4.0. James Farr and Lewis Moore were named as legatees.[1175]

1171. Md. Inventories, 30:195; Md. Administrations, 32C:96.
1172. Donnelly, 181.
1173. Md. Wills, 14:221.
1174. Md. Wills, 14:467.
1175. Md. Wills, 18:238 ; Md. Inventories, 9:446; Md. Administrations, 7:96, 512.

Children of Francis and Elinor (Spink) Nevitt:

15. Francis⁴ Nevitt, m. Elinor Mills, daughter of Peter and Margaret (Dant) Mills and niece of William Dant. Elinor married (2) John Dant.[1176] The Peter Dant who wrote his will on 4 April 1741 named his wife Margaret but no daughter Elinor.[1177]
16. [daughter], m. John Riley, who signed as next of kin on her father's inventory.
17. Elizabeth Nevitt.
18. Mary Nevitt, or is this the daughter who m. John Riley?[1178]

13. **Richard⁴ Nevitt**, son of John and Sarah Nevitt, was born c1700 and died in 1724. He married **Mary Montgomery**, who married second [-?-] McAtee, by whom she had a daughter Rosamond; Mary died by 21 December 1774.

Richard's estate was appraised on 3 September 1724 by John Beale and Mark Mackferson at £79.2.1, and approved by John Nevitt, brother of the deceased. The widow Mary filed an account on 16 August 1725 with a balance of £105.3.2, with payments of £54.5.7, but no distribution to heirs.[1179]

Mary McAtee of Charles County died leaving a will dated 8 November 1774 and proved 21 December 1774. She made bequests to her children Elizabeth Tennison, Ann Birch, Rosamond McAtee, and son John Nevitt; also to grandchildren William Miles Nevitt, John Tennison, John Nevitt, Jr., Charles Nevitt, and William Miles Nevitt (the latter the son of deceased son Richard). Son John was appointed executor, with William Miles Nevitt of Richard to serve if John died. The personal estate was valued by Peter Dent and Daniel McPherson at £187.2.3¼, with William Miles Nevitt and Ann Burch signing as kinsmen.[1180]

Children of Richard and Mary (Montgomery) Nevitt, born Prince George's County:

19. Anne⁵ Nevitt, b.1720; d. 1804; m. Oliver Burch (1713-1795), son of Justinian and Susannah (David) Burch.
20. John Nevitt, b. 1722; d. 1808 Nelson Co., Ky.
21. Richard Nevitt, b. 1724; d. 1772.

1176. Claimed by Donnelly, 181. If Elinor m. Dant, she died before 1763 as she is not mentioned in his will, although a Mary Mills is. Md. Wills, 31:1048.

1177. Md. Wills, 23:532.

1178. The 1743 will of a John Riley of St. Mary's Co. names a wife Mary, but it may not be that of this John Riley. Md. Wills, 23:460.

1179. Md. Inventories, 10:20; Md. Administration Accounts, 7:90.

1180. Md. Wills, 40:168; Md. Inventories, 121:311.

22. Elizabeth Nevitt, m. [-?-] Tennison; had son John.

JOHN PRICE

1. **Colonel John**[1] **Price** was born c1608, giving his age as about 40 in 1648.[1181] He died by March 1661. He married, perhaps late in life, **Anne (-?-) Bushell**, widow of Thomas Bushell.[1182] Newman suggests the possibilities: (1) that he may have been one of the two John Prices transported to Maryland in 1633-1634 by the Wintour Brothers, and (2) that he left the province, but immigrated to Maryland again by 1636, bringing servants.[1183]

On 18 February 1638/39, when domiciled in St. Michael's Hundred, he was elected to the first General Assembly.[1184] In June 1647 he was Captain of the Fort at St. Inigo's. In January 1659/60, as Colonel John Price, he was appointed a member of the Upper House of the Assembly by Lord Baltimore.[1185]

Colonel John Price of St. Mary's County died leaving a will dated 10 February 1660 and proved 11 March 1660/61 by the witnesses Reverend William Wilkinson, Thomas Dent, and William Hatton. Price devised land on Herring Creek to son-in-law Joseph Bullett, who was then under age.[1186] The residue of his entire estate was bequeathed to his daughter Anne Price (not yet 18), who was appointed executor. Personalty was bequeathed to Herbert Howman and William Styles. William Hatton, Daniel Clocker, George Makall, and Thomas Dent were appointed overseers.[1187]

Only child of Colonel John and Anne Price:
+ 2. Anne[2] Price, b. 1658.

2. **Anne**[2] **Price** was born in 1658, only child and sole heir of Colonel John

---

1181. *Archives*, 4:358.

1182. Md. Land Warrants, 19:375; Chancery Court Proceedings, 2:59, 66-70. Thomas Bushell of St. Mary's Co. died leaving will dated March 1653, proved 12 Feb. 1661, mentioning, but not naming, wife and children. Md. Wills, 1:157. Further research is needed to confirm the identity of Anne's first husband.

1183. Newman, *Flowering*, 246-248. Md. Land Patents, ABH:10, 66.

1184. *Archives*, 1:29, 32.

1185. See Newman, *Flowering*, 246-248, 328, for other details concerning his activities.

1186. Newman suggested that surname might have been "Bushell." But it is clearly written "Bullett," and a man of this name was of record in Charles County. This puts into question the identity of Anne Price's first husband.

1187. Md. Wills, 1:141.

and Anne Price of St. Mary's County. In 1674 she married **Richard Hatton, Jr.**, son of Richard and Margaret Hatton. At Chancery Court 11 December 1674 Richard Hatton and Ann, his wife, age 16, daughter and sole heir of John Price, who died c1660, sued [overseers] Thomas Dent, William Hatton, George Macall, and Daniel Clocker for possession of her estate.[1188]

Richard Hatton established his plantation at *Poplar Hill*.[1189] He died leaving a will dated 5 February 1675 and proved 14 February 1675. He left personalty to Isaac Booth, son of the widow Booth, to Richard Goodaker and Richard Ringe. He named his wife Anne, and his son Richard at age 18. He also named a cousin Elizabeth Henson. The testator's brothers, William Hatton and Randolph Hanson were named overseers. The will was witnessed by John Ditchfield and Thomas Renalds.[1190] The estate of Richard Hatton was appraised on 16 April 1676 by William Harper and William Watts who valued his personal property at 38,817 pounds of tobacco.[1191] William Hatton, executor of Richard Hatton, filed an account of the administration of the estate on 20 October 1677. Assets were valued at 23,610 pounds of tobacco. Richard Rings was one of the legatees.[1192] William Hatton, brother of Richard, filed subsequent accounts of the administration of the estate on 9 July 1678 and 10 August 1686.[1193]

Child of Richard and Anne (Price) Hatton:
3. Richard[3] Hatton III, under 18 in 1675.

ROBERT SMITH

1. **Robert**[1] **Smith**, almost surely arrived on the *Ark* and the *Dove* in 1634, and was probably transported, but we have no record of the passage. He was a freeman and gentleman of St. Mary's County by 23 November 1638 when he declared his intention to marry **Rose** [-?-] **Gilbert**,[1194] the widow of Richard Gilbert [see his account]. Gilbert arrived on the *Ark* and the *Dove,* but then returned to England; he was back in Maryland, having financed his own passage, bringing his wife Rose and her daughters

---

1188. *Archives*, 51:445-446, 450-455.
1189. Newman, *Flowering*, 328.
1190. Md. Wills, 2:403.
1191. Md. Inventories and Accounts, 2:215.
1192. Md. Inventories and Accounts, 4:445.
1193. Md. Inventories and Accounts, 5:195; 9:137.
1194. Md. Patents, ABH:37, 1:334, 2:206.

Elizabeth and Grace, as well as two servants, Walter Waterling and Thomas Thomas. He died by November 1638, before he had claimed any land for transporting himself, family, and servants. This made it possible for Robert Smith to claim the land due Gilbert.

While in St. Mary's County, Smith held a leasehold on Governor Calvert's *Manor of Trinity* by 1646, when his rent to the Proprietor was in arrears. Both he and his wife appear frequently in the records for not paying taxes or for unpaid wages to his laborers. Rose, who was literate, testifed in court in 1651 and was on a jury in 1656; she was a midwife and testified on behalf of abused wives.[1195]

Smith demanded land on 28 February 1649/50, requesting 50 acres for his service to Lord Baltimore, 100 acres for Thomas Thomas, 300 acres in the right of his wife Rose Gilbert and her daughters Elizabeth and Grace, 100 assigned to him by Walter Waterling, and 50 acres for a maid servant.[1196] He received a patent for 600 acres in 1659,[1197] which was located on St. Michael's River near Morgan Creek in Kent County [later Talbot County]. He named the tract *Smeath*.

Smith made his will on 4 May 1671; it was proved in Talbot County on 19 December 1671. He made bequests of livestock to his grandchildren Mary Waterlin [daughter of Grace Gilbert and Walter Waterling], Ann Walters, daughter of Christopher Walters, deceased, and Elizabeth King, daughter of Mark King deceased. He devised the plantation where he lived to Robert King, oldest son of Mark King, and enough land to make 200 acres. To Robert Walters he devised the plantation where Robert's father Christopher Walters lived, with the parcel that the testator marked out to belong to it. To daughter Ann Emory he devised the plantation where she lived for life, and after her death to John King, youngest son of Mark King. The residue was divided into three parts and devised to Robert Walters, John King, and James Symonds as they came of age. Apparently these were various farms on *Smeath*, because his name is not in the land records indexes of Kent County or Talbot County.[1198] William Coursey acted as executor (although Tristan Thomas was also appointed) and indicated on 16 September 1672 that he was holding a cow for Ann Walters, the daughter of Christopher Walters, being a debt due Arthur

1195. Newman, *Flowering,* 253-254.
1196. Md. Patents, 2:606.
1197. Md. Patents, 4:220, 10:281.
1198. Newman, *Flowering,* 254-256.

Emory, given to Ann Walters by Emory.[1199]

The will is ambiguous at best, but apparently Robert had two daughters. He had more than one child in 1649 when "one of the said Smith's children" was given a calf by John Hilliard. Mark King died leaving minor children, and by 1669 Arthur Emory was guardian to his orphans. Both King and Christopher Walters lived on Smith's plantation, and Walters was dead by 1669/70; his orphan was also under the guardianship of Emory.[1200]

Children of Robert and Rose (-?-) (Gilbert) Smith:[1201]

+ 2. Ann[2] Smith, b. c1639.
+ 3. [daughter] Smith, m. Christopher Walters.

2. **Ann[2] Smith,** daughter of Robert and Rose Smith, was born c1639 and died between 1663 and 1692; she married first **Mark King** and second by c1668 **Arthur Emory.** Emory was born in England and immigrated to Maryland by 1666 with wife Mary and two children.[1202] In 1667 he received from Lord Baltimore several grants of land on the Choptank, Wye, and Chester rivers in Talbot and Queen Anne's counties.[1203]

Mark King is first of record in 1660 when he witnessed the gift of Robert and Rose Smith to Elizabeth Brooke, daughter of Francis, and was able to sign his name.[1204] He died before 1668, leaving minor children. At the June Court 1669 Arthur Emory as guardian to King's children acknowledged the livestock owned by the children.[1205] On 31 December 1673 Arthur and Anne sold to William Bell 100 acres of *Chance* in Broad Creek.[1206] Anne had died by 19 July 1692 when Arthur Emory conveyed to his son by Anne, Arthur Emory: 100-acre *Emory's Neglect,* 100-acre *Emory's Addition,* 50-acre *Butterfield,* 140 acres plus half of *Emory's Paxton.*[1207]

Arthur Emory's will was dated 11 July 1693 and proved 5 August 1693

1199. Md. Wills, 1:466; *Archives,* 54:540, 576-577. The devise to James Symonds, minor son of Thomas Symonds, suggests a relationship, but none has been found to date.

1200. *Archives,* 54:458-9, 497; *Testamentary Proceedings,* 3:336.

1201. Ledlie I. Laughlin, "Early Generations of the Emory Family," typescript, MHS, 1965.

1202. Md. Patents, 10:391.

1203. [No author], "Genealogical Notes on the Emory Family of Maryland," *Maryland Historical Magazine* 23:363-372; reprinted in *Maryland Genealogies,* 432-441; Md. Patents, 12:61.

1204. *Archives,* 3:256.

1205. *Archives,* 54:440.

1206. Talbot Co. Land Records, 1:283.

1207. "Emory Family," 434.

in Kent County, Delaware. He named his eldest son Arthur Emory, Sr., and youngest son Arthur Emory, Jr., the elder son being appointed executor.[1208]

Children of Ann (Smith) by Mark King:

4. Robert[3] King, eldest child, old enough to witness a deed in 1685.[1209]
+ 5. John King.
6. Elizabeth King.

Children of Ann (Smith) by Arthur Emory:

+ 7. Arthur Emory, Jr.

3. [-?-][2] **Smith**, daughter of Robert and Rose (-?-) (Gilbert) Smith, married **Christopher Walters**, born c1639,[1210] who died by March 1669/70 when his estate was sued. According to Newman, he also lived on Smith's plantation. He deposed on 25 October 1651 that he was present when Thomas Lisle fell out of a tree on John Halfhead's plantation on the Patuxent River; he was a servant of John Halfhead at the time.[1211]

The administration of his estate was granted to Francis Staunton of London, with Robert Smith appraiser. His orphan Ann Walters was placed under the guardianship of Arthur Emory, who in 1671 petitioned the court of Talbot County for 600 pounds of tobacco out of his estate for board and schooling.[1212]

Children of Christopher Walters and [-?-] Smith:

+ 8. Robert[3] Walters.
9. Ann Walters, b. c1664.

5. **John[3] King**, son of Mark and Anne (Smith) King, was born by 1665-1666 and died in 1713. He married first by 1686 **Elizabeth Skinner**, daughter of Andrew Skinner, and second by 1697 **Juliana Thomas**, daughter of Tristram and Ann Thomas, born 15 October 1671 in Talbot County and died c1719.[1213]

On 23 August 1686 Andrew Skinner conveyed to his daughter

1208. Delaware Archives, 16:176, Register of Wills, A:6, cited in Leon de Valenger, *Calendar of Kent County, Delaware, Probate Records, 1680-1800* (1944, reprint 1995). The application papers of Timothy Field Beard, in the Society's files. Previous compilers have assumed that these two sons were instead father and son. Arthur Emory, Sr., who died testate in 1699 naming four children, Md. Wills, 6:268, married Catherine Vanderfort, who m. second [-?-] Prior. Md. Wills, 27:33.

1209. Talbot Co. Land Records, 5:11.

1210. *Archives,* 10:154.

1211. Newman, *Flowering,* 219, citing *Archives,* 10:154.

1212. Testamentary Proceedings, 3:336. *Archives,* 54:497.

1213. "Emory Family," n.p.

Elizabeth, wife of John King, 120-acre *Timberneck*, and on 3 November 1686, 320-acre *Rockcliffe*. By the will of Robert Smith, John King inherited one-third part of *Smeath*. On 21 September 1697 he released all claims to the land to his brother-in-law Robert Walters.[1214]

The will of John King of St. Paul's Parish, Queen Anne's County, was dated 18 July 1713 and proved 29 September 1713. He devised to wife Juliana 320-acre *Rockcliffe* for life, of which 175 acres were devised to daughter Anne and the residue to an unborn child. To daughter Sophia was devised 150 acres in Tuckahoe, and to daughter Sarah was devised 200 acres of *Pharsalia*. Arthur Emory and John Blunt were appointed executors, with John Burden, William Mackan, and Robert Walters witnessing. The estate was appraised by Robert Walton and Jacob Covington on 20 August 1714 at a value of £20.19.11. On the same day Juliana King, executrix, filed another inventory of an additional £182.19.1.[1215]

Five years later, Juliana King made her will on 18 September 1718, with the probate on 26 February 1719/20, naming daughters Sarah and Sophia and granddaughter Anne Meredith, not yet 16; with her brother [-in-law] Arthur Emory appointed executor. William Meredith, James Cross, and Thomas Jones witnessed. An account was filed on 11 October 1721 showing an inventory of £164.0.8 and naming legatees Sarah King, Ann Meredith, and Sophia King.[1216]

Children of John and Juliana (Thomas) King:
+   10. Sarah[4] King, b. 1704.
+   11. Ann King, m. William Meredith.
+   12. Sophia King, living 1774.

7. **Arthur[3] Emory**, Jr., son of Arthur and Anne (Smith) Emory, was born c1669-1670 and died 22 September 1747. He married first **Anne Thomas**, who died 10 November 1721, and second **Jacqueline Littilen**. He was a member of the first Queen Anne's County Court in 1708 and a vestryman of St. Paul's Parish in 1704, and is buried at Ingleside, also called *Emory's Fortune,* near Queenstown.[1217]

On 8 November 1677 he bought from William and Judith Hemsley 300-acre *Hemsley* in Talbot County, and on 8 November 1713 he bought from

1214. Talbot Co. Land Records, 5:80, 7:259.
1215. Md. Wills, 13:598; Md. Inventories & Accounts, 36B:52, 36A:186.
1216. Md. Wills, 15:65; Md. Inventories, 4:101.
1217. "Emory Family," 434-435.

John and Catherine Spry 20 acres of *Forrest Lodge* near Coursey Creek.[1218] On 5 November 1723 he conveyed to his daughters Anne, Sarah, Mary Anne, and Juliana Emory, several negroes, to be delivered to the girls at age 21, and negroes to his son Arthur, with reversion to Thomas. The next day he gave to his son Arthur 500-acre *Welsh Ridge*, with the same reversion, and to son John the 300-acre tract *Hemsley*, 125-acre *Emory's Neglect*, 50-acre *Emory's Addition*, 200-acre *Butterfield*, and 20 acres of *Forrest Lodge*, with reversion to sons Arthur and Thomas; negroes were also included in the conveyance. On 1 June 1731 Arthur, Sr., bought from Thomas and Elizabeth Wilkinson 116-acre *Hap Hazard*, and on 27 October 1746 he gave his son Thomas 100-acre *Paxton* on the west side of Thomas' Branch.[1219]

The will of Arthur Emory, gentleman, was dated 18 July 1747 and proved 25 November 1747. Bequests and devises to his children were: Thomas: £10; James: 200 acres from *Trustram Addition* and *Corsey Upon Wye*; Gideon: parts of *Fortune, Saint Paul,* and *Carraman's Creek*; John, Arthur, Ann Sudler, Sarah Carter, Juliana Kemp, and Letterlien Kirby: 5 shillings each, and five slaves each to Gideon and James. His wife and son James were given slaves and appointed executors, with Wm. Emory, Thomas Emory, and John Emory witnessing. John Brown and William Elbert valued the personal property on 2 January 1747/48 at £505.19.9, with John Emory, Jr., Gideon Emory, and Benjamin Kirby signing as kinsmen. The inventory was filed on 10 March 1748.[1220]

Children of Arthur and Anne (Thomas) Emory:[1221]

+ 13. Ann[4] Emory.
+ 14. Mary Ann Emory.
+ 15. Sarah Emory.
  16. John Emory, m. Sarah Marsh; no children; John Emory's estate was administered 10 June 1762, with a balance of £1807.12.9, and distributed on 10 June 1762 by Sarah and Thomas Emory, executors, with Gideon Emory and Thomas Marsh as securities. Legatees were: Arthur Emory (nephew), Sarah Emory, Mary Emory (dau. of Thomas), Gideon Emory, Juliana Kemp, Tiley Kemp, Henry Carter (son of Richard Carter), and James Emory. The balance was distributed, with one-third to the widow and residue to Thomas Emory after decease of his [unnamed] wife.[1222]

1218. Talbot Co. Land Records, 3:84; Queen Anne's Co. Land Records, ETA:178.

1219. Queen Anne's Co. Land Records, IKB:212-3, 215, RTA:80, RTC:185.

1220. Md. Wills, 25:177; Md. Inventories, 35:497.

1221. "Emory Family," 435; Laughlin, 9, 16-17, 21.

1222. Md. Balance Books, 3:124.

+ 17. Arthur Emory.
+ 18. Thomas Emory.
+ 19. Juliana Emory.
   Children of Arthur and Jacqueline (Littelin) Emory:
+ 20. Gideon Emory.
   21. Littelien [also read as Littelier], m. by 18 July 1747 (probably Benjamin) Kirby.
+ 22. James Emory.

8. **Robert**[3] **Walters**, son of Christopher Walters and his wife, married **Elizabeth** [-?-] and possibly **Amelia** [-?-].[1223] On 4 May 1697 John King of Talbot County gave to Robert Walters a release on all King's claim to part of *Smeath,* willed to him by Robert Smith. On 23 June 1697 Robert and Elizabeth Walters sold 50 acres of the tract to John Etherington of Talbot County, planter. The deed was acknowledged by Walters and John King on behalf of Elizabeth Walters, who gave her power of attorney to John King.[1224]

Robert Waters [*sic*] of Queen Anne's County died by 27 February 1744 when his personal estate was appraised by William Campbell and John Brown and valued at £171.15.7; James Walters and Samuel Walters signed as kinsmen. Amelia Cooper, administratrix, filed the inventory on 13 June 1744. On 2 November 1746 an account was filed by Amelia, wife of Thomas Cooper, showing payments of £198.2.6.[1225]

Robert Walters is tentatively placed as the father of:
+ 23. Robert[4] Walters, b. c1693.
   24. Richard Walters.
+ 25. James Walters, b. c1706.
   26. John Walters.
   27. Samuel Walters.

10. **Sarah**[4] **King,** daughter of John and Juliana (Thomas) King, was born c1704 and died by November 1776. She married **William Emory,** son of Arthur and Catherine Emory. He died by 1752. Sarah Emory deposed on 5 October 1768 naming her husband, now deceased, her son John Emory, and her husband's brother John Emory, the surveyor.[1226] She deposed again on 31 March 1772 that she was not yet ten years old when her

---

1223. Because the widow has first refusal of the administration on her late husband's estate, Amelia is possibly but not definitely the second wife of Robert Walters.

1224. Talbot Co. Land Records, 7:258-9.

1225. Md. Inventories, 31:61; Md. Administration Accounts, 22:442.

1226. Queen Anne's Co. Ejectment Records, Emory, Gideon.

father John King died. Also that her mother lived as a widow for about five years, and died in the house where her father lived, where John Downes lives now. A year after her mother died, the deponent and her sister Downes, wife of the present plaintiff, were boarded at Major William Turbitt's, under the care of Arthur Emory. John Beck married her sister. Also mentioned was Richard Walters, eldest son of Robert. After Richard died, his brother Jno. Walters inherited the land. John King's elder brother was Robert King, who was proved heir-at-law of his grandfather Robert Smith.[1227]

On 28 March 1733 William and Sarah Emory sold to John Emory 100 acres of *Hawkins' Pharsalia* in Tully's Neck. On 29 July 1752 Sarah Emory, widow, sold to John Bracco, gentleman, the same tract, being the residue of 200 acres devised to her by her father John King. On 24 June 1765 Sarah released all claim to the tract *Smeath* to John and Sophie Downes, her sister.[1228]

The will of Sarah Emory was dated 7 November 1776 and proved 14 November 1776. She bequeathed several negroes to her daughter Sophia Emory, son William Emory, grandchildren Elijah Emory and Mary Emory (of John), as part of their father's estate. To grandchildren William and Elizabeth Emory, she also bequeathed negroes, and the residue of her estate was divided one-third each to son William, daughter Sophia, and the children of son John. Vachel Downes, executor, was appointed guardian of grandson Elijah. Witnesses were Thomas Emory, son [-in-law] Arthur Emory, Solomon Wright, Jr., and John Barneclo.[1229]

Children of William and Sarah (King) Emory:

28. John[5] Emory, d. between 1765 and 1767; m. Anne Emory, dau. of John and Ann.[1230]

29. Sophia Emory, m. Arthur Emory; she gave to her mother three negroes on 9 Oct. 1751.[1231]

30. William Emory.

11. **Ann[4] King**, daughter of John and Juliana (Thomas) King, was born c1695 and died in 1775. She married by 1715 **William Meredith**, born 1692 and died in Queen Anne's County by 1745. He gave his age as 51

1227. *Ibid.*, Downes, John and Sophia.

1228. Queen Anne's Co. Land Records, RTA:197, RTG:95, 150.

1229. Md. Wills, 41:98.

1230. Barnes, "The Emory Family," 33-34.

1231. Queen Anne's Co. Land Records, RTD:95.

in 1743.[1232] The will of William Meredith was dated 24 February 1728/29 and proved 14 November 1745, naming his children William, Mary, Elizabeth, John, and Margaret, and wife Anne; she with Robert Norris Wright was appointed executrix. Joseph Harris and Charles Wiggins witnessed.

Ann Meredith's will was dated 19 August 1775 and proved on 23 October 1775. She named her son William, daughter Mary Meredith, and the heirs of Elizabeth Devens, all of whom were bequeathed one shilling. The residue of the estate was bequeathed to her daughter, Margaret Hewitt, the executrix. James Fowler, Joshua [Whitticar?], and William Walters witnessed.[1233]

Children of William and Anne (King) Meredith:
31. William[5] Meredith, b. c1714; d. 1792-1793; m. 9 Aug. 1748 Juliana Hutchinson.[1234]
32. John Meredith, bp. 1741.
33. Mary Meredith.
34. Elizabeth Meredith, m. [-?-] Devens.
35. Margaret Meredith, m. [-?-] Hewitt.

12. **Sophia**[4] **King,** daughter of John and Juliana (Thomas) King, married first **John Beck** after 1718 and second **John Downes,** who is probably the one who died by February 1774. Sophia and John Downes had no known children. The will of John Beck of Queen Anne's County was dated 25 March 1738/39 and proved 16 January 1739/40. He devised 50 acres of *Smeath* to his son John, and made other bequests to his children James and Sarah. Wife Sophia and son John were appointed executors, with James Cox, William Emory, John Walters, and John Lockerman, Jr., witnessing. On 18 February 1739 the widow Sophia demanded her thirds of both the real and personal estate, in lieu of only the personal estate bequeathed to her. William Campbell and Hercules Cooke appraised the inventory of the personal estate on 20 March 1739/40 at £640, which was filed by Sophia on 20 May 1740, and an additional inventory of £104.1.6 on 23 July 1741. An account was filed on 9 November 1741, "during the minority of her son John," showing payments of £26.1.9.[1235]

John Downes died by February 1774, when John Kerr and John Serdey

---

1232. Queen Anne's Co. Land Commission, 2:247.
1233. Md. Wills, 24:239-41; 40:469.
1234. *Eastern Shore Vital Records,* 2:59.
1235. Md. Wills, 22:143; Md. Inventories, 25;66, 26:107; Md. Administration Accounts, 18:426.

[*sic*] appraised his estate at £1166.16.7, with Charles Downes, Jr., and Vachel Downes signing as kinsmen. Sophia was administratrix; no legatees were mentioned.[1236]

Children of John and Sophia (King) Beck:
36. John King[5] Beck.
37. James Beck.
38. Sarah Beck.

13. **Anne**[4] **Emory**, daughter of Arthur, Jr., and Ann (Thomas) Emory, possibly born c1705, married first, possibly around 1724, **Joseph Sudler**. She married second by 10 August 1756 **Sewell Long**.[1237]

Joseph Sudler witnessed the will of James Sudler, presumably his brother, on 9 December 1753. Joseph was a magistrate for Queen Anne's County.[1238] Joseph Sudler died on Kent Island, Queen Anne's County. His will was dated 23 June 1744 and proved 25 June 1756. He named his wife Anne and son, to whom was devised the land where I live, *Sudler's Fountain, Sudler's Island,* and *Sudler's Purchase* after the death or remarriage of Anne. To sons John, Joseph, and Thomas was devised a total of 800 acres, not named, some on the Chester River. To children Benjamin and Mary Ann were bequeathed slaves. William Price, Elias Meconnikin, and Joann Christian witnessed the will. On 10 August 1756 Joseph Smith and N. Walters valued the personal property at £2267.6.5, with Emory and Thomas Sudler signing as next of kin. Ann Long, executrix and wife of Sewell Long filed the inventory on 20 December 1760. The account was filed on 22 April 1761, showing payments of £362.8.1. The balance of £1726.15.0 was distributed on 21 September 1761 to the legatees: Emory, Joseph, John, Thomas, Benjamin, Mary Ann, and the widow Ann. The residue was divided, with the widow getting her thirds and the rest to the children: John, Thomas, Benjamin, and Mary Ann.[1239]

The will of Sewell Long of Kent Island was dated 25 February 1774 and proved 31 March 1774. He named a son David Long, grandson Sewell Long Sudler, son-in-law Thomas Sudler, daughter Ann Sudler, and granddaughter Mary Ann Sudler, devising to his wife a riding chair and

---

1236. Md. Inventories, 118:297, 124:225.

1237. Louis C. Sudler, *The Sudler Family of Maryland* (Chicago, 1977) cites Md. Administration Accounts, 46:272.

1238. Md. Wills, 29:114; *Archives*, 23:367.

1239. Md. Wills, 30:101; Md. Inventories, 73:80; Md. Administration Accounts, 46:272; Md. Balances, 6:206.

mare, plus £30.0.0. Son David Long and son-in-law Thomas Sudler were appointed executors, with Isaac and Thomas Winchester and Thomas Elliot witnessing. Jacob Carter and Thomas Elliott valued the personal estate at £709.0.2 on 15 April 1774, with Jean and Samuel Seon signing as kinsmen. The inventory was filed on 21 February 1775.[1240]

Children of Joseph and Ann (Emory) Sudler:[1241]

39. Emory⁵ Sudler, b. Queen Anne's Co. c1725; d. c1797; m. Martha Smith, who d. by 28 Jan. 1799, dau. of Thomas and Mary (Frisby) Smith.
40. John Sudler, d. 15 Feb. 1787; m. Anne Seon.
41. Joseph Sudler, d. 1779; m. Susanna Carter.
42. Thomas Sudler.
43. Benjamin Sudler, b. 1751; d. 1784; m. (1) Mary Walters; m. (2) Elizabeth [-?-].
44. Mary Anne Sudler, m. Sewell Handy.

14. Mary Ann⁴ Emory, daughter of Arthur, Jr., and Ann (Thomas) Emory, born c1705-1710, married first **Samuel Griffith** and second **James Sudler, Jr.**, and third **Edward Brown**.

Samuel Griffith of Queen Anne's County made a nuncupative will on 28 March 1734, proved 4 April 1734, in which he bequeathed a horse to Letitia White. The will was brought to court and sworn to by Matthew Griffith, age 22, and Mrs. Mary Winchester, age 29, brother and sister of the deceased. James Sudler, Jr., who married the widow, reported that he had delivered the legacy to the legatee.[1242]

James Sudler died on Kent Island leaving a will dated 9 December 1753 and proved 25 March 1754/55. He named his children James and Mary, both minors, to whom were bequeathed slaves. His wife Mary was appointed executrix, and Sudler stipulated that if both children died without heirs, his estate was to fall to his brothers and sisters. He also mentioned his son-in-law [stepson] Samuel Griffith. Joseph Sudler, Jo. Harvey, and William Price witnessed. An account was filed on 21 November 1755 by Mary, now the wife of Edward Brown, showing an inventory of £883.13.10 and payments of £125.4.10. Another account was filed on 22 October by "Margaret" [*sic*], wife of Edward Brown, which stated that James Sudler, one of the legatee, received two negroes.[1243]

1240. Md. Wills, 39:887; Md. Inventories, 119:270.
1241. Sudler, n.p.
1242. Md. Wills, 21:202; Md. Administration Accounts, 14:38.
1243. Md. Wills, 29:114; Md. Administration Accounts, 38:244, 41:236.

Children of Samuel and Mary Ann (Emory) Griffith:
45. Samuel[5] Griffith, alive in 1753.
Children of James and Mary Ann (Emory) Sudler:
46. James Sudler.
47. Mary Sudler.

15. **Sarah[4] Emory**, daughter of Arthur, Jr., and Ann (Thomas) Emory, married **Richard Carter**. They had at least one child, named in the distribution of the estate of John Emory, Jr.
    Known child of Richard and Sarah (Emory) Carter:
    48. Henry[5] Carter, b. by 10 June 1762.

17. **Arthur[4] Emory III**, son of Arthur, Jr., and Ann (Thomas) Emory, married **Sarah Turbutt**, daughter of Michael and Sarah (Foster) Turbutt,[1244] who died before 1761. Arthur, of Queen Anne's County, was named in the will made 12 January 1761 of his brother [-in-law] John, as having at least one son, Arthur. On 26 August 1749 Matthew Dockery, gentleman, and his wife Sarah, conveyed to Arthur Emory (now styled Senior) 100-acre *Moore's Hope* on Chester Mill Branch, and 208 acres of *Moore's Hope Addition*.[1245] He is probably the Arthur Emory who gave to his son Arthur, gentleman, half (300 acres) of *Hemsley*, half (125 acres) of *Emory's Neglect*, half (50 acres) of *Emory's Addition*, half (200 acres) of *Butterfield*, half (20 acres) of *Forrest Lodge*, and other land.[1246]
Arthur Emory of Queen Anne's County died leaving a will dated 20 September 1761 and proved 5 October 1765. In this document, he named his children: Thomas, Arthur, Ann wife of James Clayland, and Margaret Downes; also grandchildren Arthur Emory, James Clayland, Solomon Wright, Coursey Wright, Elizabeth Emory, and Sarah Wright, as well as his brother John Emory. He mentioned the tracts *Welch Ridge, Haphazard, Hemsley* (near Queen Town, which was given to the testator by deed of gift from his father); *Moore's Hope* and *Addition*, bought from Matthew Dockery. Thomas and Arthur Emory were appointed executors, with John Davis, Matthew Dockery, and William Allaband witnessing. The estate, with a balance of £345.10.10. was distributed on 8 September 1768 by the two executors, with Gideon and Arthur Emory, Jr., as sureties, to: children Thomas, Arthur, Ann Clayland, Margaret Downes, grandchildren Arthur Emory, Elizabeth Emory, James Clayland, Solomon

---

1244. Laughlin, 19.
1245. Queen Anne's Co. Land Records, RTC:392.
1246. Queen Anne's Co. Land Records, RTG:64, 65.

Wright, Coursey Wright, and Sarah Wright. After the legacies were paid, the balance was distributed equally among the four children: Thomas, Arthur, Ann, and Margaret.[1247]

Children of Arthur and Sarah (Turbutt) Emory:

49. Thomas[5] Emory.
50. Arthur Emory.
51. Ann Emory, m. James Clayland.
52. Margaret Emory, m. [-?-] Downes.

18. **Thomas[4] Emory**, son of Arthur, Jr., and Ann (Thomas) Emory, died 15 August 1765. He married first **Mary (Price or O'Neal)** and by 1750 he was married to **Sarah Lane**, and by 1766 to **Martha [-?-]**, whose will was proved 8 December 1766.[1248]

Thomas Emory of Queen Anne's County died leaving a will dated 18 January 1765 [date of probate not given]. He named his children Thomas Lane Emory, Richard, Ann, Mary Carradine, and Sarah Emory, and brother John Emory, and cousin John Emory. He mentioned a tract in Kent County on the Delaware River that he bought from Colonel Wm. Hopper and Emory Paxton. Executors appointed were brother Gideon Emory and Arthur Emory, son of brother Arthur. Witnesses were Thomas Clayland, Ann Wells, Ann Wilkinson, and Mary Chambers. Arthur Emory renounced as executor.[1249]

Martha Emory of Queen Anne's County left a will dated 1 September 1766 and proved 8 December 1766. To her daughters-in-law Ann and Sarah Emory equally, she bequeathed slaves "and all other things that may hereafter be assigned to the testator as her full one-third part of her husband's estate, when they arrive to age 16." She stated that Thomas Caradine and his wife should have care and educating of the girls, and Caradine should have full use of goods and chattels during their minority or to the day of their marriages.[1250]

Gideon Emory, the acting executor, filed an account of Thomas Emory's estate on 29 January 1774, citing two inventories, one of £638.4.10 and the other of £114.9.0, with payments of £433.3.10. The representatives of the deceased were the widow Martha, Mary wife of Thomas Carradine, Thomas Lane Emory (of age), and Richard and Sarah

---

1247. Md. Wills, 33:356; Md. Balance Books, 5:153.

1248. An unidentified Thomas Emory m. at Chester Meeting House on 9 June 1749; Chester Quaker Meeting records.

1249. Md. Wills, 33:360.

1250. Md. Wills, 35:155.

Emory (under age). The minor Ann was dead.[1251]

Children of Thomas and Mary Emory:

53. Mary[5] Emory, m. Thomas Carradine.

Children of Thomas and Sarah (Lane) Emory:

54. Thomas Lane Emory, b. 1751; d. 2 Feb. 1828;[1252] m. Elizabeth Hopewell.
55. Richard Emory, b. c1753.
56. Ann Emory, d. by 1774.
57. Sarah Emory, d. a minor in 1775.

19. **Juliana**[4] **Emory**, daughter of Arthur, Jr., and Ann (Thomas) Emory, married first [-?-] **Kemp** and second by 10 June 1762 **Christopher Thomas**.[1253] Christopher Thomas of Queen Anne's County made his will on 5 March 1776; it was filed at the county probate office on 18 January 1777. He devised to son Trustram the plantation where he lived, Juliana to have her thirds of it while a widow, and negroes were bequeathed to the other children: Edward, Ann, Juliana, and Mary Kent. His wife and son Edward were appointed executors, with Philemon Young, William Dimond, and Perry Dawson witnessing.[1254]

It is not certain if all of Christopher Thomas's children were by his marriage to Juliana Emory, but they are listed here as possible descendants. Applicants to the Society must establish that Juliana was the mother. She may have had Kemp children as well.

Children of Christopher Thomas:

58. Trustram[5] Thomas.
59. Edward Thomas.
60. Mary Thomas, m. [-?-] Kent.
61. Ann Thomas.
62. Juliana Thomas.

20. **Gideon**[4] **Emory**, son of Arthur, Jr., and Jacqueline (Littelin) Emory, was born c1731 and died in 1784. He married **Mary Marsh**, daughter of Thomas Marsh in 1716.[1255] On 6 August 1768 Gideon's sister-in-law Sarah Marsh Emory made her will, naming Gideon, his wife Mary, and their children: William, Gideon, Tilley [Matilda?], and John.[1256]

1251. Md. Administration Accounts, 71:84.

1252. Francis B. Culver, "Some Old Bible Records of the Emory Family of Maryland," *Maryland Genealogies*, 430-1.

1253. Md. Administration Accounts, 48:70.

1254. Md. Wills, 41:380.

1255. "Emory Family," 435.

1256. Md. Wills, 39:624.

Children of Gideon and Mary (Marsh) Emory:
  63. William Wilson⁵ Emory.
  64. Gideon Emory.
  65. John Emory.
  66. Matilda/"Tilley" Emory.
  67. James Emory.

22. **James⁴ Emory**, son of Arthur, Jr., and Jacqueline (Littelin) Emory, was born after 1731 and died in 1762, when his inventory was filed. He married **Mary** [-?-] who married second Marcellus Keene, and died by 1785.[1257] William Elbert and James Hammond appraised the personal property of James Emory, gentleman, on 5 February 1762, setting a value of £842.16.10. Arthur and Thomas Emory signed as kinsmen, Mary Emory, administratrix, filed the inventory on 10 June 1762.[1258]

Child of James and Mary Emory:[1259]
  68. Littelin/Lettillier⁵ Emory.

23. **Robert⁴ Walters**, of Kent Island, Queen Anne's County, planter, tentatively placed as a son of Robert and Elizabeth Emory, was born c1693, and died in 1763. He deposed in 1745 giving his age as 52.[1260] He married **Elizabeth** [-?-]. On 15 July 1745 Robert Walters and wife Elizabeth conveyed to their son Jacob 90 acres of land near where Alexander Walters now lives. On 27 March 1751 John Allen Woodell and wife Mary conveyed 200-acre *Jamaica* and part of *Mount Hope* to Robert Walters.[1261]

Robert Walters left a will dated 14 January 1763 and proved 17 February 1763, in which he devised the tract *Dundee* to his sons John and Benjamin. He also named his son Alexander and the latter's children Robert and Susanna; also his son James to whom was devised the tract *Jamaica* and 50 acres of *Hope,* and gave slaves to his children Ruth, Mary, Anne, and Jacob; also named were granddaughter Ann Blunt and daughters Susannah Latham and Rachel Kirby, son Jacob and wife Elizabeth. The balance of the estate went to son John, who with wife Elizabeth were appointed executors. Witnesses were Francis Bright,

1257. Laughlin, 23.
1258. Md. Inventories, 78:59.
1259. Laughlin, 23.
1260. Queen Anne's Co. Land Commissions, 2:268.
1261. Queen Anne's Co. Land Records, RTC:111,534.

Francis Bright, Jr., and Charles Wells or Webb.[1262]
Children of Robert and Elizabeth Walters:
69. John[5] Walters.
70. Benjamin Walters.
71. James Walters.
72. Capt. Jacob Walters, b. c1716; d. Anne Arundel Co. by Nov. 1774; m. (1) Sarah Day and (2) by 18 May 1765 Eleanor [-?-].
73. Rachel Walters, m. [-?-] Kirby.
74. Alexander Walters, b. c1716; d. testate 1773; m. Susannah [-?-].
75. Susannah Walters, m. by 14 Jan. 1763 [-?-] Latham.

25. **James**[4] **Walters**, son of Robert and Elizabeth Walters, was born c1706 and died after September 1766 when he deposed, giving his age as 60, that Arthur Emory was guardian to Sarah King and Sophia King, mentioning his own brothers Richard and John. On 1 April 1772 at age 66 he deposed again stating that when he was a boy, his father Robert Walters was living, and that William Meredith married the eldest daughter of John King; he stated he was born in 1705 and was above 33 years when his father died.[1263]
Probable children of James Walters:
76. Ruth[5] Walters.
77. Mary Walters.
78. Anne Walters.
79. Jacob Walters.

ANN SMITHSON

1. **Ann**[1] [-?-] was transported to Maryland as a maid servant by Captain Jerome Hawley, probably in 1634. She soon married **John Smithson**, who immigrated in 1635.[1264] The nuncupative will of John Smithson of St. Mary's County was proved on 27 August 1638, having been witnessed by John Metcalfe and William Lewis. He left his entire estate to his wife Anne, and appointed her executrix.[1265]
Before 30 October 1649 Ann Smithson married, second, **John Norman**, who claimed 100 acres due John Smithson for transporting himself into the province in 1635, the said Norman having married Smithson's widow. Norman also claimed 50 acres in his own right, as servant to Captain

---

1262. Md. Wills, 31:827.
1263. Queen Anne's Co. Ejectment Records: Downes, John and Sophia file.
1264. Md. Land Patents, 2:514; ABH:24.
1265. Md. Wills, 1:2; *Archives*, 4:45-46.

Cornwallis, and 50 acres in right of his wife who had been a servant to Captain Hawley.[1266] John Norman married, second, Agnes Neale, a servant of Roger Brooke.[1267] A tenant on St. Clement's Manor, Norman died in 1656, administration on his estate being granted to his widow, Agnes Norman, on 17 June 1656.[1268]

Child of John and Ann Smithson:

2. Anne[2] Smithson, identified as daughter-in-law of John Norman in 1656; m. before 1658, [-?-] Brown.[1269]

Children of John and Ann Norman:

3. Mary Norman, given a heifer in 1649.[1270]
4. John Norman, freeholder on St. Clement's Manor in 1659 and 1660.[1271]

ROBERT VAUGHAN

1. **Robert**[1] **Vaughan** was employed by Governor Leonard Calvert in Maryland before 10 July 1634, on which date he witnessed the will of George Calvert, Esq. He died intestate on Kent Isle in 1668. He married by 1651 **Mary** [-?-],[1272] who married second, Thomas Ingram, and later Jeremy Eaton.[1273]

On 9 October 1640 Captain Robert Vaughan demanded 50 acres of land due him for his services to the Governor.[1274] On 20 August 1650 500-acre *Parson's Point* was surveyed for him on Kent Isle and also a 1000-acre plantation in what is now Queen Anne's County.[1275] In 1658 he was granted 300-acre *Kimbolton* on west side of Longford Bay, and 300-acre *Ruerdon* on east side of Longford Bay. His 1000-acre tract, called *Coxe's Neck*, beginning at the head of Flunt Point Creek, Crayford Manor, was

---

1266. Md. Land Patents, ABH:24, 46, 402; 2:514; 3:22.

1267. Md. Land Patents, ABH:402; 1:166.

1268. *Archives*, 10:45. For additional details concerning John Norman, see Newman, *Flowering*, 258-260.

1269. *Archives*, 10:465.

1270. *Archives*, 4:508.

1271. *Archives*, 53:627, 699. Not the John Norman of Charles County, who was age 28 in 1662.

1272. Capt. Robert Vaughan in 1649 claimed head rights for immigrating to Maryland amd transporting his now wife, whom he married by 1651, and others. Md. Land Patents, ABH:175; Qo:221.

1273. Newman, *Flowering*, 269, 280.

1274. Md. Land Patents, ABH:90, 130; 1:99. He assigned the warrant to George Pye three days later.

1275. Md. Land Patents, 2:567.

confirmed to Vaughan on 29 May 1668.[1276]

Robert Vaughan was present at the Assemblies of 1637/38, 1641, 1647/48, 1649, 1650, and subsequent Assemblies. He was a member of the Council from 1648 to 1651, and a Justice of the Provincial Court from 1648 to 1651. From 1650 to 1652 he was Commander of Kent Isle. Vaughan was in joint charge of a pinnace captured by William Claiborne, and was instrumental in helping to capture Kent Isle for Lord Baltimore in 1638. Vaughan was a loyal supporter of Lord Baltimore against the encroachments of William Claiborne, Richard Ingle, and the Puritans. In 1642, as an elected delegate, he requested that the Assembly be divided into two houses, with the elected delegates having equal power to those attending by special writ.[1277]

On 18 October 1647 Frances Coxe of Kent Island made her will, naming Robert Vaughan executor, and instructing him to hold her estate in trust for her children.[1278] On 21 October 1656 he was appointed an overseer of the will of Thomas Hawkins.[1279] On 17 November 1668 Robert Vaughan and wife Mary, of Kent County, gave a power of attorney to John Wright to make over to Richard Pether, tailor, 300-acre *Ruerden*.[1280]

Robert Vaughan died between 24 November 1668 and 26 January 1668/69.[1281] At the time of his death he owned about 2,250 acres of land, and the total estimated value of his estate was at least 55,734 pounds of tobacco.[1282]

Thomas Ingram of Kent County made his will on 13 September 1669 leaving to his wife Mary the property which had belonged to the estate of her late husband Captain Robert Vaughan. To [his step son] William Vaughan he devised land at Choptank at age of 21 years.[1283]

Children of Robert and Mary Vaughan:[1284]

   2. Charles[2] Vaughan, b. 30 Nov. 1655; d. intestate, Talbot County, by 23 May 1685 when his estate was valued at £98.8.0;[1285] witnessed deed 19 Jan.

1276. Md. Land Patents, 11:459; Newman, *Flowering*, 268.

1277. *Biographical Dictionary of the Maryland Legislature*, 2:850.

1278. Md. Wills, 1:13.

1279. Md. Wills, 1:352.

1280. Talbot Co. Land Records, 1:59-60.

1281. At Kent County Court 26 Jan. 1668/69 Mrs. Mary Vaughan was styled "relict of Capt. Robert Vaughan." *Archives*, 54:253.

1282. *Biographical Dictionary of the Maryland Legislature*, 2:850.

1283. Md. Wills, 1:408.

1284. Newman, *Flowering*, 279-282. There is no evidence that Thomas Vaughan of Talbot Co. 1676-1684 was a child of Robert Vaughan.

1285. Md. Inventories and Accounts, 8:443.

1673;[1286] sold 300-acre *Kimbolton* to Hans Hanson.[1287]
3. William Vaughan, d. by Oct. 1684; was under age when father d. in 1668; m. Elizabeth [-?-] (m. second, by Oct. 1688 Richard Jones). Will of William Vaughan of Kent Co. dated 15 Sept. 1684, proved 20 Oct. 1684, mentioned two [unnamed] children, son to be of age at 14; daughter to have 200-acre *Parson's Point*; wife and two children to have residue of estate. James Ringgold named overseer.[1288] The widow Elizabeth, wife of Richard Jones, filed account of administration of William Vaughan's estate 17 Oct. 1688. Inventory value £107.15.0, payments totaled 9,596 pounds of tobacco.[1289] The two children d. without issue.[1290]
+   4. Mary Vaughan, b. c1655.

4. **Mary**[2] **Vaughan**, daughter of Captain Robert and Mary Vaughan, was born c1655 and died 11 December 1704 at Ellendale, Kent County. She married, first, **Edward Burton**, and second, as his second wife, c1673, Major **James Ringgold** of Kent Island, born c1637,[1291] died by 28 September 1686.[1292] After Ringgold's death in 1686, Mary married, third, [-?-] **Spears**.

Major James Ringgold, son of Thomas Ringgold, lived at *Huntingfield*, Kent County. He was twice married; his first wife has not been identified.[1293] James Ringgold established a town in Kent County near Gray's Inn Creek in 1675.[1294] On 22 August 1676, an indenture was made between James Ringgold, of Kent County, gentleman, and Samuel Tovey, late of the City of Bristol in England, merchant, and now of Kent County.[1295] On 20 November 1678, Samuel Tovey of Kent County conveyed to James Ringgold and wife Mary, of Kent County, for 5 shillings, part of the land in Great Neck on Grays Inn Creek in Chester River. The deed mentioned part of a tract of 100 acres granted and intended to be granted by the said James Ringgold to the said Samuel Tovey and part of a tract of 1,200 acres formerly granted by patent to

1286. Talbot Co. Land Records, 1:186.

1287. Kent Co. Land Records, A:459.

1288. Md. Wills, 4:65.

1289. Md. Inventories and Accounts, 10:181.

1290. Title to William's land reverted to his sister Mary's family. Newman, *Flowering*, 280.

1291. Age c23, James Ringgold deposed 20 Dec. 1660. *Archives*, 54:190.

1292. *Biographical Dictionary of the Maryland Legislature*, 2:849.

1293. Christopher Johnston, Ringgold Family Charts, Johnston Collection, Md. Historical Society.

1294. Md. Land Patents, 19:599.

1295. Kent Co. Land Records, A:381.

Thomas Ringgold, father of the said James and called Huntingfield.[1296]

The will of James Ringgold was dated 18 May 1686 and proved 28 September 1686. To sons William and John was devised 600-acre *The Plaines*. To youngest son Charles was devised 150-acre *Ringgold's Fortune*. To son James was devised the dwelling plantation, provided son Thomas refuses to give him 300 acres of northern portion of 600 acres of land given by deceased father, Thomas Ringgold, to said son Thomas. If son James by reason of being the eldest son of the now only daughter of Captain Robert Vaughan, deceased, inherits lands of said Vaughan, then testator gives to son Thomas the entire tract of 600 acres together with plantation. Personalty was given to daughter Barbara Lanham and to William Williams, to children aforesaid, and to daughter-in-law Rebecka Borten. To wife Mary was given personalty and half of the dwelling plantation. She was to administer the estate jointly with Colonel Henry Coursey.[1297] Accounts of the administration of the estate of Major James Ringgold were filed on 22 October 1686 and 9 September 1687. An additional account was filed on 8 May 1694 by executor Mary Speares.[1298]

Child of Edward and Mary (Vaughan) Burton:

+   5. Rebecca[3] Burton, m. by Aug. 1688, William Kemp.

Children of James and Mary (Vaughan) Ringgold:[1299]

+   6. James Ringgold, b. c1670, d. 15 March 1704/5.
+   7. William Ringgold, d. 1754.
     8. John Ringgold.
+   9. Charles Ringgold.

5. **Rebecca³ Burton**, daughter of Edward and Mary (Vaughan) Burton, married by August 1688 **William Kemp**. He married, second, Martha Eubanks on 11 May 1711 at Treadhaven Meeting House.[1300] On 20 August 1688 William Kemp and his wife Rebecca conveyed to Robert Smith 100 acres surveyed by Edward Burton, father of the said Rebecca.[1301] The will of William Kemp, joiner, of St. Michael's Parish, Talbot County, was dated 10 March 1728 and proved 14 November 1729. To son William was devised 223-acre *Mable Enlarged* and part of *Kemp's Lot*. If William should die without issue, the land was to pass to the

1296. Kent Co. Land Records, A:514.

1297. Md. Wills, 4:232.

1298. Md. Inventories and Accounts, 9:224, 457; 13A:213.

1299. Newman, *Flowering*, 281.

1300. F. Christos Christou, Jr., and F. Edward Wright, "The Kemp Family," in *Colonial Families of the Eastern Shore of Maryland* (Westminster, Md.: Family Line Publications, 1998), 4:144.

1301. Talbot Co. Land Records, 5:180.

testator's three eldest daughters, Elizabeth, Rachel, and Martha, who were to pay his two youngest daughters Jane and Constant 3,000 pounds of tobacco each at age or marriage. Wife Martha and son William were named executors. John Blackett, William Sewell, and Elizabeth Hughes witnessed the will.[1302]

Child of William and Rebecca (Burton) Kemp:

+ 10. William[4] Kemp, Jr., b. before 1711.[1303]

6. **James[3] Ringgold**, eldest son of Major James Ringgold by his second wife, Mary (Vaughan), was born c1675, and died shortly before 15 March 1704/5. He married **Mary Harris**, daughter of Moses Harris. After Ringgold's death she married, second, Thomas Godman.[1304]

The will of James Ringgold of Kent Island was dated 27 October 1704 and proved 15 March 1704/5. To wife Mary, appointed executrix, he gave half of his personal estate and the use of one-third of his real estate during her life. To his three children Moses, Mary and James he bequeathed the residue of estate and the entire real estate upon the death of his wife, with whom they are to remain during their minority.[1305] The list of his debts was filed c1704/5.[1306] An account was filed on 28 February 1711 by executrix Mary Godman, wife of Thomas Godman, listing payments totaling £152.5.10.[1307]

The will of Moses Harris of Talbot County, dated 16 February 1712, named the two children of daughter Mary Godman, wife of Thomas Godman, by former marriage with James Ringgold, Mary and James Ringgold.[1308] The will of Thomas Godman of Kent Island was dated 1 March 1728/29 and proved 15 May 1730. He appointed James Ringgold as executor, and directed that ten mourning rings were to be ordered and one was to go to James Ringgold, and one was left to James's sister, Mary Wright.[1309]

Children of James and Mary (Harris) Ringgold:

11. Moses[4] Ringgold.

1302. Md. Wills, 19:825.

1303. Probably of age when named executor of father's 1728 will.

1304. Robert Barnes and F. Edward Wright, "The Ringgold Family," *Colonial Families of the Eastern Shore of Maryland* (Westminster, Md.: Family Line Publications, 1996), vol. 2.

1305. Md. Wills, 3:660.

1306. Inventory in Md. Wills, 3:546.

1307. Md. Inventories and Accounts, 33A:202.

1308. Md. Wills, 13:455.

1309. Md. Wills, 20:85.

+ 12. Mary Ringgold, m. (1) Samuel Wright, (2) Robert Blunt.[1310]
+ 13. James Ringgold of Kent Island, d. 1740.

7. **William³ Ringgold**, son of Major James and Mary (Vaughan) Ringgold, was born in 1677 and died in 1754.[1311] William Ringgold, age c51, deposed in August 1726 regarding the bounds of a tract called *Arcadia*.[1312] On 25 June 1743, Mr. William Ringgold, age c66, deposed regarding the bounds of a tract called *Fancy*.[1313] William Ringgold of Kent County, age c71, deposed in April 1747 that when his grandfather, Thomas Ringgold, came out of England, he purchased a tract called *Crawford*.[1314]

William Ringgold married **Martha** [-?-].[1315] On 13 November 1699 William Ringgold and his wife Martha, of Talbot County, conveyed to Thomas Ringgold, of Kent County, 200 acres, taken up by his father Major James Ringgold in 1677, called *The Plaines*.[1316] At the November 1731 Court, William Ringgold of St. Paul's Parish, with many others unknown, were charged with, on 29 August 1729, having broken 20 panels of a fence made with rails, of the value of 100 pounds of tobacco, erected to enclose the corn growing of Thomas Ambrose, owner of the tract *Queen Charlton*, allowing horses, steers, and bulls to eat and consume the corn to the great damage of Thomas Ambrose. Ringgold was acquitted.[1317] William Ringgold of Kent County, gentleman, on 24 August 1739 conveyed to his son-in-law Esau Watkins and his daughter Sarah, wife of aforesaid Esau, part of a water lot #11 in Chester Town.[1318] On 25 April 1743, William Ringgold of Kent County, gentleman, conveyed to his son James Ringgold, of the county aforesaid, part of a tract called *The Plaines*.[1319]

The will of William Ringgold was dated 10 November 1753 and proved on 1 April 1754. The heirs named were son James Ringgold, son Thomas Ringgold (who received one seat in a pew in the addition to St. Paul's Parish Church), daughter [Rebecca] Ringgold (who also received one seat

---

1310. Queen Anne's Co. Land Records, RTB:121.

1311. Barnes and Wright, "The Ringgold Family."

1312. Kent Co. Land Records, JS#X:43.

1313. Kent Co. Land Records, JS#24:439.

1314. Provincial Court Ejectment Papers for Queen Anne's Co., MSA S 549, case of Elizabeth Barnes *versus* Frisby.

1315. "The Ringgold Family."

1316. Kent Co. Land Records, M:109B.

1317. Kent Co. Court Proceedings, MSA C 1091, CM 669, JS#WK:261.

1318. Kent Co. Land Records, JS#22:392.

1319. Kent Co. Land Records, JS#24:319.

in the addition to St. Paul's Parish Church where she now sits), and son John Ringgold (appointed executor). The will was witnessed by Chas. Scott, Ann Scott, and Samuel Wickes.[1320] Mr. William Ringgold's estate was appraised in 1754 by W. Hynson and John Wickes, and was valued at £297.8.6. James Ringgold and Thomas Ringgold signed as creditors; Thomas Ringgold and Rebecca Ringgold signed as kinsmen. Executor John Ringgold filed the inventory on 2 July 1754.[1321] On 17 February 1756 the estate was appraised again by William Hynson and John Wickes, and valued at £50.9.5. Executor John Ringgold filed the inventory on 9 April 1756.[1322] On 9 April 1756 John Ringgold filed an account of the administration of the estate. Legatees were son Thomas and daughter Rebecca.[1323]

Children of William and Martha Ringgold:[1324]
+ 14. Susanna[4] Ringgold, bp. 26 Oct. 1712; m. Benjamin Wickes.
+ 15. James Ringgold, d. 1766.
+ 16. John Ringgold.
+ 17. Thomas Ringgold, living in 1753.
  18. Rebecca Ringgold.
+ 19. Sarah Ringgold, m. (1) (probably John) Johnson, (2) Esau Watkins.

9. **Charles[3] Ringgold**, son of Major James and Mary (Vaughan) Ringgold, died by 1723. On 17 January 1705 he married **Elizabeth Parke**, who married, second, Philip Davis. Charles Ringgold died intestate in Kent County shortly before 8 September 1723, when an account of the administration of his estate was filed by Elisabeth Davis, wife of Philip Davis. An inventory of £279.19.5 was cited, and payments made by Elizabeth Davis totaled £22.14.9.[1325]

Children of Charles and Elizabeth (Parke) Ringgold:[1326]
+ 20. James[4] Ringgold, b. 30 June 1709.
  21. Mary Ringgold, bp. 14 Dec. 1712.[1327]
  22. Charles Ringgold, b. 27 April 1713. Charles Ringgold, age c35, deposed on 16 April 1750 regarding bounds of tracts *Fare Harbour* and *New Ferry*. He recalled that about three years earlier Morgan Hurt desired him to show him

---

1320. Md. Wills, 29:221.
1321. Md. Inventories, 57:381.
1322. Md. Inventories, 60:476.
1323. Md. Administration Accounts, 39:148.
1324. "The Ringgold Family;" Register of St. Paul's Parish, Kent Co., MSA SC-1642.
1325. Md. Administration Accounts, 5:240.
1326. "The Ringgold Family;" Register of St. Paul's Parish, Kent Co., MSA SC-1642.
1327. Parish register identified her as daughter of Charles and *Mary* Ringgold.

the bounded tree of Thomas Joce's land.[1328]
23. Vincent Ringgold, b. 12 Aug. 1716.

10. William⁴ Kemp, Jr., is placed as a son of William and Rebecca (Burton) Kemp, because if he were old enough to be named executor in 1728, he was probably born before 1711. He married **Mary Ann** [-?-], who was identified as his widow on 8 February 1779.

On 25 December 1742 William Kemp leased part of *Mabel* on Harrises Creek to Edward Colwell for seven years. Kemp was to find a carpenter, timber, and nails, to build a 30 foot tobacco house.[1329] On 8 November 1759 William Kemp of Talbot County, blacksmith, conveyed 45½ acres of *Mabel* to Joseph Denny.[1330] By 10 September 1765 Kemp was living in Dorchester County when he sold the residue of *Mabel* and *Mabel's Addition* to Matthew Tilghman.[1331] On 8 February 1779 Mary Ann Kemp conveyed to Matthew Tilghman her right of dower in her late husband's lands, *Mabel* and *Mabel's Addition*, which William Kemp had sold to Tilghman.[1332]

Possible child of William and Mary Ann Kemp:
24. Benjamin⁵ Kemp. To him on 26 Oct. 1776 were conveyed part of *Timber Neck Addition* and *Taylor's Ridge* by Robert Kemp, being same land which Benjamin Kemp and his wife Sarah had conveyed to Robert Kemp the previous Sept. 1776.[1333]

12. Mary⁴ Ringgold, daughter of James and Mary (Harris) Ringgold, married first, by 1727/8, **Samuel Wright**, and second, by 8 August 1737, **Robert Blunt**.[1334]

On 15 December 1729 Rachel Brown of Kent County, widow, conveyed to Samuel Wright of the said county, planter, the dower or third part of a tract which Colonel Edward Scott left in his last will to his son William Scott, land called *Stepney Heath Manner*. Samuel Wright was the possessor of the other two-thirds parts as it was allotted by Edward Scott, administrator of the said Colonel Edward Scott to the aforesaid Rachel

1328. Kent Co. Land Records, JS#26:368.
1329. Talbot Co. Land Records, 15:328.
1330. Talbot Co. Land Records, 19:4.
1331. Talbot Co. Land Records, 19:342.
1332. Talbot Co. Land Records, 21:76.
1333. Talbot Co. Land Records, 20:351, 556-557.
1334. Queen Anne's Co. Land Records, RTB:121; Md. Wills, 20:85 (Godman), 21:563 (Wright).

Brown.[1335]

The will of Samuel Wright of Kent Island, Queen Anne's County, was dated 12 April 1735 and proved 20 May 1736. The heirs named were children Samuel, Anne, John, Sarah, Frances, Elizabeth, and Susannah Kirby, and wife Mary, executor. The will was witnessed by Ralph Elston, James Chambers, and Alice White.[1336] Mary Wright, widow and executor of Samuel Wright, and now wife of Robert Blunt, filed an account of the administration of Samuel Wright's estate on 8 August 1737. An inventory value of £523.10.3 was mentioned, and payments totaled £76.10.0.[1337]

By deed dated 29 November 1737 James Ringgold conveyed to Robert Blunt and Mary his wife two tracts, *Coxes Neck* and *Parson's Point* on Kent Island.[1338]

The will of Robert Blunt of Queen Anne's County was dated 5 November 1764 and proved 16 March 1765. He named his children Elizabeth Sudler and James Ringgold Blunt co-executors and Sarah Kerby. He mentioned the tract *Partnership*, lying in Queen Anne's County. The will was witnessed by William Legg, Susannah Walters, and Penelope Wright.[1339]

Children of Samuel and Mary (Ringgold) Wright:
25. Samuel[5] Wright, d. testate[1340] by May 1767;[1341] estate accounts filed 1769 and 1771.[1342] Daughter Ann m. by 1784, Jacob Ringgold.[1343]
26. Anne Wright.
27. John Wright.
28. Sarah Wright.
29. Frances Wright.
30. Elizabeth Wright.
31. Susannah Wright, m. [-?-] Kirby.

Children of Robert and Mary (Ringgold) Blunt:
32. Elizabeth Blunt, m. [-?-] Sudler.
33. James Ringgold Blunt.
34. Sarah Blunt, m. [-?-] Kerby.

13. **James[4] Ringgold**, son of James and Mary (Harris) Ringgold, was born

1335. Kent Co. Land Records, JS#X:399.
1336. Md. Wills, 21:563.
1337. Md. Administration Accounts, 14:376.
1338. Queen Anne's Co. Land Records, RTB:121-122.
1339. Md. Wills, 33:166.
1340. Will dated 22 Aug. 1766, left entire estate to daughter Ann. Md. Wills, 35:449.
1341. Inventory dated 25 May 1767. Md. Inventories, 99:77.
1342. Md. Administration Accounts, 61:276; 66:138.
1343. Judgments, 65:182; Md. Chancery Court Records, MSA S 517, 14:151.

c1710 and died 1740. He married **Mary** (possibly **Carroll**).[1344] She married, second, by 6 October 1742, James Sudler.

On 14 August 1732 James Ringgold, Jr., age c22, deposed regarding bounds of a tract called *Fare Harbor*; he stated he was in company with Arthur Miller, Jr., to Robert Dunn's landing, and, when they came to the land, Michael Miller told him that in the water lay the bounded tree of Gibs land.[1345]

The will of James Ringgold of Kent Island, Queen Anne's County, was dated 24 October [-?-] and proved 17 April 1740. To his son Thomas and his heirs he devised the upper part of *Coxes Neck*; in the event of Thomas's death without heirs, land to pass to testator's son William and heirs and failing such, to the male heirs of testator's daughters Sarah, wife of John Carter Jr., and Mary. To son William and heirs he devised the residue of *Coxes Neck*. Should he have no heirs said land to pass to heirs of Thomas or male heirs of daughters aforesaid. To wife Mary, executrix, one-third of the estate. Personalty bequeathed to children: Thomas, Sarah Carter, Mary, Rachel, and Susanna. The will was witnessed by William Elliott, Robert Wilson, Henry Carrill, and Elizabeth Wilson.[1346] J. Wickes and Marmaduke Goodhand appraised the personal property of Mr. James Ringgold on 7 July 1740, and evaluated it at £447.4.0. James Sudler and wife Mary filed the inventory on 14 August 1740.[1347] The account of the administration of the estate of James Ringgold of Queen Anne's County was filed on 6 October 1742 by Mary, wife of James Sudler. Payments totaled £60.17.0.[1348]

Children of James and Mary Ringgold:[1349]

35. Thomas[5] Ringgold, d. 1795; m. Mary Sudler; had issue.[1350]
36. William Ringgold, b. 9 July 1720; m. 11 May 1741, Rebecca Brown (d. Kent Island after 1790); had son Thomas Ringgold (b. 1750; d. by 1816; m. 1796, Sophia Spencer).
37. Sarah Ringgold, m. John Carter.
38. Mary Ringgold.
39. Rachel Ringgold.

1344. "The Ringgold Family;" Francis B. Culver, ed., *Society of Colonial Wars in the State of Maryland: Genealogies of the Members and Services of Ancestors* (Baltimore: Williams & Wilkins Co., 1940), 2:294.

1345. Kent Co. Land Records, JS#16:254.

1346. Md. Wills, 22:161.

1347. Md. Inventories, 25:172.

1348. No heirs were mentioned. Md. Administration Accounts, 19:256.

1349. "The Ringgold Family."

1350. Kent Co. Wills, 7:616; Culver, *Society of Colonial Wars ...*, 2:293.

40. Susanna Ringgold.

14. Susanna⁴ Ringgold, daughter of William and Martha Ringgold, was baptized 26 October 1712. She married **Benjamin Wickes**, son of Samuel and Frances Wickes.[1351] Benjamin Wickes of Kent County died shortly before 14 April 1750, when his estate was appraised by James Piner, Jr., and Philip Milton, and valued at £230.7.9. Joseph Nicholson and Thomas Ringgold signed as creditors. Samuel Wickes and John Wickes signed as kinsmen. Administrator James Ringgold, Jr., filed the inventory on 23 November 1750.[1352] The account of administration of the estate of Benjamin Wickes of Kent County was filed by James Ringgold, Jr., on 17 September 1751. Payments totaled £173.7.9.[1353] On 17 September 1751 distribution of Benjamin Wicks' estate was made by James Ringgold, Jr., administrator. Sureties were Christ. Bateman and James Deoran.[1354]

Children of Benjamin and Susanna (Ringgold) Wickes:[1355]

41. Samuel⁵ Wickes, b. 21 Oct. 1732; had son Simon Wickes.[1356]
42. Mary Wickes, b. 26 Jan 1735.
43. Joseph Wickes, d.s.p. 1784; m. Margaret [-?-] who survived him; his will, dated 15 Apr. 1784, proved 18 Aug. 1784, left his negro man to Simon Wickes, surveyor, who was to set him free, and rest of estate to wife Margaret.[1357]
44. Benjamin Wickes.
45. Martha Wickes.

15. James⁴ Ringgold, son of William and Martha Ringgold, was born c1705 and died 1766. On 4 December 1735 James Ringgold, age c30, deposed regarding the bounds of tract called *The Plains*.[1358] In St. Paul's Parish, Kent County, on 2 December 1726, James married **Mary Tovey**.[1359] William Ringgold stated that some time after his brother Thomas's death, James Ringgold, son of Wm., who had married Mary Tovey, offered land to Rebecca Ringgold.[1360]

1351. Robert Barnes and F. Edward Wright, "The Wickes Family," *Colonial Families of the Eastern Shore of Maryland*, 1:345.

1352. Md. Inventories, 44:136.

1353. Md. Administration Accounts, 31:46.

1354. Md. Balance Books, 1:3.

1355. "The Wickes Family;" St. Paul's Parish Register, Kent Co.

1356. Wickes Family Chart, Christopher Johnston Collection, Md. Historical Society.

1357. Kent Co. Wills, 7:68.

1358. Kent Co. Land Records, JS#18:199.

1359. "The Ringgold Family;" St. Paul's Parish Register, Kent Co.

1360. Kent Co. Land Records, DD#1:615.

The will of James Ringgold, Jr., of Kent County, was dated 30 December 1765 and proved 3 June 1766. He mentioned children: William, James, John, Anne, Martha, Mary, and Sarah. He also named Sarah Porter, daughter of Richard Porter, deceased. Tracts mentioned were *Timely Discovery*, *The Plains*, and *Pontridge*. Son James Ringgold appointed executor. The will was witnessed by John Moore, Will Hinds, Henry Thomas, and James Strong.[1361] George Presbury and James Pinner appraised the estate of James Ringgold on 17 October 1766 and valued his personal property at £960.9.7. Thomas William Ringgold and Thomas Ringgold signed as kinsmen. Executor James Ringgold filed the inventory on 18 October 1766.[1362]

Children of James and Mary (Tovey) Ringgold, recorded at St. Paul's Parish, Kent County:[1363]

46. Martha[5] Ringgold, b. 16 Nov. 1727.
47. William Ringgold, b. 19 July 1729.
48. Mary Ringgold, b. 5 March 1732.
49. James Ringgold, b. 22 Aug. 1734; buried Sept. 1735.
50. Anne Ringgold, b. 23 Dec. 1736.
51. John Ringgold.
52. Sarah Ringgold, m. [probably] Richard Porter.

16. **John[4] Ringgold**, son of William and Martha Ringgold, died by February 1780. He married **Mary** [-?-]. The will of John Ringgold was dated 14 August 1779 and proved 11 February 1780. He named his only child, Ann Carvill, and his grandchildren: Ann, Elizabeth, Jane, Polly, Martha, Mary, and John. The residue of his estate was bequeathed to his wife, who was to be executrix, and then to his daughter Ann. James Frisby, Thomas B. Hands, and James Ringgold witnessed the will.[1364]

Child of John and Mary Ringgold:

53. Ann[5] Ringgold, b. June (probably c1735); m. [-?-] Carvill; children named in grandfather John Ringgold's will.[1365]

17. **Thomas[4] Ringgold**, son of William and Martha Ringgold, was living as late as 1755. At the Kent County June 1747 Court Thomas Ringgold was charged for cutting and selling five timber trees and 200 fence logs

1361. Md. Wills, 34:43.
1362. Md. Inventories, 89:133.
1363. St. Paul's Parish Register, Kent Co.
1364. Kent Co. Wills, 6:133.
1365. Kent Co. Wills,, 6:133.

from the land of Philip Davis. He was fined 2 shillings 6 pence.[1366] On 13 May 1755 Thomas Ringgold of Chester Town, attorney-at-law and heir of his grandfather James Ringgold, formerly of Eastern Neck, gentleman, deceased, conveyed to John Ringgold, gentleman, son and devisee of William Ringgold, deceased, 200 acres of a tract called *The Plains*, which his father William by his last will devised to him.[1367]

19. **Sarah**[4] **Ringgold**, daughter of William and Martha Ringgold, married, first, (probably **John**) **Johnson**, and, second, on 11 April 1737 in St. Paul's Parish, Kent County, **Esau Watkins**.[1368] Esau died by December 1757, probably having married second, Mary [-?-]. The will of John Johnson of Kent County was dated 7 April 1737 and proved 7 May 1737. He named his nephew, son of Thomas Howard of Philadelphia, his sister Mary, his [step] mother-in-law Susannah Johnson, and his wife Mary [*sic*], executrix. The will was witnessed by Andrew McKittrick, John Kennard, and John Wallace.[1369] William Ringgold of Kent County, gentleman, on 24 August 1739 conveyed to his son-in-law Esau Watkins and his daughter Sarah wife of aforesaid Esau, part of water lot # 11 in Chester Town.[1370] On 12 July 1742 Esau Watkins of Chester, Kent County, blacksmith, and his wife Sarah, conveyed to James Calder of the same place, attorney at law, water lot #11 in Chestertown.[1371]

The will of Esau Watkins, blacksmith, of Chestertown, Kent County, was dated 23 August 1757 and proved 17 September 1757. He named his wife Mary, and his children John and Sarah Watkins. Son John, not yet 20, was to be a ward of Dr. William Murray. Wife Mary was appointed executrix. The will was witnessed by Margaret and Mary Moore and Sarah Graves.[1372] On 13 December 1757, Esau Watkins' estate was appraised by Samuel Grooms, Sr., and James McClean, and valued at £501.12.8. James Anderson and Thomas Ringgold signed as creditors. Sarah Watkins signed as kin. Executrix Mary Watkins filed the inventory on 15 December 1757,[1373] and the account of administration on 15 February

---

1366. Kent Co. Court Records, JS#24:378.

1367. Kent Co. Land Records, JS#28:144.

1368. St. Paul's Parish Register, F. Edward Wright, *Eastern Shore Vital Records, 1642-1825* (Westminster, Md.: Family Line Publications), 2:29.

1369. Md. Wills, 21:790.

1370. Kent Co. Land Records, JS#22:392.

1371. Kent Co. Land Records, JS#23:449.

1372. Md. Wills, 30:358.

1373. Md. Inventories, 64:141.

1762. Out of the inventory, payments of £154.18.7 were made. One legatee mentioned was William Rippin. The account also mentioned the [unnamed] widow and two children.[1374]

Child of John and Sarah (Ringgold) Johnson:

54. Sarah[5] Johnson, b. Shrewsbury Parish, Kent Co., 9 July 1737.[1375]

Possible children of Esau and Sarah (Ringgold) Watkins:

55. John Watkins, b. after Aug. 1737.
56. Sarah Watkins.

20. **James[4] Ringgold**, son of Charles and Elizabeth (Parke) Ringgold, was born 30 June 1709.[1376] At the Kent County June 1733 Court, James Ringgold of St. Paul's Parish, son of Charles Ringgold, was found guilty of committing fornication on 10 June 1732 with Dorcas Cleaver and begetting a bastard child. He was fined 30 shillings.[1377]

ROBERT WISEMAN

1. **Robert[1] Wiseman** may have been the "Mr. Wiseman" who was among the "very near twenty gentlemen of fashion" who held shares of stock in Lord Baltimore's holding company, and may have been one of the five gentlemen who remained in Maryland after their arrival in 1634.[1378] Father White's *A Relation of Maryland*, a pamphlet published in London in 1635, included "The names of the Gentlemen adventurers that are gone in person to this Plantation: . . . Mr. Henry Wiseman, son to Sir Thomas Wiseman, Knight."[1379] Wiseman, his name again written as "Henry," appeared only once in the Maryland records, when, in 1641/42, he attended the Assembly.[1380] Newman concluded that the name of the adventurer was inadvertently written Henry instead of Robert.[1381]

Robert Wiseman was accompanied by a servant Joseph Edlowe.[1382] Wiseman died at his home on Wiseman's [now Chancelor's] Point in St. Mary's County shortly before April 1650. He may have been the Robertus

1374. Md. Administration Accounts, 48:170.
1375. Shrewsbury Parish Register, in *Eastern Shore Vital Records*, 2:13.
1376. "The Ringgold Family."
1377. Kent Co. Court Records, JS#WK:385.
1378. Newman, *Flowering*, 15, 163.
1379. Reprinted in Clayton C. Hall, *Narratives of Early Maryland 1633-1684* (New York: Charles Scribner's Sons, 1910), 101.
1380. *Archives*, 1:118, 120.
1381. Newman, *Flowering*, 273 fn.
1382. Newman, *Flowering*, 15, 163, 193-194, 273. *Archives*, 10:10-11.

Wiseman who married **Ann Capell** at Roding, County Essex, England, on 29 September 1619. Robert Wiseman was a son of Sir Thomas Wiseman and Alice Myles of Canfield, County Essex.[1383]

Henceforth always named as *Robert* Wiseman of St. Mary's Hundred, he was first of record at the Assembly of 25 January 1637/38 when he gave his proxy to Lieutenant William Lewis.[1384] Shortly afterwards he assigned some property.[1385] By 14 February 1638/39 he was seated in Mattapanient Hundred among the inhabitants who chose their burgess to the General Assembly.[1386] He continued to be mentioned in Maryland records in the period 1642-1649.[1387]

Robert Wiseman died shortly before 16 April 1650, on which date his former servant, Joseph Edlowe, deposed concerning Wiseman's nuncupative will and death. Edlowe stated that he asked Wiseman to make some settlement of his estate, as Edlowe perceived Wiseman to be a man not likely to live long. Wiseman asked Edlowe to take any estate in [Wiseman's] possession and "manage it the best way he could" in order to pay his debts. Any "overplus" was to be used for his son John Wiseman, the sole legatee.[1388] On 5 June 1650 letters of administration were issued to Joseph Edlowe.[1389]

Only known child of Robert Wiseman:

+ 2. John[2] Wiseman.

2. **John[2] Wiseman**, son of Robert Wiseman, was a minor at the death of his father in 1650. He died in St. Mary's County shortly before 13 July 1704. He married **Catherine Miles**, daughter of Francis Miles, gentleman. She married, second, by 1705, Richard Shirley, by whom she had a child.[1390]

The will of Francis Miles of St. Mary's County, proved on 23 September 1700, bequeathed personalty to daughter Catherine Wiseman,

1383. *Visitation of Essex, Harleian Society Publications*, 13:129-130, 171, 326; Newman, *Flowering*, 273 footnote; Robert Barnes, *British Roots of Maryland Families* (Baltimore: Genealogical Publishing Co., 1999), 473.

1384. *Archives*, 1:3.

1385. Letter from Secretary Lewger to Lord Baltimore, Jan. 1638/39, in Calvert Papers, Md. Hist. Soc., no. 195.

1386. *Archives*, 1:116.

1387. Summarized in Newman, *Flowering*, 274.

1388. Md. Wills, 1:24.

1389. Newman, *Flowering*, 274-275.

1390. Newman, *Flowering*, 275, 305-306.

and named grandson Robert Wiseman, son of John Wiseman.[1391]

The will of John Wiseman of St. Mary's County was dated 6 December 1703 and proved 13 July 1704. To eldest son John he devised the dwelling plantation and half of the land bought from Hugh Hopewell. To youngest son Robert he devised the residue of land bought from Hopewell. To daughter Mary Manning he devised 100 acres near Accomack Valley on Patuxent main road. He bequeathed personalty to [unnamed] youngest daughter. He named wife Catherine as residuary legatee during widowhood and executrix, and appointed son-in-law Cornelius Manning overseer.[1392] The estate of John Wiseman was appraised at £182.10.10, and included four slaves and a number of books.[1393] Catherine, wife of Richard Shirley, filed accounts of the administration of John Wiseman's estate on 20 September 1705 and 17 May 1708. In the first account, assets of £292.9.11 were cited, and payments totaled £13.10.0. In the second account, payments totaled £2.4.6.[1394] The final account of John Wiseman's estate was filed on 20 July 1720 by Catherine Shurley, wife of Mr. Richard Shurley. Payments totaled £301.18.11, and included those made to eldest son John, son Robert, daughter Catherine who married John Greenwell, and to John Baker. The balance was distributed, with one-third to the widow and the residue to the [unnamed] children of the deceased.[1395]

Children of John and Catherine (Miles) Wiseman:[1396]

   3. John[3] Wiseman, d.s.p.; will dated 26 Jan. 1715/16, proved 18 Apr. 1716; he named stepfather Richard Shirley (executor), mother Catherine, and brothers Robert Wiseman and Richard Shirley, sister Catherine Greenwell, and cousin Francis Miles.[1397]

+ 4. Mary Wiseman, m. Cornelius Manning.

+ 5. Robert Wiseman.

+ 6. Catherine Wiseman, m. John Greenwell.

4. **Mary[3] Wiseman**, daughter of John and Catherine (Miles) Wiseman, died by 17 June 1719. She married by 6 December 1703, **Cornelius Manning**, who died in St Mary's County in 1721.[1398] Cornelius married,

---

1391. Md. Wills, 6:375.

1392. Md. Wills, 3:242.

1393. Md. Inventories and Accounts, WB#3:589.

1394. Md. Inventories and Accounts, 25:52; 28:223.

1395. Md. Administration Accounts, 3:71.

1396. Newman, *Flowering*, 305-310.

1397. Md. Wills, 14:238; Md. Inventories and Accounts, 37A:164; 37B:133-134.

1398. Newman, *Flowering*, 306-308.

second, Mary, widow of George Simcon, and third, Elizabeth [-?-], who later married William Combs.[1399]

On 17 June 1719 Cornelius Manning, administrator of Mary Manning, who had been the executor of George Simcon of St. Mary's County, filed an account of the administration of Simcon's estate.[1400] The will of Cornelius Manning of St. Mary's County was dated 10 April 1721 and proved 15 August 1721. He named his son Cornelius, daughters Mary Mills and Anne (not yet 16, to care of her grandmother Shurly), John, son of John Manning, deceased, and wife Elizabeth, who with John Mills was named executor. Manning also named William, son of Edward Morgan, and George Thorold. The will was witnessed by Archibald Johnson, Mary Johnston, Rudolph Simon, and William Johnson.[1401] William and A. Thompson appraised Cornelius Manning's personal property on 14 October 1721, and valued it at £444.13.10. Mary Morgan and Mary Simms signed as kinsmen. Executors Mary Manning and John Miles filed the inventory on 4 December 1721.[1402] An account of the administration of the estate of Cornelius Manning was filed on 13 August 1722 by William Coomes and his wife Elizabeth and John Mills. An inventory of £444.3.10 was listed, and payments totaled £353.5.8. Among those who were paid were Mrs. Mary Tant for John and Mary Manning, orphans, Rodolph Simmons for himself and his sister Dorothy Simmons.[1403] A second account was filed 19 March 1723 and mentioned Mr. George Thorrold as a legatee.[1404]

Children of Cornelius and Mary (Wiseman) Manning:[1405]

+   7.   Cornelius[4] Manning.
+   8.   Mary Manning, m. (1) John Mills, (2) Enoch Combs.
     9.   Ann Manning.

5. **Robert[3] Wiseman**, son of John and Catherine (Miles) Wiseman, died by August 1737. He married **Elizabeth Heard**, daughter of William Heard. She died in St. Mary's County in 1763.[1406]

Elizabeth Wiseman filed an account of the administration of the estate

---

1399. Margaret K. Fresco, *Marriages and Deaths: St. Mary's County, Maryland, 1634-1900* (Ridge, Md.: the author, 1982), 198.

1400. Md. Administration Accounts, 2:27, 43.

1401. Md. Wills, 17:6.

1402. Md. Inventories, 6:238.

1403. Md. Administration Accounts, 4:237.

1404. Md. Administration Accounts, 5:393.

1405. Newman, *Flowering*, 307.

1406. Newman, *Flowering*, 308-309.

of Robert Wiseman on 21 August 1738. An inventory of £372.12.0 was listed and a second inventory, worth £30.0.0, was also listed. Payments totaled £446.6.2. The balance was distributed, with one-third to the widow, and the balance to the orphans: John, Edward, William, Richard, Mary, Ann, and Elizabeth.[1407]

Daughter Elizabeth Wiseman was named in the will of Elizabeth Heard of St. Mary's County dated 30 April 1745.[1408] The will of Elizabeth Wiseman of St. Mary's County was dated 25 October 1762 and proved 20 February 1763. She named son John, daughter Ann Van Rishwick and her children Monica and Wilfrid Van Rishwick, son Richard and his son Robert, daughter Elizabeth Downie, daughter Mary Leigh and her daughter Peggy Leigh. Son Richard was named executor. Mary Kough and Henrietta Heard were witnesses.[1409] Elizabeth Wiseman left an estate valued at £299.8.6, which executor Richard Wiseman, with Jeremiah Rhodes and Mark Heard as his sureties, distributed on 30 October 1765. After the legatees received their legacies, the balance was distributed to the children of the deceased: John, Richard, Mary Leigh, Ann Van Rishwick, and Elizabeth Downie.[1410]

Children of Robert and Elizabeth (Heard) Wiseman:[1411]

    10. John[4] Wiseman.
    11. Edward Wiseman.
    12. Richard Wiseman.
+ 13. Mary Wiseman, m. Joseph Leigh.
+ 14. Ann Wiseman, m. (1) Thomas Van Rishwick, (2) George Medley.[1412]
    15. Elizabeth Wiseman, m. David Downie. His will dated 7 Apr. 1764, proved 7 May 1764, named wife Elizabeth and brother John Downie; wife Elizabeth and Richard Wiseman appointed executors.[1413]
    16. William Wiseman, probably d.s.p.

6. **Catherine**[3] **Wiseman,** daughter of John and Catherine (Miles) Wiseman, married by 12 August 1704, **John Greenwell,** who was born c1680-1681,[1414] son of James and Grace (Taylor) Greenwell, and died

1407. Md. Administration Accounts, 16:295.

1408. Md. Wills, 28:10.

1409. Md. Wills, 31:863.

1410. Md. Balance Books, 4:147.

1411. Newman, *Flowering*, 308.

1412. Fresco, *Marriages and Deaths: St. Mary's County*, 317.

1413. Md. Wills, 32:263.

1414. Gent., of St. Mary's Co., he gave age as c40 in 9 June 1721 deposition. Md. Chancery Court Records, CL:738.

shortly before 15 July 1741.

The will of John Greenwell of St. Mary's County was dated 22 December 1738 and proved on 15 July 1741. He devised *Pile's Woodyard* to sons John Wiseman Greenwell, John Basil Greenwell, and James Greenwell. He devised to son Joshua the tract *Last Shift*, and to son John Baptist the 100-acre *Rochester*. Wife Catherine was named executor and he mentioned "younger children."[1415] The inventory of his estate, dated 21 August 1741, was valued at £216.15.16. John Basil Greenwell and John Wiseman Greenwell signed as kinsmen. Catherine Greenwell, executor, filed the inventory on 1 September 1741.[1416]

Children of John and Catherine (Wiseman) Greenwell:[1417]

+ 17. John⁴ Wiseman Greenwell, b. 1705; m. Mary Pike, daughter of Archibald and Lucy Pike.[1418]
+ 18. John "Basil" Greenwell.
+ 19. James Greenwell.
  20. Joshua Greenwell, d.s.p. 1750; will dated 24 Feb. 1749/50, named brother Basil, sisters Susanna and Ann Lettice (who were to have his land, 100-acre *Last Shift*), and nephew James Manning; brother John named executor.[1419] His estate was appraised at £11.10.0 by John Hammond and John Cole 4 Sept. 1750. Mary Manning and "Philly" Greenwell signed as creditors, and John Baptist Greenwell and John Basil Greenwell signed as kinsmen. John Wiseman Greenwell filed inventory 28 Dec. 1750.[1420]
+ 21. John Baptist Greenwell.
+ 22. Mary Greenwell, m. by 1749, John Manning.
  23. Susanna Greenwell, may be the Susannah Greenwell whose estate was appraised 1 Sept. 1761 by James Pike and John Hammond, and valued at £73.17.6. Basil Greenwell signed as kinsman, and John Wiseman Greenwell, administrator, filed inventory on 1 Sept. 1761.[1421]
  24. Anne Lettice Greenwell, d. unmarried by 28 Feb. 1753 when estate appraised at £50.8.2;[1422] account of administration filed by brother John Wiseman Greenwell 30 July 1754; payments made to Thomas James, Basil Greenwell, and Susannah Greenwell.[1423]
+ 25. Robert Greenwell, named in 1737 will of Richard Shirley.

1415. Md. Wills, 22:368.

1416. Md. Inventories, 26:333.

1417. Mary L. Donnelly, *Colonial Settlers of St. Clements Bay, 1634-1780, St. Mary's Co., Md.* (Ennis, Texas: the author, 1996), 110; Newman, *Flowering*, 309.

1418. Fresco, *Marriages and Deaths: St. Mary's County*, 130.

1419. Md. Wills, 27:326.

1420. Md. Inventories, 44:248.

1421. Md. Inventories, 76:322.

1422. Md. Inventories, 54:50.

1423. Md. Administration Accounts, 36:410.

7. **Cornelius⁴ Manning**, son of Cornelius and Mary (Wiseman) Manning, married **Jane** [-?-] by 1754.[1424] His will was dated 2 August 1764 and proved 3 September 1764 in St. Mary's County. He named his wife Jane (executrix), children Robert, Monica, Frances, Mary, and John; son-in-law John Greenwell, and daughter Ann Elizabeth wife of William Fenwick (and their son Cornelius Fenwick). Manning mentioned the tract *Nan's Oak*, bought from John Smith. Peter Ford, Jr., William Williams, Francis Williams, and Mary Combs witnessed the will.[1425] Jane Manning filed an account of the administration of the estate of Cornelius Manning on 15 December 1766. Citing an inventory of £114.15.3, she listed payments of £624.18.9.[1426] After all debts were paid, executrix Jane Manning had a balance of £1088.4.5 to distribute, which she did on 15 December 1766. Peter Ford, Jr., and Robert Fenwick were sureties. The legatees were: John Manning, Robert Manning, Cuthbert Fenwick, Ann Elisabeth Fenwick, Monica Manning, Francis Manning, Mary Manning, John Greenwell, and the widow Jane Manning. Robert Manning received one-fifth of the stock and one-sixth part of household furniture. The residue went to the widow.[1427]

Children of Cornelius and Jane Manning, born in St. Andrew's Parish, St. Mary's County:[1428]

    26. John⁵ Manning, b. c1745; d. testate 1815, Perry County, Mo.; m. (1) Susan Wimsatt, (2) c1780, Anastasia Ormsby; had eleven children.[1429]

    27. Robert Manning.

    28. Ann Elizabeth Manning, m. Robert Fenwick.

    29. Ignatius Manning, b. 23 Dec. 1754; not named in father's 1764 will.

    30. Monica Manning, b. 26 Oct. 1759.

    31. Frances Manning, b. 10 Jan. 1762.

    32. [Mary?] Manning, m. John Greenwell.

8. **Mary⁴ Manning**, daughter of Cornelius and Mary (Wiseman) Manning, died 21 March 1769. She married, first, **John Mills**, and, second, **Enoch**

1424. He married either: Jane Brooks [Talbot Co. Wills, 1:459; Timothy O'Rourke, *Md. Catholics on the Frontier*, 748], or Jane (Ford) Greenwell, widow of Ignatius Greenwell (d. 1757) and sister of Monica, Ignatius, and Athanatius Ford [Charles and Laverne Fenwick, *The Greenwell Family*, unpublished, at St. Mary's Co. Hist. Society].

1425. Md. Wills, 32:272.

1426. Md. Administration Accounts, 55:326.

1427. Md. Balance Books, 5:11.

1428. Elsie G. Jourdan, *Colonial Records of Southern Maryland* (Westminster, Md.: Family Line Publications, 1997), 102, 127; Timothy J. O'Rourke, *Maryland Catholics on the Frontier* (Parsons, Kansas: Brefney Press, 1973), 747.

1429. O'Rourke, *Maryland Catholics on the Frontier*, 747, 749.

Combs, who died 4 June 1756.[1430] The will of John Mills of St. Mary's County was dated 31 August 1728 and proved 6 November 1728. He named son John, not yet 21, daughter Mary, and Francis Lloyd. Wife Mary was executrix, John Greenwell, Henry Winset, and Cornelius Manning were witnesses.[1431] Mary, wife of Enoch Combs, filed an account of the administration of the estate of John Mills on 20 January 1729. An inventory of £375.2.2 was listed, and payments totaled £69.12.3.[1432] John Mills may have been the son of Nicholas Mills of St. Mary's County, whose will, dated 11 November 1728, named grandchildren John and Mary Mills, and daughter-in-law Mary Mills, widow. Cornelius Manning was one of the witnesses.[1433]

The will of Enoch Combs of St. Mary's County was dated 18 April 1756 and proved 6 July 1756. He named sons Enoch, William, Bennett, and Ignatius, and wife Mary. Wife Mary and son Enoch were named executors. The will was witnessed by William Williams, Nicholas Mills, and James Roach.[1434] James Roach and John Gale appraised Enoch Combs' personal estate on 6 July [1756?]. They set a value of £1211.11.3 on his property. Mary Waughop and Elenor Medley signed as kinsmen. Mary and Enoch Combs, executors, filed the inventory on 4 November 1756.[1435] An account of the administration of the estate of Enoch Combs was filed by Mary and Enoch Combs, executors, on 2 November 1757. The inventory cited above was offset by payments of £1304.11.11. His estate was distributed to the widow, Enoch (of age), William (of age), Ignatius (age 18), and Bennett Combs (age 10).[1436]

The will of Mary Combs of St. Mary's County was dated 8 November 1769 and proved 12 April 1769. She named her sons Bennett, William, and Ignatius, and granddaughters Mary Walbred Combs and Elizabeth Combs. Her three sons were named executors. The will was witnessed by Josiah Langley, Luke Crisman, and James Pike.[1437]

Children of John and Mary (Manning) Mills:

33. John[5] Mills, minor in 1728 (according to father's will); probably d. before

---

1430. Combs family Bible record, cited in Fanny Combs Gough, *The History of 'Glen Mary' and the Descendants of Enoch Combs amd Allied Families* (1940), typescript, 21.

1431. Md. Wills, 19:500.

1432. Md. Administration Accounts, 10:180.

1433. Md. Wills, 19:616.

1434. Md. Wills, 30:121.

1435. Md. Inventories, 62:127.

1436. Md. Administration Accounts, 41:258; Md. Balance Books, 2:73.

1437. Md. Wills, 37:261.

Apr. 1756 (not named in stepfather's or mother's wills).
34. Mary Mills, may have also d. by Apr. 1756.

Children of Enoch and Mary (Manning) Combs:

35. Enoch Combs, of age in 1757; d. by March 1761; m. Catherine [-?-]. Cars. [*sic*] Manning and Peter Ford, Jr., appraised personal effects of Enoch Combs 11 March 1761; Ignatius and William Combs signed as kinsmen; Catherine Combs, administrator, filed the inventory 2 June 1761.[1438] On 18 Feb. 1762 Catherine Combs filed an account of the administration of his estate; out of the inventory totaling £1026.2.10, payments of £104.16.2 were made. James Combs was one of those who was paid.[1439] When Catherine Combs distributed the balance of £1121.14.5 on 10 Feb. 1762, the Prerogative Court office noted that the "representatives were unknown."[1440]

36. William Combs, of age in 1757; d. in St. Mary's County by Apr. 1774; m. Mary Eleanor Taney [see #115 on page 56]; his will dated 22 Jan. 1774, proved 4 Apr. 1774, named sons Raphael and William, wife Mary, and other children; wife Mary and brother Ignatius named executors.[1441] Robert Fenwick of John and Joseph Jenkins appraised personal property of William Combs at £6550.15.5; Ignatius and Bennett Combs signed as kinsmen; Mary Eleanor Combs, executrix, filed inventory 4 Aug. 1774.[1442] Five children recorded in St. Andrew's Parish, St. Mary's County.[1443]

37. Ignatius Combs, b. 24 Nov. 1740, age 18 in 1757; d. 10 Oct. 1790; m. Mary Fenwick 3 Sept. 1761; she b. 10 March 1746, daughter of John and Monica (Ford) Fenwick; d. 5 Jan. 1813 in 67th year.[1444] Ignatius was 2nd Lt., Lower Battalion, St. Mary's Co. Militia in Aug. 1777; took the Oath of Fidelity in 1778.[1445] Will dated 16 Sept. 1790, proved 8 Feb. 1791; named children Enoch, Bennett, Samuel, John Perry, Lewis, Cornelius, Monica, Mildred, and Eleanor. Wife Mary to have whole estate during widowhood, and to be executrix.[1446] Issue: thirteen children.[1447]

38. Bennett Combs, age 10 in 1757; by 1765 m. Elizabeth [-?-]; two children recorded St. Andrew's Parish, St. Mary's Co.[1448]

1438. Md. Inventories, 74:258.

1439. Md. Administration Accounts, 47:379.

1440. Md. Balance Books, 3:116.

1441. Md. Wills, 39:734.

1442. Md. Inventories, 119:131.

1443. Jourdan, *Colonial Records of Southern Maryland*, 131.

1444. Combs family Bible record, in Gough, *History of 'Glen Mary' and the Descendants of Enoch Combs*, 21, 23-24.

1445. Henry C. Peden, Jr., *Revolutionary Patriots of Calvert and St. Mary's County* (Westminster, Md.: Family Line Publications, 1996), 61.

1446. St. Mary's Co. Wills, JJ#1:520.

1447. Combs family Bible record.

1448. Jourdan, *Colonial Records of Southern Maryland*, 132.

13. **Mary⁴ Wiseman**, daughter of Robert and Elizabeth (Heard) Wiseman, died in St. Mary's County in 1794. By 1762 she married **Joseph Leigh**.[1449] Joseph Leigh died in St. Mary's County in 1785.[1450]
   Child of Joseph and Mary (Wiseman) Leigh:
   39. Margaret⁵ Leigh, m. Matthew Heard, son of Mark Heard.

14. **Ann⁴ Wiseman**, daughter of Robert and Elizabeth (Heard) Wiseman, married, first, before 1753, **Thomas Van Rishwick**, and, second, **George Medley**.[1451] Thomas Van Rishwick, son of Thomas and Anne (Carberry) (Cissell) Van Rishwick, was born in St. Mary's County, and died by March 1762. On 9 March 1762 the inventory of his estate was taken, leaving an estate valued at £128.6.10. Ann Reswick was the administrator.[1452] Ann, "now wife" of George Medley, filed an account of the administration of Thomas Van Reswick's estate on 25 May 1763. Out of the inventory cited above, payments of £39.13.3 were made.[1453]
   Ann "Vanrishwick" and her children Monica and Wilfrid were named in the administration account of Elizabeth (Heard) Wiseman, Ann's mother, filed on 30 October 1765.[1454]
   George Medley was the son of George and Ann (Tant) Medley.
   Children of Thomas and Ann (Wiseman) Van Rishwick, born in St. Andrew's Parish, St. Mary's County:[1455]
   40. Monica⁵ Van Reswick, b. 19 Aug. 1753; d. unmarried; will proved 5 May 1773, naming parents and brother Wilfrid.[1456]
   41. Wilfrid Van Reswick, b. 12 Jan. 1756; d. by 1787; m. Eleanor Fenwick, daughter of John and Monica (Ford) Fenwick; Eleanor m. (2) Francis Herbert.[1457] Had daughter Monica Van Reswick.
   Child of George and Ann (Wiseman) Medley:
   42. Augustine Medley, b. St. Andrew's Parish, St. Mary's Co., 26 Sept. 1762.[1458]

17. **John⁴ Wiseman Greenwell**, son of John and Catherine (Wiseman) Greenwell, was born in 1705. He married **Mary Pike**, daughter of

---

1449. Donnelly, *Colonial Settlers of St. Clements Bay*, 126.
1450. St. Mary's Co. Wills, JJ#1:28, 356; St. Mary's Co. Administration Accounts, 1810-1815, 95.
1451. Fresco, *Marriages and Deaths, St. Mary's County*, 317.
1452. Md. Inventories, 79:270.
1453. Md. Administration Accounts, 49:609.
1454. Md. Balance Books, 4:147.
1455. Jourdan, *Colonial Records of Southern Maryland*, 116.
1456. Md. Wills, 39:341.
1457. Donnelly, *Colonial Settlers of St. Clements Bay*, 252.
1458. Jourdan, *Colonial Records of Southern Maryland*, 95.

Archibald and Lucy Pike.[1459] On 31 January 1750 Archibald Pike of St. Mary's County made his will naming, among others, a daughter Mary Greenwell.[1460] On 15 July 1747 John Wiseman Greenwell and John Wiseman signed the inventory of Richard Shirley as kinsmen. A Charles Greenwell signed as one of the creditors.[1461] On 19 April 1750 he signed the inventory of Archibald Pike as a kinsman.[1462]

18. **John "Basil"**[4] **Greenwell**, son of John and Catherine (Wiseman) Greenwell, died by August 1764 in St. Mary's County. He married **Eleanor** [-?-], widow of [-?-] Clark. She married, third, James Wheatley. The will of John Basil Greenwell was dated 10 September 1761 and proved 13 October 1761. To son Joshua was devised 100-acre *Evans' Quarter*, and, after the death of testator's wife Eleanor, if Joshua was to have no heirs, land was to pass to testator's son James, and then to Richard Langhorn Clark. To son James was devised 200-acre *Pile's Wood Lane*. An unnamed daughter-in-law was bequeathed tobacco. Wife Eleanor was named executrix. The will was witnessed by Monica Medley, Mary Norris, and James Pike.[1463] On 5 March 1762 the estate of John Basil Greenwell was appraised by James Pike and John Cole. John Wiseman Greenwell and John Baptist Greenwell signed as kinsmen. Eleanor Wheatley, now wife of James Wheatley, was the executrix.[1464] Eleanor Wheatley, wife of James Wheatley, filed an account of the administration of the estate on 1 August 1764. Out of the inventory of £143.5.3, payments of £36.13.9 were made.[1465] On 1 August 1764 Eleanor Wheatley, executrix, and "now wife" of James Wheatley, distributed the estate. There was a balance of £171.5.11. After the legacies were paid to the widow Eleanor, to an unnamed daughter-in-law, and son-in-law Richard Clark, the balance was distributed as follows; one-third to the widow, and two-thirds to the two sons, equally, Joshua and James.[1466]

Children of John Basil and Eleanor Greenwell, baptisms recorded in St. Andrew's Parish, St. Mary's County:[1467]

1459. Fresco, *Marriages and Deaths, St. Mary's County*, 130.
1460. Md. Wills, 27:198.
1461. Md. Inventories, 35:371.
1462. Md. Inventories, 44:259.
1463. Md. Wills, 31:498.
1464. Md. Inventories, 77:64.
1465. Md. Administration Accounts, 51:362.
1466. Md. Balance Books, 4:65.
1467. Jourdan, *Colonial Records of Southern Maryland*, 97.

43. Joshua Leonard⁵ Greenwell, b. 5 Nov. 1756.
44. James Greenwell, b. 15 Jan. 1761.

19. James⁴ Greenwell, son of John and Catherine (Wiseman) Greenwell, may possibly be the James Greenwell who married **Hannah** [-?-].

The will of James Greenwell of St. Mary's County was dated 27 April 1770 and proved on 24 July 1770. He named his wife Hannah as executrix, and his first son John, second son Clement, third son James, and youngest son Joseph. He also named his daughters Dorothy and Elizabeth. He named his fourth son Barnaby and fifth son Bennett, and son William. He disposed of the tracts *Holly Tree* and *Greenwell's Defense*. Benjamin Gough, James Gough, Jr., and James Pike witnessed the will.[1468] Hannah Greenwell filed an account of the administration of the estate of James Greenwell on 20 October 1772, citing an inventory of £217.8.8, and listing payments of £13.5.0.[1469] Hannah Greenwell, executrix, with Enoch and Ignatius Fenwick, sureties, distributed a balance of £226.5.3 on 21 October 1772. Legatees were sons John, Clement, and James Greenwell, and the balance went to the widow for her lifetime.[1470]

Children of James and Hannah Greenwell, some of whose births were recorded in St. Andrew's Parish, St. Mary's County:[1471]

45. John⁵ Greenwell.
46. Clement Greenwell.
47. James Greenwell.
48. Barnaby Greenwell.
49. Dorothy Greenwell.
50. Bennett Greenwell, b. 28 Aug, 1755.
51. William Greenwell, b. 12 July 1757.
52. Joseph Greenwell, b. 3 Aug. 1759.
53. Elizabeth Greenwell, b. 23 July 1763.

21. John Baptist⁴ Greenwell, son of John and Catherine (Wiseman) Greenwell, died by 15 February 1774. He married **Susannah** [-?-].[1472] On 14 August 1756 John Baptist Greenwell filed the inventory of John Clark's estate, which had been signed by John Wiseman Greenwell and John Baptist Greenwell as kinsmen.[1473] The inventory of John Baptist

1468. Md. Wills, 38:54.
1469. Md. Administration Accounts, 67:140.
1470. Md. Balance Books, 6:168.
1471. Jourdan, *Colonial Records of Southern Maryland*, 101, 127.
1472. Donnelly, *Colonial Settlers of St. Clements Bay*, 115.
1473. Md. Inventories, 61:341.

Greenwell's estate, dated 15 February 1774, showed a value of £117.19.0. Archibald and Elizabeth Greenwell approved the inventory, and Susannah Greenwell, administratrix, filed it on 29 November 1774.[1474]

Children of John Baptist and Susannah Greenwell, baptisms recorded in St. Andrew's Parish, St. Mary's County:[1475]

54. John Basil[5] Greenwell, b. 17 Aug. 1764.
55. Mary Ann Greenwell, b. 17 March 1767; m. Bernard Newton.
56. Henrietta Greenwell, bp. St. Andrew's Episcopal Church, St. Mary's Co., 27 Feb. 1770; m. John Redman.
57. Cornelius Greenwell, bp. St. Andrew's, 14 Feb. 1773.

22. **Mary**[4] **Greenwell**, daughter of John and Catherine (Wiseman) Greenwell, married by 1749 **John Manning**. Child of John and Mary (Greenwell) Manning:

58. James[5] Manning, b. by 1749.[1476]

25. **Robert**[4] **Greenwell**, son of John and Catherine (Wiseman) Greenwell, died in Baltimore County at about 4 o'clock in the morning of 10 April 1756, according to testimony before the Baltimore County Court.[1477]

On 16 April 1747 he witnessed the will of Richard Shirley of St. Mary's County; Shirley directed that he advise the widow on the sale of land and payment of debts.[1478] The nuncupative will of Robert Greenall was proved at Baltimore County Court in April 1756. Martha Childs, aged about 36, and Mary Childs her daughter, aged about 16, testified that they heard Robert Greenall say that he left his brother Cutbert Greenall as executor and desired he would take care of his children, that he give the eldest son all his lands in St. Mary's County.[1479] The inventory of the estate of Robert Greenwell of Baltimore County was dated 27 July 1756, valued at £409.6.6, approved by Edward and James Mattingly as kinsmen, and filed by executor Cuthbert Greenwell on 27 November 1756.[1480] Cuthbert Greenwell filed an additional inventory on 26 April 1758, adding £79.16.9.[1481] Cuthbert Greenwell, executor, filed an account of the

---

1474. Md. Inventories, 18:221.

1475. Donnelly, *Colonial Settlers of St. Clements Bay*, 115; Jourdan, *Colonial Records of Southern Maryland*, 129.

1476. Bequeathed a box by will of uncle Joshua Greenwell [#20 above] dated 24 Feb. 1749/50. Md. Wills, 27:326.

1477. Baltimore Co. Wills, 1:494. Name spelled "Greenall."

1478. Md. Wills, 25:100.

1479. Baltimore Co. Wills, 1:494; Md. Wills, 30:81-82.

1480. Md. Inventories, 62:119.

administration of Robert Greenwell's estate on 26 April 1758. Payments of £91.4.6 were reported. The account mentioned three children: Joshua, age 11, Robert, age 8, and Juliana, age 6.[1482]

Children of Robert Greenwell:

59. Joshua[5] Greenwell, b. c1747.
60. Robert Greenwell, b. c1750.
61. Juliana Greenwell, b. c1752.

1481. Md. Inventories, 65:234.
1482. Md. Administration Accounts, 41:423.

PART THREE

OTHER EARLY ARRIVALS

This section contains biographies of the 1633-1634 passengers of the *Ark* and the *Dove* who are not yet known to have had descendants. Their inclusion here should not be considered as forestalling further investigation and research. Also mentioned here are some later arrivals who were previously claimed as passengers, but whose presence in Maryland in 1634 can not be proven. Some spurious or doubtful claims of descendants, if appearing in the genealogical literature, are also noted.

Thomas Allen was an indentured servant transported to Maryland in 1633 by Leonard Calvert, who claimed Allen as a headright in 1641.[1483] He is not to be confused with the Thomas Allen who died in 1648 and was one of Claiborne's men on the Isle of Kent in 1633.[1484]

John Altam/Althem, a member of the Jesuit Order, was transported to Maryland in 1633 by Thomas Copley.[1485] John Altham, styled "gentleman" and "Mr.," of St. Mary's Hundred did not appear at the Assembly held at St. Mary's beginning 25 January 1637, having been excused from giving voice in the Assembly because of sickness.[1486] He died in Maryland on 5 November 1640.[1487]

William Andrews, servant, was transported to Maryland in 1633 by Leonard Calvert,[1488] but he did not attend the Assembly of 1637 or the following Assemblies, and is presumed to have died or departed.[1489] He is not to be confused with men of this name mentioned in 1651 and later.

John Ashmore was transported to Maryland in 1633 by Leonard Calvert.[1490] He did not attend the Assembly of 1637, and he does not

---

1483. Md. Land Patents, ABH:98.
1484. Newman, *Flowering*, 165-166, for records of Thomas Allen of Isle of Kent.
1485. *Archives*, 3:258; Md. Land Patents, 1:19, 37, 166.
1486. *Archives*, 1:2, 5.
1487. Newman, *Flowering*, 166.
1488. Md. Land Patents, 1:121, ABH:98.
1489. Newman, *Flowering*, 166.
1490. Md. Land Patents, 1:121, ABH:98.

appear in any testamentary proceedings or land records.[1491]

William Ashmore was transported to Maryland in 1633 by Thomas Copley.[1492] He was on the pinnace *St. Margaret*, and was shot on 10 May 1635 by William Claiborne's men. He was killed instantly.[1493] An inquest was held concerning the shooting of William Ashmore.[1494]

James Barefate/Barefoot, gent., a Catholic, died 1633 en route to Maryland along with twelve others because of over-indulgence at Christmas.[1495]

John Baxter was one of the "gentlemen of fashion."[1496] He died by 20 February 1637/8.[1497] He was married at the time of his death. The inventory of his estate listed a letter to his wife with a small silver seal. Justinian Snow administered the estate.[1498] There is no record of issue.

Ralph Bayne/Bean(e) was one of the fifteen men transported to Maryland in 1633 by Leonard Calvert.[1499] He died testate in 1655. He married **Elizabeth [-?-]**.[1500] On 21 February 1638 Ralph Beane made his mark when he and other inhabitants of St. George's Hundred chose David Wickliffe to represent them in the Maryland Assembly.[1501] Beane took the oath of fealty on 15 March 1648.[1502] He witnessed the will of Thomas Peteate of St. Mary's County on 19 January 1650.[1503] On 7 March 1650 Ralph Beane revoked a letter of attorney given to George Manners and appointed his brother Walter Beane to be his attorney.[1504] He died leaving a will dated 12 November 1654 and proved 24 April 1655. He named a

---

1491. Newman, *Flowering*, 166.

1492. *Archives*, 3:258; Md. Land Patents, 1:20, ABH:64.

1493. *Archives*, 1:17-18; 4:22-23.

1494. *Archives*, 10:22-23.

1495. Newman, *Flowering*, 172.

1496. As referred to by Lord Baltimore.

1497. Newman, *Flowering*, 172.

1498. *Archives*, 4:76, 104-105.

1499. Md. Land Patents, 1:121; ABH:98.

1500. A general reference is Scott D. Breckenridge, "Bayne Family Memorandum," (Lexington, Ky., 1980), manuscript, filing case A, Md. Historical Society.

1501. *Archives*, 1:30.

1502. *Archives*, 3:228.

1503. Md. Wills, 1:67.

1504. *Archives*, 10:59.

daughter Sarah (under age) and a brother Walter who was to have all of his estate in Maryland or Virginia. All his property in England was to go to his wife Eliza. He also mentioned an unnamed sister and "Curbies three children." George Cerye Smith of Southwark and Joseph Ward at the Sign of the White Hart in England were named overseers. Mary Calvert and John Hatch witnessed the will.[1505] The widow Elizabeth Beane married second, by 9 August 1658, John Tonge of St. Thomas Southwark, Surrey. On that day they gave a receipt to Walter Beane of the same parish.[1506] Ralph Bayne/Beane was the father of:

1. Sarah[2] Beane, evidently remained in England.

Thomas Beckworth/Beckwith was transported to Maryland in 1633 by Captain Thomas Cornwalys as a servant.[1507] Nothing else is known about him.[1508]

Henry Bishop was transported to Maryland in 1633 by the Jesuits as an indentured servant.[1509] Free by 1638, he served on the grand jury in 1638, 1643, and 1644, was on a committee in 1640, and was a burgess in 1639 and 1642.[1510] He and Simon Demibiel were named executors and residuary legatees by the 24 March 1640 will of Leonard Leonardson of St. Mary's County.[1511] On 8 January 1644/5 Richard Garnett demanded 900 pounds of tobacco from Simon Demibiel, due Garnett by account from Demibiel and Henry Bishop his mate, *late deceased*.[1512] He is not known to have been married or to have had issue, and is not to be confused with Henry Bishop, Sr., a Virginian who later settled in Somerset County.

John Bolles, gentleman, was secretary or agent sent by Lord Baltimore to accompany the settlers in 1633, and, upon their arrival in Maryland, to read the letters patent and other rights. He witnessed the will of George Calvert, Esq., in Maryland on 10 July 1634. On 26 August 1636 Lord Baltimore granted a 1000-acre land warrant to him. No further record is

---

1505. Md. Wills, 1:60.
1506. *Archives*, 65:181.
1507. Md. Land Patents, 1:110; ABH:94.
1508. Newman, *Flowering*, 174.
1509. Md. Land Patents, 1:20, 37, 38, 166; 2:604; ABH:36; *Archives*, 32:258.
1510. For details of his activities, see Newman, *Flowering*, 174-176.
1511. Md. Wills, 1:5; *Archives*, 1:168.
1512. *Archives*, 4:292.

found for him.[1513]

Richard Bradley was transported to Maryland in 1633 as a servant.[1514] In 1635 he was listed as a creditor of the estate of William Smith, deceased. He was dead by 7 March 1638/9, when Thomas Franklin returned the inventory of his small personal estate.[1515] He was unmarried and left no issue.[1516]

John Bryant/Briant arrived in Maryland in 1634, transported by the Jesuits.[1517] At the Maryland January 1637 Assembly Richard Garnett held John Bryant's proxy.[1518] He became a planter in Mattapanient Hundred, where he was killed by a falling tree on 31 January 1637. On 22 February 1637 administration of his estate was granted to Richard Garnett, who filed the inventory of Bryant's small personal estate on 28 April 1638.[1519] He may have been survived by a widow. In 1639 a "widow Briant" received 40 pounds of tobacco owed to her from the estate of Mr. Egerton, and in 1640 the "widdow Bryant" received 10 pounds of tobacco from the estate of Michael Lums.[1520] There is no evidence of any issue.

Matthew Burrowes/Burraws was transported to Maryland as a servant in 1633 by Captain Thomas Cornwalys.[1521] No further record is found.

John Carle was a sailor who deserted the *Dove* while in Virginia on 22 November 1634.[1522]

Christopher Carnell, his surname variously spelled as "Carnock," "Carnol," and "Carnoll," was transported to Maryland in 1633 by Thomas Copley, Esq.[1523] In 1641 he was a freeholder in St. Mary's Hundred, and attended the General Assembly at its opening day on 23 March 1641/42.[1524] At the

---

1513. Newman, *Flowering*, 176.
1514. Md. Land Patents, 1:121; ABH:98.
1515. *Archives*, 4:32-33.
1516. Newman, *Flowering*, 176.
1517. Md. Land Patents, 1:20, 37-38, 166; ABH:36; *Archives*, 3:258.
1518. *Archives*, 1:4.
1519. *Archives*, 4:23, 30-31.
1520. *Archives*, 4:107, 113.
1521. Md. Land Patents, 1:110; ABH:94.
1522. *Maryland Historical Magazine* 4:251-255.
1523. *Archives*, 3:258; Md. Land Patents, 1:29, 37-38, 166; ABH:66.
1524. *Archives*, 1:120, 176.

Assembly held 6 September 1642 he was one of several persons fined 20 pounds of tobacco for not appearing personally or sending a proxy.[1525] Christopher Carnell of St. Mary's County died leaving a will dated 25 November 1661 and proved 17 June 1662. He left his estate to John Pyper, executor, in trust for the testator's daughter Elizabeth Carnell.[1526] John Goldsmith was named overseer. Samuel Harris, John Norman, and Samuel Debson witnessed the will.[1527]

Thomas Charinton was transported to Maryland in 1633 by the Wintour brothers.[1528] At the Assembly held in January 1637 Captain Robert Evelyn exhibited his proxy for Charinton and other planters of St. George's Hundred.[1529] Charinton attended the Assembly on the morning of 21 March 1641, but that afternoon appointed George Pye as his proxy.[1530] On 2 August 1642 he was assessed 33 pounds of tobacco.[1531] He died shortly before 3 August 1642, on which date letters of administration on his estate were granted to Captain Thomas Cornwalys. The inventory of his small personal estate, taken 23 August 1642 in the presence of Cuthbert Fenwick and Richard Gardiner, was filed on 3 December 1642.[1532]

Richard Cole was transported to Maryland in 1633.[1533] Subsequent records indicate that one or more additional men of this name were transported to Maryland in 1635, "since 1635," and in 1641.[1534] Various records pertaining to men named Richard Cole in the period 1641-1660 can not be identified as the one who arrived in 1633.[1535]

John Cook, according to Newman, was one of Jerome Hawley's retainers in Maryland 1633/34.[1536] A servant, John Cook testified on 27 October 1638 that he was present at an agreement between James Hitches,

---

1525. *Archives*, 1:169. For other records, see Newman, *Flowering*, 185-186.
1526. No further record is found for the orphaned Elizabeth Carnell.
1527. Md. Wills, 1:155.
1528. Md. Land Patents, 1:20, 38; ABH:66.
1529. *Archives*, 1:3.
1530. *Archives*, 1:116-117.
1531. *Archives*, 1:146. For a few other records of Charinton, see Newman, *Flowering*, 186.
1532. *Archives*, 4:95.
1533. Md. Land Patents, 1:20, 38; ABH:65.
1534. Md. Land Patents, 1:26, 129; ABH:60, 102.
1535. Summarized in Newman, *Flowering*, 187.
1536. Newman, *Flowering*, 187. No record of Hawley's transportees is extant.

servant, deceased, and Thomas Hebden.[1537] He had not completed his four years of service at the time of Hawley's death in 1638, but he had attained his freedom by 24 May 1639, when he was a debtor of the estate of Justinian Snow. In May 1640, as a carpenter's servant of Jerome Hawley, deceased, he recovered £9 for wages.[1538] He is not further traced, and is not to be confused with John Cook of St. Mary's County, transported in 1636 by Captain Cornwalys.

Thomas Cooper was transported c1633 to Maryland as a servant of Thomas Greene, Esq.[1539] He died intestate prior to 5 June 1640,[1540] presumably unmarried and without issue. On 5 August 1640 the court ordered Robert Clark to sell Thomas Cooper's goods at an outcry. In November 1642 Robert Clark, administrator of Thomas Cooper, deceased, demanded of John Smith of Kent payment for Cooper's goods.[1541]

Edward Cranfield, Esq., was listed by Lord Baltimore as one of the seventeen "gentlemen of fashion" who sailed to Maryland in 1633,[1542] but no record of him has been found in Maryland.[1543]

John Curke was to be paid £1 a month for services on the *Dove* in 1633.[1544] Richard Kempton of Tower Wharf, London, sailor, aged 24, in May or June 1636 he deposed that Captain Curle [*sic*] had died before the pinnace reached Virginia.[1545]

Thomas Dorrell, said to have been a kinsman of Thomas Greene, Esq., was listed by Lord Baltimore as one of the "gentlemen of fashion" who came to Maryland in 1633. There is no land patent record for him and he died before the Second General Assembly of 1637/38.[1546] In 1638/39

1537. *Archives*, 4:49.

1538. *Archives*, 4:59.

1539. Md. Land Patents, 1:17, 27, 41; 2:346; ABH:6, 67.

1540. *Archives*, 4:64.

1541. *Archives*, 10:150.

1542. "A Relation in Maryland," (London, 1635), reprinted in Hall, *Narratives of Early Maryland*, 101.

1543. Newman, *Flowering*, 190.

1544. *Maryland Historical Magazine* 1:353; Newman, *Flowering*, 15.

1545. Examinations in Equity Cases, vol. 52, cited by Peter W. Coldham, *English Adventurers and Emigrants, 1609-1660*, 65.

1546. Newman, *Flowering*, 191.

Secretary Lewger wrote "about Mr. Dorrell's goods . . . no will yet proved, no administration taken out, no inventory of the goods, some remaining in my hands."[1547] No Maryland issue or heirs have been identified.

Peter Draper, gentleman, immigrated to Maryland c1633[1548] as secretary or steward to Leonard Calvert.[1549] In August 1642 he was assessed 30 pounds of tobacco.[1550] In September 1642 he was one of several planters "suspended from amercement" [i.e., excused from paying a fine].[1551] He died after April 1643 and before April 1644, when Secretary Lewger administered his estate and sold his land rights.[1552] In June 1644 Mary Courtney recovered 350 pounds of tobacco and a cask from the estate of Peter Draper.[1553] No Maryland issue or heirs have been identified.

Richard Duke was transported to Maryland in 1633 by the Wintour brothers.[1554] He was born c1613, according to the age "35 years or thereabouts," which he gave in a deposition in June 1648.[1555] In 1636 he was granted "condition" in Portsmouth for *Duke's Place* in St. Mary's County. This was finally surveyed for him in October 1649.[1556] This tract was never claimed by any heirs of Richard Duke, was escheated to the proprietor, and was resurveyed as part of the tract *Peer* before 1737.[1557] He was a freeman by March 1641 when he attended the Assembly.[1558] He was out of the province in 1642.[1559] In November 1649 William Bretton deposed that Richard Duke had left the province with his partner John Lancelett, "that they would go upon a plantation of their own."[1560] His many debts owed to other planters were noted in the period 1638-1650.[1561]

1547. Calvert Papers, Fund Pub. no. 28, p. 199.

1548. Md. Land Patents, 1:20, 63, 121; ABH:79, 98.

1549. Newman, *Flowering*, 191.

1550. *Archives*, 1:143.

1551. *Archives*, 1:169.

1552. Additional records are summarized in Newman, *Flowering*, 191-192.

1553. *Archives*, 4:279.

1554. Md. Land Patents, 1:20, 38; ABH:65-66.

1555. *Archives*, 4:392.

1556. St. Mary's Co. Rent Rolls, 37.

1557. St. Mary's and Charles Cos. Rent Rolls, 1639-1771, 283. This escheat record indicates the probability that Duke did not leave heirs in Maryland.

1558. *Archives*, 1:116.

1559. *Archives*, 1:169, 179.

1560. *Archives*, 4:533.

1561. *Archives*, 4:48, 122, 181, 340, 385, 437, 498, 521; 10:96, summarized with other records by Patricia Dockman Anderson, "Richard Duke Revisited," in *Md. Genealogical Society Bulletin* 39

There is no evidence that he is the man of this name who immigrated to Maryland in 1653 with a wife and two children,[1562] or the man of this name who was transported to Maryland in 1666.[1563]

Joseph Edlow, definitely of record as a servant in Maryland in 1637 and progenitor of the Edlow family of Maryland, was a freeman at the time of the General Assembly on 1637/8.[1564] There is no record evidence which would prove conclusively that he was among the first settlers in 1633-1634,[1565] but he is said to have accompanied Robert Wiseman.

Richard Edwards was chirurgeon on the *Ark*. In 1634 Governor Calvert authorized payment for his services.[1566] It is not known how long he stayed in Maryland; he did not attend the early assemblies.[1567]

Robert Edwards was transported to Maryland in 1633 by Richard Gerard, who assigned his service and rights to Ferdinand Pulton.[1568] He was a freeman by 1640 when he voted for Thomas Gerard to represent St. Clement's Hundred. In 1640 he lost his suit against Gerard for wages due him. In 1643 he sued Robert Percy for 100 pounds of tobacco. In December 1643 he was assessed 35 pounds of tobacco. He took the oath of fealty on 2 January 1646/47. His last record in Maryland was on 25 January 1646/47, when he demanded tobacco and corn from the estate of John Langworth. He received no land grants and there is no record of the administration of his estate.[1569]

John Elkin was transported to Maryland c1633 by John Saunders.[1570] Name also read as "Elbin." As a freeholder in St. George's Hundred, in August and September 1642 he was fined for failure to appear or name

---

(Fall 1998): 522-527.

1562. Md. Land Patents, ABH:331.

1563. Md. Land Patents, 10:277. See Anderson's "Richard Duke Revisited" article for further discussion.

1564. See Newman, *Flowering*, 193-196, for discussion of the contradictory evidence concerning Edlow's arrival year.

1565. Detailed records of him are provided in Dr. Lois Green Carr, Men's Career Files, MSA SC 5094, PIN 1250-1253.

1566. Lechford Papers, *Fund Publication No. 35*, 25; *Maryland Historical Magazine* 5:61.

1567. Newman, *Flowering*, 196.

1568. Md. Land Patents, 1:20, 38; ABH:66.

1569. Records summarized in Newman, *Flowering*, 197.

1570. Md. Land Patents, 1:20, 38; ABH:65.

a proxy at the Assembly.[1571] In 1642 he was arraigned in court for the felony murder of the Indian king of Yowocomoco. He was found innocent because the jury thought he had killed in self-defense. After 2 December 1642 he was transported to the York River in Virginia by Michael Peasley.[1572]

Nicholas Fairfax, Esq., was one of the "gentlemen of fashion" who accompanied Governor Calvert on the voyage to Maryland in 1633.[1573] He was one of the twelve men who died on the voyage, probably from dysentery and fever, aggravated by over indulgence in beer and wine during the Christmas feast on board the ship. He assigned all his rights in the province to Thomas Greene.[1574]

William Fitter came to Maryland with his employer Thomas Cornwalys in 1633.[1575] He returned to London by April 1636 when he testified on behalf of Lord Baltimore in the suit with Richard Orchard, one-time master of the *Dove*. At that time Fitter was styled "William Fitter of Maryland in the West Indies, Gent., aet. 55." He is not traced further.[1576]

Francisco, a mulatto, was brought to Maryland by Andrew White as one of his servants. Newman states that he was apparently part Portuguese, and part African. He may have been the same as the "Fra. Molcto [or Fra., mulatto]," who was transported in 1633 by Thomas Copley.[1577] No further record is found in Maryland.

Lewis Fre(e)mond was transported to Maryland in 1633 by Thomas Copley.[1578] At the Assembly held January 1638 he was one of several planters of Mattapient Hundred summoned to choose a proxy.[1579] In August 1642 he was assessed 33 pounds of tobacco.[1580] Though at first he could not sign his name, by about 1650 he was able to act as interpreter

---

1571. *Archives*, 1:144, 170.
1572. Newman, *Flowering*, 200.
1573. Md. Land Patents, 1:17, 41, 42; 2:346; ABH:67.
1574. Newman, *Flowering*, 15, 32, 157, 200.
1575. Md. Land Patents, 1:110; ABH:94.
1576. Newman, *Flowering*, 203-204.
1577. *Archives*, 3:258; Md. Land Patents, 1:166; ABH:66.
1578. Md. Land Patents, 1:20, 37, 38; ABH:65.
1579. *Archives*, 1:28.
1580. *Archives*, 1:146.

to Robert Brooke. In 1654 he deposed, signing his name "Lewis ffroman," and giving his age as 29 years. He was last heard of in August 1658 when he, as "Lew ffroeman," sued Robert Holt.[1581]

John Games, the gunner on the *Dove* in 1633, he was paid 12 shillings per month. He went "clear away from the *Dove*" while the vessel was in Virginia 22 November 1634. John Games of Ratcliffe, Middlesex, sailor, aged 34, deposed between 9 May and 15 June 1636 that he had been hired by Richard Orchard, master of the ship, in 1633 to serve on the *Dove* for a voyage from London to the West Indies and Virginia. In 1634 Leonard Calvert sent the *Dove* from Maryland to Massachusetts Bay, New England. On the way, the ship stopped in Virginia to have its bottom refurbished and to take on a new pilot. On the return trip, contrary winds forced the ship into Point Comfort, Virginia.[1582]

Thomas Gervase, probably French, was one of two lay members of the Jesuit Order transported to Maryland in 1634 by Father White. He died in 1637.[1583]

Stephen Gore was brought to Maryland in 1633 by Captain Cornwalys.[1584] No further record is found for him in Maryland.

Thomas Grigston was transported to Maryland in 1633 by Richard Gerard.[1585] No further record is found for him in Maryland.

John Halfhead was born c1605.[1586] He was transported to Maryland in 1633/34 as one of Father White's indentured servants.[1587] He died by 4 February 1675/76, the date his estate was inventoried. He married first, **Ann** [-?-], a free woman who was dead before 1649.[1588] He married second, by 1649, **Julian** [-?-], born c1623, who had been a bond servant

---

1581. Various records summarized in Newman, *Flowering*, 209-210.

1582. *Maryland Historical Magazine* 1:353; 4:251-255; Examinations in Equity Cases, vol. 52, cited by Peter W. Coldham, *English Adventurers and Emigrants, 1609-1660*, 65.

1583. Calvert Papers, in *Fund Publication No. 7*, 117, 126.

1584. Md. Land Patents, 1:110; ABH:94.

1585. Md. Land Patents, 1:20 (name spelled "Grigsta"), 38; ABH:66.

1586. The surname "Halfhead" is common in Bedfordshire, England, in the 17th century.

1587. Md. Land Patents, 1:121; ABH:35, 98.

1588. Md. Land Patents, ABH:35; 2:579.

of Mr. White.[1589] He married third, by 1665, **Elizabeth** [-?-], who was born c1616.

John Halfhead was the provincial brickmason, probably responsible for the construction of many of the early St. Mary's County structures and for the training of the apprentice brickmasons.[1590] Aged about 45 or 46, he made a deposition in court on 25 October 1651, concerning an accidental death at his plantation on the Patuxent River.[1591] Julian "Haffhead," aged 34 years or thereabouts, testified at the provincial court held at Patuxent on 3 November 1657. She made her mark in signing the document. Her husband also testified and made his mark with "JJ."[1592] John Halfhead served on a grand jury in 1637, was a freeman of St. Mary's Hundred by the time of the January 1637[/38] Assembly,[1593] and attended the Assembly in 1647/48.[1594] In her will, dated 28 December 1673, Mary Pine of Kent County bequeathed personalty to John Halfhead and his wife.[1595]

John Halfhead's 250-acre plantation called *Halfhead on the Hill* on the south side of the Patuxent River next to Joseph Edloe was surveyed for him on 2 March 1649[/50], based on 100 acres due to him for his service, 100 acres in right of Ann his first wife, a free woman, and 50 acres more in right of his now wife Julian, who had been a servant to Mr. White.[1596] By deed dated 9 December 1665 Barnaby and Joseph Edloe sold to John Halfhead of Calvert County, planter, 100 acres adjoining Halfhead's plantation in Calvert County. This transaction was the basis for Halfhead's suit in the June 1669 Chancery Court against Joseph Edloe, dismissed in Court on 19 December 1671, when Halfhead was ordered to pay Edloe 2,000 pounds of tobacco for costs. Edloe's countersuit against Halfhead, presented at the June 1670 Court, was dismissed at the 9 April 1672 Court, where the case was dismissed for want of prosecution and Edloe was ordered to pay Halfhead 2,000 pounds of tobacco for costs of the suit.[1597]

John Halfhead, styled "Senior," died shortly before 4 February 1675, on which date George Thompson and Joseph Edloe appraised his personal

1589. Md. Land Patents, 2:579; ABH:35, 98.

1590. Newman, *Flowering*, 219-220, which see for a full account of John Halfhead.

1591. *Archives of Maryland*, 10:155; Md. Patent Records, F&B (1640-1658): 287-288.

1592. *Archives*, 10:549-551; Md. Land Patents, A&B (1650-1657): 339.

1593. Newman, *Flowering*, 219; Md. Patent Records, Z&A (1637-1651): 18.

1594. *Archives*, 1:214-215.

1595. Md. Wills, 2:1.

1596. Md. Land Patents, ABH:118; Q:208; Z&A:608. His "demand" for the land warrant was made on 27 Feb. 1649[50]. Patents, Z&A:579.

1597. Chancery Court Proceedings, in *Archives*, vol. 51, many references.

estate at 25,562 pounds of tobacco.[1598] On 9 February 1675/76 John Halfhead and his wife Elizabeth, now deceased, were mentioned as the former owners of *Halfhead's Folly*, which they had sold to George and Susanna Aynsworth.[1599] On 29 January 1676 John Halfhead, administrator, filed an account of the administration of the personal estate of John Halfhead, Senior, of Calvert County, listing payments totaling the amount of the inventory.[1600]

The only known child of John Halfhead was:

John[2] Halfhead, Jr., son of John Halfhead by either his first or second wife, was an adult by 1676, when he administered his father's estate, but he died in St. Mary's County on 6 January 1677/78, having been accidentally killed by the fall of a tree.[1601] He married **Jane [Maddox?]**,[1602] who "married immediately after his death" and before the filing date, Henry Elliott.[1603]

Jane "Halfehead" witnessed the will of Spencer Hales of Calvert County on 20 March 1675.[1604] On 28 October 1677 John Halfhead was named as administrator and sole legatee by the will of Nicholas Clements, which was proved on 12 November 1677.[1605]

On 11 January 1677/78 administration on the estate of John Halfhead of St. Mary's County was granted to his widow Jane. She stated that he had been struck speechless and senseless by a fall from a tree and had died a few days later.[1606] The personal estate of John "Halfehead" of St. Mary's County was appraised at a value of 15,265 pounds of tobacco. The administration account was filed on 28 July 1679 by Jane Elliott, wife of Henry Elliott, whom she "married immediately after [Halfhead's] death." Payments and disbursements totaled 25,266 pounds of tobacco value, including a payment to Dr. Jacob Lockerman for medical services.[1607]

In his petition to the Chancery Court on 10 July 1678 Henry Elliott explained that John Halfhead had owned a 400-acre tract called *Brushy*

1598. Md. Inventories and Accounts, 1:500.

1599. *Archives*, 66:77.

1600. Md. Inventories and Accounts, 3:63.

1601. Maryland Chancery Court Proceedings, in *Archives*, 51:250-253.

1602. Hodge's Card File, Supposed Marriages, at MSA; does not cite source of surname "Maddox."

1603. Md. Testamentary Proceedings, 9:445, 517. Md. Inventories and Accounts, 6:222.

1604. Md. Wills, 2:410.

1605. Md. Wills, 5:306.

1606. Md. Testamentary Proceedings, 9:45.

1607. Md. Inventories and Accounts, 6:222. Md. Testamentary Proceedings, 9:519.

Neck in St. Mary's County, and had died intestate and without issue, whereby the land became escheatable to the Lord Proprietor. Elliott requested that letters patent be issued, granting the tract to him.[1608] The Court ordered inquisition was held on 12 August 1678 at the house of Henry Elliott, where it was determined that Halfhead had purchased the 300-acre tract from Gwyther on 7 April 1677 for 13,000 pounds of tobacco plus an annual rent of five bushels of corn; that he died on 6 January [1677/78] without making a will; that he left no heir; and that Elliott and his wife Jane, since their intermarriage, have lived on and improved the property. On 10 March 1678/79 the opinion of the Court was that the land and premises are escheated for want of heirs.[1609]

Jane's next husband Henry Elliott of St. Mary's County did not long survive. His will was dated 13 September 1679, by which he named his wife Jane executrix and sole legatee. He was dead by 18 October 1679, the date his will was proved.[1610] His personal estate, valued at 18,600 pounds of tobacco, was appraised on 13 November 1680 by John Evans and Thomas Courtney.[1611]

The fact that John Halfhead's land reverted to Lord Baltimore, for want of heirs, and the fact that the name Halfhead disappears from Maryland records after 1678, make it probable that the line died out or moved to another colony.

Thomas Harington was brought to Maryland in 1633.[1612] Newman states that the name was actually Charinton, and had been incorrectly transcribed.[1613]

Jerome Hawley, eldest son of James and his first wife, Susannah (Tothill) Hawley of Boston near Brentford, County Middlesex, was born 1580, and died in Maryland in summer 1638. He married first, **Judith Hawkins**, and second, **Elinor (Brereton) de Courtney**, widow of Thomas de Courtney and mother of Sir William de Courtney.[1614] Jerome was a brother of Henry Hawley, Governor of Barbados, and William Hawley, one-time

1608. Maryland Chancery Court Proceedings, in *Archives*, 51:221-222.
1609. Maryland Chancery Court Proceedings, in *Archives*, 51:250-253.
1610. Md. Wills, 10:75.
1611. Md. Inventories and Accounts, 7A:229.
1612. Md. Land Patents, 1:38.
1613. Newman, *Flowering*, 186.
1614. A. H. T. Cory, "Some Unpublished Hawley-Halley Data," *Maryland Historical Magazine* 34 (1939): 175-179 (to be used with caution). Laura Hawley, *Hawley, Halley, Holley Resource Book* (Bowie, Md.: Heritage Books, 2003), 59-62.

Deputy Governor of Barbados, and later of Carolina and Maryland, and he was also related to Gabriel Hawley, Surveyor General of Virginia. Jerome was a friend of George Calvert, Lord Baltimore, and was one of the three commissioners who assisted Leonard Calvert on the *Ark* and the *Dove* expedition to Maryland, in which he had a one-eighth share. Prior to sailing on the *Ark* he was granted two manors: 6000-acre *St. Jerome* and *St. Helen*. He maintained his home called *St. Peter* in St. Mary's Hundred. Later he was appointed Treasurer of Virginia by King Charles I.[1615]

His will, made shortly before sailing to Maryland in 1633, appointed as executors his brother William Hawley of Grossmont, Monmouthshire, Arthur Dodington, and Lewis Hele. According to a 1649 letter from his brother James to brother William, Thomas Cornwallis had seized Jerome's estate in Maryland, and William was "next heir to Jerome," whose only child, a daughter, was living at Brabant.[1616] Cornwallis filed the inventory of Hawley's personal estate, total value £944.13.0.[1617] At the Prerogative Court of Canterbury in January 1651 Thomas Cornwallis, as principal creditor, was granted administration on the estate of Jeremiah Hawley of Maryland. Before 1650, as heir of Jerome, brother William Hawley settled on *St. Jerome Manor*.[1618] In 1655 Jerome's step-son, Sir William Courtney of Newhouse, Wiltshire, upon the death of his mother, Mrs. Eleanor Hawley. claimed the manors of *St. Jerome* and *St. Helen*.[1619]

The only surviving child of Jerome and Judith (Hawkins) Hawley was a spinster daughter living at Brabant in 1649. After her uncle William Hawley's death she filed a claim to her father's estate.[1620]

Thomas Heath was transported to Maryland in 1633 by Father White.[1621] On 22 September 1635 he witnessed the will of William Smith.[1622] No further record is found for him in Maryland.

1615. Biography in Newman, *Flowering*, 226-229.

1616. Newman, *Flowering*, 228.

1617. *Archives*, 4:100-101.

1618. *Archives*, 10:250.

1619. *Archives*, 10:444.

1620. Newman, *Flowering*, 229. The claim (in Cory's "Hawley Data" cited above) that Clement Haley of Maryland in 1675 was descended from Jerome Hawley may be discarded as clearly spurious.

1621. Md. Land Patents, 1:20, 37, 38, 166; ABH:65.

1622. Md. Wills, 1:1.

Captain John Hill was one of the "gentlemen of fashion" who accompanied Governor Calvert on the voyage to Maryland in 1633.[1623] Nothing else is known about him, and he is distinguished from the following servant.[1624]

John Hill was transported to Maryland in 1633 as a servant by Thomas Copley.[1625] In February 1637/8 he claimed a voice as a freeman in the Assembly.[1626] In 1638 he was a juror. On 29 August 1638 John Halfhead claimed 690 pounds tobacco of the crop of John Hill, identified as a "fugitive."[1627] On 16 December 1642 a John Hill was assessed 22 pounds of tobacco as an inhabitant of Kent.[1628] Newman states that, although there was a John Hill who had settled on Kent [Island], John Hill, the 1633 passenger, probably settled in Westmoreland County, Virginia, where, with John Hallowes [a fellow passenger], he was named in the will of Thomas Boys.[1629]

John Hilliard was transported to Maryland in 1633 by Father White.[1630] His earliest activities and employment in Maryland are summarized by Newman. By 1660 he had became an overseer for William Bromhall of Calvert and Kent counties, who died testate. At a session of the Prerogative Court in 1660, William Turner presented a petition stating that John Hilliard, overseer of the servants of William Bromhall, "hath clandestinely runne away out of this Province." There were other John Hilliards who came to Maryland, and no evidence has been found identifying any family for this John Hilliard.[1631]

Richard Hills was transported to Maryland c1633 as a servant.[1632] His activities are summarized by Newman.[1633] He was last of record in Maryland when, on 29 June 1649, he transferred his plantation to Richard

1623. "A Relation of Maryland" (London, 1650).
1624. Newman, *Flowering*, 229.
1625. Md. Land Patents, 1:20, 37-38, 166; ABH:66; *Archives*, 3:258.
1626. *Archives*, 1:13.
1627. *Archives*, 4:46.
1628. *Archives*, 3:126.
1629. Newman, *Flowering*, 229-230; Westmoreland Co., Va., Wills, 1:51.
1630. Md. Land Patents, 1:20, 166.
1631. Newman, *Flowering*, 230.
1632. Md. Land Patents, 1:121; ABH:98.
1633. Newman, *Flowering*, 230-231.

Browne,[1634] and assigned a bill to George Manners.[1635] His later history is unknown, and he is distinguished from later settlers of the same name.

James Hockley was brought to Maryland as a servant in 1633 by Leonard Calvert, who demanded land in 1640 for transporting him and then assigned his rights to Peter Draper.[1636] No further record is found for him in Maryland.[1637]

Benjamin Hodges was transported to Maryland in 1633 as a servant for John Sanders, who assigned his land rights to Ferdinand Pulton.[1638] No further record is found for him in Maryland, and there is no evidence that he had descendants.[1639]

Thomas Hodges was transported into Maryland in 1633 by Mr. Copley.[1640] No further record is found for him and he is distinguished from later settlers of the same name.

John Holdern was transported to Maryland in 1633 as a servant of Captain Cornwalys.[1641] In August 1642 he was assessed 30 pounds of tobacco in St. Mary's Hundred.[1642] In the fall of 1642 John Holderne claimed 75 pounds of tobacco as his pay for service in an expedition.[1643] At the September 1642 General Assembly he chose Captain Thomas Cornwalys as his proxy.[1644] No further record is found for him in Maryland.[1645]

Henry James was transported to Maryland in 1633 by the Wintour brothers.[1646] On 25 January 1637 he was one of the St. Mary's Hundred freeholders who chose William Lewis as their proxy at the General

---

1634. *Maryland Historical Magazine* 7:388.

1635. *Archives*, 10:38.

1636. Md. Land Patents, 1:63, 121; ABH:98.

1637. Newman, *Flowering*, 232.

1638. Md. Land Patents, 1:38; ABH:65.

1639. Newman, *Flowering*, 232.

1640. Md. Land Patents, 1:19-20.

1641. Md. Land Patents, 1:26; ABH:60.

1642. *Archives*, 1:142.

1643. *Archives*, 3:119.

1644. *Archives*, 1:167.

1645. Newman, *Flowering*, 232.

1646. Md. Land Patents, 1:38; ABH:66.

Assembly.[1647] In February 1638, signing by mark, he chose James Cauther and John Price as his proxies.[1648] Unmarried and without issue, Henry James died between 27 April 1645, the date of his will, and 23 September 1646, when it was proved. He devised his home and plantation to Thomas Yewell, bequeathed personalty to Thomas Allen (for the use of James's [unnamed] goddaughter), and named Robert Sedgrave as residuary legatee and joint executor with Thomas Yewell. Matthew Rodan and Isaac Edwards witnessed the will.[1649] His leasehold plantation in St. Gabriel's Manor, reported on 14 January 1646/47 as an arrear of manorial rent, was to be escheated to the Lord of the Manor.[1650]

Mary Jennings was transported to Maryland in 1633 as a servant for Father White.[1651] She may have been one of the young women who was nearly drowned while washing Father White's linen shortly after the landing at St. Clement's Island. No further record is found for her.[1652]

Richard Kempton, boatswain, was engaged on 16 October 1633 at £1.2.0 a month. He went "clear away" from the *Ark* while in Virginia in November 1634.[1653] A sailor, resident of Tower Wharf, London, aged 24, he deposed between 9 May and 15 June 1636 that he had been hired as a boatswain of the *Dove*, and that Captain Curle had died before the pinnace reached Virginia.[1654]

John Knowles was transported to Maryland by Father White as one of two lay members of the Society of Jesus. He died 24 September 1637 of a fever.[1655] According to the patent records, he immigrated in 1637.[1656]

Samuel Lawson, mate on the *Dove*, was engaged 16 October 1633 at £2.10.0 per month. He left the *Dove* while in Virginia.[1657]

1647. *Archives*, 1:3.
1648. *Archives*, 1:29.
1649. Md. Wills, 1:33.
1650. *Archives*, 10:93.
1651. Md. Land Patents, 1:19, 166; *Archives*, 3:258.
1652. Newman, *Flowering*, 233.
1653. *Maryland Historical Magazine* 1:353; 4:251-255.
1654. Examinations of Equity Cases, vol. 52, in Peter W. Coldham, *English Adventurers and Emigrants, 1609-1660*, 65.
1655. Calvert Papers, *Fund Publication No. 7*, 117, 126.
1656. Md. Land Patents, 1:17, 20, 38; ABH:66.
1657. *Maryland Historical Magazine* 1:353; 4:251-255.

William Lewis came to Maryland as a free immigrant, possibly as one of the 26 servants transported by Father White,[1658] but he is not recorded in Maryland before 25 January 1637/38, when he appeared as a freeholder at the opening day of the General Assembly.[1659] On 2 November 1638 he made oath that he was not contracted to any other woman, and there was no impediment of consanguinity, affinity, or any other lawful impediment to his intended marriage with **Ursula Gifford**. He was granted a license to marry her.[1660] Lewis was present at the Assembly of January-March 1637/38, with five proxies. He was a proxy to Robert Clarke at the January 1647/48 Assembly.[1661] On 3 July 1638 William Lewis, with John Medcalfe and Richard Browne, posted bond for 3,000 lbs. of tobacco, in case Lewis should offend the peace of the colony, or the inhabitants thereof by injurious and unnecessary arguments or disputations in matters of religion, or if he should use any ignominious words or speeches touching the books or ministers authorized by the Church of England.[1662] They probably left St. Mary's with Governor Calvert and were in exile during the Ingle and Clayborne insurgency.[1663] On 15 October 1646, upon his return to Maryland, Lewis demanded land for transporting himself and his wife and six servants.[1664] On 29 December 1646 he testified before the Assembly as a soldier of Governor Calvert returning to Maryland from Virginia.[1665] He was killed at the Battle of Severn in 1655.[1666] On 23 September 1657 administration on the estate of William Lewis was granted to George Gutteridge who had married Lewis's widow.[1667] According to a 1667 record, Lieutenant William Lewis died without heirs, and his 3,000-acre manor was escheated to the Lord Proprietary.[1668]

Richard Loe was one of the servants transported to Maryland by Thomas Cornwalys in 1633.[1669] By the time of the Second General Assembly of 1637 he had become a freeholder in St. Michael's Hundred. On 18

1658. Newman, *Flowering*, 233-234.
1659. *Archives*, 1:2.
1660. *Archives*, 4:50-51; Md. Land Patents, 1:133.
1661. *Archives*, 1:2, 217.
1662. *Archives*, 4:39.
1663. Newman, *Flowering*, 234.
1664. Md. Land Patents, 2:512.
1665. *Archives*, 1:209.
1666. Letter from Verlinda Stone, in Hall, *Narratives of Early Maryland*, 266.
1667. *Archives*, 10:523.
1668. Newman, *Flowering*, 234.
1669. Md. Land Patents, ABH:94.

February 1638 at Saint Inigo's, Richard Loe was among the freemen who chose the Saint Michael's Hundred burgesses.[1670] He died by 2 May 1638 when John Medley was granted letters of administration on his estate. In 1642 Mr. Baldridge filed the inventory of his personal estate, appraised at a total value of 2,158 pounds of tobacco, and included a servant, a sword, a book, a dog, and a hen with five chicks.[1671] He apparently was unmarried and died without issue. It should be noted that a later Richard Loe immigrated in 1640 and was granted land in August 1641.[1672]

Richard Lusthead was transported to Maryland in 1633 as a servant of the Jesuits.[1673] In Maryland he married **Elizabeth Garnett**, who had been brought into Maryland in 1637, at the age of 19 years, by her father Richard Garnett,[1674] and was a sister of Luke Garnett/[Gardiner].[1675] The few records which he generated during his brief tenure in Maryland are summarized by Newman.[1676] Presumably predeceased by his wife, he died shortly before 3 August 1642, when letters of administration on the estate of Richard Lustead were issued to Captain Thomas Cornwalys,[1677] and his small personal estate was appraised on 23 August 1642 in the presence of Cuthbert Fenwick and Richard Gardiner, and filed on 3 December 1642.[1678] On 10 March 1650/51, Luke Gardiner claimed land "due to Richard Luslick [*sic*], servant to Mr. Copley, who married my sister, deceased,"[1679] thus indicating that Richard Lusthead left no children or heirs.

John Marlburgh was transported to Maryland in 1633 by John Saunders.[1680] He was in St. Mary's County on 25 November 1642 when he was assessed 2 pounds of tobacco. In December 1642 he was assessed 8 pounds of tobacco.[1681] After his 1643 assessment of 35 pounds of tobacco, there is no further record of him.

1670. *Archives*, 1:15, 28-29.
1671. *Archives*, 4:57, 74.
1672. Md. Land Patents, 1:119.
1673. Md. Land Patents, 1:20, 37, 38, 166; ABH:65.
1674. Md. Land Patents, 1:62. Richard Garnett was also known as Richard Gardiner.
1675. Md. Land Patents, 1:168.
1676. Newman, *Flowering*, 235.
1677. *Archives*. 4:71.
1678. *Archives*, 4:94
1679. Md. Land Warrants, 1:167.
1680. Md. Land Patents, 1:38; ABH:65.
1681. *Archives*, 3:120, 123.

Christopher Martin was transported to Maryland in 1633 or 1635 in the retinue of Captain Cornwalys.[1682] He married **Eleanor** [-?-]. As a St.Mary's Hundred freeholder, he attended the January 1637/38 Assembly. At the Provincial Court on 30 March 1638 he released and quitclaimed James Cloughton of all actions and suits whatsoever.[1683] On 8 October 1641 Leonard Calvert granted administration on the estate of Christopher Martin to his widow Eleanor.[1684] In June 1642 the personal estate of Christopher Martin, tailor, was appraised jointly with that of the administrator [and business partner?], Joseph Edloe, planter, Martin being credited with "one halfe of the goods and chattles."[1685] No further record is found for the widow Eleanor Martin or any children.[1686]

John Metcalfe, gentleman, was stated by Cecilius Calvert in 1635 to have been one of the "gentlemen of fashion" who had sailed for his Province.[1687] On 16 September 1650 Metcalfe claimed land rights for having immigrated to Maryland "in July last was 15 yeares" [*i.e..* July 1635].[1688] He was not mentioned in Maryland before 25 January 1637/38, and did not claim land rights under the Conditions of 1633. His many activities and civil offices are summarized by Newman,[1689] who does not cite any record which would indicate that Metcalfe was among the first arrivals. No record is found for any family, and there is no probate record for him in Maryland.

Charles Middleton was transported to Maryland as a servant in 1633 by Governor Leonard Calvert.[1690] There is no other record of him in Maryland.

Fra. Molcto was transported to Maryland in 1633 by Thomas Copley. See "Francisco, a mulatto," above.

1682. Md. Land Patents, ABH:244; 4:623.
1683. *Archives*, 4:26.
1684. *Archives*, 4:66.
1685. *Archives*, 4:93.
1686. Newman, *Flowering*, 236.
1687. Newman, *Flowering*, 236.
1688. Md. Land Patents, ABH:50, 206; 3:77.
1689. Newman, *Flowering*, 236-238.
1690. Md. Land Patents, 1:121; ABH:98.

Roger Morgan was transported to Maryland in 1633 by Captain Cornwalys, who proved a claim to land in 1641.[1691] There is no other record of his life in Maryland.

Thomas Munns, was transported to Maryland in 1633 by Richard Gerard, who conveyed his right to land to Ferdinand Pulton.[1692] On 23 April 1649 Thomas Munnes testified regarding his employment by Richard Husbands, mariner.[1693] Thomas [Munni?] witnessed the will of Thomas Tucker on 4 November 1659.[1694] No further record is found.

John Norton the Elder and **John Norton the Younger** were transported to Maryland from Virginia by Captain Cornwalys in 1633.[1695] There is no proof that they were father and son, or that they were related. As a freeman of St. Mary's Hundred one John Norton attended the Assembly of 1637/38.[1696] One of the John Nortons appeared in records in 1638/39 and 1642.[1697] In September 1642 he failed to attend the Assembly and assigned his rights to Captain Cornwalys.[1698] In 1643 and again in 1644 he was sued for debt,[1699] after which there is no further record for a man of this name in Maryland until 1655.[1700]

Richard Orchard, master of the *Dove*, was engaged on 30 September 1633 at £4.0.0 a month. He and the crew deserted the *Dove* in Virginia. Lord Baltimore sued him in England, on charges of disobeying orders, but Lord Baltimore lost the suit.[1701] This master of the pinnace *Dove* was the subject of a complaint by Leonard Calvert and Jerome Hawley, owners of the ship. Before 9 May 1636, Sir John Harvey, Governor of Virginia, deposed that Calvert and Hawley complained that Richard Orchard had left his ship and behaved insolently. Orchard and his men had refused to return to their ship unless their outstanding wages were paid. Calvert and Hawley refused payment until the *Dove* returned to Maryland. In the case

---

1691. Md. Land Patents, 1:26.
1692. Md. Land Patents, 1:38 "Munns"; ABH:66 "Minns."
1693. *Archives*, 10:9.
1694. Md. Wills, 1:93.
1695. Md. Land Patents, 4:623; ABH:244.
1696. *Archives*, 1:3.
1697. *Archives*, 1:28, 145.
1698. *Archives*, 1:170, 176.
1699. *Archives*, 4:202, 286.
1700. Newman, *Flowering*, 245-246. A John Norton and wife Elizabeth immigrated in 1655.
1701. *Maryland Historical Magazine* 1:353; 4:251-255.

of Cleborne *versus* Clobery *et al*, Richard Orchard of Wapping, Middlesex, sailor, aged 40, deposed between 5 March 1639/40 and 10 November 1642 that he had lived in Maryland and Virginia and had often seen the patent granted to Lord Baltimore for the Province of Maryland. He stated that the Isle of Kent or Isle of Contentment of Virginia was north of the 40 degree line and the greater part, therefore, outside the bounds of Maryland.[1702]

Michael Perril was engaged as the servant for the *Dove*'s master on 16 October 1633 at 10 shillings per month.[1703]

Nicholas Perry, a seaman, was engaged on the *Dove* in 1633 at £1.0.0 a month.[1704] He came from Jernematha [*sic*], Isle of Wight, and was a sailor, aged 26, when he deposed between 9 May and 15 June 1636 that he had gone as quartermaster of the *Dove*.[1705]

Robert Pike was transported to Maryland as a servant in 1633 by Governor Leonard Calvert.[1706] No further record is found for him in Maryland.

John Price, Sr., *alias* White John Price, and **John Price, Jr.**, *alias* Black John Price, were transported to Maryland in 1633 by the Wintour brothers, who later assigned their head rights to Ferdinando Pulton.[1707] Neither man is further identified in Maryland, and should not be confused with the well-documented[1708] Captain (later Colonel) John Price, born c1608, who immigrated to Maryland in 1636, and died testate shortly before 11 March 1660/61 (date his will was proved), survived by a minor daughter Anne Price.[1709]

1702. Examination in Equity Cases, vol. 57, cited by Peter Wilson Coldham, *English Adventurers*, 104.

1703. *Maryland Historical Magazine* 1:353; 4:251-255.

1704. *Maryland Historical Magazine* 1:353; 4:251-255.

1705. Examinations in Equity Cases, vol. 52, cited in Coldham, *English Adventurers and Emigrants, 1609-1660*, 65.

1706. Md. Land Patents, 1:121; ABH:98.

1707. Md. Land Patents, 1:38; ABH:66. "Black" indicated the man with the darker or swarthy complexion, not an African. Newman, *Flowering*, 246-247.

1708. Records summarized in Newman, *Flowering*, 247-248, 328.

1709. Md. Wills, 1:141.

Lodowick Price was transported to Maryland as a servant in 1633 by Governor Leonard Calvert.[1710] There is no further record of him in Maryland.[1711]

Thomas Price was not a passenger on either the *Ark* or the *Dove* when they sailed from the Isle of Wight, England, in November 1633 and arrived in Maryland the following March. He was transported to Maryland as a servant by Thomas Pasmore, possibly from Virginia, on the second voyage of the *Ark*, which left England about 29 September 1634 and arrived in Maryland in early December 1634, stopping first in Virginia.[1712] No further record traces of this Thomas Price are found in Maryland in the period 1634-1655.[1713] Other men of this same name were transported to Maryland in the 1660s and 1670s.[1714]

Thomas Price, who died by 9 April 1703 in St. Mary's County, was probably the father of the Thomas Price who filed the inventory and account of Thomas Price, Sr. His personal estate was valued at £15.9.7 by William Aisquith and John Milles; debts amounted to £14.14.0. His presumed son Thomas died about five months later, when Thomas Davis and William Smith appraised his estate at £59.15.0, with payments of £37.17.5., administered by Elizabeth Price, on 1 March 1704.[1715] She may have been his widow. No evidence was found that Thomas, Jr. had children, and more particularly that he was the father of Edward and grandfather of Francis Price mentioned in the 17 April 1686 will of Robert Phillips of Anne Arundel County.[1716] No evidence was found that these men were related to Mordecai Price of Anne Arundel County, who married c1710 Mary Parsons and was associated with Anthony Holland, who both had an interest in the tract *Locust Neck* devised by Robert Phillips to Edward and Francis Price.[1717]

1710. Md. Land Patents, 1:121; ABH:98.

1711. Newman, *Flowering*, 248.

1712. Md. Land Patents, 1:25, 73; ABH:82; Newman, *Flowering*, 47.

1713. The earliest records are itemized in Dr. Lois Green Carr Men's Career Files, MSA SC 5094, nos. 3397-3398.

1714. Ten entries listed in Md. Land Patents, indexed in Skordas, *Early Settlers of Maryland*, 374.

1715. Md. Inventories and Accounts, 22:79; 25:149.

1716. Md. Wills, 6:295.

1717. Calvert Rent Rolls, 137.

Francis Rabnett was transported in 1633 by the Wintour brothers.[1718] At the 11 November 1635 meeting of the Privy Council, Governor Harvey of Virginia denied favoring the assertion of one Rabnet of Maryland that it was lawful to kill a heretic king. Harvey had apprehended Rabnet, but the evidence against him of Mr. Williams, a minister, was not admitted.[1719] He was living in November 1642 when, as an inhabitant of Kent Island, he was assessed 4 pounds of tobacco. In December of that year, he was assessed 20 pounds of tobacco.[1720] In February 1642 Thomas Weston demanded 1,200 pounds tobacco and cask from Rabnett.[1721] He was last mentioned in Maryland on 18 July 1643, when he was sued by Giles Brent for a debt of 1,300 pounds of tobacco.

John Robinson, a carpenter, was transported to Maryland as a servant in 1633 by Captain Cornwalys.[1722] At the Assembly of 1637/38 he was admitted as a freeholder,[1723] and served on a coroner's inquest panel at Mattapanient.[1724] Apparently unmarried and without issue or heirs, he died shortly before 1 December 1643, on which date Richard Wright administered his estate.[1725]

Francis Rogers was transported to Maryland in 1634 by Thomas Copley.[1726] He is not further mentioned in the province.[1727]

William Saire, Esq., was mentioned as one the "gentlemen of fashion" who came to Maryland with the first settlers. But there is no further record of him in Maryland.[1728]

1718. Md. Land Patents, 1:38; ABH:66.

1719. *Calendar of State Papers, American and Colonial Series, 1574-1660*, edited by W. Noel Sainsbury (Longman & Green, 1860), in Peter W. Coldham, *The Complete Book of Emigrants, 1607-1660* (Baltimore: Genealogical Publishing Co., 1987), 172.

1720. *Archives*, 3:121, 124. Several earlier records are summarized in Newman, *Flowering*, 248-249.

1721. *Archives*, 4:184.

1722. Md. Land Patents, 1:110, 130; ABH:94.

1723. *Archives*, 1:4.

1724. *Archives*, 4:9. His few additional records are summarized in Newman, *Flowering*, 249.

1725. *Archives*, 4:214-215, 284.

1726. Md. Land Patents, 1:20, 37, 166; *Archives*, 3:258. Identified as "Mr. Rogers."

1727. Newman, *Flowering*, 250.

1728. Newman, *Flowering*, 250.

Stephen Salmon (or Sammon) was transported to Maryland as a servant of Thomas Cornwallis in 1633, for whom he claimed land rights in 1640/41.[1729] He completed his service in about 1643, at which time he was assessed or paid 50 pounds of tobacco for a campaign against the Indians.[1730] On 2 January 1646/47 he took the oath of fealty.[1731] His [unnamed] wife claimed land for her service in 1649.[1732] He served on juries in November 1650 and February 1650[/51].[1733] On 20 February 1650[/51] he was granted a warrant for 250 acres at Cedar Point on Potomac River.[1734]

Stephen Salmon died before 2 December 1651, on which date Walter Peake, administrator of the estate of Stephen Salmon, was sued at the Provincial Court by William Stone.[1735] On 22 January 1652/53 his estate was sued by Robert Brooke for 600 pounds of tobacco. The will of Thomas Diniard of St. Mary's County, dated 1 November 1659, bequeathed personalty to "Thomas Salmon son of Stephen Salmon."[1736]

Child of Stephen Salmon:

Thomas² Salmon, son of Stephen Salmon, is not further traced. He can not be identified as the man of this name who immigrated to Baltimore Co., Md., in 1667, was a planter, ordinary keeper, merchant, and county court clerk; Cecil Co. member of Lower House, 1674; died testate in Cecil Co. July 1675.[1737] Newman speculated that he might have been the cooper of this name, attached to the Jesuit mission at Newtowne, who died without issue in 1695, leaving his small estate to the priests.[1738]

John Saunders, Esq., one of the "gentlemen of fashion," immigrated to Maryland in 1633,[1739] but died in 1634,[1740] his estate being administered by

---

1729. Md. Land Patents, ABH:383.

1730. *Archives*, 3:138.

1731. *Archives*, 3:174.

1732. Md. Land Patents, ABH:35, 41. Stephen claimed 50 acres in right of his wife bought of Mrs. Troughton. Md. Patent Records, Z&A (1637-1651): 624.

1733. *Archives*, 10:57. See Newman, *Flowering*, 250-251, for brief account of Stephen Salmon.

1734. Md. Patent Records, Z&A (1637-1651): 572, 624; A&B (1650-1657): 104.

1735. *Archives*, 10:113.

1736. Md. Wills, 1:82.

1737. Papenfuse *et al*, *A Biographical Dictionary of the Maryland Legislature, 1635-1789* (Baltimore: Johns Hopkins University Press, 1985), 2:710.

1738. Newman, *Flowering*, 251.

1739. Md. Land Patents, ABH:65.

1740. Records are summarized by Newman, *Flowering*, 251-252.

his business partner, Thomas Cornwalys. The administration account mentioned a brother Valentine Saunders as heir.[1741]

Robert Sherley was transported to Maryland as a servant of Father White in 1633.[1742] Thomas Copley later claimed land rights for his transportation.[1743] There is no further record of him in Maryland.[1744]

Robert Simpson, a surveyor, was transported to Maryland as a servant of Father White in 1633,[1745] and was employed to survey the planned town.[1746] He did not attend the Assembly of 1637 and is not further mentioned in Maryland.[1747]

Thomas Smith was transported to Maryland in 1633 by the Wintour brothers.[1748] He did not attend any of the early assemblies, and is not further mentioned. He is not to be confused with Thomas Smith, gent., of Kent Island, a Virginian executed by 1638 for piracy, leaving a wife Jane and daughters Gertrude and Jane.[1749]

William Smith, gent., immigrated to Maryland in 1633.[1750] He died testate at St. Mary's shortly before 22 September 1635, the date his will was proved. He appointed his wife **Anne** as executrix and residuary legatee.[1751] He left a personal estate valued at £135.18.6. His widow Ann filed the inventory and an account on or about October 1638, and was not again mentioned in Maryland.[1752]

Mathias Sousa, a mulatto probably of African and Portuguese origin, was transported to Maryland in 1633, one of nine indentured servants claimed as headrights by Thomas Copley and brought by Father Andrew White, the Jesuit missionary. In 1639 Ferdinando Pulton requested a land

---

1741. *Archives*, 4:14.
1742. Md. Land Patents, 1:20, 37, 38, 166.
1743. *Archives*. 3:258.
1744. Newman, *Flowering*, 252.
1745. Md. Land Patents, 1:19, 37, 38, 166; ABH:65; *Archives*, 3:258.
1746. Calvert Papers, *Funds Publication No. 28*, 138.
1747. Newman, *Flowering*, 261. Name also spelled "Sympson."
1748. Md. Land Patents, 1:38; ABH:66.
1749. *Archives*, 4:507; Newman, *Flowering*, 134, 256.
1750. Md. Land Patents, 1:17, 41-42; 2:346; ABH:6, 67.
1751. Md. Wills, 1:1. The first will recorded in Maryland.
1752. Newman, *Flowering*, 256-257.

warrant for these servants' rights, assigned to him by Father White.[1753] Pulton employed Souza as skipper of a small vessel, permitting him to trade with the Susquehannock Indians.[1754] In 1638/39 he owed the estate of Justinian Snow.[1755] At the 23 March 1641/42 meeting of the Maryland Assembly "Matt das Sousa" appeared as a freeholder.[1756] He was next employed by John Lewger as master of a ketch, indenturing himself for a four-month term. Lewger took him to court in November 1642, and Sousa was ordered to fulfill his indentureship.[1757] Also in 1642 he was sued by John Hollis for a debt of 500 pounds of tobacco, and the sheriff was ordered to seize the "person of Mathias de Sousa."[1758] At that point he disappeared from Maryland.

Thomas Stratham was transported to Maryland in 1633 by Thomas Copley.[1759] His name also read as "Slatham," he witnessed the will of William Smith, gent., which was proved on 22 September 1635.[1760] He was not summoned to the Assembly of 1637, and there is no further record of him in Maryland.[1761]

John Tomson was transported to Maryland in 1633 by Father White.[1762] Early records of men of this name, variously spelled "Thompson," "Tompson," and "Tomkins," are summarized by Newman,[1763] who concluded that this man died unmarried and without issue shortly before 7 May 1649, the date his will was proved. His will, dated 19 February 1648[/49], devised his plantation to George Ackrick and James Walker, and appointed them executors.[1764]

Richard Thompson was transported to Maryland in 1633 by Father White,[1765] and is not further recorded in Maryland. He should not be

---

1753. Md. Land Patents, 1:19, 37, 38, 166; ABH:65-66. Name also read as "Zause."
1754. *Archives*, 4:138.
1755. *Archives*, 4:85.
1756. *Archives*, 1:120.
1757. *Archives*, 4:138.
1758. *Archives*, 4:155.
1759. Md. Land Patents, ABH:65; *Archives*, 3:258.
1760. Md. Wills, 1:1.
1761. Newman, *Flowering*, 252.
1762. Md. Land Patents, 1:20.
1763. Newman, *Flowering*, 265-266.
1764. Md. Wills, 1:12; *Archives*, 4:337.
1765. Md. Land Patents, 1:37-38; ABH:65.

confused with the later arriving Richard Thompson, gent., of Kent Island, who married Ursula Bisshe and died in Northumberland County, Virginia, in 1649.[1766]

William Thompson, gent., first recorded in Maryland in the 1640s, died testate in New Town in 1650, leaving a widow and children.[1767] But he cannot be identified as being among the first arrivals.

James Thornton was transported to Maryland in 1633 by Thomas Copley.[1768] After his testimony during hearings against William Lewis in 1638,[1769] there is no further record of him in Maryland.[1770]

Cyprian Thorowgood, gent., recorded in Maryland only in the period 1637-1643,[1771] cannot be placed among the first arrivals. He returned to England. At London on 18 July 1646 Cyprian Thorowgood of Wendon, Co. Essex, aged 40, deposed concerning events in Maryland.[1772]

Roger Walter was transported to Maryland by Captain Thomas Cornwalys, who in 1641 claimed land for bringing him in 1633.[1773] Walter did not attend the Assembly in 1637/38, and there are no other references to him.[1774]

John Ward was transported to Maryland in 1633,[1775] as one of the retainers of Richard Gerard, but he did not attend the early Assemblies and is not further mentioned. He cannot be identified as the man of this name who arrived in 1647.[1776]

1766. Newman, *Flowering*, 261-262; Louise C. Morrell, essay on "Richard Thompson of Kent Island," in Society files.

1767. Newman, *Flowering*, 262-263.

1768. Md. Land Patents, 1:20.

1769. *Archives*, 4:38.

1770. Newman, *Flowering*, 263.

1771. Records summarized in Newman, *Flowering*, 263-264.

1772. Public Record Office (England), Chancery Court document C2/Chas. I/C15/23, abstracted in Peter W. Coldham, "Genealogical Gleanings in England," *National Genealogical Society Quarterly*, 69 (1981): 121.

1773. Md. Land Patents, ABH:1:26; ABH:60. Skordas indexes arrival year as 1635.

1774. Newman, *Flowering*, 269.

1775. Md. Land Patents, 1:38; ABH:66.

1776. Newman, *Flowering*, 269.

John Wells was recorded in Maryland records only when he witnessed the will of George Calvert at St. Marie's on 10 July 1634.[1777] He should not be confused with the man of this name who immigrated in 1653.

Father Andrew White, a Jesuit priest, came to Maryland in 1633.[1778] His important services during his tenure in Maryland ended when he was transported back to England by the Puritan rebels in 1644.[1779]

Evan Wilkins was transported to Maryland as a servant in 1633 by Leonard Calvert.[1780] No further record is found.[1781]

Frederick Wintour and **Edward Wintour** immigrated to Maryland in 1633,[1782] bringing seven adventurers, whose head rights they assigned to Ferdinand Pulton. They were described by Lord Baltimore as brothers, sons of Sir John and Lady Anne Wintour. Last mentioned in Maryland in June and July 1634, they did not attend the January 1637/38 Assembly, and their later histories are not determined.[1783]

Robert Wintour was commander of the *Ark* on its 1633 voyage to Maryland. In July 1637 he transported seven servants to Maryland.[1784] On 8 April 1638 he agreed to lease five servants to George Evelin.[1785] He died shortly before 4 September 1638, on which date his personal estate was appraised.[1786] An account of the administration of his estate was filed on 4 September 1639 by Secretary John Lewger.[1787] No family or heirs have been identified.[1788]

1777. Newman, *Flowering*, 269-270.

1778. Md. Land Patents, 1:19, 37, 166; ABH:65.

1779. Records summarized in Newman, *Flowering*, 270-271.

1780. Md. Land Patents, 1:121.

1781. Newman, *Flowering*, 271. Name also read as "Watkins."

1782. Md. Land Patents, ABH:66.

1783. Newman, *Flowering*, 271.

1784. Md. Land Patents, 1:18.

1785. *Archives*, 4:27.

1786. *Archives*, 4:88-89.

1787. *Archives*, 4:106.

1788. Newman, *Flowering*, 271-273. Undocumented summary of his history and career, in Edward C. Papenfuse *et al*, *A Biographical Dictionary of the Maryland Legislature, 1635-1789* (Baltimore: The Johns Hopkins University Press, 1985), 2:905.

INDEX

Compiled by Jane Fletcher Fiske, FASG

In the following index of persons, married women appear under their maiden names (if known) as well as under their married names. Surnames have been standardized to some extent and variants cross-referenced. The small letter "n" indicates a footnote on the page referenced.

ADDITIONS AND CORRECTIONS

Compiled by Donna Valley Russell and George Ely Russell

John Briscoe. Pages 18-19. There is no primary documentary record evidence to establish the presence of a John[1] Briscoe in Maryland before 1648. Furthermore, there is no reliable record evidence to place Philip Briscoe in Maryland before about 1669, and no evidence of the identity of the parents of either John[2] or Philip[2] Briscoe. Contrary to the statement in footnote 92, Pye's journal article *does not refute* the cogent conclusions explained in Bell's very convincing previous article. Claims of descent from John Briscoe are now disallowed by the Society.

John Curle. Page 218. Delete "Curke" and "[sic]." The mariner's surname was "Curle."

Richard Duke. Pages 219-220. Richard Duke and his partner next appeared in Westmoreland County, Virginia, where in ca. 1652 the account of Abraham Johnson with Major John Hallows included one hogshead [of tobacco] at Mr. Richard Duke's. On 10 July 1654 Richard Duke signed a bond promising to pay Andrew Monroe 571 pounds of tobacco. The bond was recorded on 27 February 1657/58. Richard Duke was dead in Westmoreland County by 1 August 1655, on which date his widow Jane Duke agreed that her son Richard Duke would be indentured to and serve John Dodman of Westmoreland County, gent., and his wife Elizabeth or their son John Dodman, for eleven years from the 25th December next and until 25 December 1666, at which time they will give Richard a "good and gentle cow with one cow calfe by her side."[1] In Westmoreland County, 30 Dec. 1663, Richard Duke witnessed a deed of gift from William Fryzar of Appomattocks.[2]

Cuthbert Fenwick. Page 85. Enoch[4] Fenwick's mother has not been identified. Delete "and Cassandra (Brooke)." Delete "He married Susannah Ford who died in St. Mary's County in 1784." Insert "He married **Elizabeth Miles** before 1767."

Thomas Greene. Page 112, 4th line. Delete "widow of Nicholas Harvey."
Page 114. 4. **Robert[2] Green** died by 1716 (not in wife's will). Delete "He may have married second Katherine Severen." Delete sentence beginning "Robert Green may have moved...." Replace footnote 813 with: Md. Wills, 14:229; Md. Add new paragraph: "Robert's widow Mary Green left a will dated 12 May 1716 (no probate date) devising to sons Thomas and James: *Guyther's Purchase* as now divided between them. If either die without issue, his share to pass to his widow during widowhood and then to grandson Thomas Squires; if he dies without issue, to next heir of daughter Squires. To Sarah Squires: kitchen utensils and livestock, she to enjoy part of the tract belonging to son James. John Squires to have liberty to clear and plant same at wife's pleasure. To

---

[1]Westmoreland Co. Court Proceedings, 1653-1657, pages 41, 52, in Beverley Fleet, *Virginia Colonial Records*, 1:663, 669. Westmoreland Co. Deeds, Wills, Patents, Etc., 1653-1659, page 99a.

[2]*Ibid.*, 1665-1677, page 98a.

Jane Campbell: livestock. To grandson Thomas Squires: livestock at age 18. Son James appointed executor. Witnesses: Daniel and Alice Clocker and John Baker." Md. Wills, 14:229.

Pages 114-115. Revise children of Robert and Mary (Boarman) Green:

13. Sarah Green m. John Squires. Delete "Patrick McAtee." Their son Thomas Squires inherited   *Guyther's Purchase.*

14. Ann Green. Delete; no evidence of this child.

15. William Green. He is not the William Green born 1690 in Baltimore County. See Robert Barnes, *Baltimore Families*, p. 276.

16. Robert Green, d. by 11 April 1751 in Charles Co. Administrator was Thomas Green. Admin.   Accounts, 32:172.

17. James Green, m. Agnes [--?--], who m. (2) William Cutler. His administration account dated   30 June 1721, St. Mary's Co., named William Cutler and James White as appraisers; Mary Van   Swearingen as a creditor; with next of kin Thomas Campbell and John Squires; Wife Agnes was   administratrix. A second account dated 5 Aug. 1723 named legatee Thomas Squires, son of John;   Administrator Agnes now Agnes Cutler.

___. Add child Jane/Jean Green, named in her mother's will as Jane Campbell. On 8 Feb. 1723   Jean Campbell was administratrix of her husband, Thomas Campbell's St. Mary's Co. estate. Md.   Wills, 118:213. This document dated 19 Jan. 1723/4 and proved 28 Jan. 1723/4 named wife Jean   executrix, she to inherit the real estate; 3 minor sons James, Richard, and Joshua; son John 1000   lbs. tobacco, and dau. Jeane. By 3 March 1724 Jean had married (2) Stephen Martin. Md. Wills,   18:213.

Page 119. 11. **Elizabeth³ Green**. 4th line. Add after "... 100 acres of land" "adjoining land of John Thompson on main run of Port Tobacco Creek, now in his possession."

Page 119. 12. **Mary³ Green**. 3rd line. Delete "(part of *Green's Forest*)" Replace with: "(being part of *Green's Inheritance* by main branch of Port Tobacco Creek)"

Page 120. 17. **James³ Green**. Delete this account in its entirety. This man is not a descendant of Thomas Greene of the *Ark & Dove*. He is the son of John Green and Charity Hagan; this Greene is a 1682 arrival to Md. who settled in Prince George's Co. Children nos. 68-76 are ineligible. Delete their accounts on pp. 133-134. Replace James's account with the following:

Page 120. 17. **James³ Green**, son of Robert and Mary (Boarman) Green, died c1721. He married **Agnes** [-?-], who married (2) William Cutler. His estate was valued by William Cutler and James White, and named as kinsmen Thomas Campbell and John Squires. Agnes Cutler, wife of William Cutler, was administratrix; legate was Thomas Squires, son of John. Md. Administrations, 4:160, 5:200, dated 30 April 1722 and 5 Aug. 1723.

Nicholas Harvey. Page 140, 5th line. Insert "a" before "Thomas Greene by 1653." Footnote 932, add "CC:534." 2nd paragraph, 4th line. Change "2 January 1635" to "2 January 1634[/35]." Footnote 933. Add: "Hotten, *Original Lists of Persons of Quality 1600-1700*."

Richard Hill. Pages 227-228. Before 1651 Richard Hill settled at Apomattox in Washington Parish, Westmoreland [old Northumberland] County, Virginia, where he was frequently mentioned in land, probate, and other court records.[3] His will, dated 26

---

[3]See John Frederick Dorman's abstracts of *Westmoreland County Deeds, Wills, Patents, Court Order*

November 1675, bequeathed his estate to his wife **Mary** and to his kinsman Mr. Richard Hill, son of Major Nicholas Hill, deceased, of Isle of Wight County, Virginia. He died shortly before 18 March 1675/76, on which date his estate was appraised. Mary, his relict and executrix, married William Robinson before 20 August 1677, on which date they recorded an account of payments from Hill's estate.[4]

John Hilliard/Hiller. Page 227. He was born ca. 1607-1608.[5] He was transported to Maryland in 1633 by Father White, and was later claimed as a headright by Thomas Copley, Esq.[6] His earliest activities and employment are summarized by Newman. In 1643 he was employed by John Hollis/Hallows of St. Michael's Hundred, Maryland, but later of Appamatucks, Northumberland (Westmoreland after 1653) County, Virginia, by 1648. He later become an overseer for William Bromhall of Calvert and Kent counties, Maryland, who died intestate. At a session of the Maryland Prerogative Court, William Turner presented a petition stating that John Hilliard, overseer of the servants of William Bromhall, had "clandestinely runne away out of this Province."[7]

Beginning in 1649 Mr. John Hiller/Hillier/Hilliard/Hillyer/Hyllyard, was frequently mentioned in Northumberland County and (after 1653) Westmoreland County, Virginia, court records.[8] He lived at Round Hill in Appomattocks on the Potomack River, near Machotock River and adjoining the property of Thomas Boyce and Francis Gray/Grey.[9] On 25 August 1656 Robert Wyard of Westmoreland County, taylor, put out his daughter Dorothy to serve Mr. John Hiller and **Ann** his wife until of age or married.[10] In Westmoreland County on 29 October 1656, John Lancellot[11] gave his power of attorney to Mr. John Hiller, authorizing him to appear in all causes for him.[12] By a deed of gift dated 5 June 1657, John Hiller, gent., gave to John Rosier the younger, a cow "which my late wife desired me to give unto him."[13]

The will of John Hiller, being not very well in body, was dated 12 October 1657, and proved in Westmoreland County on 20 February 1657/58. A widower, he bequeathed his estate to his daughter Elizabeth, wife of John Rosier, and their son John Rosier, Jr.[14] At Westmoreland County Court on 30 October 1678, Anthony Bridges was ordered

Books, Etc., many volumes.

[4]Westmoreland Co. Deeds, Patents, Etc., 1665-1677, pages 248-248a, 265a, 313a. Westmoreland Co. Court Order Book, 1675/6-1688/9, page 61.

[5]According to age 50 given in deposition in 1658.

[6]Maryland Land Patents, F&B (1640-1658):19-20, 166.

[7]Harry W. Newman, *Flowering of the Maryland Palatinate* (Washington, 1961), page 230.

[8]Northumberland Co. Court Records, 1650-686, various references. Westmoreland Co. Court Records, 1653-1657, various references.

[9]Grey was formerly of St. George's Hundred, Maryland.

[10]Westmoreland County Court Records, 1653-1657, page 63. Witnessed by John Rosier and Thomas Boys. Recorded 15 Sept. 1656.

[11]Also formerly of Maryland.

[12]Fleet, *Virginia Colonial Records*, 1:676.

[13]Westmoreland County Court Records, 1653-1657, page 79. Recorded 5 June 1657.

[14]Westmoreland County Deeds, Wills, Patents, Etc., 1653-1659, pages 98-98a. Before 19 June 1665 Elizabeth (Hiller) Rosier married Anthony Bridges of Washington Parish, Westmoreland County, gentleman. Her son

to possess himself with the estate of Mr. Jno. Hillier, and to appraise the same and return it to Court. George Weeden and Francis Gray appointed to appraise the estate.[15]
    Only child of John Hilliard:
    Elizabeth Hilliard, m. (1) Rev. John Rosier,[16] (2) Anthony Bridges.

Richard Lowe. Page 161, footnotes 1125 and 1127. Replace "Two Captains, Two Ships:" with "The Master of the *Ark*:"

Thomas Munns. Page 233. Thomas Munns was brought into Westmoreland County, Virginia, by 1653, when Colonel Richard Lee was granted a land patent for his transportation to Virginia of six persons, including Thomas and William Muns.[17] He was mentioned in Westmoreland County court records, in association with Marylanders Ralph Beane, John Tew, and John Hallowes in the period 1654-1659.[18] The will of Thomas Munns of Westmoreland County, planter, "being weake in body," was dated 24 April 1659. He bequeathed his estate to his wife **Elizabeth** and his daughter Elizabeth, who was under age 21. The will was proved 20 July 1659.[19] In 1660-1661 James Bauldridge[20] and his wife Elizabeth had possession of Munns' property in Appomattox Parish.[21]

Francis Rabnett. Page 236. May possibly be identical with the Francis Robinet, son of William Robinet, baptized at Errol, Perthshire, Scotland, 10 Dec. 1620.[22]

Robert Sherley. Page 238. Robert Sherley settled in Westmoreland County, Virginia, where he frequently served as a witness to deeds and as a juror in the period 1657-1663.[23]

Mathias Sousa. Pages 238-239. A very detailed discussion of the few records of this man is provided by David S. Bogen in "Mathias de Sousa: Maryland's First Colonist of African Descent," *Maryland Historical Magazine* 96 (2001): 68-85.

30. **Ignatius Wheeler**. Page 126, 4th line. Delete "daughter of Francis Marbury."

23. **Leonard Wheeler**. Pages 123-124. The will of widow Elisabeth Wheeler, dated Prince George's County 5 June 1772 and proved 10 June 1783, made bequests to

John Rosier/Rosyer, Jr., married Mary Williamson by November 1671.

[15]Westmoreland County Court Order Book 1675/6-1688/9, page 134.

[16]See George Ely Russell, "Hiller and Rosier Families of Virginia," in *The American Genealogist* 85 (2011): 9-21.

[17]Virginia Land Patents, 3:15.

[18]Westmoreland Co. Court Records, 1653-1657, various references.

[19]Westmoreland Co. Deeds, Wills, Patents, Etc., 1653-1659, page 133a.

[20]See page 14 for the Bauldridge family of Maryland.

[21]Westmoreland Co. Deeds, Wills, Etc., 1653-1659, page 23; 1661-1662, page 4a.

[22]Errol Parish Register.

[23]John Frederick Dorman, *Westmoreland Co., Va., Records, 1658-1661, 1661-1664*, various references.

children: Leonard, Clement, Mary Ann, Elisabeth, Charity, and Elinor Wheeler.[24]

---

[24]Prince George's Co. Probate Records, T#1:150 (will), ST#1:226 (administration), ST#2:115.

CPSIA information can be obtained at www.ICGtesting.com
Printed in the USA
BVOW012258300412

289077BV00005B/54/P